D1565105

QUARTERS

QUARTERS

To Josh,

THE ACCOMMODATION OF THE BRITISH ARMY AND THE COMING OF THE AMERICAN REVOLUTION

John Gilbert McCurdy

JOHN GILBERT McCURDY

26 Sept 2019

CORNELL UNIVERSITY PRESS
Ithaca and London

First published 2019 by Cornell University Press

Printed in the United States of America

Library of Congress Cataloging-in-Publication Data

Names: McCurdy, John Gilbert, 1972– author.
Title: Quarters : the accommodation of the British Army and the coming of the American Revolution / John Gilbert McCurdy.
Description: Ithaca : Cornell University Press, 2019. | Includes bibliographical references and index.
Identifiers: LCCN 2019002331 (print) | LCCN 2019004115 (ebook) | ISBN 9781501736612 (pdf) | ISBN 9781501736629 (epub/mobi) | ISBN 9781501736605 | ISBN 9781501736605 (cloth ; alk. paper)
Subjects: LCSH: Soldiers—Billeting—United States—History—18th century. | Soldiers—Billeting—North America—History—18th century. | Requisitions, Military—United States—History—18th century. | Requisitions, Military—North America—History—18th century. | Great Britain. Army—Barracks and quarters—History—18th century. | United States—History—Colonial period, ca. 1600–1775. | United States—History—Revolution, 1775–1783. | United States—History, Military—18th century. | United States. Constitution. 3rd Amendment—History.
Classification: LCC UC403 (ebook) | LCC UC403 .M33 2019 (print) | DDC 973.3/113—dc23
LC record available at https://lccn.loc.gov/2019002331

Contents

Preface and Acknowledgments

If you ever find yourself in Ypsilanti, Michigan, get a bite to eat at Sidetrack.

During a meal at Sidetrack in 2012, I noticed, across the street in front of a long-abandoned building, a new historical marker, for "The Barracks." As the marker explains, the building once housed Civil War recruits. Yet I was less intrigued by Company H, First Michigan Infantry, than I was by the name. "The Barracks" seemed incongruous in a modern American community, especially across the street from Sidetrack and a mile from my university. I thought of barracks as segregated from civilian life and ensconced in military bases like Fort Leavenworth. A barracks in Ypsilanti? The only thing more preposterous would be soldiers marching in the city.

Quarters is my attempt to explain why "The Barracks" is so unusual. Having grown up near an active US Army base, I always have been aware of how the military both penetrates and evades civilian life. Placing that question in a historical context, I have concluded that the civilian-martial relationship is ultimately spatial and that our perceptions of it emerge from the eighteenth century, particularly the twenty years preceding the American Revolution. From 1755 to 1775, professional soldiers were a common sight in many American cities, yet after the war, troops disappeared along with the military infrastructure. Although they resurfaced at moments of mobilization, like the Civil War, they have never been the permanent fixtures they once were.

Quarters fulfills my long-standing desire to write a book about the American Revolution. Digging in such well-worked fields is a daunting prospect, and when I started this project, I had no idea what insights I could add. I often tell my students who can't find a research topic to go sit in an archives and read until they find something interesting. In January 2011, I took my own advice and went to the William L. Clements Library. After several false starts, I settled on quartering because no one had ever written a book about the Quartering Act and because of the exquisite details in the Thomas Gage Papers. As with any good research project, *Quarters* has opened a number of new intellectual avenues for me, including the study of place, as well as

Atlantic and military history. Eight years later, I am even more convinced of the consequence of the Revolution to present-day US culture.

There are many people and institutions to thank for this book.

More than anything, this book is the product of two universities: Eastern Michigan University and the University of Michigan. Since 2005, EMU has been my academic home, and I have delighted in working with excellent students and colleagues. EMU provided me with a sabbatical and a faculty research fellowship, as well as several travel grants to visit archives and conferences. It also provided a Provost's Research Support Award to defray the costs of publishing this book. I am grateful to the advice and insights of my colleagues, including George Cassar, Kathleen Chamberlain, James Egge, Jesse Kauffman, John Knight, Richard Nation, Mary-Elizabeth Murphy, Steven Ramold, Tomoyuki Sasaki, and Philip Schmitz. Julia Nims, Alexis Braun Marks, and other members of EMU's Bruce T. Halle Library provided books and articles, and tracked down interlibrary loans.

This book also could not have been written without the resources of the University of Michigan–Ann Arbor. The William L. Clements Library has amazing collections and a world-class staff, including Brian Leigh Dunnigan, Clayton Lewis, and Cheney Schopieray. The U of M also provided me with an Eisenberg Institute Residency Research Grant, which introduced me to the scholarship of place and put me into conversation with exceptional scholars, including Howard Brick, Gregory Dowd, June Howard, Susan Juster, John Shy, Scott Spector, Alexandra Stern, and Hitomi Tonomura. I am also grateful for Michigan's Hatcher Graduate Library.

I was humbled to receive the support of institutions outside of Michigan. I am appreciative of a Massachusetts Society of the Cincinnati award from the Massachusetts Historical Society and a Library Resident Research Fellowship from the American Philosophical Society. I had the good fortune to present parts of my research to the Omohundro Institute of Early American History and Culture, the Society of Early Americanists, the Organization of American Historians, the Massachusetts Historical Society, and the Colonial Society of Massachusetts. In addition to the above-named institutions, I spent many blissful hours researching at the Henry Huntington Library, the New Jersey State Archives, the New-York Historical Society, the New York Public Library, the South Carolina Department of Archives and History, the South Carolina Historical Society, and the UK National Archives at Kew.

I thank the Albany Institute of History and Art, the Burton Collection at the Detroit Public Library, the Library Company of Philadelphia, the Library of Congress, the Massachusetts Historical Society, and the William

L. Clements Library for permission to reprint images in this book. Material from chapters 2 and 5 previously appeared in my article, "From Fort George to the Fields: The Public Space and Military Geography of Revolutionary New York City," *Journal of Urban History* 44, no. 4: 625–42, reprinted by permission of SAGE Publications.

At Cornell University Press, I worked with an excellent staff of editors including Susan Specter, Glenn Novak, and Carmen Gonzalez. Michael McGandy deserves special credit for shepherding this book to completion. I thank the readers for their insightful comments on my manuscript and advocacy for its publication.

Daniel Polley was instrumental in helping with my translations from the French. I thank Stephanie Sambrook for her excellent maps and Daniel Bowlin for his research assistance.

During my time working on this book, I met many wonderful scholars who challenged my thinking and made this book stronger. They include Laura Ferguson, Eliga Gould, Derek Gregory, Robert Gross, Eric Hinderaker, Woody Holton, Matthew Klingle, Hyun Wu Lee, Tracy Neumann, Daniel Richter, Alan Taylor, Kacy Tillman, Tim Williams, Kariann Yokota, Serena Zabin, and Rosemarie Zagarri. Even better are those early American historians who are also dear friends. I am blessed to share laughs and learning with George Boudreau, David Hancock, and Ann Little.

Many friends, congregants, and neighbors have provided a support network, including Shane Dillon, David and Sally Epskamp, Damian Evilsizor, Dario Gaggio, Collin Ganio and Suzanne Davis, Dawn DeZan, Suzanne Fliege, Charles and Diane Jacobs, Anne Kirk, Gary Kotraba, Beverly McCurdy, Marcia McCrary, Angelo Pitillo, Daniel Polley, Helmut Puff, Doug Ross and Larry Barker, Sinderella, JoAnn Kennedy Slater, Liz Taylor, and Brenda Wilson. I'm saddened that two of the people who read *Citizen Bachelors* did not live to see *Quarters*: Gilbert McCurdy and Michael Drake.

Last but never least is Anthony Mora. On July 28, 2011, I met Anthony on break from the Clements, and he has been there ever since. I could not have done any of this without him, so I dedicate this book him.

A NOTE ON QUOTATIONS, TERMINOLOGY, AND MONEY

I have modernized the quotations to contemporary American English. For example, I removed capital letters from the middle of sentences, translated ampersands, updated and Americanized the spelling, and added punctuation where it did not alter the original meaning. I also have translated sources from the French into English. I am conscious that such changes can compromise meaning, but inconsistency in the original documents and their transcriptions renders precision elusive.

I have updated place names where such changes are minimal and widely accepted, such that Charles Town, South Carolina, becomes Charleston, and Elizabethtown, New Jersey, becomes Elizabeth. However, where place names changed dramatically, such as Fort Duquesne (Fort Pitt) and La Gallette (Oswegatchie), I have used the preferred name of the time, with a reference to the current name in parentheses. I have retained the French spelling for place names in Québec.

For Native American groups, I have opted to use the contemporary nations' preferred demonyms, with historical labels in parentheses where appropriate.

I describe the colonists who lived in the thirteen British colonies that became the United States as "Americans," given the preference for the demonym in current parlance. I describe the area north of the St. Lawrence River as "Canada" and the people as "Canadians," reserving "Québec" for the British colony and "Québécois" for its Francophone colonists. I also have adopted the eighteenth-century convention of referring to the region that became the United States as "the old colonies" or "the thirteen colonies," but Québec, Nova Scotia, and Florida as "the new colonies." The terms "backcountry" and "periphery" shifted over time, and I address this in chapter 4.

For military units, I note primarily regiments and companies in the British army. In 1765, a company in the North American Establishment was ordered to consist of a captain, two subalterns, four noncommissioned officers, a drummer, and forty-seven privates, while a regiment was to contain eight infantry companies and one company of grenadiers. However, companies and regiments varied in size and composition, and were notoriously under-manned in the late 1760s.

In terms of money, where known, the figures are British pounds sterling (£). In the instances where the amounts appear in colonial currency, I have indicated this. I have not converted the values, although I have tried to make comparisons to assist the reader.

QUARTERS

Introduction

The Importance of Place in the Age of Atlantic Revolutions

It was sunset when the army entered William Thompson's home. Thompson lived in the Boston suburb of Brookline, Massachusetts, and according to his deposition, at least forty armed soldiers appeared at his door late on December 14, 1775. The troops had been ordered to seize Thompson's residence for quarters—that is, military accommodations. But William Thompson resisted. He disputed the constitutionality of the soldiers' orders, informing them that "it was his dwelling house, his castle." When the army threatened to take the house by force, Thompson rebuked this as "contrary to the sacred right of every freeman to the enjoyment of his property and domestic security." Thompson then offered alternative quarters; should the troops "march to the next public house," then he would pay for their room and board. Rejecting this, a sergeant struck the front door with his musket, breaking the lock and forcing the house open. Troops swarmed in with bayonets drawn, dislodging Thompson and his family.[1]

Securing quarters is an essential task of any army. To maintain an effective fighting force, armies secure campsites or buildings where troops can sleep, eat, and store their personal effects. Whether they be tents, houses, or barracks, quarters are as central to military readiness as weapons and discipline. Yet as the experience of William Thompson reveals, how the army acquires quarters can be a flashpoint between soldiers and civilians. When the

1

army came, it expected Thompson to surrender his house without question. Although he protested the loss of property, this was not Thompson's primary complaint; indeed, he was willing to part with financial property if the soldiers went away. Instead, Thompson objected to the invasion of his home. His language and defense of the structure indicates that he viewed his domicile as inviolable regardless of military orders, exigencies of war, or even brute force. The presence of his family made the home different from another building, as did an ideal that Thompson termed "domestic security," or what we might call privacy. In his deposition, Thompson proclaimed his willingness to render his "utmost efforts in behalf of his country," but he believed that quartering soldiers in his home was something that no government could sanction.

Historians long have understood quarters as central to the American Revolution. Like taxation without representation or restrictions on trade, the practice of quartering soldiers elicited complaints from the American colonists, who cited it as a cause for independence. But the story is more complicated than that. First, the history of quarters is longer than the Revolution. Lodging soldiers in one's home was an ancient practice, and it was only in the seventeenth century that Britons began to speak of "private houses" as off-limits to soldiers. In North America, centuries of social and legal change culminated in an intense debate over quarters between the French and Indian War and the Revolutionary War. Second, evicting military power from the home had consequences for other places. When William Thompson offered to board troops in a nearby public house, he was unconcerned about how this would affect that place. But the protection of the home from quartering sacrificed taverns to the army and led to the construction of massive barracks. Indeed, by the time soldiers came to Thompson's house, quartering was a broad issue that touched all places in American society, not just the home. Third, quarters were most controversial when they involved British soldiers, but it was not only redcoats who required accommodations. The troops that William Thompson lodged were provincial troops marching for Massachusetts. The objection to quarters was larger than anti-British sentiment, and it outlasted the Revolution, such that quartering *all* troops in houses was prohibited in the US Constitution. Similarly, the colonial American experience was not universal. Canadians and Native Americans also quartered troops, but their experiences set them apart from the thirteen colonies.

This book explores the history of quartering and its role in the coming of the American Revolution. Although the most significant aspect of this story is the passage and implementation of the Quartering Act, the story is larger than one law. By investigating how troops were housed and fed, this book connects the social experience of quartering to the politics that led to independence. It does so by thinking about notions of place. Quartering forced people throughout the British Atlantic to contemplate the meaning of the spaces they inhabited and to renegotiate places they had taken for granted. Not only did this process create a nation—it changed American ideas about the home and the city. Few since 1775 have relived the ordeal of William Thompson, but the effects of quarters in Revolutionary America continue to touch us where we live.

The Quartering Act and the American Revolution

Despite its importance to the coming of the American Revolution, quartering has not received the in-depth examination that it deserves. Some historians have considered quartering as a legal issue, concluding that Americans' opposition to the British army resulted from a constitutional objection to standing armies, while others have examined it in a limited context such as the garrisoning of Boston in 1768.[2] Yet these treatments have been incomplete, as they focus on small parts of the story. Indeed, quartering is one of the very few aspects of the American Revolution never to be the topic of a scholarly monograph.

The lack of scholarship on quarters has led many historians to mischaracterize events. Nowhere is this clearer than in the history of the Quartering Act, alternately known as the Mutiny Act for America or the American Mutiny Act. In 1765, Parliament issued a law requiring that colonists provide accommodations, supplies, and transportation to British soldiers. Several academic monographs, popular histories, and college textbooks have claimed that the Quartering Act forced British soldiers into American homes against the will of the inhabitants. Some even have speculated about the unconscionable implications of the law, arguing that once it opened the door to colonial homes, British troops ate out sustenance, destroyed property, and sexually assaulted women.[3] A better cause for revolution would be hard to imagine, except that none of these allegations were true. The Quartering Act *prohibited* British soldiers from entering private houses, and records indicate that the army faithfully complied with this stipulation. However, keeping troops out of the home was not the only issue at hand. Once soldiers were confined to barracks, the American colonists struggled with the implications of quarters for their cities and the borderland, ultimately concluding that accommodating British troops was a condition of empire to be rejected in favor of being an independent nation.

This book places quartering (also known as billeting) at the center of the story. It traces the practice from its colonial roots, through the French and

Indian War and the passage of the Quartering Act, to the start of the Revolutionary War. Quarters were not limited to one city or colony, but were
in widespread use through British North America; thus this book employs
a wide-angle lens to understand the practice. Moreover, billeting was both
a legal issue and a sociopolitical one. The presence of soldiers, whether in
one's house or nearby barracks, was an intensely intimate experience. This
book asks how quartering troops shaped American politics.

A social history of quarters provides a new perspective on the coming of
the American Revolution. Before it became a reason for independence, quartering was the product of a complex dialogue between Britain and the colonies. Taking troops into one's home was common in North America before
the French and Indian War. While most of the soldiers quartered before 1756
were other colonists, the arrival of British regulars did not turn Americans
against the practice. Instead, they welcomed redcoats as necessary to their
security within a rapidly expanding empire. Although the Quartering Act
was drafted without their consent, the colonists acquiesced out of self-interest.
For this reason, the American Mutiny Act represents an imperial relationship very different from that of the Stamp Act or Tea Act. American opposition was neither immediate nor visceral, but slow and uneven. Although
the deployment of four regiments to Boston in 1768 initiated intercolonial
opposition to the law, the Quartering Act was effective until 1775. When
Americans declared independence, they assailed the king "for quartering
large bodies of armed troops among us," but it had taken them two decades
to see billeting redcoats as an example of British tyranny.[4]

A social history of quarters also provides a new perspective on the consequences of the American Revolution. While taking troops into one's home
was common in the colonial era, the practice has been nonexistent in the
nation that followed. When British regulars first arrived, they billeted in at
least ten of the thirteen colonies, occupying private residences in several.
A flurry of barrack construction soon followed that removed the soldiers
from houses. The Quartering Act confirmed this solution, marking the first
and only time that Parliament recognized Americans' right to privacy. At the
end of the Revolutionary War, the newly formed United States upheld this
principle. With the ratification of the Third Amendment to the Constitution in 1791, the US explicitly prohibited quartering troops in houses except
in special circumstances. The military has not tested this right, making the
amendment one part of the US Constitution never to be the center of a
Supreme Court decision.

In the final accounting of the American Revolution, the constraints
placed on military power by the founders are a source of pride. The US

Constitution gave financial control over the army to an elected Congress and made a civilian commander in chief. The Second Amendment and the militia (National Guard) made the citizenry central to the nation's defense. But we have missed the cultural constraints. Not only have soldiers been removed from the house; they have been eradicated from major centers of population. While Britain quartered thousands of troops in America's largest cities in peacetime, the United States has never repeated this feat. Although military power has been central to US prominence, it has also been carefully concealed from civilians, heeding the lessons of the American Revolution two hundred years later.

Transatlantic Quartering

Understanding quarters requires placing the subject in a transatlantic context. One of the most important shifts in the scholarship of the American Revolution in the last generation has been the influence of Atlantic world studies and global history. A recent study of the Tea Act carried its readers to Asia and Europe before returning to Boston for the infamous tea party.[5] A transatlantic approach can help us to better understand the history of quartering and its consequences. The American colonies were not the only locales to confront billeting, but the uniqueness of their response set them apart from the rest of the British Atlantic.

Quartering was brought to America by English colonists, and it was broadly similar to the practice in the mother country. By the early seventeenth century, there was already widespread distrust of the practice in England, specifically forced and free quartering. During the Glorious Revolution, Parliament erected legal constraints on billeting in the form of the English Mutiny Act, which decreed that all soldiers be lodged in public houses, never private ones. However, a segregation of houses made little sense in the colonies, where housing was inadequate. Accordingly, when thousands of British regulars arrived in the 1750s, the colonists built barracks. Barracks, in turn, distinguished the colonies from the mother country, where such structures were constitutionally problematic. Over the next twenty years, different approaches to quartering continued to distance Britain and America. Although colonists hailed barracks as a salvation in the 1750s, they turned against them in the 1770s as symbols of British oppression, and, after the Treaty of Paris, either pulled them down or repurposed them for civilian uses, such as schools. Britons also changed their minds in the process, engaging in a barrack-building frenzy in the 1790s. Permanent military quarters never returned to Boston or New York, but were common in London in the 1800s.

The American experience with billeting also contrasts sharply with the experience of Britain's other North American colonies. When Britain acquired Québec and Florida in 1763, it dispatched thousands of soldiers to patrol the non-English populations. However, the new colonies had little military infrastructure, so the troops quartered in private houses. Indeed, the irony of misremembering the Quartering Act's violation of domestic privacy as a cause for revolution is that British soldiers actually billeted in homes in Québec and Florida, two places that did not rebel against the empire. The heavy presence of redcoats in the new colonies also blunted critiques of British military power. While the US prohibited billeting in houses, similar protections were not forthcoming in the places that remained part of the British Empire.

Beyond the Atlantic coast, quartering also took on different dimensions. West of the Appalachian Mountains and in the British West Indies, non-English populations dampened calls for legal protections against quarters. In the backcountry, the struggle between Native Americans, French colonists, and American settlers produced a conflicted vision of billeting. During interracial struggles like Pontiac's War, all places were available for quarters. While the British army avoided housing soldiers with Indians, it invaded French colonial homes; later, quartering became an argument for and against colonizing the backcountry. In the Caribbean, barracks were vigorously pursued in colonies like Jamaica and Antigua, where 90 percent of the population was enslaved people of African descent. This also improved islanders' views of British military power and set the West Indies apart from North America. Despite the importance of slavery to the economy of the mainland, the Americans never built barracks for soldiers among the new nation's southern plantations or looked to the US Army as a permanent slave patrol.

In sum, a social history of quarters invites a transatlantic interpretation. British soldiers were as much the sinews of empire as was money, but the problem of finding a place to house and feed them was solved differently by the constituent parts. Although the communities of Canada, the backcountry, and the Caribbean differed as to the specifics of billeting, it is possible to distinguish between those places that declared independence in 1776 and those that did not. Historians have pointed to the role that military power played in the division of Britain's North American empire, and a closer look at quartering allows us to see this in greater detail.[6]

Place in Revolutionary America

So why was Americans' experience with quarters so different from that of the rest of the British Atlantic? Although we should not discount critiques of military power and resistance to parliamentary governance, the unique response of the Americans was a product of place making. The opposition to billeting British soldiers in houses resulted from changing notions of the home as a place of domestic privacy. When Americans directed the redcoats to barracks, they created new places that changed the colonial city. Quartering also prompted Americans to think more broadly about other places, including the empire and borderland. In time, opposition to the Quartering Act even allowed Americans to imagine themselves as an independent nation.

Geographers have explored notions of place extensively, creating an immense literature for understanding the meaning we attach to sites, as well as the effects that places have on us.[7] War strongly affects our environment; thus the subfield of military geography considers the influences that soldiers, weapons, and martial codes have on notions of place. Military geography can shed new light on quartering in the Revolutionary era. At the heart of Americans' debate over quarters was a basic question: where do soldiers belong? In the eighteenth century, the professional soldier was the deadliest weapon of war. In an era before drone strikes and nuclear missiles, warfare was more intimate, as a musket was only as effective as the man wielding it. Accordingly, where a soldier was allowed to go determined military power. The Americans understood this when thousands of British regulars arrived in 1755 and the colonists built barracks to keep them out of their houses. For the next twenty years, the debate over quarters was a discourse of military geography; as Americans and Britons sparred over where soldiers belonged, they delineated civilian and martial places. Although this was a fictive division, it proved critical to later understandings of American military power.[8]

Consequently, the history of quarters is the history of place. Asking where soldiers belonged and understanding the divergent answers reveal not just why Americans believed quartering to be a cause for independence, but allow us to understand the changing notion of place in Revolutionary America. Moreover, they reveal the centrality of military geography to creating the places we take for granted. Although much has been written on the home and the city, geographers and historians have ignored the effects that soldiers had on these places and how the removal of troops changed them. Ultimately, military geography allows us to connect places and understand their interrelated development. Removing soldiers from the home changed the city, while placing troops in the center of town challenged the empire and created a nation. For this reason, this book explores quartering chronologically and spatially.

Chapter 1 begins in the house. For centuries, soldiers billeted in undifferentiated houses. The rise of a standing army in England in the seventeenth century led to a distinction of private and public houses, with troops confined to the latter. When British troops came to America for the French and Indian War, the English segregation of houses was not possible, so troops entered private homes. This experience outraged colonists, who had begun to think of their domiciles as places where the family was protected against violent intrusion. To protect their houses, the Americans sought alternative quarters for British soldiers.

Chapter 2 enters the barracks. Beginning in 1756, the four largest American cities and several smaller towns built massive barracks for British troops. Most stood unimpeded on the city common, coloring the communities that hosted them. The proliferation of barracks set the Americans apart from England as well as new colonies in Canada and Florida. Barracks also strengthened the argument that the home should be sacrosanct against state intrusion. However, barracks enabled the British army to retain regulars in the colonies after the war ended, making the American city a permanent part of Britain's military geography.

Chapter 3 examines empire. The Quartering Act of 1765 was part of an effort by the British government to pull the colonies into a unitary empire. As originally envisioned, the statute extended English rights and responsibilities to the colonists, and applied to all parts of British North America. However, local circumstances undermined imperial unity. The American Mutiny Act proved unenforceable in Québec, while financial considerations encouraged the British army to concentrate troops in New York, New Jersey, and Pennsylvania. Opposition to the law also diverged, and New York was singled out for punishment. Despite the statute's imperial design, it was enforceable only by recognizing that the British Empire was not one place but many places.

Chapter 4 moves out to the borderland. Victory in the French and Indian War added lands west of the Appalachian Mountains to the British Empire, lands that were inhabited by Native Americans and non-English colonists. The British army was critical to maintaining the region, such that specific provisions were added to the Quartering Act to extend the law to the backcountry. Quartering also shaped how colonizers came to think about the North American interior. The accommodation of troops was central to the arguments of both proponents and opponents of colonization, but the division over the use of military power in the backcountry led to the persistence of the borderland.

Chapter 5 returns to the cities and towns where most British troops were stationed. Redcoats lived peaceably alongside colonists in several North American communities, exemplifying the spirit of the Quartering Act that delineated places in order to make it possible to share the city. However,

British soldiers dominated Canadian cities in ways that set Québec apart from New York. Moreover, Britain's decision to use British troops to enforce parliamentary law in Boston in 1768 soured urban relations. As the Americans began to imagine their cities and towns as purely civilian places, they turned against the Mutiny Act for America.

Chapter 6 considers the American nation that emerged from the discourse of quarters. Following the Boston Massacre of 1770, the colonists distanced themselves from the British army. As they built American armies, they took responsibility for their own defense and displaced the need for redcoats. They also explored intercolonial cooperation when the occupation of Boston in 1774 made the Quartering Act a rallying point for opposition to Britain. Colonial armies and cooperation eluded Canada and the other British colonies, effectively setting the US apart from the rest of Britain's North American empire when shots were fired at Lexington in 1775.

The epilogue carries the lessons of the eighteenth century forward to the present. The outbreak of the Revolutionary War ended the protections and obligations of the Quartering Act, thus creating a situation where soldiers forced their way into the home of William Thompson. But the Revolution was an aberration rarely repeated in the 250 years that followed. Instead, the military geography forged between 1755 and 1775 has had a lasting impact on American ideas of the home, the city, and the nation.

CHAPTER 1

Houses

The Rise of Domestic Privacy

Richard Nicolls needed a place to quarter soldiers. In August 1664, Colonel Nicolls and three hundred soldiers descended upon the Dutch colony of New Netherland, intent on claiming new territory for England. Arriving at Long Island, Nicolls sent word to New Amsterdam that his troops would enter the capital within forty-eight hours. The colonists rallied to defend their city, but with a moldering fort and few troops, New Netherland was no match for the English. When word came that Nicolls would guarantee the colonists' personal rights and property should they surrender, the city capitulated without a fight. On September 8, the English army entered Manhattan. Nicolls installed himself as governor and changed the name of the city and colony to New York. But before he could do much else, Nicolls had to find a place for his soldiers to live.[1]

Colonel Nicolls likely had some experience quartering troops. Nicolls was a career officer who had come of age as a Royalist commander in the English Civil War, and two decades of military service had taught him that billeting was a delicate matter. It required locating places where soldiers could sleep and take their meals without offending the local population, especially those who supplied the places. During negotiations for surrender of the city, Nicolls agreed that "the townsmen of Manhattan shall not have any soldier quartered upon them without being satisfied and paid for them."[2] In so doing, Nicolls disavowed both forced quartering and free quarters. However,

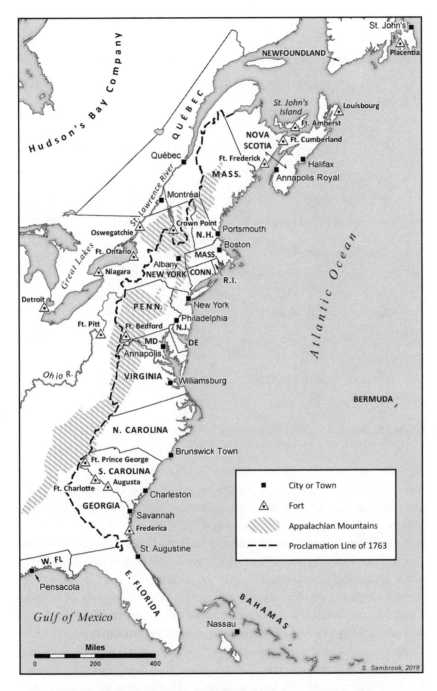

MAP 1. British North America, ca. 1765. S. Sambrook, 2018.

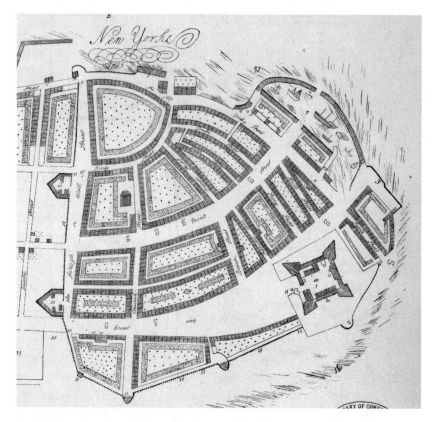

FIGURE 1.1.   New York in 1695. John Miller, *New Yorke 1695* [New York: Lith. G. Hayward, 185?]. Library of Congress, Geography and Map Division, 93680196.

neither Nicolls nor the people negotiating the surrender of the city made any spatial distinctions about accommodations. Instead, all houses would be made available to quarter English soldiers.

Upon entering New York, Nicolls and his troops investigated the fort that stood at the southern tip of the city for quarters. The fort was the nucleus of the settlement, containing a church, the governor's residence, and a small barracks (figure 1.1). However, the barracks was barely capable of holding a third of the troops, so Nicolls looked elsewhere. In the articles of surrender, the colonists had agreed that "if the fort be not capable of lodging all the soldiers," then the burgomasters (city leaders) would "appoint some houses capable to receive them."[3] Accordingly, Nicolls submitted his request for accommodations to the burgomasters, and before long, Isaac Grevenraet offered his house for the troops. A merchant of some means, Grevenraet owned a commodious building on Broadway two blocks from the fort, and he rented this house to Nicolls for a handsome sum. Grevenraet and his family did not live in the building, and thus he felt no compunction to keep it habitable; the building's fireplaces did not work, and its unglazed windows let in the cold. The house also likely contained no furniture. Grevenraet's house thus offered the English soldiers a roof over their heads but little else.[4]

Warehousing got the troops through the winter, but the following spring, Governor Nicolls reassessed the situation. In March 1665, he informed the burgomasters that it was no longer acceptable to provide empty houses, as this deprived the troops of proper meals, ablutions, and warmth. "It was therefore necessary to quarter the soldiers in the burghers' houses," Nicolls concluded. Nicolls offered to pay householders two guilders per week per soldier, but the colonists received the governor's request poorly. Appearing before the city council, New Yorkers complained of the troubles the troops had already caused them. Mary Verplanck charged that a soldier had stolen her Bible and sold it. Bartholdus Maan described how two men came to his house for wine, and while waiting for their drink, "they put their hands on his wife's belly." When Maan objected, a fight broke out. The soldiers called for reinforcements, who came to Maan's house, cut him with their swords, and "smashed the windows in pieces." Not surprisingly, when the burgomasters called a meeting of forty-nine householders to see who would billet troops, twenty-two refused, and another sixteen departed without an answer. Such defiance angered Nicolls, who rebuked city leaders for having "not done their duty in quartering the soldiers in the burghers' houses." Brushing aside warnings that "the commonalty dread receiving the soldiers," he sent a captain to inspect the colonists' houses and list those capable of accepting troops. Nicolls also made quartering more attractive by raising the compensation from two guilders to five, although he paid for this out a house tax he laid on the city. Eventually, admonitions and financial persuasion induced enough New Yorkers to open their houses to the English troops, and soon all were billeted.[5]

By sending troops into the colonists' houses, Governor Nicolls followed the accepted English protocol for quartering soldiers. As was true in England and its American colonies, New York had an insufficient supply of permanent military lodgings such as barracks, so the best place for a soldier's bed and table was a house. This was possible because the house was a multipurpose structure with few of the features that later characterized the home. Indeed, New Yorkers' objections to quarters were legal and personal, not spatial. They disliked how accommodating soldiers intruded on their lives and property, but they made no claims that their domiciles should be exempt from the practice.

There was little privacy in a seventeenth-century house. Probate and archaeological records indicate that most late Dutch colonial houses consisted of two rooms, with an attic for storage. All manner of activities occurred in these rooms, including manual labor, meal preparation, washing, prayers, and dining. In such houses, firm spatial divisions were impractical. Even the furniture served multiple functions. Instead of a dining table and chairs, most New Yorkers ate off chests that also stored clothes and personal effects. Perhaps the only thing that made a residence distinct from another building like a warehouse was that it contained a bed. Most early New York domiciles had a *bedsteden* or box bed partitioned off from the rest of the house by paneling. The *bedsteden* was the one place in the house without multiple uses and the only place where the family could expect not to be disturbed.[6] Nicolls respected these sensibilities, exempting fifteen houses from quartering because they were "wanting double bedding and pillows." The colonel would not put troops into bed with the colonists.[7]

Nor was the house particularly gendered. Although women were more likely to work where they lived, there was nothing particularly feminine about a residence. Seventeenth-century New York was composed of patriarchal households, but there was little sense that the domicile was a place where the weak and dependent were protected. Indeed, Nicolls had no problem billeting troops in houses with female heads. Many of the complaints that followed the troops into the houses came from women like Tryntje Walingsen, who charged soldiers with stealing her farm implements. Several widows and wives complained about having soldiers living with them, but the city leaders ignored these pleas, even ordering Annetje Kock "to lodge two soldiers."[8]

It is telling that neither Nicolls nor the burgomasters insisted that the troops be quartered in public houses instead of residences. As an experienced commander, Nicolls would have known that taverns, which were accustomed to providing meals and beds to strangers, were better prepared than families to accommodate soldiers. Nor was there any shortage of such facilities, as the last Dutch governor estimated that "one full fourth of the city of New Amsterdam has been turned into taverns." However, public houses were not substantially different from domiciles. Although publicans were required to hold a license, they often plied their trade in their residences. Often it was the woman of the house who produced the alcoholic beverage and ran the business. In February 1666, Mrs. Mils lost her license to sell alcohol when several "very drunk" soldiers stumbled "out of her house" and started a fight. Functionally, it made little sense to quarter troops in a tavern instead of a domicile, as there was little difference between the two.[9]

The imposition of troops on New Yorkers did not last long. Shortly after entering New York, Governor Nicolls dispatched part of his army to other New York communities, including Albany. As the number of soldiers in the capital dwindled, they relocated to the barracks in the city's fort, later renamed Fort George. Nicolls himself remained in New York for four years, promulgating New York's first written legal code. He departed in August 1668 and returned to active service in the English army, dying four years later in a Dutch naval incursion.[10]

The experience of quartering English soldiers had a profound effect upon New Yorkers. At the convening of the colony's first elected assembly in 1683, the delegates approved a Charter of Liberties and Privileges, which promised "that no freeman shall be compelled to receive any mariners or soldiers into his house and there suffer them to sojourn, against their wills provided always it be not in time of actual war within this province." Although this essentially reiterated Nicolls's prohibition on forced quartering, it was the first time that an American colony stated this principle as a constitutional right. Moreover, once the right was enunciated, spatial dimensions emerged. Following a colonial insurrection that witnessed the arrival of more English troops, New Yorkers in 1691 repeated their objection to quarters. This time, however, they denied the protection to "innholders and other houses of public entertainment, who are to quarter for ready money." In this, the colonists distinguished between houses. Whereas those places that sold room and board had to billet troops, those that did not engage in such commerce were absolved from this obligation. The constitutional right was a spatial one; quartering itself was not banned, only quartering in certain places.[11]

The experience of New York is characteristic of quarters in the seventeenth-century Anglo-Atlantic world. The practice was a necessary part of maintaining an army, especially during wartime when a massive force was defending a city, or, in the case of New York, capturing and holding it. Although often temporary, quartering was unpopular, even when efforts were made to avoid forced and free quartering. Most distinctively, quartering took place in the house. Because barracks were small, and uninhabited buildings like warehouses lacked beds, the residence was the foremost site for billeting. Yet in the late seventeenth century, attempts to limit quartering emerged that were primarily spatial. As people in England and the American colonies claimed a constitutional right against accommodating soldiers, they insisted that there was something unique about the domicile that privileged it, something that did not apply to other buildings.

The history of quarters begins with the house. Between 1664 and 1756, the primary site for quartering soldiers became the one place where the practice was expressly forbidden. The stunning reversal of long-accepted practice was the result of changes in the army and the house. Before the 1660s, the English army was often provisional, and quarters mostly a short-term inconvenience. But the arrival of a standing army, first in England then in the American colonies, created a fighting force too large and powerful to be quartered in residences. At the same time, the house as a place changed. In the 1660s, most houses in England and the colonies were two-room, multipurpose structures. With little expectation of privacy, it made sense to add soldiers to the houses. But late seventeenth-century changes in architecture, gender, and labor differentiated houses, distinguishing public from private, and remaking the residence as a site of domestic tranquility. Soldiers became antithetical to the home, a violent presence unwelcome in a place where women and dependents were to be protected. In effect, as the army expanded, it became important to protect the domicile from becoming part of the military geography.

The alteration of the army and the house was concluded in England by 1700 but remained incomplete in the American colonies fifty years later. Accordingly, when thousands of British regulars arrived to fight in the French and Indian War, a single solution was not possible. Instead, Philadelphia limited billeting to public houses, New Jersey allowed troops to enter private homes, and Boston sought alternative sites. The diversity of approaches to quartering concealed a unifying theme: like Britons, Americans wanted to keep soldiers out of their domiciles. Quartering thousands of troops during the French and Indian War revealed how difficult this was to achieve, and its allows us to reframe the Quartering Act as part of a longer history of American efforts to keep British soldiers out of their homes.

The transformation of the house was one of the most profound developments of the early modern era. Geographers and philosophers have written much on the importance of the home, specifically the deep meaning we attach to the places in which we live, or, to repeat the cliché, what makes a house a home. Historians have also explored changing ideas of the house, observing how the home emerged as the site of domestic privacy between the seventeenth and nineteenth centuries. The expansion of houses from a few rooms to many allowed for greater differentiation of space within the structure, while the emergence of a culture of refinement introduced the fashion of segregating personal practices like sleeping and bathing from communal activities like political debates and worship. Changes in labor brought about by the market revolution removed men's work from the house, thus creating the ideal of the home as a place for women and children to be protected from the public sphere. Missing from this history is the role that quarters played.

The experience of housing troops between 1664 and 1756 introduced a language of privacy and notions of constitutional protections for the home that outlasted the presence of British troops.[12]

English and American Billeting

Ancient in origin, quartering arrived in England with the Norman invasion of 1066. William the Conqueror brought an army from the continent, and these troops had to be accommodated. The defeated Saxons had no permanent lodgings for soldiers, as they had long relied on the *fyrd* (militia) to defend their kingdom. Although the newly crowned King William I built castles like the Tower of London for his troops, most ended up in houses. Quartering continued to be an irregular burden for English householders for the next seven centuries.[13]

Almost as old as quartering were complaints about the practice. Householders most often protested forced quartering—that is, when soldiers entered the house without the occupants' permission. They also complained about free quarters, or how they were undercompensated or not compensated at all for the burden of providing soldiers with meals, beds, and supplies. Out of forced and free quartering grew a variety of offenses. In William Langland's late-fourteenth-century allegorical poem *Piers Plowman*, a man charges that he "had his wife taken" by soldiers as well as "my poultry and pigs." He dares not "fight or complain" against the better-armed king's men, and for all his suffering, he receives "no farthing there for."[14] For many in medieval England, *Piers Plowman* rang true. The army invaded their houses and saddled them with armed soldiers who might abuse female inhabitants, steal their property, and offer nothing in return.

Over time, complaints from householders prompted the English government to establish some limits on quarters. Ending the practice of free quartering came first. When the army placed a soldier in a house, it was required to provide tickets or billets that the householder could take to the government for payment. For this reason, quartering troops became known as billeting. Unfortunately, billets could be worthless if the government refused to honor them, and this happened with some regularity. The English kings were more reluctant to end forced quartering, although some communities secured promises against the practice. In the City of London's charter of 1130, King Henry I guaranteed that "none shall lodge within the walls, neither of my household, nor any other, nor [shall] lodging [be] delivered by force."[15]

Missing entirely from both complaints and limits on quarters was a concern for the house as a place. Billets were freely distributed to owners of domiciles as well as taverns. The army preferred houses that were licensed to sell food and provide lodging, but many such establishments doubled as residences. Accordingly, quartering troops in a pub was often no less intimate than placing troops with a family. The restrictions on forced quartering also had little to say about the house as a place. The protections of city charters were corporate rather than individual. London could refuse to grant accommodations, but there was no corollary right for householders.[16]

The English populace began to think more spatially about quarters in the seventeenth century with the advent of a standing army. In medieval England, armies grew and shrank with some regularity, depending on the military challenge of the moment. However, a lengthy civil war and a series of foreign conflicts introduced an ever-present fighting force, or a standing army. In place of occasional recruits, a standing army consisted of professional or regular soldiers, trained in the use of deadly weapons fueled by gunpowder, such as muskets and cannons. Nor did a standing army disband when a particular conflict was over; rather, it continued to exist even in peacetime.[17]

The rise of a standing army made the medieval style of quartering untenable. Whereas billeting had been a temporary imposition in the fourteenth century, the constant presence of troops in the seventeenth century meant that a householder might have to quarter soldiers indefinitely. Contemporary events confirmed this new reality. Problems began in the 1620s when King Charles I commenced hostilities with Spain and France. Disappointed with the army's poor performance in battle, Parliament turned against the king and refused to vote money for billeting. In response, King Charles quartered troops in English houses without obtaining permission from householders or providing any compensation. Quartering persisted through the English Civil Wars of the 1640s. Although Parliament cited such abuses when it declared war on the king, both Roundheads and Cavaliers routinely demanded free quarters. The Restoration of the monarchy in 1660 brought little relief. Wars against the Netherlands in 1665–1667 and 1672–1674 provided a new pretext for billeting, as did the suppression of Covenanters in Scotland in 1679–1680.[18]

The increase of quartering led to new restrictions on the practice. In response to the actions of Charles I, Parliament issued the Petition of Right in 1628. Written as a statement of constitutional principle, the petition denounced the king's crimes against the English people, including "great companies of soldiers and mariners" whom "the inhabitants against their wills have been compelled to receive into their houses."[19] For the first time, quartering was framed as a violation of the English constitution and an individual's rights. Although the lofty aims of the Petition of Right were swept away when Charles went to war with Parliament, the notion of a personal liberty against billeting retained currency among English lawmakers. In the Disbanding Act of 1679, Parliament again denounced quartering as unconstitutional, stating that "it shall and may be lawful for every such subject and inhabitant to refuse to sojourn or quarter any soldier or soldiers notwithstanding any command, order, or billeting whatever."[20]

Spatially, these protections were vague. In neither the Petition of Right nor the Disbanding Act did Parliament identify exactly which houses were off limits to soldiers. Theoretically, a shop or tavern was as protected against quartering as a domicile. Moreover, the Petition of Right and the Disbanding Act were statements of constitutional principle rather than enforceable statutes, a point made abundantly clear when King James II started billeting soldiers in houses when he ascended the throne in 1685. Despite Parliament's location of a personal right against forced billeting, the undifferentiated house remained the favored site for quarters.[21]

The constitutional protection against quartering did not become meaningful until it took on a spatial dimension. Three years after James II resumed quartering, the English people turned against the monarch and chased him from the country. In a turn of events known as the Glorious Revolution, James's daughter and her Dutch husband arrived to replace the fugitive king. However, before Parliament would recognize the couple as King William III and Queen Mary II, it insisted that they support a statement of constitutional principles. The resulting English Bill of Rights of 1689 excoriated James II for "quartering soldiers contrary to law," effectively labeling all forced and free quartering unconstitutional. William and Mary also agreed that henceforth "raising or keeping a standing army within the kingdom in time of peace" could exist only "with consent of Parliament."[22] Parliament then promptly demonstrated its prerogative to regulate military affairs by passing the English Mutiny Act.

The Mutiny Act of 1689 was the first statute to regulate quarters throughout England. The law repeated verbatim the Petition of Right and the Disbanding Act, reiterating that free and forced quartering were unconstitutional. More important, it detailed the measures by which these constitutional liberties would be protected. Instead of free quarters, all "officers and soldiers so quartered and billeted . . . shall pay such reasonable prices." Rather than allowing the army to choose houses, the law transferred control over billeting to civilian authorities, empowering the local "constable, tithing man, or such like officer or magistrate" to determine where troops belonged. Most significantly, the English Mutiny Act introduced a new spatial division as to which types of houses would be available for soldiers. Henceforth all troops were to quarter "in inns, livery stables, alehouses, victualling houses" or other establishments licensed to sell alcohol, "and in no private houses whatsoever."[23] The Mutiny Act thus drew a line between types of houses: *private* houses were sacrosanct and could not be used for billeting, but *public* houses could not refuse to quarter troops. For the first time in the history of English quarters, all houses were not the same, and it was this spatial distinction that protected the liberties of English subjects.

The English Mutiny Act's reformation of quarters coincided with the emergence of the legal recognition of privacy. In *Semayne's Case* of 1604, a London sheriff had offered to break down the door of a residence and retrieve goods against the will of a householder. Commenting on the case, Attorney General Sir Edward Coke famously opined that "the house of everyone is to him as his castle and fortress, as well as his defense against injury and violence, as for his repose." It was not just that the house was private property; rather, the actions that occurred within the structure privileged it and entitled a man to defend it with his life. Coke's words gained popularity over the seventeenth century, leading Chief Justice Sir Matthew Hale to criticize the use of warrants that did not precisely specify the place to be searched. Yet these protections of place remained nascent, and warrantless searches continued well into the eighteenth century. It was only in the context of quartering that householders could exercise a right to privacy.[24]

The English army accepted the Mutiny Act without question. In truth, the rise of a standing army had made medieval-style billeting impractical for the army. A professional, regular fighting force prized discipline and efficiency, aims that were thwarted by scattering troops around a village. By quartering in public houses alone, the army could standardize the troops' beds, meals, and supplies, and better maintain an effective fighting force. Moreover, the army swelled in size. While medieval armies struggled to reach 15,000, the English army averaged 76,000 under William and Mary, and grew to nearly 150,000 in 1713. This gave rise to a massive military bureaucracy and further aspirations of professionalization. Indeed, some military planners envisioned massive barracks to hold the troops and keep them disciplined. The front line also moved out of England and across the globe as William and Mary vastly expanded their empire. As English armies set out to conquer Blenheim, Québec, and Palashi, billeting in private houses looked positively quaint.[25]

To be sure, the spatial dimensions of the English Mutiny Act of 1689 were not absolute. In England, the dichotomy of private and public could be more theoretical than practical. Many houses that sold alcohol continued to double as domiciles, while private householders could choose to billet troops. The differentiation of houses also did not extend to places outside England. Although monarchs forbade "any free quarter" in Scotland, English troops routinely quartered in a variety of houses in the northern kingdom.[26] Chillingly, in 1692, English soldiers billeted in Scottish homes executed at least thirty-eight members of Clan MacDonald in what came to be known as the Massacre of Glencoe.[27] The Act of Union of 1707 that melded England and Scotland into Great Britain had no effect on billeting, and well into the eighteenth century the British army documented "many inconveniences" that arose "by the soldiers being quartered in private houses" in Scotland.[28] There were no protections for the Irish.

In North America, the absence of a standing army obviated the need for quarters and blunted a division between types of houses. When the Pilgrims settled in Plymouth in 1620, they quickly made peace with the Wampanoag Indians, only to discover that congenial relations with one indigenous group put them at odds with another. Accordingly, a month after the first Thanksgiving, Governor William Bradford reported that the colonists "agreed to enclose their dwellings with a good strong pale." As the Plymouth faithful fought for salvation, they also prepared for war in this world. Their meetinghouse was the first floor of a fort "made with a flat roof and battlements, on which their ordnance were mounted." While the men of the colony led wives and children in daily prayers, they also drilled regularly, constantly ready in case of attack. Out of this type of experience, the colonial militia emerged. Unlike a standing army, the militia was inherently local, temporary, and amateur. Plymouth and nearly every colony that followed required men ages sixteen to sixty to serve in the militia. They had to own firearms and attend regular training musters.[29]

A militia had no need for quarters. Typically, the militia's work was local, so fighting men could return to their own beds and take meals at their own tables. On the rare occasion that a battle took militiamen farther afield, billeting was rarely a concern, as there were few colonial houses beyond the palisades. Indeed, the general scarcity of housing meant that groups of non-family members often lived together and that unique purposes for buildings were rarely observed; the multifunctionality of the Plymouth meetinghouse was replicated in domiciles, taverns, and other buildings. In the earliest years of colonization, military geography permeated the landscape. In a society in which every man was a soldier, every place was quarters.

Fifty years after Plymouth was planted, the English colonies had expanded in ways that altered their defensive needs and ideas about quartering. By the 1670s, colonial settlement had pushed from a few Atlantic outposts west to the Appalachian Mountains. This increasingly put the Americans in conflict with new groups of Native Americans and other European colonists. As warfare stretched from Maine to the Carolinas, the colonial governments recruited young, able-bodied men for provincial armies. Unlike militiamen, provincial soldiers required quarters. In the backcountry, the colonies built blockhouses and forts that contained meager barracks for the provincials; but while training or marching into theater, provincial armies billeted in houses. When Captain Benjamin Gibbs led troops into battle during King Philip's War (1675–1678), the Massachusetts General Court ordered that "his troops shall be quartered, at the charge of the country, in the several towns in this jurisdiction." In this and subsequent instances, the colony demanded quarters without specifying the legalities of the practice or compensation rates.[30]

On occasion, English soldiers joined the provincials. Beginning with Richard Nicolls's occupation of New York in 1664, small numbers of English soldiers arrived in North America to seize new territory or suppress insurrections. As was the case with Nicolls's troops, these soldiers often remained in America and became part of the local defense. Successors to Nicolls's forces still barracked at New York City and Albany ninety years after the first contingents arrived, recruiting new soldiers from among the colonists and subsisting on the charity of local civilians. These troops were known as independents, to distinguish them from the regulars of Britain's standing army. By 1754, there were seven companies of independents in North America, divided between New York and South Carolina. Confined to barracks and lacking military adventurism, the independents did not raise many questions about quartering.[31]

The demand for quarters intensified after 1689 when Great Britain's wars against France and Spain roiled North America. As more provincial soldiers marched into battle, the colonies began to limn some rules for billeting that emulated English practice. First, forced quartering was prohibited. New York had been the first to make this point explicit in its 1683 Charter of Liberties, and Massachusetts followed suit a decade later. "No officer," read the Bay colony's 1693 law, "shall quarter or billet any soldier or seaman upon any inhabitant within this province, without his consent."[32] Second, the determination of which houses would quarter troops was to be made by civilian authorities, not military commanders. In 1746, the Connecticut General Court resolved that a captain seeking quarters could select houses only "with the advice of one justice of the peace." Third, there was to be no free quarters. Instead, the colonies appropriated considerable financial resources to ensure that every householder who billeted troops was compensated.[33] In 1747, Massachusetts allocated £3,682 in colonial money, the equivalent to 10 percent of the colony's annual tax revenue, for billeting troops headed to Canada.[34]

The one place that Americans broke with the English was over which houses were available for quarters. While England's Mutiny Act explicitly prohibited billeting in domiciles, colonial lawmakers eschewed any practical distinction between public and private houses. Certainly, taverns were preferred; Massachusetts and New York denied licensed public houses the option of refusing to billet soldiers. But the preference for taverns was impractical, especially in small towns and rural areas. Upon leading provincials out of Boston in May 1758, Major Artemas Ward "lodged at Hasting's" in Brookfield, then "lodged at Gideon Lyman's" at Northampton, before he ran out of houses to inhabit and "encamped" in the Massachusetts wilderness.[35] To be sure, Americans complained about billeting, often objecting to low rates of compensation or the behavior of the soldiers. "Public housekeepers" in Pennsylvania claimed that the meager billeting money "makes it impossible for them to subsist," while the *New-York Weekly Journal* termed quartering "a vexatious thing" because the "insolent inmates" invariably delivered "a mischief scarcely supportable."[36] What the American colonists did not claim, however, was the inviolability of their residences or their constitutional right to keep soldiers out of them.

This was about to change.

A Home Is Not a House

Esther Edwards Burr cherished the privacy that her home afforded her. In 1754, Burr resided in Newark, New Jersey, and was the wife of the town's Presbyterian minister and president of the school that would become Princeton University. As befitted a woman of her status, Burr lived in one of the most elegant houses in Newark, a two-story Georgian structure with thick walls and wide windowsills known as the Parsonage. Although the Parsonage no longer stands, records indicate it resembled Morristown's Schuyler-Hamilton House, depicted in figure 1.2. Esther Burr kept a daily log of her life in the Parsonage, recording a constant flow of visitors through the house, including ministers and the governor. She was responsible for entertaining these guests as well as managing a household that included an infant daughter, a French teacher, and several college students. At times, Burr tired of so many people in her house. "Phoo, folks always coming," she noted in her journal. Fortunately, the size of the Parsonage allowed Burr enough space to separate her boarders into different rooms, and even gave her the opportunity to distance her personal affairs from her duties as Newark's head hostess. One night in October 1754, as Burr entertained guests, a female visitor said she wished to discuss something in confidence. "I told her we would

FIGURE 1.2. Schuyler-Hamilton House, Morristown, New Jersey. Historical American Buildings Survey, *Schuyler-Hamilton House, 5 Oliphant Place, Morristown, Morris County, NJ* (1933). Library of Congress, Prints and Photographs Division, HABS NJ,14-MORTO,3-.

walk upstairs if she pleased so we went up," Burr recorded, and the two women withdrew to discuss some delicate family matters.[37]

Esther Burr lived only ten miles from New York City, but the Parsonage was a world away from the small Dutch houses where Colonel Nicolls had billeted soldiers ninety years earlier. Quartering in the colonies had not changed much since the 1660s, but the house had. In the seventeenth century, colonial houses were small and crowded. Most contained two rooms: a chamber for storage and a hall for a variety of activities, including artisanal labor, meal preparation, and sleeping. On average, six to eight people squeezed into a house, such that parents, children, servants, slaves, and visitors shared the interior spaces, often living, working, and sleeping together. But by the middle of the eighteenth century, the size and use of the house had begun to change. As Americans acquired better building supplies, and new skilled artisans appeared, the two-room structures were replaced by larger buildings, often with two stories and six or more rooms. The larger interior spaces, in turn, affected how people lived. Additional floors and rooms separated the family from non-family members; visitors were detained in parlors, while slaves removed to separate cabins. This change occurred first among the urban elite who could displace remunerative work to a shop and transform their domiciles into places where the care of the family was the only purpose. In short, they made the house a home.[38]

It was women who stood at the forefront of this change. As men removed their work from the home, domestic matters became women's sole responsibility. Esther Burr had a taste of these changing sensibilities as her husband was often traveling, leaving her alone to manage the household. Even with the help of a servant, Burr frequently lamented how "I am really hurried" by "domestic affairs" like child care, meal preparation, and housework.[39] Although the doctrine of separate spheres did not appear until the nineteenth century, the home was already emerging as a feminine space by 1750 because it promised privacy. Not only did the home shield women from the vagaries of politics and the marketplace; it became a place to be defended because it contained dependents like women.[40]

While Esther Burr entertained guests at the Parsonage, the French and Indian War began. In May 1754, an army of Virginia provincials led by Lieutenant Colonel George Washington marched on French forces near the forks of the Ohio River. The Ohio Country sat at the forefront of British and French colonial expansion, and the two empires sought to control the trade with Native Americans in the region. Washington's provincials proved no match for a combined force of French regulars, Canadian militiamen, and Shawnee and Lenape (Delaware) warriors, surrendering at Fort Necessity in July.[41] As news of the French and Native American victory reached the American colonies, preparations for war began, even in New Jersey. In October, more than a thousand men gathered on the Newark town common to drill for war. "There never was such a training in this town before," observed Burr, who ventured two blocks from her house to survey the activities. Although "the noise of drums, guns, and trumpets" gave her a headache, she was proud of the martial valor of Newark's men. A massive war was imminent, although Burr was spared billeting troops in the Parsonage.[42]

As war preparations continued, Esther Burr's thoughts turned to her father, Jonathan Edwards. Reverend Edwards was New England's greatest revivalist, the man who had preached the Great Awakening of Northampton, Massachusetts, in the 1730s. Since then, Edwards had turned to missionary work and moved his family to Stockbridge to minister to Mahican and Mohawk Indians. "What will become of my dear father and his afflicted family!" Burr fretted as reports of skirmishes near Stockbridge reached Newark. Worried that she would never see her parents again, Burr prepared to visit western Massachusetts. Although she had saved enough money by the summer of 1755, Burr postponed her trip once she discovered she was pregnant. In February 1756, she gave birth to a son, Aaron, and six months later,

Esther Burr and the future vice president of the United States set out for Stockbridge.[43]

From Newark, Burr first traveled to New York City, where she sought a ship to take her up the Hudson River. Two years had passed since Burr saw soldiers drilling in Newark, and in that time, the skirmish at the forks of the Ohio had swollen into a world war. As a devout Presbyterian, Esther Burr cheered Great Britain's determination to take on France and defeat "our popish enemies," but the war impeded her progress. At one point, she purchased passage on a sloop, but had to surrender her place on the ship when it was "obliged to carry some of the forces that lately arrived." For nearly a week, Esther Burr and her traveling companions waited in New York City for alternate transport.[44] During this time, Burr likely boarded at a tavern or inn in the city. Much as the home had changed since the 1660s, so too had public accommodations. While Colonel Nicolls saw little difference between private and public houses, in the ninety years that passed, the two had become increasingly distinct. In New York City, the number of public houses increased dramatically, from 78 in 1722 to 287 in 1759, a rate of increase that was matched by other cities and some rural areas. The larger number of public houses encouraged a greater variety of establishments that catered to differences of rank, ethnicity, and party. One historian has observed that the increasing number of public houses depressed the expectations of householders to provide visitors with beds. In her journal, Esther Burr notes visiting several friends in New York for dinner, tea, or a visit, but never mentions sleeping at their houses.[45]

After a week in Manhattan, Burr sailed north and then hired a carriage to take her overland to Stockbridge. Outside of Albany, she ceased travel for the Sabbath and found accommodations at "a Dutch house in the woods." For a woman accustomed to the spatial divisions of the Parsonage, Burr must have felt like she had gone back in time. "The whole house is but one room," she noted disapprovingly, adding that the only way she could find solitude was to go for a walk in the forest. At night, Burr readied to sleep amid her host's "large family" when the war abruptly intruded. The single-room house became even smaller when a recruiting party appeared with "fifty soldiers to sup at this house and lodge."[46] There was no distinction between private and public houses in the woods, nor was any place spared from military control. Instead, quartering in undifferentiated houses persisted much as it had for the last century.

The next day, Esther Burr reached Stockbridge, where she was warmly embraced by Reverend Edwards and the family. Much to Burr's consternation, the Edwardses were not living in a private home, but a fort. After a series of nearby skirmishes, the Indian proselytes had departed for battle, while Stockbridge's white inhabitants had flooded the Edwardses' house at the center of town and surrounded it with palisades. This situation allowed little differentiation of space or much more privacy than the small Dutch house in the woods. Esther Burr did not like being so close to the war. She admitted being "overcome with fear" when Native Americans warriors billeted in the house, but she was not much more comforted when seventeen provincial soldiers did the same. In Newark, Burr had the luxury of keeping the soldiers on the common, but in Stockbridge, there was no distinction between martial and civilian spaces. She was astonished at how unfazed her relatives were about quartering, how her father preached four services every Sunday and wrote theology, while her mother and sisters prepared beds and meals for the troops. After a week, Burr admitted that she was "almost homesick" and began preparing to return to New Jersey.[47]

The experience of Esther Edwards Burr says much about how the American house as a place had changed and not changed by the 1750s. For an elite woman living in a two-story building in a large town, the house had become a home. It was the place of infants, not soldiers; where dinners were for distinguished guests, not random strangers. The home promised privacy—if not the entire structure, then places within it. For Burr, the English Mutiny Act with its divisions of private and public houses made sense. But her journey to Stockbridge showed her that not everyone in the colonies enjoyed domestic privacy. In rural hamlets, the house remained undifferentiated, a multipurpose structure much as it had been in the seventeenth century. Esther Burr would not have made these observations but for the intrusion of the war. Billeting soldiers was an anachronism to her, an unconscionable expansion of military geography that inhibited the house from becoming a home. Burr was not the only colonist to make this connection. Instead, the need for quarters prompted by the French and Indian War initiated an intercolonial dialogue about the house as a place. By the time Burr returned to Newark, most Americans had concluded that soldiers did not belong in the home.

The North American Establishment

With the start of the French and Indian War, the British government decided that North America needed a proper British army, a decision that had profound effects on colonial quartering policy. In September 1754, news of Washington's defeat at Fort Necessity reached the first lord of the treasury (and de facto prime minister)[48] Thomas Pelham-Holles, the first Duke of Newcastle. Newcastle had little interest in war with France, but he had no intention of surrendering the Ohio Country to Britain's archenemy. Accordingly, the prime minister devised a strategy of quick and decisive action whereby an overwhelming force of British regular soldiers would seize the Ohio Country and frighten the French into abandoning their Indian allies. While Newcastle promoted his strategy among members of Parliament at Westminster and cabinet officials at Whitehall, his plan was improved upon by Prince William Augustus, the Duke of Cumberland and commander in chief of the forces. Cumberland liked the idea of sending British regulars to North America but not Newcastle's limited action. Instead, he ordered the 44th and 48th Regiments of Foot from Ireland to Virginia with orders to recruit soldiers in the southern colonies until each unit totaled seven hundred men. He also asked the Massachusetts governor, William Shirley, to raise two regiments of a thousand men each in New England. Cumberland then enlarged Newcastle's plan to include a strike against French forces at Lake Champlain and in Nova Scotia.[49]

With this, the British government created the North American Establishment. Since the early the seventeenth century, American warfare had been left in the hands of colonists, either militiamen or provincial troops. However, the defeat at Fort Necessity elicited calls for a central military authority. At the Albany Congress in the summer of 1754, Pennsylvania assemblyman Benjamin Franklin proposed uniting the colonies to form a continental army to be led by a "military man" appointed by the king.[50] Although the colonial legislatures rejected the Plan of Union, William Shirley advocated the idea of an American army to London. At Whitehall, the idea of military reforms for the colonies also found powerful supporters, but instead of leaving matters to colonial forces, the cabinet preferred that a British army take over the war. The Ohio Country was too valuable to trust to the provincials, and Washington's surrender suggested that Americans did not have the fortitude to protect Britain's growing empire. In place of colonial troops, regular soldiers recruited in Britain and America would wage war against France. This army would be trained in military maneuvers, equipped with the latest weapons, and led by British officers. It was the first step toward assembling a standing army in the colonies.[51]

An army of thousands of British regulars scattered across a continent required leadership. In 1754, the colonial governors were the ultimate military authority in America. They commanded the militiamen and provincial soldiers, as well as any British soldiers stationed within their colony's borders. However, having a dozen commanders in chief was too chaotic for British objectives, so Whitehall created the position of commander in chief of all His Majesty's forces in North America. To occupy this august post, the cabinet selected Major General Edward Braddock, a forty-year veteran with considerable administrative experience. Braddock was given command of all British regulars headed to or raised in the colonies, as well as the seven companies of independents in New York and South Carolina. It was an impressive centralization of military authority in a place where warfare had been decentralized for a century and a half.[52]

The creation of the North American Establishment marked a new chapter in Britain's campaign to assert greater control over the colonies, but the effort was incomplete.[53] Although London commanded the soldiers, it devolved other aspects, such as quarters, to the Americans. In October 1754, Secretary of State for the Southern Department Thomas Robinson notified the colonial governors of the impending arrival of British regulars, as well as their responsibility for "quartering the troops, impressing carriages, and providing all necessaries for such forces." In effect, the colonists were responsible for arranging quarters and paying for them. Although it appears that Whitehall expected the Americans to follow English prohibitions on forced and free quartering, Robinson was silent as to where the nearly four thousand regulars being raised for North America would be quartered. Tellingly, he mentioned neither the English Mutiny Act nor its prohibition on quartering in private houses.[54]

Without money or rules from London, the governors turned matters over to the colonial assemblies. By 1754, all thirteen American colonies possessed a legislature (known alternately as the general assembly or general court), which typically consisted of an elected house of representatives and an appointed council.[55] Like little parliaments, the assemblies assumed responsibility for military affairs, especially levying taxes to pay for soldiers, fortifications, and quarters. Following Washington's defeat, the legislatures passed laws recruiting provincial troops and appropriating money to billet them. As in previous conflicts, the assemblies planned on quartering soldiers of the colonial forces in houses. However, when they received word that British regulars were headed to the colonies, American lawmakers reassessed the situation. The initial responses to quartering the North American Establishment were anything but uniform. In February 1755, the Maryland General Assembly approved funds to transport the British army into battle, as well as money to defray "quartering soldiers in public houses."[56] Maryland, which had never distinguished types of houses when billeting provincial troops, now defended private homes from lodging British soldiers. By contrast, the Massachusetts General Court voted £800 colonial money to build barracks on Castle Island in Boston Harbor and directed that all British regulars quarter there. In so doing, Massachusetts reversed its earlier differentiation of houses, as by building barracks it exempted both residences and taverns from billeting. The other colonial assemblies were not so spatially specific. The New Jersey General Assembly voted funds to support regulars as they marched through the colony, but made no mention of where British soldiers were to be accommodated. As a result, New Jersey protected neither private nor public houses, effectively opening both to quartering.[57]

In February 1755, General Braddock arrived in Virginia, where the regulars joined him a month later. The commander in chief sailed the 44th and 48th Regiments up the Potomac River to Alexandria, Virginia, and then marched them overland until they were within a hundred miles of the French Fort Duquesne (later Fort Pitt) at the forks of the Ohio River. Questions of quarters were carefully avoided in Braddock's expedition. As they marched west, the regulars camped in the open fields, and when they reached Fort Cumberland, they barracked in a rough outpost. As they waited for the weather to warm, the size of Braddock's force swelled to twenty-two hundred, which created a shortage of supplies. However, the colonial governments were slow to respond to the general's demands, and soon Braddock was grousing about parsimonious Americans. When the soldiers began to consider seizing what they needed from the nearby inhabitants, Benjamin Franklin went to Fort Cumberland and brokered a peace. In one of his earliest acts of diplomacy, the Pennsylvania assemblyman persuaded the colonists to supply the troops willingly. Nevertheless, Braddock did not want the colony to forget his kindness in requesting only transportation and supplies.[58] "My commission empowers me to settle the winter as I shall think most proper," he reminded Pennsylvania's Governor Robert Hunter Morris, adding that should the colony not be more generous, "I will repair by unpleasant methods" to quarter troops in colonial homes.[59]

Braddock never had a chance to put his threat into action. On July 9, 1755, the commander in chief and nearly five hundred of his soldiers were slain by a combined force of French, Canadian, Abenaki, Lenape, and Shawnee troops at the Battle of the Monongahela, ten miles southeast of Fort Duquesne. "O, the dreadful, awful news! General Braddock is killed and his army defeated," wrote Esther Edwards Burr when she heard what happened. "O my dear, what will, what must become of us!"[60] Many on both sides of the Atlantic received Braddock's defeat with similar horror and dread. With the general dead and the North American Establishment in disarray, Whitehall's hope of quick victory was dashed. More immediately, Braddock's defeat created an army of thirteen hundred wounded warriors who had to be removed from the Ohio Country and transported to some place where they could heal and regroup. Before the end of July, Colonel Thomas Dunbar rounded up what was left of the 44th and 48th Regiments and marched them east to Philadelphia in search of quarters.[61]

In the summer of 1755, Pennsylvania confronted the challenge of quartering British regulars. As Colonel Dunbar marched redcoats across Pennsylvania, he formally requested quarters from Governor Morris. Dunbar made sure to disavow Braddock's earlier threats of forced quartering, noting "all I desire is that the troops" receive lodging consistent with "quarters in England." News that a British army would soon be quartered in their houses sat particularly poorly with the citizens of Philadelphia, whose mayor and alderman icily observed "that we know of no law that authorizes us to make such provisions."[62] In response, the Pennsylvania assembly stepped in to write just such a law. With regulars only a few days away from the capital, the legislature embraced Dunbar's professed desire to quarter troops as they would be in England. The law announced that as "British subjects," the people of Pennsylvania had the right "not to be burdened with the sojourning of soldiers against their will." Quoting directly from the English Mutiny Act, the law declared it lawful for any colonist "to refuse to quarter any soldier or soldiers, notwithstanding any demand, warrant, or billeting whatsoever." The statute went on to insist that provisions of the Mutiny Act then in force "in that part of Great Britain called England shall be duly observed and put in execution in this province."[63] In passing such a law, Pennsylvania joined the other colonies in sacrificing public houses in order to privilege domiciles.

Pennsylvania's quartering law went unchallenged by the British army. Reaching Philadelphia in late August 1755, Colonel Dunbar encamped healthy soldiers at the southern edge of the city and hospitalized ailing troops in a house he rented from Jacob Duché at the handsome rate of £15 for six months. This deference to domestic privacy impressed the city's inhabitants, who welcomed the soldiers warmly.[64] "The Philadelphians' hearts and houses were open to us, in the most affectionate and tender manner," remembered Private Duncan Cameron of the 44th Regiment. The colonists were fascinated by the soldiers' drilling and artillery firing, and they invited the officers to a ball at the statehouse. It no doubt helped that the regulars did not linger long. A month after arrival, Colonel Dunbar marched the army north to Albany.[65]

Braddock's defeat tilted Great Britain toward all-out war with France. A second loss in the Ohio Country combined with shifting alliances in Europe to bring about a global conflict subsequently labeled the Seven Years' War. Soon, the ministry at Whitehall was directing British forces in Europe, Asia, and Africa. Nevertheless, the British government remained committed to the French and Indian War, the North American theater of the conflict.

Whitehall immediately set about rebuilding the North American Establishment by dispatching the 35th and 42nd Regiments of Foot to the colonies.
The British government also ordered the creation of the Royal American
Regiment, subsequently labeled the 60th, to raise four battalions of a thousand men each in America. Once again, the colonists prepared to quarter
thousands of British regulars with no consensus about where such soldiers
belonged.[66]

To lead the regulars in the colonies, the British government tapped Major
General John Campbell, the Earl of Loudoun, to serve as commander in
chief. Loudoun was a Scot who had inherited his father's peerage in his twenties. A lifelong bachelor, Loudoun had devoted his life to the army. He shared
Braddock's extensive military administrative experience, as well as his predecessor's preference for forceful leadership that made him seem prickly if
not tyrannical. In many ways, Loudoun was the colonies' first exposure to a
powerful British imperialist, and the colonists complained bitterly about his
demands; for this reason, historians have often depicted Loudoun's efforts
as an opening salvo in the Revolutionary War. Indeed, the colonists quickly
located a vocabulary of constitutional rights in their communications with
the commander in chief that foreshadowed the crises of the 1760s and 1770s.[67]

Chief among Loudoun's conflicts with the colonists was quarters. Arriving to command an army that was losing the war, the Earl of Loudoun
refused to accept any limitation on where a soldier could be billeted. Specifically, he asserted that spatial distinctions had been obliterated by the declaration of war. "Although in time of peace quartering of troops is confined to
public houses," the general explained to one governor, "in time of war the
practice has always been in every country without exception, that no house
has been exempted from quartering the troops."[68] Accordingly, Loudoun
rejected the privileging of residences in Maryland and Pennsylvania, as well
as Massachusetts's protection of all houses. Moreover, unlike Braddock and
Dunbar, Loudoun was prepared to challenge directly the colonists' limits on
quarters. In response, the Americans moved to strengthen the protection of
the house from state intrusion.

In July 1756, Lord Loudoun arrived in New York. The new commander in
chief found the situation dire. Massachusetts's Governor William Shirley had
taken command after Braddock's defeat and concentrated the army along
Lake Ontario and Lake George. It was an act of futility. Less than a month
after Loudoun arrived, the French general the Marquis de Montcalm captured Fort Oswego (near Fort Ontario), decimating the 50th and 51st Regiments, and allowing France to consolidate its control over the Great Lakes
and the Ohio Country. Accordingly, Loudoun headed north for Albany to

take command from Shirley. There, he discovered some ten thousand men drilling for war. However, the men were so poorly disciplined that the general decided to winter in Albany and train for battle the following spring.[69]

Loudoun's conflict with the colonists over quarters began in Albany. With soldiers outnumbering civilians by a ratio of five to one, the general brushed aside any distinction between houses. He ordered a survey of Albany's buildings and determined that the city could billet fifty soldiers in public houses and from fifteen hundred to two thousand in domiciles.[70] The townspeople reacted defiantly. Mayor Johannes Hansen informed Loudoun that he had "no right to quarters, or storehouses, or anything else from them." Loudoun dismissed Hansen as "a fool" and pressured the local magistrates to billet troops. The inhabitants "shut out several officers," and one householder "threw an officer's baggage into the streets, and barricaded the door." Loudoun responded by sending soldiers to put the officer in the man's house by force and then threatened that if any others resisted, he would "take the whole house for a hospital, or a store house." It was a breathtaking show of force that completely disregarded the colony's sixty-five-year-old prohibition of quartering in private houses.[71]

Albany was a particularly poor place to billet regulars. Numerous writers noted the small size of Albany's houses and the intimacy within them. Most inhabitants resided in one-or two-room wooden structures with few accoutrements.[72] When traveling through the region in early 1761, Warren Johnson remarked how "a Dutch parlor has always a bed in it, and the man and woman of the house sleep in it."[73] Such intimacy was aggravated by the addition of soldiers.

Growing up in Albany, Anne MacVicar Grant recalled how a "young colonel" took a fancy to a woman who lived in the house where he billeted. "Artless and fearless of consequences," the two began a flirtation that was harmless at first. However, when the colonel received word he would depart Albany, the young woman "tore her hair in frantic agonies at his departure," and the relationship sped up considerably. "Being very impetuous, and unaccustomed to control," the woman gave herself sexually to the colonel, which her father discovered much to his horror. Seeking to "cover the disgrace of his family," the father pressed the officer to marry his daughter, but the colonel refused, and he departed with his regiment. "This unexpected refusal threw the whole city into consternation," Anne Grant concluded. "One would have thought there had been an earthquake."[74]

Lord Loudoun was not unaware of these problems. Describing Albany as a place "where I am obliged to quarter more troops than the people can support," the commander in chief noted how he took only "house room" from the inhabitants, supplying firewood and beds at the army's expense.[75] To some extent, Albany's location midway between New York City and Montréal condemned it to have troops until the end of the French and Indian War. However, the size and poverty of the city convinced Loudoun that he should send as many British regulars out of Albany as he could. In the fall of 1756, the general sent word to the governors of Massachusetts, New York, New Jersey, Pennsylvania, and Maryland to expect some portion of the North American Establishment for the following winter. Loudoun selected these colonies because they had large populations and thus had more houses for quarters and more money for supplies. "My plan is to quarter the whole, and give no *slaap gelt*, which will be a saving to the government," Loudoun announced proudly to Whitehall, using a Dutch term for billeting money.[76]

For the next two years, the North American Establishment spread across the colonies. Entire regiments wintered in colonial cities, while recruiting parties and columns of regulars marching to battle billeted intermittently in small towns and rural areas. As he had in Albany, the Earl of Loudoun insisted that any colonial restrictions on quartering were irrelevant, invalidated by war. The colonists, however, resisted Loudoun's spatial imprecision as they sought to protect their domiciles from quartering. To be sure, the colonies' unique quartering laws and varied infrastructures meant that some troops were confined to public houses, some entered domiciles, and some were diverted to other buildings. Regardless of where the British regulars billeted, however, the Americans insisted on the spatial protections that their English brethren enjoyed. Through petitions, laws, and personal actions, the colonists sacrificed public houses, surrendered municipal buildings, and built barracks to protect their homes.

Public Houses in Philadelphia

In October 1756, the Earl of Loudoun began to dispatch British regulars out of Albany. The North American Establishment had been demoralized and decimated by recent losses. The defeat at Fort Oswego had reduced the 50th and 51st Regiments to three hundred soldiers total, while the recently created Royal American Regiment had fewer than fifteen hundred men, far below its authorized size of four thousand. Consequently, Loudoun divided the army, sending contingents to cities and towns on the Atlantic coast. He ordered the 50th and 51st to Boston, and dispersed the Royal Americans across New York, New Jersey, Philadelphia, Delaware, and Maryland. The troops were to stay in the American colonies for the next six months. During this time, Loudoun expected veterans of the previous campaigns to heal, while recruiting parties would build up the North American Establishment to full strength.[77]

Preceding the troops' deployment, Loudoun sent formal requests for quarters to the colonial governors. In each missive, the commander in chief reiterated his argument that in time of war no distinction could be made between types of houses. When the governors forwarded Loudoun's request to the colonial assemblies, however, American lawmakers took exception to such spatial imprecision. Regardless of war or peace, they asserted, private houses were barred to British troops. However, this was rarely the end of the matter. Keeping troops out of residences required that the colonies provide alternative accommodations, but this was not an option for all cities and towns. With hundreds of regulars descending upon them, the colonists found that protecting private homes required perseverance and creativity.

Philadelphia attempted to avoid billeting in domiciles by following the English practice of distinguishing public from private houses, and for the most part the city succeeded. Philadelphia had wrangled with quarters in 1755 when Colonel Dunbar arrived with the remnants of Braddock's expedition, and the Pennsylvania assembly issued an effective, if succinct, law directing soldiers to public houses. Accordingly, when the Earl of Loudoun sent word in September 1756 that Philadelphia should expect the first battalion of the Royal American Regiment, Pennsylvania lawmakers received the news calmly. Ignoring Loudoun's comment that troops were quartered in all houses "in Great Britain in time of war," they planned to maintain the English Mutiny Act's distinction of houses and quarter regulars in taverns.[78]

But there was a problem. Shortly after Loudoun informed Philadelphia to expect regulars, the colony received word that Britain's Privy Council had disallowed the Pennsylvania quartering law of 1755. The British government insisted on reviewing all laws passed by the American colonies, typically delegating this task to a group of civil and ecclesiastical ministers including the cabinet known as the Privy Council, or to the Board of Trade, which acted on behalf of the Privy Council.[79] In the case of Pennsylvania's quartering law, the councilors found the colonists' differentiation of place problematic. Attorney General William Murray cited "the tendency of this act . . . to cramp the public service and obstruct the defense of the province" in his recommendation that the council quash the law, effectively agreeing with Loudoun that there could be no restrictions on quartering "in time of war."[80] However, the Pennsylvania assembly was unmoved. In December 1756, the House of Representatives approved a law that was an even more stirring defense of private houses than the 1755 version had been. If the previous statute had been too succinct, the 1756 version repeated the Mutiny Act verbatim, including the point that civilian officials alone would "quarter and billet the officers and soldiers in His Majesty's service in inns, livery stables, alehouses, victualing houses," and "in no private houses whatsoever."[81] Like England, Pennsylvania would have a clear distinction of houses when it came to quarters.

The intransigence of the Pennsylvania assembly worried Governor William Denny. Denny was an Oxford-educated Englishman and a veteran of the British army who arrived in Philadelphia just as the quartering controversy was heating up. When the assembly first proposed its quartering bill, Denny cautioned that it was "the same as that lately repealed by His Majesty in council," but he signed the bill into law anyway. Denny did, however, find the legislature's math a bit odd. He examined lists of tavern licenses and calculated that there would not be enough room in the public houses alone to quarter a battalion. The House of Representatives rejected this point. A house committee had also examined the same list of licenses, and it concluded there were "no less than 117" taverns in Philadelphia, a sufficient number to quarter the four hundred troops expected in the city.[82] Denny responded that this count was overly optimistic; the number of public houses had been inflated as a result of publicans' "mistaken notion that they were to be paid a shilling a day for every head," which was three times the going rate for civilians. Some Philadelphia tavern keepers had volunteered their own homes, even though many had "large families, and not a bed to spare."[83] Philadelphia mayor Attwood Shute agreed. With troops expected any day, he "apprehended those houses would not be sufficient to entertain so great a number."[84] But the assembly was unmoved.

Local concerns may have contributed to Pennsylvania's rigid stance. The colonial legislature was dominated by members of the Society of Friends, whose Quaker theology encouraged a sharp division of public and private houses. First, the Friends were notably hostile to Philadelphia's rapidly expanding tavern culture. In 1744, a grand jury chaired by Benjamin Franklin expressed its "great concern" with "the vast number of tippling houses within this city, many of which they think are little better than nurseries of vice and debauchery."[85] As previous efforts to reduce the number of public houses had failed, the 1756 quartering law may have been an attempt to tax some taverns out of existence. Second, the Friends placed greater value on the home as a place than most colonists did. The Quakers were pioneers of domesticity, attaching profound spiritual significance to the family and child rearing. Seventeenth-century probate inventories reveal that Friends spent more money on furniture, especially beds, than their Anglican neighbors, a distinction that grew over time. In their quest to create the home as a place where the family could be nourished, Pennsylvanians would have been more hostile than most Americans to billeting soldiers in private houses.[86]

In December 1756, Colonel Henry Bouquet arrived in Philadelphia with five hundred enlisted men and forty-seven officers from the Royal American Regiment. This was a third more troops than even the assembly's optimistic calculations claimed the city's taverns could accommodate; plus, Bouquet was anxious to recruit more soldiers. Confronting the prospect of troops exposed to the vagaries of a Philadelphia winter, Governor Denny gave Bouquet a warrant "to provide quarters for the soldiers in private houses."[87] The assembly was outraged. "We cannot conceive it will, when well considered, be thought advisable, to quarter the soldiers by force on private houses rather than by law on public houses," the House of Representatives railed against the governor. "The king's troops must be quartered," Denny responded.[88]

On December 20, Governor Denny appeared before the House of Representatives to debate quarters. Once again, the discussion revolved around temporal versus spatial divisions. Like Loudoun, Denny contended that "in time of war, and in cases of necessity, it was usual in England to quarter soldiers on private houses." As proof, he "instanced Carlisle," a somewhat dubious reference to King James II's forced billeting in the 1680s. Legislators responded that the troops could have been sent to suburban taverns or other buildings instead of private homes, as was also "the custom in England." Denny conceded that this was indeed true, but he added that the cost of such quarters was "the expense of the town or city," and Philadelphia had not agreed to pay any such money.[89] The debate ended without resolution, only "an abundance of heat, passion, and rudeness," including Benjamin Franklin's "several offensive, indecent, and rude expressions" that were too colorful to be entered into the assembly record.[90]

While the governor and the assembly exchanged unpleasantries, Colonel Bouquet squeezed as many soldiers into Philadelphia's taverns as possible, but by Christmas, sixty-two men still lacked quarters. With snow beginning to fall, the mayor and the battalion quartermaster inspected every tavern in the city, only to discover that the situation was worse than they had imagined.[91] Of the billeted soldiers, ninety-four slept on piles of straw, and seventy-three "had nothing to lay on and not sufficient quantity of covering."[92] Even officers could not find quarters. Many of the troops had contracted smallpox, which threatened to infect the whole city. The mayor and quartermaster also discovered that thirty-five publicans claimed that they had no room for the troops, although this may have reflected the meager compensation rate for billets approved by the assembly. They also discovered that Governor Denny's warrants for billeting troops in private homes were useless because the sheriff refused to execute them. When Lord Loudoun heard that soldiers "in Philadelphia are extremely ill quartered," he communicated his displeasure to Denny. He appealed to the governor's experience in the army when he may have billeted in a private house, before closing with a threat. If houses were not procured, "I will instantly march a number sufficient to that purpose and find quarters for the whole."[93]

The prospect of forced quartering hastened a solution to the impasse in Philadelphia. Remaining insistent that private houses could not be opened to British regulars, the assembly turned over the recently completed Pennsylvania Hospital to Bouquet for use as barracks. This provided temporary accommodations, but Denny and the assembly continued to negotiate a lasting solution. In March 1757, the assembly passed and the governor signed a quartering law that once again codified the distinction between houses. Although the law did not explicitly mention private houses, it stated that the English Mutiny Act applied to Pennsylvania, thus making the same point more subtly. Henceforth, all public houses would pay a tax on the "wine, rum, brandy or other spirits by him or her sold," the revenue of which would compensate publicans who quartered troops. The law also penalized tavern keepers who chose to go out of business instead of billeting troops. If a publican gave up his or her license, then he or she would be "incapable of receiving any such license thereafter."[94]

Philadelphia's determination to place British regulars in public houses required some creativity and sacrificed one of the city's great civic institutions. Nevertheless, the city had rejected Loudoun's notion of place, doing so through colonial law. Proof of Philadelphia's success came in January 1758 when Britain's Privy Council considered the colony's quartering law and allowed it to stand.[95] The home was not part of Philadelphia's military geography.

Yet Philadelphia was unique. In addition to being controlled by Quakers, Philadelphia was the largest city in British North America, with more than sixteen thousand inhabitants and three thousand houses. It was the political capital of Pennsylvania and the economic center of the region. More than most colonial cities, Philadelphia embraced refinement, boasting dozens of Georgian mansions as well as civic institutions like the Pennsylvania Hospital. It also offered a conviviality that few other places could match, with well over a hundred licensed taverns in operation. As a result, Philadelphia had the physical space to quarter a regiment of regulars without having to intrude upon private houses, as well as the cultural capital and political power to defend its rights in the face of the British army. Not every place in America was so well equipped.[96]

Private Houses in New Jersey

Where Philadelphia succeeded, towns in the surrounding colonies failed. In dividing the North American Establishment, the Earl of Loudoun sent word to New Jersey, Maryland, and Delaware to prepare winter quarters for two battalions of the Royal American Regiment. None of these colonies possessed a city as large or as vibrant as the Pennsylvania capital. Annapolis was the largest town in the three colonies, at perhaps one-fourth the size of Philadelphia. Most other towns in the region contained a few hundred houses, nearly all of which were residences. Like the house in figure 1.3, most of the region's houses were two-room structures, while those few that served as taverns typically had little separation between public and private spaces. A shortage of public houses was compounded by a lack of municipal buildings and forts with barracks. In these colonies, British regulars billeted almost exclusively in private houses.[97]

In October 1756, Loudoun dispatched the fourth battalion of the Royal American Regiment to New Jersey, as well as an independent company to drum up recruits. Upon receiving a request for quarters from Loudoun,

FIGURE 1.3. Wood Tavern, Roadstown, New Jersey. Historical American Buildings Survey, *Wood Tavern, Roadstown, Cumberland County, NJ* (1933). Library of Congress, Prints and Photographs Division, HABS NJ, 6-ROATO,1-.

Governor Jonathan Belcher applied to the colonial legislature for guidance. As the House of Representatives was in recess, the provincial council told Belcher "to prepare winter quarters" and left the details to him.[98] Accordingly, the governor recommended that the troops be divided among four towns, the largest of which contained between two and three hundred houses. With little other direction from the colonial government, hundreds of regulars spread across New Jersey, billeting in whatever houses they could find.[99]

As British regulars entered their houses, the people of New Jersey complained to their elected leaders. When the House of Representatives reconvened in December 1756, it received petitions from six towns "relating to the soldiers quartered among them." Apparently, the troops had found insufficient space in the towns identified by Governor Belcher and moved on to Perth Amboy, New Brunswick, Princeton, Trenton, Bordentown, and Burlington. Trenton representative Joseph Yard told the assembly of the harassment he had faced in his own home. According to Yard, a captain appeared at his house and demanded accommodations for a soldier. When Yard refused, "the said officer taking a musket in his hand, rushed against the said complainant, and forced his way into the house, and put in one of his soldiers." The soldier departed after a few days, but left his luggage behind. When rumors reached the army that Yard had turned out the soldier, an officer and troops returned "and then said officer went into every room of said complainant's house, and then ordered one of his sergeants, to see that the soldier was lodged in a good feather bed."[100] Joseph Yard's experience exhibited all the worst excesses of forced quartering unregulated by civilian authority. Not only did the army invade Yard's house; it refused to recognize the difference between public and private spaces within his home.

The House of Representatives sat for only a week in December 1756 and adjourned before addressing the complaints of Joseph Yard and other New Jersey householders. However, when the assembly reconvened in March 1757, lawmakers set some rules for quartering in the future. No longer would there be free or forced quartering. When regulars returned, householders would be compensated out of the colonial treasury, and types of houses would be distinguished. The House of Representatives resolved unanimously "that the quartering soldiers in any private house within this colony, is expressly contrary to the Act of Parliament."[101] But it was an empty promise. Not only had the regulars already departed, but the legislature had not specified where soldiers should go instead.[102]

In the fall of 1757, British regulars returned to New Jersey for a second winter. Now that the colonial government had established some rules, quartering proceeded in a more orderly fashion. Officers applied to civilian authorities for houses rather than simply taking them; they were more faithful about issuing billets for householders to redeem for payment. Despite the new rules, however, problems remained. Troops swarmed several towns, overwhelming the inhabitants with "sick and ailing soldiers."[103] "There being no hospitals or barracks prepared for their reception," the provincial council remarked, the soldiers were placed in homes with "great inconveniences to the inhabitants."[104] The result was particularly rough on those colonists who were poor and who had "small houses and numerous families, with not more than one room." Again, the assembly collected petitions from aggrieved colonists, but failed to provide a remedy.[105]

Surviving records from Trenton for the winter of 1757–1758 allow a rare view inside the practice of quartering. Beginning in the middle of November, soldiers and officers from the 48th Regiment of Foot trickled into town. By the end of the year, there were more than 200 infantrymen, grenadiers, ensigns, and lieutenants living in Trenton. At least 250 more arrived between January and April 1758, after which they all departed. The small town, which had 100 to 130 dwellings at the time, few of which were taverns, was overwhelmed by so many soldiers. Men crowded into nearly every house, so that 121 of the town's families hosted at least one soldier at some point. More than half the families accommodated seven soldiers or more over the course of the winter, although because the soldiers came and went with some regularity, most families had only two to four soldiers living with them at any one time. This could be nonetheless imposing in a county where the average household contained six people.[106]

Quartering proceeded with little regard for a homeowner's religion, sex, or wealth. Some regulars quartered with pacifist Quaker families and others with Presbyterians. One-fifth of households were headed by or owned outright by women. Some regulars lived with "the widow Skirm," and others with individuals who could not sign their own names. Some made themselves at home with the leading men of the county like Dr. Ralph Norton, town treasurer Andrew Reed, esq., and Assemblyman Joseph Yard. While the destitute avoided billeting troops, wealthier residents had additional responsibilities. Andrew Reed and Moore Furman supplied a makeshift hospital with chamber pots, blankets, and candles, while Theophilus Severns and William Morris procured over a hundred cords of wood for the hospital and guardhouse.

The troops constantly moved in and out of Trenton, creating a destabilizing influence that upset normal family relations. Nine soldiers arrived on Christmas Day 1757, and another forty-one appeared in the week that followed, marring a time traditionally reserved for celebrations and rest. One in twelve soldiers spent only one night in Trenton, and half spent less than two months quartered with the colonists, but more than a hundred lingered on for five months. Even within the town, the soldiers were constantly on the move. One soldier who arrived in November stayed at Charles Axford's house for three months before going to William Adams's, before moving again to Joseph Hall's in April. Some householders may have become fond of the troops. This was most likely true for houses that hosted officers, although at least three residents listed the names of privates on the receipts, perhaps indicating a degree of familiarity.

The records do not offer much insight into what life was like inside the Trenton homes where soldiers billeted. It appears that homeowners were responsible for providing beds and blankets for the troops. These beds, each one shared by two soldiers, probably were not far from the residents' sleeping spaces, as Trenton was "nothing remarkable," according to one visitor.[107] The soldiers likely took their meals with the family at the dinner table and ate food prepared by the woman of the house. Interestingly, the colonial government compensated homeowners at the rate of only two shillings sixpence per week for a private. This low rate of reimbursement might indicate that the army provided food for the soldiers. If so, this would certainly have lightened the burden of quartering, although householders likely had to pay for extra candles and firewood out of billeting money provided by the colonial government.[108]

A similar scene played out in Maryland and Delaware. The third battalion of the Royal American Regiment wintered between the two colonies in 1756–1757.[109] As in New Jersey, the colonial governments divided the troops among several small towns with "scarcely any public houses," according to one captain.[110] Accordingly, the soldiers went into private houses, where they irritated the colonists. In February 1757, the Earl of Loudoun received a petition from the inhabitants in Georgetown, Maryland, on behalf of a householder for whom billeting had gone horribly wrong. As Georgetown lacked "barracks or other conveniences," several soldiers billeted in "a dwelling house with four rooms on the lower floor" until a candle left carelessly unattended by a soldier caused a fire that "utterly consumed the dwelling house" and several outbuildings. The neighbors demanded Loudoun compensate the householder, insisting "this burden too heavy to be borne by one individual."[111] Nor was this the only private house in Maryland damaged by British troops before they departed in the spring.[112]

The following winter was equally difficult when the second battalion of the Royal Americans sought quarters in Maryland. Loudoun insisted that all five hundred regulars be stationed in Annapolis, although they quickly overwhelmed the colonial capital. According to Maryland's Governor Horatio Sharpe, the "the number of families that reside in this place are far short of a hundred," and most were too poor to provide beds and supplies for the soldiers. As a result, leading men of the town were "obliged to receive or provide lodging, fire, and necessaries for fifteen or twenty men each."[113] Not only did Loudoun ignore the pleas from Annapolis, but the Maryland legislature offered no help. Political wrangling between the two houses of the Maryland General Assembly kept any quartering bill from becoming law, and Annapolis was forced to billet troops in private houses for free.[114]

Practically, the distinction between public and private houses in New Jersey, Maryland, and Delaware was prevented in the billeting of British regulars under Lord Loudoun. Privacy was denied to residences, while long-standing guarantees against forced and free quartering were ignored. Lawmakers were unable or unwilling to challenge the commander in chief, while New Jersey's legal prohibition on quartering in private houses went unheeded. Where the assemblies proved inadequate, the people demonstrated leadership, demanding that the army be held accountable for damaging residences and assaulting individuals. Through actions and petitions, the inhabitants struggled to protect the domicile from soldiers, even if they ultimately failed to do so.

Alternative Quarters in Boston

In their efforts to keep British soldiers out of private houses, lawmakers in Pennsylvania and New Jersey followed the English example. In the spirit of England's Mutiny Act, they sought a legal distinction between public and private houses, sacrificing the former to privilege the latter. However, as New Jersey demonstrated, this distinction was ineffectual in places that lacked enough taverns to accommodate all the troops. Yet not all colonies followed the mother country. Instead, Americans in urban areas proposed an alternative: quartering troops in forts, barracks, or public buildings. In so doing, they privileged all houses as a way of keeping British regulars out of residences. Several cities attempted this strategy, although none was entirely successful, in part because it required that they have large amounts of uninhabited buildings capable of housing hundreds of troops. New York City and Charleston tried to keep regulars out of all houses, but only Boston proved successful at providing alternative quarters.

In early 1757, the Earl of Loudoun informed Boston that it should expect three hundred soldiers from the 50th and 51st Regiments for the remainder of the winter. The troops' reception in the capital of Massachusetts worried Loudoun, who apparently had been warned to expect defiance in Boston. The general's fears were not entirely unwarranted, as Massachusetts had been without a royal governor since William Shirley had departed the previous fall. Yet even without a chief executive, the General Court of Massachusetts successfully answered Loudoun's call for quarters. Two years earlier, the assembly had voted to build barracks for British soldiers. The barracks stood on Castle Island, a fortified outpost in Boston Harbor, some three miles from the city and a half mile from the mainland.[115] When the General Court received news that regulars were headed to Boston, it directed the soldiers to the Castle Island barracks and voted they "be provided with as many beds as were necessary for the forces, and wood and candles."[116]

Massachusetts's response angered Loudoun, who assailed a colony's prioritization of place over time. Indeed, restricting the understaffed regiments to Castle Island undermined the reason they were sent to Boston in the first place: to recruit new soldiers. Recruiting parties were made up of an officer, one or two sergeants, and a drummer, who journeyed from town to town seeking soldiers for the British army.[117] Confining troops to Castle Island made this impossible. However, Loudoun had no time to challenge quartering in Massachusetts; shortly after the 50th and 51st arrived, the troops departed for battle along the Great Lakes and in Canada. But six months later, the soldiers returned. In August 1757, Loudoun told Boston to expect a thousand men from a Scottish regiment for the winter. As so many troops exceeded the space in the barracks, Massachusetts would have to allow quartering in houses.[118]

Arriving along with Loudoun's demand was a new governor for Massachusetts: Thomas Pownall. Alone among the men whom Whitehall dispatched to govern the colonies, Pownall understood Americans' spatial sensitivities. He had studied imperial affairs at Cambridge and improved upon this education with a series of posts in North America, including lieutenant governor of New Jersey. During his time in the colonies, Pownall had befriended Benjamin Franklin, and the two forged a friendship based on their shared vision of greater Anglo-American unity. When the French and Indian War began, he went to work for the Earl of Loudoun, serving as his secretary before becoming governor of Massachusetts. These experiences gave Pownall a keen understanding of Americans' aversion to quartering troops in their houses.[119]

Upon receiving Loudoun's request for quarters, Pownall sent the matter to the General Court. The governor reaffirmed the power of the colonial assembly, noting that all decisions about quartering "must originate with the House of Representatives." But he also insisted that it was pointless for lawmakers to oppose quartering, because "the troops are sent hither for the preservation and security" of the colony, and because it was cruel to leave the soldiers "destitute of quarters." Pownall went on to request that the assembly consider billeting troops in places other than Castle Island. "In Scotland and Ireland it has been found necessary to quarter troops on private houses," Pownall noted, baiting the House with a non-English comparison, adding that whether the soldiers would best be accommodated by "quartering partly on private houses, and partly on public, you are the best judges."[120] If Massachusetts truly wanted to be like England, then Boston would have to quarter troops in its public houses.

Pownall's clever approach inspired action among Massachusetts lawmakers, but they refused to open Boston's taverns to soldiers. Rather, the House of Representatives voted "that there be an addition of about one hundred feet in length to the new barracks on Castle Island, which will then contain a thousand privates." The legislature also agreed to build a house at Castle Island for officers, and to provide beds, kettles, bowls, spoons, lamps, firewood, and candles. Although lawmakers groused about how their constituents already paid taxes "vastly out of proportion to any other colony," they nonetheless appropriated £400 colonial money for the new buildings and supplies.[121] Writing to Loudoun, Pownall tried to put the best face on Massachusetts's obstinacy. "It is of more consequence to gain the point of quarters," the governor advised, than "to engage unsuccessfully in disputes about regaining the Crown's rights."[122]

Governor Pownall's practical response to the situation in Boston did little to calm the commander in chief. Three months after Massachusetts refused to billet soldiers in any house, Loudoun dispatched recruiting parties to Boston in order to force a resolution. However, the colonists were no more prepared to billet recruiters than they were regular soldiers. "On my arrival here I applied to the selectmen and to . . . justices [of the peace] for billets for my party which they have refused," Captain Nicholas Cox informed his commanding officer.[123] Pownall was sympathetic to the recruiting parties, but he refused to violate colonial law, so he directed the troops to Castle Island. The recruiters were baffled. Confining them to barracks thwarted "the purpose of this service on which they were sent."[124] Pownall was furious with Loudoun, but he was unwilling to challenge him. Instead, the governor asked the legislature for a law to billet recruiting parties in colonial houses.[125]

In November 1757, the Massachusetts General Court agreed to the commander in chief's demand for quarters at least in part. The assembly passed a law allowing "recruiting officers and recruits" but no other British soldiers to billet in public houses "licensed for the selling within doors wine, rum, or other strong liquors." The act empowered civilian authorities alone to select the taverns and provided recourse in case "any person shall find himself aggrieved" by quartering too many soldiers. Like Pennsylvania, Massachusetts insisted that its colonists' homes were private places without explicitly making this point. The law invoked the English Mutiny Act by setting compensation rates in Massachusetts at the same levels as those "established and regulated by Act of Parliament for quartering and billeting officers and soldiers in England."[126] Yet Massachusetts's insistence on English rights upset Loudoun, who railed against the colony's differentiation of houses. He informed Pownall that the law would set a bad precedent and "turn three-fourths of the troops at once into the streets to perish." Nevertheless, the governor signed the bill into law.[127]

With the passage of the Massachusetts quartering law, recruiting parties spread out across the colony in search of new soldiers. According to Captain John Cosnan, Massachusetts made for poor recruiting, as New Englanders preferred to fight as provincial soldiers rather than as British regulars. As for "billeting in this province," Cosnan noted that it proceeded, "though not without some difficulties and trouble."[128] Massachusetts publicans appreciated the high price that the army paid for billets, but they worried about quartering troops, especially those with smallpox.

Although recruiting parties could billet in Boston taverns, the barracks on Castle Island made long stints in the city unnecessary, even for recruiting parties that could easily sail back to the harbor fortress. In this way, Boston's public houses were uniquely protected within Massachusetts. When Governor Pownall received word in March 1758 that "a body of His Majesty's troops" would be marching through the province on its way to the front, he asked the General Court for a remedy.[129] The legislature responded with a law requiring "every taverner or innholder" to lodge and feed regulars. However, the law exempted publicans "within the town of Boston," directing the troops to Castle Island instead.[130] As regulars marched through Massachusetts, it became apparent that smaller towns suffered more than Boston from quartering. In June 1758, the General Court received a petition from people in Worcester requesting a tax exemption because they had "suffered greatly in the year past, by billeting five thousand men for many days."[131] Without barracks, the publicans in small towns like Worcester lacked the type of spatial protections that Bostonians enjoyed.

Massachusetts's strategy for keeping British regulars out of houses was also attempted in New York City. When Loudoun announced that the second battalion of the Royal American Regiment would spend the winter of 1756–1757 in the colonial capital, the assembly set about writing a quartering law. Although New York had maintained a legal distinction between public and private houses since 1691, recent events prompted many to question this point. Indeed, some lawmakers wondered if British regulars should to be quartered in any house at all. According to Governor Sir Charles Hardy, billeting was "so hard upon the poor tavern keepers" that they could not do so "without ruin to them and their families."[132] Instead of quartering in public houses, the New York assembly suggested that the troops go into barracks at Fort George and several blockhouses in the region. When Loudoun heard this plan, he rejected it, contending that New York City's military infrastructure could accommodate only two-fifths of the total number of troops that the second battalion was set to raise.[133] Accordingly, the governor and legislators worked out a compromise that introduced a gradation of places. British soldiers in need of quarters would first be directed to barracks, and if these proved insufficient, they would be billeted "in such inns, livery stables, alehouses, victualling houses, and all houses selling rum, brandy, cider, or any other spirituous liquors." Should both options be exhausted, then the troops would be billeted "in such private houses" as selected by local authorities.[134]

Charleston also attempted to divert regulars to alternative quarters. In the 1740s, the capital of South Carolina had received an independent company of British soldiers and had built a small brick barracks to accommodate them. Although the independents departed for Virginia at the start of the French and Indian War, Charleston hoped that its barracks would protect it from having to billet British regulars in the city's homes. However, when Colonel Henry Bouquet arrived with seven hundred Royal Americans in June 1757, he pronounced the barracks insufficient and demanded the colony provide quarters. Attempting to keep soldiers out of their homes, the South Carolina Commons House ordered that "the late free school be also fitted up, and other suitable houses hired for their reception, until the whole number of troops shall be accommodated." While he waited for quarters, Bouquet encamped the soldiers outside town.[135]

Before South Carolina could fix up the school, however, a second regiment appeared. In September 1757, Lieutenant Colonel Archibald Montgomerie and a thousand Highland Scots arrived. As the number of soldiers in Charleston doubled, the weather turned nasty. "The continual rains have driven us out of the camp, and our men are quartered in town very badly," Bouquet lamented. As soldiers started to desert, the colonel took matters into his own hands. He led soldiers into the city, where they "were quartered in a half finished church without windows, in damp storehouses upon the quay, and in empty houses where most of the men were obliged to lie upon the ground without straw." Although South Carolina lawmakers assured Bouquet that they were working on a solution, the colonel continued to quarter troops himself. By October, he had squeezed five hundred men into the barracks and scattered the rest among the city's public houses. However, this was still not enough room, so, as the colonel informed Loudoun, "the Highlanders have 187 men quartered in private houses." As Bouquet confessed to Loudoun, quartering was "the eternal struggle in America."[136]

The efforts of lawmakers in Massachusetts, New York, and South Carolina were a sincere attempt to keep soldiers out of American houses by offering alternative locations. Like Americans elsewhere, legislators in these colonies placed the greatest priority on protecting private houses and offered them only as a last resort if all other buildings were occupied. Ultimately, however, Boston, New York, and Charleston failed to keep troops out of all houses, with regulars even entering private houses in Charleston. Yet the idea of alternative quarters remained popular in these colonies and quickly gained traction in others. If British regulars quartered in private houses because there was not enough room in the public houses, forts, barracks, and public buildings, then new structures had to be built. By the fall of 1757, several American colonies were hard at work constructing massive barracks for the British regulars.

Houses

It would be incorrect to claim that quartering created the home or introduced the notion of domestic privacy. These were long-term changes that were still in their infancy in the eighteenth century. Yet the advent of a large, professional army, first in England and then in America, initiated a dialogue on billeting from which people concluded that soldiers should be barred from domiciles. As Esther Edwards Burr observed, the home was a place where women and children were protected, where a person found solace and peace. Although not all houses had these attributes, Burr recognized that the intrinsic quality of the home was incompatible with quarters. Lawmakers codified the home as a place of domestic tranquility through quartering laws, and in so doing promoted a notion of constitutional rights and a differentiation of public and private that protected the home long after the soldiers departed.

Yet the military geography of British North America had only begun to change in 1756. Despite Americans' insistence that the home was different from other houses, they lacked the infrastructure to make this a reality. The Earl of Loudoun's determination to quarter troops in all houses, as well as the colonies' lack of taverns, prevented the English Mutiny Act from providing a way for the colonists to protect their homes. Accordingly, they sought an alternative: barracks. Barracks effectively removed houses from the colonies' military geography, creating a firm divide between places where soldiers belonged and places they did not. Making the home a civilian place later resurfaced in the Quartering Act's prohibition of billeting in private houses.

CHAPTER 2

Barracks

Constructing a Colonial Military Infrastructure

John William Gerard De Brahm believed that the best way to protect a city was to surround it with a wall. Born in Germany around 1717, De Brahm was well educated in the tactics of war, having applied his expertise to numerous military campaigns from France to Turkey. By 1745, he was perhaps the most important military planner in Europe, holding the title of captain engineer to Holy Roman Emperor Charles VII. But De Brahm also suffered from a conflict of conscience. By 1748, he had renounced the Roman Catholicism of his masters and converted to Lutheranism. With religious conflict still smoldering in Europe, De Brahm headed to Georgia. His reputation preceded him, and soon the colonists demanded that De Brahm draw maps, survey settlements, and, above all, fix their fortifications.[1]

No place needed De Brahm's expertise more than Charleston. On September 15, 1752, the capital of South Carolina was hit by "the most violent and terrible hurricane."[2] It decimated houses and ripped churches apart, although the chief concern of Governor James Glen was the tempest's destruction of the city's defenses. Before the storm, Charleston had been surrounded by earthen walls and palisades, with protruding bastions and demi-lunes made of earth, wood, and brick. The hurricane obliterated these defenses, so Glen invited De Brahm to refortify the city. De Brahm complied with a design worthy of an imperial city, one that enclosed Charleston

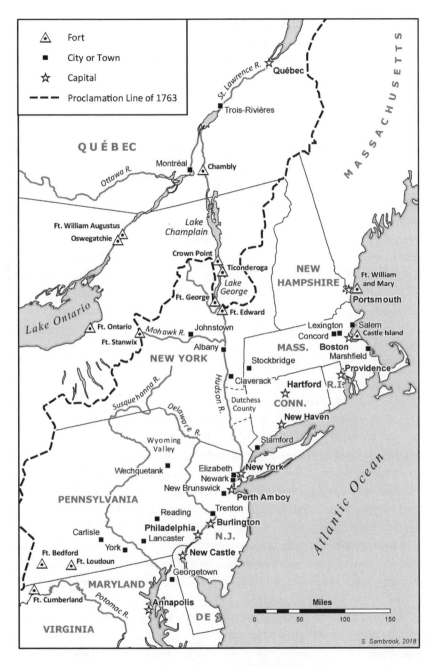

MAP 2. Northeastern British North America, ca. 1765. S. Sambrook, 2018.

"with ramparts, forming regular bastions, detached or joined with curtains," mounted with hundreds of cannons. The Ashley and Cooper Rivers would further protect three sides of the city, while on the fourth, De Brahm envisioned a canal and two forts to protect the settlement "against an insurrection of the Negroes or Indian war." The colonists were unimpressed. The plan was too massive: certainly too expensive. De Brahm estimated it would cost just under £300,000: five times South Carolina's annual budget. The assembly called De Brahm a "foreigner" and sent him away.[3]

Three years later, South Carolina's dismissal of De Brahm's walls looked foolish. As the French and Indian War began, lawmakers feared for their capital and invited the German engineer to return and execute his plan. However, now it was the colonists who disapproved. When De Brahm began erecting bastions in late 1755, the inhabitants of Charleston exhibited violent hostility toward the project. According to De Brahm, the workers were unmanageable and ineffective. One man hated Germans, "striking, cursing and treating with indignations" all such people, including De Brahm himself. The general public was just as antagonistic. At one point, De Brahm had to hire sentries to guard against idle "young people" and a saboteur who rushed the fortifications "with a fire brand in his hand," intending to raze them. He also blamed "cart people" for damaging the fortifications when they braced the gates "at purpose to keep them open."[4] It was all too much for De Brahm, who abandoned Charleston's walls and returned to Georgia.[5]

Charleston's rejection of fortifications was neither irrational nor simply parsimonious; it was spatial. Europe was populated by cities surrounded by massive walls, and this was the model that De Brahm sought to transfer to America. But such military geography made no sense for Charleston. In the middle of the eighteenth century, Charleston was the primary American port for rice, indigo, and slaves; between 1748 and 1775, the value of colony's exports quadrupled. This growing market economy demanded a physical and mental openness that ran counter to the very idea of an enclosed city. Charleston could not thrive unless goods and people flowed freely through the city. Walls might serve German cities, but Charleston needed a more fluid defense.[6]

The solution was barracks. Since 1745, at least one independent company of fifty British soldiers had been stationed in Charleston. To house the independents, the South Carolina legislature appropriated thousands of pounds to build rows of brick rooms and kitchens to house and feed the soldiers. The barracks were located inside Charleston, only two blocks from the city center, and this proximity allowed the soldiers to circulate throughout the town. The colonists welcomed the troops, employing them as a night watch and asking them to man a guardhouse in the middle of town. The independents provided protection that was far more fluid than city walls, as well as cheaper and less obtrusive. Although the British army withdrew the soldiers in 1754, Charlestonians remained hopeful that new troops would arrive to defend their city. The colonists did not want city walls, they wanted barracks.[7]

Barracks constitute a second aspect of military geography that is crucial to understanding quarters. When the Earl of Loudoun billeted thousands of British regulars in America during the French and Indian War, the colonists responded spatially. In order to keep troops out of their homes, they directed them to taverns, forts, and public buildings. When these proved inadequate, Boston offered a model for the future: barracks large enough to contain all British soldiers. Between 1756 and 1758, massive barracks arose in the four largest American cities, as well as in a half dozen smaller towns. Boston alone isolated its barracks on an island; all others followed Charleston's lead of placing the structures in central public spaces like the town common.

The sudden prominence of barracks was remarkable. The massive edifices set the American colonies apart from the mother country, where such structures were viewed as a tyrannical violation of the English constitution. In America, the opposite was true; the colonists built barracks to effect a constitutional right to keep soldiers out of their houses. Permanent military quarters also set the old colonies apart from the new. Whereas the thirteen American colonies had the resources to prevent billeting by building barracks, people in Canada, Florida, and the backcountry did not; thus they were forced to accommodate troops in their homes. Over time, Americans came to question the wisdom of barracks. They had placed a permanent piece of military geography in their population centers, and this invited the British army into their cities and towns. Shortly after the French and Indian War, this decision led the army to barrack troops whose purpose was not to protect the colonies but rather the colonists' enemies.

The history of barracks as a place is less complete than that of the house. Philosopher Michel Foucault famously considered barracks as a tool of discipline that helped transfer punishment from the body to the soul, but US historians have generally been uninterested in barracks. Perhaps because the use of permanent military quarters has not changed much in two thousand years, we assume that barracks reveal little about the societies they inhabit. But barracks have meaning, both to their inhabitants and those around them, and this meaning has changed radically since the Revolutionary War. In eighteenth-century America, barracks were lauded by colonists as a physical means of effecting their constitutional rights. They were public buildings that enabled Americans to encounter British military power and provided them a spatial means to contain that power. In sum, barracks were critically important to changing notions of military geography and the American Revolution. If the first prerequisite for the Quartering Act was Loudoun's decision to billet troops in houses, then the second was barracks.

English Objections and Colonial Adaptation

Barracks have existed since ancient times. The biblical book of Nehemiah records a *bêt haggibbōrîm* ("house of the mighty men") in Jerusalem in the fifth century BC, while the Romans built the Castra Praetoria in the reign of Tiberius five centuries later.[8] Interest in barracks rapidly accelerated in the seventeenth century with the advent of standing armies in Western Europe. As Spain and France assembled massive bodies of troops, it proved impossible to billet all soldiers in houses, so they built permanent military quarters. Both kingdoms built their first barracks in conquered territory and later added them to their own countries. They derived names for such buildings from the Latin term for "quarter" (*cuartel* in Spanish and *caserne* in French), although both also employed an old term for "hut" or "small house" (*barraca* in Spanish and *baraque* in French). By the eighteenth century, European governments were enthralled with barracks, building more structures for their ever-growing armies. By 1775, France barracked two hundred thousand soldiers.[9]

The appeal of barracks was their disciplinary space. Large armies required discipline, something that scattering troops among private households could never achieve. Inside barracks, a soldier's every move could be monitored and corrected until he became a cog in a military machine. Confining soldiers to barracks also had the effect of separating them from the civilian population, which promoted better discipline as well. In occupied territories, barracked troops had fewer conflicts with hostile civilians; at home, permanent quarters quieted complaints about the size and intrusiveness of a standing army. Barracks removed soldiers from the gaze of civilians, allowing harsh and cruel discipline to go unscrutinized by nonmilitary personnel, thus rendering the army increasingly independent.[10]

Barracks were idealized to be gendered places. Premodern warfare presumed the separation of the sexes, both as a means of protecting women from combat and concentrating masculine power for battle. Indeed, ancient barracks may have existed more to exclude women from war than to contain warriors. Seventeenth-century warfare remained heavily gendered, and the appearance of permanent quarters fostered a manliness that billeting in houses had not permitted. The rise of barracks as distinctly masculine places corresponded to and may have encouraged the feminization of the home. Practically, however, women and families entered barracks along with the soldiers, and prevented a complete separation of the sexes.[11]

England came late to barracks. Although the Romans built quarters alongside Hadrian's Wall, and William the Conqueror constructed houses for his army, barracks in medieval England were small, remote, and concealed behind stone walls. This practice continued even after England assembled a standing army. When the Tudor monarchs bolstered the country's defenses in the sixteenth century, they added permanent quarters to coastal citadels like Plymouth Castle and Tilbury Fort, usually in the form of casemates—that is, rooms built into the fort walls. King Charles II built the first free-standing structure to be labeled a "barracks" at the Tower of London in 1669, and William and Mary added permanent quarters for the guards at Hampton Court Palace. All these barracks were separated from the civilian population, safely confined within stone fortresses or relegated to the periphery.[12]

English resistance to barracks was ideological. As Great Britain sank into a century-long series of wars with France, monarchs pushed for barracks, but Parliament refused to fund them. The Whigs who dominated the House of Commons viewed barracks as symbols of tyranny. They feared that creating permanent quarters would leave the country "saddled with a perpetual standing army," while placing barracks among the people would give soldiers new opportunities to oppress them.[13] Even at the height of the Seven Years' War, Britons remained suspicious. A letter in the *London Evening-Post* in 1760 warned that "putting our soldiery into barracks, instead of quarters, would make them a more distinct and separated body of men." It was far better to continue billeting troops in public houses in order to check the army's dominance.[14]

Such high-minded Whig ideals did not go unchallenged, especially by those English men and women who had to provide quarters. During the Seven Years' War, "grievous complaints" of publicans appeared in newspapers as "the quartering of soldiers, is to them so great a detriment that they are ready to despair."[15] Some cited the low rates of compensation that the army provided, while others claimed soldiers disrupted their business. When dragoons billeted in Eastbourne and Pevensey, a group of East Sussex innkeepers petitioned the prime minister for relief, claiming that because of the soldiers, "we thereby have not had room to entertain passengers or other guests, nor even lodging for our own families."[16] Despite these complaints, Whig arguments held sway. It was not until the 1790s that continental-style barracks appeared in England.[17]

As with billeting, constitutional protections against barracks did not extend to Ireland or Scotland. Indeed, the very reason that Whigs did not want barracks in England was exactly why they placed them in the dependent kingdoms: to impose military rule on civilians. In 1702, construction began on the Royal Barracks in Dublin. When completed seven years later, it was the largest barracks in Europe, with quarters for a thousand men, along with parade grounds, stables, and workshops. Less palatial barracks filled smaller towns, although their presence was hardly inconsequential: by 1704, Ireland contained forty-three barracks for infantry companies and thirty for cavalry. Whether in the capital or a distant county, Irish barracks were built in the center of town in order to demonstrate England's dominance and to allow the soldiers to act as police. Scotland also filled with barracks, especially after the Jacobite uprising of 1715. Although Scottish barracks tended to be confined within castle walls, they were constructed in or near major population centers, thus inserting the British army into Scottish society.[18]

A desire to control non-English populations also prompted the construction of barracks in the Caribbean. By 1671, England had established colonies in the Bahamas, Barbados, Jamaica, and the Leeward Islands (consisting of Anguilla, Antigua, Barbuda, Montserrat, Nevis, Saint Kitts, and the British Virgin Islands). The island colonies were almost entirely occupied by sugar plantations worked by African slaves, and this gave rise to fears of slave revolt. A slave conspiracy in Antigua in October 1736 brought five companies of British regulars to the island. After repeated complaints from officers about how the "want of barracks" exposed the men to "violent heats" and caused many to desert, the Antiguan assembly built barracks near the capital of St. John's.[19] Uprisings by escaped slaves in Jamaica in the 1730s likewise brought six companies to the island. Jamaica also built barracks to accommodate the troops, although instead of concentrating them at the capital, lawmakers spread soldiers throughout the island to monitor slaves on plantations. Twenty years later, the arrival of British regulars for the Seven Years' War prompted islanders to throw up additional quarters throughout the Caribbean.[20]

Britons also added barracks to the North Atlantic. Since the early seventeenth century, Britain had vied with France for control of Nova Scotia, Newfoundland, and other lands at the Gulf of St. Lawrence. In 1749, Britain erected a massive military installation at Chebucto Harbor and named it Halifax. Wary of the Francophone Acadian colonists in the region, the first British colonists at Halifax were accompanied by Colonel Edward Cornwallis and the 47th Regiment of Foot. Cornwallis planned an eighty-foot-long artillery barracks at the center of town to stand alongside St. Paul's Church and the courthouse. The military tenor of Halifax increased after Braddock's defeat, when it became a staging ground for the French and Indian War. In response, the army built "three new forts with barracks," including one on "Citadel Hill, which is to be 365 feet long and 35 wide, of two stories."[21]

In contrast to Canada and the Caribbean, the thirteen American colonies followed the English model of keeping barracks small, remote, and concealed. Permanent quarters stood in Boston, New York, and Albany, but these were confined to islands or hidden inside forts. Colonial expansion led to the construction of backcountry outposts, which typically contained barracks, but most were only large enough to accommodate a skeleton crew of defenders. Indeed, the temporary character of provincial armies made the type of permanent military quarters that populated Halifax and Jamaica unnecessary in the American colonies. Perhaps because of the rarity of British regulars for most of the colonial era, Americans rarely repeated Whig arguments against barracks. There were thus few ideological impediments to bringing quarters out of forts, enlarging them, and placing them in the center of town when independent companies arrived in Charleston in the 1740s and regulars appeared throughout the colonies a decade later.[22]

Building Urban Quarters

Americans' demand for barracks began as soon as the French and Indian War began. At first, the colonies kept new barracks small and remote. Maryland's Fort Cumberland and New York's Fort Edward were built on the colonial frontier, with barracks concealed behind walls and placed at a great distance from the colonial capitals. However, once the Earl of Loudoun began wintering thousands of British regulars in coastal cities, Americans' approach to barracks changed dramatically. Between 1756 and 1758, the colonists threw up a dozen permanent military quarters. Following Boston's example, New York, Philadelphia, and Charleston all built massive barracks. Smaller yet no less impressive barracks simultaneously rose in Albany and five New Jersey towns. It was a barrack-building frenzy that rivaled any European infrastructure project. Within three years, the American colonists had provided permanent military quarters for as many as seven thousand soldiers: more than the entire North American Establishment.[23]

The call for barracks came from a variety of sources. The initial requests originated with the colonial governors, no doubt because they were the ones responsible for keeping peace between soldiers and colonists. As soon as Pennsylvania's Governor Robert Hunter Morris received word that the first battalion of the Royal American Regiment would be spending the winter of 1756–1757 in Philadelphia, he asked the legislature "to erect a number of barracks in some convenient place sufficient for the reception of a thousand men."[24] When the same battalion headed to Charleston the following spring, South Carolina's Governor William Henry Lyttelton likewise advised lawmakers "that barracks should be constructed."[25] Colonel Henry Bouquet, the commander of the Royal Americans, appreciated the governors' prescience. The prospect of receiving "barracks instead of quarters in the houses" pleased Bouquet not only because they would "render the sojourn of the troops in the town less burdensome to the people," but because they would "give the officers better facilities for maintaining correct discipline."[26]

The colonists heartily agreed with civilian and military leaders. In early 1758, fifty-seven householders in Trenton petitioned the New Jersey General Assembly for an alternative to quartering in private houses. The petitioners, a majority of whom had billeted British soldiers that winter, humbly requested that the assembly "enable us to erect and build such sufficient and convenient barracks."[27] In their appeals, Trenton and other New Jersey localities made spatial arguments. Petitioners from Princeton complained that with "small houses and numerous families, with not more than one room," it was unfair for them "to entertain sometimes ten, twelve or fifteen soldiers for a night": thus they needed barracks.[28] Others cited cost, an argument that appealed to lawmakers. The South Carolina Commons House observed that building new barracks would be "far less expensive" than reimbursing the owners of "private houses in different and distant parts of the town."[29] Spatial and financial reasons reinforced one another, ultimately coalescing in the argument that barracks were fairer because they spread the burden across the population. A letter to the *New-York Gazette* touted barracks as the lesser of two evils, adding "that to provide for His Majesty's forces in that method, is much more equitable and just, than to have them billeted on the inhabitants."[30] New York lawyer and newspaperman William Smith Jr. put the matter succinctly: the colony appropriated funds "for the construction of barracks that private families might be delivered from the inconvenience of the soldiers billeted upon them."[31]

Once everyone had agreed on the necessity of barracks, colonial legislatures appropriated funds and delegated construction to local officials. Seeking to protect the locales that Loudoun forced to billet troops, lawmakers directed that barracks be built in the capital cities of New York, Philadelphia, and Charleston. Philadelphia's stood alone, while New York built two sets of barracks, and Charleston complemented its existing brick quarters with a large wooden structure. Barracks also went up in Albany, where thousands of British troops assembled, while New Jersey, which had no major metropolis, built five smaller structures in Elizabeth, Perth Amboy, New Brunswick, Trenton, and Burlington. In this, the colonists accepted Loudoun's reordering of the colonies' military geography. The colonial capitals, Albany, and the New Jersey towns became the permanent home of the North American Establishment.[32]

Although part of the rationale for building barracks was to save money, the colonists soon learned just how expensive the massive structures could be. New York appropriated £3,500 for barracks in the capital and another £1,000 for Albany, while the Pennsylvania legislature set aside £10,000 for barracks in Philadelphia. The charges took differential tolls on the colonies: New York's appropriation was nearly twice the cost of all salaries for the colony's public officials, but Philadelphia's barracks represented less than a tenth of Pennsylvania's military spending for 1756. Cost overruns were to be expected. The South Carolina assembly initially appropriated £4,000 for barracks in Charleston, but the builders estimated the structure would cost £10,800, excluding chimneys. Similarly, New Jersey, which appropriated £1,400 for each of its five barracks, ended up spending as little as £2,643 for quarters in Burlington and as much as £4,052 for those in Perth Amboy. These costs fell almost entirely on American taxpayers. New York City generated money through a special local tax, but other cities received provincial funds or took money out of existing fortification funds. This drove up the colonists' tax burden, which was already high because of the war.[33] The one exception was Albany. After spending the winter of 1756–1757 in a city overburdened by British regulars, Loudoun approved nearly £3,000 "to finish and complete the hospital, barracks, and storehouse building at Albany."[34]

To build barracks, the colonies turned to a variety of bodies. New York City formed an ad hoc group known as the Committee for Building of the New Barracks, while South Carolina turned matters over to the Commissioners of Fortifications, who had been responsible for Charleston's defenses for decades. These bodies contracted the work out to local laborers.[35] In Trenton, leading men of the town Joseph Yard and Theophilus Severns procured the materials to build the barracks and then hired "sundry laborers" to raise the structures, paying them three shillings a day.[36] Burlington hired skilled carpenters for piecemeal work, unskilled laborers "for digging cellars," and "a soldier for four days work digging post holes."[37] As hammers, saws, and shovels clamored up and down the Atlantic Seaboard, many local men found lucrative work in the colonial employ, driving up wages and making barracks construction an important part of the war's economic boom. Once the structures were complete, a barrack master superintended the building, repairing it when necessary and ensuring the troops were well supplied.

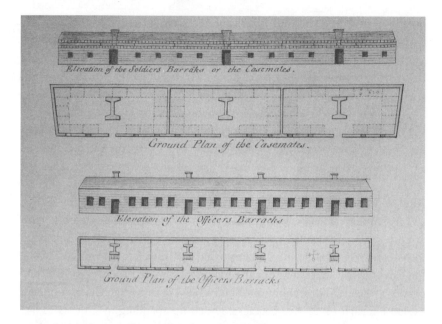

FIGURE 2.1. Barracks at Fort Ontario. William Braiser, "Plan of Fort Ontario [and environs], with the Several Alterations and Additional Works Proposed by the Chief Engineer" (ca. 1760), in *The Crown Collection of Photographs of American Maps*, ed. Archer Butler Hulbert, ser. 2, 5 vols. (Harrow, UK: Flemming, 1909), 1:18. William L. Clements Library, University of Michigan.

It is unclear what architectural plans the colonists had for building barracks, if any at all. Functionally, barracks were simple structures: essentially long rows of small rooms laid end to end, as illustrated by figure 2.1. Such edifices emulated Stoughton Hall, a dormitory on Harvard Yard, and the Moravians' sex-segregated choirs of Bethlehem, Pennsylvania. In New York City, Albany, and Charleston, colonists no doubt took inspiration from the existing barracks and simply made the new ones bigger. Building committees and barrack masters also may have sought the advice of military engineers who accompanied the British army to America, like John Montresor. Ultimately, the barracks' simplicity, as well as the speed of their construction, may have obviated the need for sophisticated plans.[38]

There was a common appearance to the barracks: all were long, thin structures with little ornamentation. Most were two stories high, although some were only one. The shape of the quarters also varied. New York built one long row of barracks on the city common, while Philadelphia, Charleston, and Albany opted for two parallel buildings. New Jersey law limited barracks to "a suitable piece of ground not exceeding one acre," so Trenton, Perth Amboy, and Elizabeth bent their quarters into the shape of a U, as

FIGURE 2.2. Barracks at Perth Amboy, New Jersey. "The Barracks," in William A. Whitehead, *Contributions to the Early History of Perth Amboy and Adjoining Country* (New York: Appleton, 1856), 256.

depicted in figure 2.2.[39] Likewise, a lack of available land at the southern tip of Manhattan resulted in an L-shaped barracks at the Battery. The capital city structures were built of wood with stone foundations, as were the barracks in Albany. Those in New Jersey were made of fieldstone, perhaps because their smaller size made this economically feasible. A number of outbuildings surrounded the barracks, such as kitchens in Charleston, guardhouses in New York, and stables, storehouses, and a hospital in Albany. Fences surrounded some of the barracks, although these appear to have been symbolic dividers rather than the ramparts of early colonial forts.[40]

The most dramatic aspect of the barracks was their size. In the capitals, colonists erected massive structures that dwarfed all other buildings, including churches and statehouses. At 420 feet long, New York's Upper Barracks were as wide as most city blocks and more than twice the size of Trinity Church. Only Fort George was larger. Plats of Charleston and Philadelphia reveal outsize barracks on ground larger than a city block. Each half of Charleston's barracks measured 40 by 430 feet and was capable of quartering a thousand troops, while Pennsylvania governor William Denny observed that Philadelphia's "barracks lately built" could house "fourteen hundred men."[41] Structures in small cities were designed to accommodate fewer soldiers: two hundred in Albany's barracks and three hundred in each of New Jersey's five structures. Yet the relative size of the barracks to these locales made them no less imposing.[42]

It is unclear exactly what the colonists thought as they watched massive barracks rise in their midst. Although the British army left evidence of the barracks' size and location in their many maps of colonial cities, the only surviving depiction by a colonist is a 1770 cartoon from New York (see figure 5.1). The perspective makes the barracks look insignificant, merely background scenery in a politically charged sketch of the common. Nor did the colonists bestow stature on the quarters through naming practices, instead employing the simplest terms possible. New Yorkers distinguished the Upper Barracks that stood on the common from the Lower Barracks at the Battery, while Charlestonians termed the 1750s structures the New Barracks to differentiate them from the existing Brick Barracks. Most referred to the edifices as "the barracks," much as a small town with only one house of worship would term the building "the church."[43]

The colonists expected all military personnel to reside in barracks. Initially, the focus was on removing enlisted men from private houses, leaving officers billeted with families. In 1758, New York City paid nearly £500 to billet officers for the winter, while Philadelphia found public houses for twenty-five lieutenant colonels, majors, captains, lieutenants, ensigns, and surgeon's mates. Generally, the colonists objected less to quartering officers than to billeting enlisted men, as the former were usually older, more refined, and paid larger sums for their accommodations. But as time wore on, Americans began pressuring even high-ranking officers to relocate.[44] To make the experience more attractive, Trenton affixed a two-story Georgian-style house to the barracks where officers could recline in comfort, sharing a dining room and an office while maintaining individual bedrooms. Not long afterward, the New Jersey assembly resolved not to "provide pay for the quartering officers."[45]

Barracking officers was particularly contentious in Charleston. When the South Carolina Commons House voted to build the New Barracks, it also appropriated funds to repair the Brick Barracks for "the reception of the subaltern officers of the troops now in this province." Governor Lyttelton found this separation confusing, as it put the officers a half mile away from the men. Accordingly, the House voted to fix up an old school near the New Barracks to quarter officers and declared that it would cover the officers' billeting costs only "until barracks shall be constructed."[46] Unfortunately, South Carolina legislators had a rather loose definition of what "constructed" meant. To lawmakers, the barracks were constructed as soon as they were begun in November 1757, even though officers' quarters were still uninhabitable the following March. Nevertheless, the House declared that it would not compensate any householders for officers billeted after November 30. This raised the hackles of Colonel Bouquet, who groused that he was forced to order "officers of the garrison to keep possession of the rooms where they had been billeted" in order to prevent householders from turning them out.[47] To lawmakers, Bouquet's denunciations were unwarranted and his solution unconstitutional. "Officers and soldiers cannot be legally or constitutionally quartered in private houses without the special consent of the owners or possessors of such houses," the South Carolina Commons House declared.[48]

The feud between Bouquet and South Carolina lawmakers blew over quickly once the officers' quarters were completed and the assembly agreed to compensate householders who had billeted officers for the winter.[49] Nevertheless, it marked the first time that Americans invoked the constitution and English liberties with respect to quarters. Significantly, the colonists did not do so to oppose the barracks as Britons had, but to justify the structures. In this, the colonists reversed the arguments of the English Whigs. Barracks had become the chief bulwark against flagrant violations of Americans' constitutional liberties, specifically the privacy of the home.

Soldiers Transform the Neighborhood

In their rush to protect their houses from British regulars, the colonists introduced new places into their landscape that dramatically altered life in America. Within the cities, barracks inserted themselves onto public spaces, making both commons and neighborhoods part of Britain's military infrastructure. Although the Americans quickly reconciled themselves to the militarization of their cities, they never entirely accepted a second unintended consequence: supplies. Barracks, it turned out, had to be outfitted so that they might be habitable for troops, and much to the consternation of the colonists, this required additional taxes and spending. Despite these added costs, the Americans remained convinced that building permanent quarters in coastal cities was the best means of protecting houses. This solution, however, disadvantaged fellow colonists who lived in small towns and rural areas when troops were stationed there. In short, barracks were far from a perfect solution to the problem of quartering.

The massive barracks immediately reshaped the urban landscape. Throughout the colonies, permanent quarters were placed outside existing forts. They were stand-alone structures that claimed new territory within the city, thus expanding military geography at the expense of civilian places. Most eighteenth-century American communities were small and compact: Charleston and New York were little more than one mile by one mile. Such tight quarters left little unoccupied space to situate the massive barracks. Even when lawmakers relegated barracks to the periphery, they were not far from the center of town. Trenton sited its barracks near the Delaware River, while Perth Amboy and New Brunswick put them on the main road out of town; but given that each of these towns consisted of fewer than a dozen city blocks, soldiers were never more than a leisurely stroll from the civilian population.[50]

The most dramatically sited of all the structures were New York's Upper Barracks, which stood on the city common, an area known as the Fields. Less than a mile northeast of Fort George, the Fields stood where Broadway split into roads leading to the suburbs of Greenwich Village and the Bowery. As late as 1748, palisades stood at the edge of the common, marking the edge of the city, but New York's rapid growth had forced the barrier down and transformed the Fields into the heart of the city. It was the site of participatory democracy where people congregated for open-air meetings, civic celebrations, and militia musters. When the Reverend George Whitefield was refused a pulpit on his first visit to the city, the great evangelist preached in the Fields to more than ten thousand listeners. Justice in the form of a gallows was meted out at one corner of the common, while the city's African American community buried their dead nearby. As figure 2.3 indicates, the Upper Barracks (26) towered over a jail (23) and almshouse (24). After the

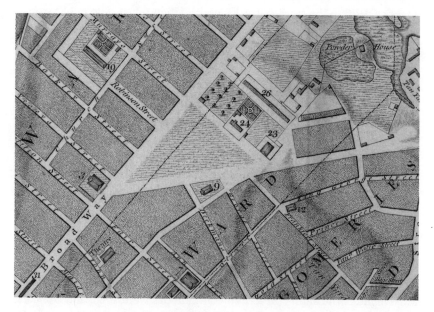

FIGURE 2.3. The Fields in New York City. Bernard Ratzer, To His Excellency Sr. Henry Moore, Bart., captain general and governour in chief in & over the province of New York & the territories depending thereon in America, chancellor & vice admiral of the same, this plan of the city of New York is most humbly inscribed (London, 1769?). Library of Congress, Geography and Map Division, 91684092.

war, the neighborhood around the Fields rapidly gentrified, with the addition of King's College (19), St. Paul's Chapel (3), and the Brick Presbyterian Church (9). From this prominent position, the Upper Barracks became integral to life in New York City.[51]

Philadelphia went in the opposite direction. In the fall of 1757, the Commissioners for Building the Barracks approved a plan, hired workmen, and dug a foundation; then suddenly they "changed their minds" and "chose another place" for quarters. The first location was west of the center of population but solidly within the city, perhaps on the long-unoccupied Centre Square that William Penn had designated to be the heart of Philadelphia. By contrast, the new location was two blocks north of the city limits, amid a field of buckwheat in the suburb of Northern Liberties. Lieutenant Colonel Frederick Haldimand disapproved of the new site, finding it impractically remote and indefensible. Barracks north of the city could not protect the city from ships sailing up the Delaware River or Indians attacking from the west. Despite this advice, "the commissioners still went on with the work."[52] The Earl of Loudoun opined that the city had no interest in a permanent military infrastructure, thus it chose to place barracks in the Northern Liberties "with a view to turn them after the war is over, either to storehouses or a manufactory."[53] This may well have been the case, as the Northern Liberties was quickly becoming a center of trade in Philadelphia. More important, the decision to move the barracks reflected the city's vision of itself and class politics. The original site stood in the path of growth and threatened to place the barracks at the civic center that was yet to come. By contrast, the Northern Liberties was one of the poorest areas in the region, with a reputation for violence. Indeed, the barracks were built within a block of Bloody Lane, so named for an infamous murder. The location of Philadelphia's barracks could not have been more different from New York's.[54]

Alone among the locales that erected barracks in the 1750s, Boston isolated its permanent military quarters, separating the edifice from the city's urban population with water. In October 1758, the Massachusetts House of Representatives appointed a committee whose members "were of opinion, that barracks be erected somewhere in the town of Boston, for the reception of a thousand men."[55] However, the idea apparently died with the committee, as the legislature took no further action on this matter. It is likely that Massachusetts lawmakers decided that the barracks on Castle Island were sufficient; Castle William contained casemates, while in 1755 the colony had built a row of rooms for enlisted men known as the Long Barracks, as well as an L-shaped officers' quarters (see figure 6.1). While these may not have been able to accommodate a thousand men, they probably could have held a regiment of three to five hundred soldiers. The legislature's willingness to consider building barracks someplace other than Castle Island suggests that Massachusetts did not have a constitutional objection to barracks inside the city. The colony's decision to barrack troops *near* Boston but not *in* Boston would not matter for another decade.[56]

Once barracks went up, they needed interior accoutrements. Colonel Bouquet had high expectations for barrack life, opining that a soldier "ought to be practically as well off in the barracks as he would be in a private home."[57] Obviously, they contained beds, typically berths attached to the walls, as indicated in figures 2.1 and 2.4. Here, men slept two to a bed. Barracks also contained places for the soldiers to cook and eat their meals. Although the army provided food, it expected the men to prepare it themselves. Each room of eight men in Charleston received an eight-gallon iron pot, a pine table, and an assortment of bowls, platters, and mugs to share. Hygiene and orderliness necessitated chamber pots, as well as cleaning items like a broom and pail, and pegs on which to hang uniforms. For warmth and cooking, each room contained a fireplace. Soldiers in Charleston's New Barracks were allotted ten pounds of candles per week for every hundred men, while the same number shared three to four cords of wood per week, depending on the season.

FIGURE 2.4. Fort Niagara Guard Room. Historic American Buildings Survey, "Interior, First Floor, Guard Room," in *Fort Niagara, French Castle, Fort Niagara State Park, Youngstown, Niagara County, NY* (1933). Library of Congress, Prints and Photographs Division, HABS NY, 32-YOUNG, 1A-.

Lastly, soldiers needed items to ward off sickness, such as salt, vinegar, and small beer, a beverage with very low alcohol content that took the place of polluted water.[58]

Responsibility for providing these supplies fell to the colonists. Typically, when troops arrived in town, the local barrack master assembled firewood and utensils from funds provided by the community. In New York, John DePeyster was routinely going to the city council for money to purchase candles, blankets, "pots, hooks, and chains" for the Upper and Lower Barracks.[59] When British regulars abruptly appeared in Philadelphia in 1758, the local government worried about the soldiers' "great distress, for want of bedding and other necessaries" and voted supplies out of the municipal treasury.[60] In these instances, cities sought reimbursement from the colonial governments. The colonies soon discovered that the cost of supplies, like the construction costs, could easily overrun initial appropriations. This led some colonies to parsimony, none more so than South Carolina. Still smarting from the cost of building the New Barracks, the province's Commons House pinched pennies with provisions. Instead of providing one blanket per soldier as requested by the army, lawmakers allotted half this supply. Colonel Bouquet ridiculed the legislature's decision "to order a blanket for two men in a country where the most covetous planter finds it his interest to allow one to the most despicable slave."[61]

The colonists' determination to rein in barrack costs fell heaviest on British soldiers. Historically, soldiers hated barracks for all the same reasons that civilians and officers liked them: they encouraged discipline by standardizing food and sleeping arrangements. Life in the barracks diminished a soldier's sense of privacy and personal space, a point made emphatic by the colonists' determination to squeeze as many men as possible into the barracks. New York's Upper Barracks were originally designed to cram twenty men in a room measuring twenty-one feet square. Such a concentration would have allowed less space per soldier than any barracks in the British Isles. Although the army was able to convince barrack master DePeyster that such conditions were inhumane, the soldiers barracked in New York and elsewhere in America remained in close quarters, no doubt pining for the comforts of billeting.[62]

In addition to living cheek by jowl with other men, barracked soldiers made room for women and children. British officers often brought their families on campaigns, housing them at their own expense. By contrast, younger and poorer enlisted men who brought wives from home or wed in the colonies barracked with their families. Women and children were thus a constant presence in the American barracks, sleeping in berths with the soldiers and sharing meals at the communal table. Civilian officials made little effort to interfere with the soldiers' familial duties, while the army actively encouraged the insertion of dependents and the unpaid labor they provided. Army regulations allowed provisions for six women per company.[63] In Charleston's New Barracks, "the nurses are soldiers' wives," commented one officer who ordered the women "to attend the sick without giving them any pay." Wives also performed gendered labor that men abhorred, specifically cooking and cleaning.[64]

Although families were common in barracks, it was not always clear who was supposed to supply wives and children after the soldiers marched off to battle. When the British army stranded dependents in the Philadelphia Barracks, "a number of soldiers' wives" were left to petition the governor for relief.[65] In Massachusetts, the arrival of soldiers' wives and children at Castle Island in October 1758 also aroused confusion. The General Court initially considered provisioning them "according to the king's allowance," but lawmakers changed course once they learned that the Crown would not compensate them for quartering dependents. Massachusetts then paid a church to distribute bread to the families while ordering that "the said women and children be sent away accordingly in the cheapest manner that may be" to join their husbands.[66]

Americans accepted the high cost of barracks and the loss of their public spaces because it removed British soldiers from their houses. Indeed, even the rising cost of supplies did not dampen the popularity of the structures as an alternative to quartering troops elsewhere. Yet barracks were an imperfect solution. The expense of building, maintaining, and supplying the edifices deterred several colonies from constructing barracks, causing billeting in houses to continue until the end of the French and Indian War. Connecticut's location between points of disembarkation and the Canadian theater meant that British regulars were constantly streaming through the colony. Instead of building barracks, however, the Connecticut General Court approved laws to quarter regulars and recruiting parties in taverns or other "particular room, house or houses" designated by local selectmen.[67] Elsewhere, individual towns were forced to quarter troops in houses. Princeton petitioned the New Jersey General Assembly with the same fervor as Trenton, asking "that barracks be erected and set up in this town," but these pleas went unanswered.[68] As a result, a cleavage emerged between communities where barracks kept soldiers out of the colonists' houses and those where such billeting persisted. Barracks promised a more equitable military geography, but not all Americans benefited from this solution.

As the British army began to push aggressively against the French and their Indian allies, the necessity of billeting in the backcountry increased, including at private houses. When Captain Christopher French arrived in South Carolina in late 1760, his detachment of the 22nd Regiment at first resided in Charleston's New Barracks. As they headed west to take on the Cherokees, however, the troops billeted in private homes, including one that French described as "a very poor place" with "nothing to be had" but some milk.[69] Although Captain French reported no conflicts with the colony's householders, the same could not be said of soldiers quartered in Claverack, New York, a small town about thirty-five miles south of Albany. In February 1760, the British army received a complaint against Lieutenant McPherson, who billeted at the home of Jeremiah Ten Broeck. According to the complaint, the officer came to Ten Broeck's bedroom door one night and demanded entrance. When Ten Broeck refused, McPherson and another officer broke down the door and grabbed Ten Broeck's wife "in such an indecent manner as is too shocking to repeat."[70] When Ten Broeck defended his wife, McPherson struck the householder several times on the head. Although an army investigation exonerated the lieutenant, this only infuriated the civilian, who called "Mr. McPherson, a liar, with many other provoking epithets."[71]

Similar confrontations took place in the Pennsylvania hinterlands. Ever since Braddock's defeat, the British army had eyed Fort Duquesne, waiting for the moment to strike. In the winter of 1757–1758, the Earl of Loudoun quartered fifteen companies in public and private houses in Lancaster, Reading, and York, about sixty miles west of Philadelphia. There they remained for two years, prompting a spirited resistance from the inhabitants. In January 1759, reports came from Reading that tavern keepers were taking down their signs, as they had "received nothing as yet for last year's quartering of soldiers."[72] Worse, people in Lancaster complained that the army used "open violence" to force "His Majesty's troops into the dwelling houses of the inhabitants." One family was so abused that they were "obliged to give up their own house, with its furniture, and seek for lodgings for themselves in the houses of their friends." When these reports made their way to the capital, the Pennsylvania General Assembly demanded answers from the British army. Lawmakers were outraged that soldiers billeted in private houses while Philadelphia's "commodious set of barracks" sat largely unoccupied. Had lawmakers known the army would quarter troops in Lancaster, then "part of the barracks would have been built in that borough."[73]

Some towns discovered that even with barracks, their houses were not protected. Albany continued to suffer from billeting, even though it boasted a barracks, a hospital, and a fort. In the spring of 1760, Boston carpenter Nathaniel Fuller spent a month in Albany building flat-bottomed cargo boats for the army. In one month, Fuller billeted all but three nights with the inhabitants, bouncing about from house to house. "Billeted at Peter Lanson's" one night, he noted in his journal, "at Elizabeth Brewar's house" the next.[74] In December, the mayor and alderman petitioned the acting governor, Cadwallader Colden, for help. Colden relayed these grievances to the commander in chief, reporting how householders were "greatly distressed by arbitrary quartering of soldiers on private homes," including one who had "nine men besides women and children quartered upon him." Observing that Albany's "barracks were capable of containing many more than are now in that city," Colden demanded all troops be barracked.[75]

The limitations of barracks became more apparent to the colonists as the French and Indian War built to a climax. By 1759, the barrack-building frenzy passed, as colonial governments began to understand the financial and spatial consequences of erecting permanent quarters in their midst. As complaints from small towns billeting soldiers made their way to the capitals, only Pennsylvania believed that additional barracks were the answer. The assembly voted to build a sixty-four-room U-shaped structure in the center of Lancaster that was completed by April 1760.[76] Conversely, when the inhabitants of Princeton and Kingston petitioned the New Jersey House of Representatives for relief from the "great hardships and expense they are put to, by travelling parties of soldiers passing and repassing through said towns," the legislature took no steps toward building barracks.[77] Other colonies also refused to enlarge their military infrastructure. The war was ending, and it was no longer necessary to quarter large numbers of regulars. However, by constructing massive barracks in the coastal cities, the colonists had made it extremely attractive for the North American Establishment to remain quartered in America long after the war was over.

Les Nouvelles-Casernes

Thomas Gage was keenly aware of the challenges of quartering troops in North America. In late 1755, Lieutenant Colonel Gage marched to Albany with the remains of the 44th Regiment of Foot following Braddock's defeat. As an officer, Gage probably rented quarters from a family in town, perhaps the Schuylers, as he quickly grew intimate with the family. Spending the winter in Albany, Gage observed the divisions that quartering created between the colonists and the British army. "If we ask for quarters, we are answered,—'it's against law, and a grievance on the subject,'" he wrote to a former commanding officer in January 1756. As a result, "the troops remained encamped in frost and snow till wooden houses were built to receive them, and forty

FIGURE 2.5.   General Thomas Gage. William Sartain, *Gen. Gage* (ca. 1899). Library of Congress, Prints and Photographs Division, LC-USZ62–40243 (b&w film copy neg.).

crammed in one room." Gage wondered why the English Mutiny Act did not extend to America, and he recommended that "all affairs here, both military and civil, want a thorough reformation." Gage spent the next four winters in Albany, ample time to contemplate quarters and to identify some solutions. It was out of this experience that Gage limned the Quartering Act.[78]

In many respects, Thomas Gage was indistinguishable from the hundreds of British officers who served in North America. He was born in 1719 or 1720, the second son of the first Viscount Gage. Like most newly created aristocrats, the Gages were ambitious and well connected, and like most second sons, Thomas was relegated to playing a supporting role. When he turned twenty-one, the family purchased him a lieutenancy in the army, and for the next fifteen years Gage experienced unimpressive successes, such as serving as an aide-de-camp in the War of the Austrian Succession, and inconsequential failures, including losing a race for Parliament. In 1754, Gage's fortunes improved when his brother succeeded as Viscount Gage and actively began promoting his career. That same year, the French and Indian War created new opportunities for advancement. After narrowly escaping Braddock's fate, Gage formed the 80th Regiment of Light-Armed Foot: five hundred rangers trained to emulate the hit-and-run tactics of their Native American opponents. Such innovation, as well as his older brother's politicking, earned Gage a promotion to brigadier general in 1758. Career triumphs were matched by personal victories when he married Margaret Kemble, the daughter of a New Jersey merchant and a member of Albany's prominent Schuyler family. In time, Gage would come to lead the North American Establishment, but quartering would never be far from his mind.[79]

No person is more important to the history of quarters in North America than Thomas Gage. Gage was the driving force behind the Quartering Act, and it was Gage who enforced the law for nearly a decade. Notably, his ideas about quartering were shaped by his experience in the colonies. Unlike Loudoun, Gage understood Americans' complaints about billeting troops in houses and may have found the practice unconstitutional. However, Gage also understood the limitations of barracks. He learned in Albany that barracked troops could suffer inhumane conditions; worse, Gage saw that without an act of Parliament, the army was dependent on the generosity of locals to keep the barracks well supplied. Gage's experience also stretched beyond the thirteen colonies. He was part of the conquest of Canada, leading thousands of troops into a hostile land where a lack of barracks prompted him to reconsider his objections to billeting in houses. Ultimately, Gage came to accept that the military geography of the thirteen American colonies was unfeasible in the territories acquired in war. Accordingly, barracks came to distinguish the old colonies from the new; and while barracks allowed Americans to make constitutional claims about the privacy of the home, the lack of permanent quarters left colonists elsewhere in British North America at the mercy of the British army.

Changes in martial space in the colonies coincided with changes in British political leadership in London. Britain's poor showing early in the Seven Years' War caused the Duke of Newcastle to lose members of his cabinet and, ultimately, the favor of King George II. Although Newcastle retained his premiership, power at Whitehall shifted to William Pitt. The second son of a wealthy but non-noble family, Pitt had made a name for himself as the most vituperative member of the opposition party in the House of Commons. He was also an enthusiastic imperialist whose vision for defeating France led the king to name him secretary of state for the southern department. To win the war, Pitt advised expanding it. Instead of skirmishing along Lake George, Britain had to attack the heart of New France at Québec, and strike French posts in the Caribbean and Asia.

To do so required more money, more troops, and new leadership. To accomplish the first two, Pitt persuaded Parliament to take out massive loans and to send money to the colonies to form provincial regiments. To accomplish the third, Pitt sacked the Earl of Loudoun, replacing him first with Major General James Abercrombie, and then with Major General Jeffrey Amherst, as commander in chief of all His Majesty's forces in North America. As Abercrombie and Amherst took control of the British army in March and September 1758, respectively, much of the American vitriol for Loudoun faded away. It helped that Parliament funded the colonies' war efforts at unprecedented levels and guaranteed that the ranks of provincial officers would be respected. It also helped that neither Abercrombie nor Amherst attempted to command the colonies like viceroys, but respectfully negotiated for quarters and supplies. In an ironic twist, by the time barracks were completed in the capital cities and in Albany and New Jersey, the billeting that had prompted their construction was no longer an issue.[80]

Meanwhile, the fortunes of the British army improved markedly. William Pitt's ambitious strategy and extravagant spending raised twenty thousand regulars and even more provincials. Clever diplomacy by British and colonial agents also brought hundreds of Native Americans to the side of King George II and, more importantly, persuaded the powerful Six Nations of the Haudenosaunee (Iroquois) to forsake King Louis XV. As a result, the French abandoned Fort Duquesne in 1758, and along with it the Ohio Valley. That same summer, General Amherst captured Louisbourg, opening the St. Lawrence Valley to a British invasion. This put the French commanding general the Marquis de Montcalm in retreat, abandoning Niagara and Ticonderoga and holing up in Québec City. On September 13, 1759, at the Plains of Abraham, British general James Wolfe defeated Montcalm, both commanders dying in a glorious tragedy that seemed fitting for the magnitude of the battle. Five days later, British forces entered Québec City, sealing the fate of New France. Over the next year, Amherst captured Montréal and seized Detroit, effectively bringing the French and Indian War to a close. Although the Seven Years' War raged on elsewhere for two more years, by the end of 1760 the British controlled all of North America east of the Mississippi River.[81]

Thomas Gage was invisible during the years of Britain's greatest triumphs. His light infantry played a supporting role in battles along Lake George in 1758, but it never lived up to its full potential. Personally, Gage demonstrated poor leadership in battle. An overabundance of caution prevented him from taking Fort La Galette (near Oswegatchie) on the St. Lawrence and delayed the fall of Montréal by a year. For this, both Pitt and Amherst censured him. But Gage was no field commander. He lacked the bravado expected of eighteenth-century generals, and he had no taste for excessive drinking, gambling, and whoring. Instead, the man whom other officers called "Honest Tom" was a born bureaucrat. While Amherst and Pitt grew bored at the details of management, Gage reveled in them. Far from battle, he worked long hours composing letters, drafting orders, and securing supplies. By the time Montréal fell in 1760, Amherst had come to appreciate his subordinate's administrative talents and appointed Gage military governor of the city. Gage happily took up residence in the Château Ramezay, the governor's palace in the center of town, and was soon joined by his wife Margaret, who bore a son in early 1761.[82]

The conquest of Canada inevitably led to a demand for quarters. Unfortunately for the British army, the military infrastructure of the new colonies was rudimentary. France had scattered a number of forts along the St. Lawrence River and the Great Lakes, while the cities of Québec and Montréal were surrounded by stone walls. Although most outposts contained small barracks, there was only one large set of permanent quarters in a city: Les Nouvelles-Casernes in the capital of Québec. Literally "the new barracks," the Nouvelles-Casernes was a 520-foot long, three-story structure, built between 1749 and 1752.[83] Yet even it was not big enough to accommodate the four thousand soldiers that had been needed to topple the capital of New France. Accordingly, when British troops entered Québec City, General James Murray "quartered them on the Canadians." Billeting proved a hardship for the war-torn city of only six or seven hundred houses. Murray also demanded supplies, especially firewood, but the Québécois, either "from inability or disaffection," proved poor at providing wood, and so the troops began pulling down their houses for fuel.[84] The suffering was even greater in Canadian cities where no barracks stood at all. When Montréal fell, orders went out for inhabitants to provide "lodgings for the soldiers," while General Gage ordered each householder to "furnish a fire to the officer or soldier lodged with him."[85] Billeting in private houses also followed the capture of Trois-Rivières and Detroit. As the war wound down, many of the British regulars withdrew, but enough remained for billeting to persist. A thousand troops remained in houses of Montréalers as late as November 1763, while six months later, Colonel John Bradstreet was astonished to discover that "the troops are lodged in at Detroit and find they have no other places but some of the inhabitants' houses."[86]

As a conquered people, the Québécois were subjected to forced and free quartering. Yet it was not just their legal status that led to billeting: Canadians lacked the knowledge, institutions, and finances to protest it. At the beginning of the war, they had not sought to keep French regulars out of their houses, and thus they lacked the experience of delineating places that defined quartering in the American colonies. In the articles of capitulation, Québec's leaders gained a promise that "the inhabitants shall be preserved in the possession of their houses," but they did not insist that soldiers be kept from those houses.[87] Moreover, Québec had no elected assembly, so there was no forum in which the colonists could voice complaints or appropriate money for barracks, as the Americans had. The French governors had taxed the Québécois without their consent to build the Nouvelles-Casernes, and the British governors continued this practice. Gage cited a 1716 tax to repair Montréal's walls, while Murray reinstated the 1749 "tax laid upon every house within the city and suburbs of Québec for repairing the barracks and keeping the same in order."[88] But these proved inadequate. Gage could gather only one-fourth of what his French predecessors had, while three years after the conquest of Québec, Murray still had not collected any money to keep the Nouvelles-Casernes habitable. Lacking the means and the ability to build barracks, the Québécois had no choice but to billet troops in their houses.[89]

Such quartering persisted even after the war ended. In February 1763, negotiators in Paris concluded a treaty, officially ending the Seven Years' War. In addition to gaining Canada, the recently crowned King George III picked up a clear title to the Great Lakes, the Illinois Country, and the Southeast. Britain had captured Havana in a 1762 raid, but traded it for Florida. In the Caribbean, the Windward Islands (Dominica, Grenada, Tobago, and St. Vincent and the Grenadines) joined the empire. However, the British government did not have much time to revel in its successes before the awesome responsibility of empire soured the mood. In particular, the large population of non-English peoples worried Whitehall, so the ministry opted to leave soldiers in the new colonies. Five regiments of British regulars were stationed in the Caribbean, while fifteen regiments on the mainland reconstituted the North American Establishment. As British troops claimed Florida, the lack of barracks again became apparent. Reports from Pensacola described only meager huts "in a ruinous condition" to shelter troops, while in St. Augustine a lack of quarters in the Castillo de San Marcos left officers "obliged to lodge themselves at some expense."[90] The situation was not much better for British troops who headed west to take control of lands beyond the Appalachian Mountains, stationing in forts like Vincennes that one report described as "a little stockade."[91]

Again, billeting British regulars in houses raised constitutional questions that proved difficult to answer. In 1763, King George III issued a proclamation that carved four new colonies out of Britain's recent acquisitions (Québec, East Florida, West Florida, and the Windward Islands) and promised each the right to "call general assemblies . . . as is used and directed in those colonies and provinces in America . . . to make, constitute, and ordain laws, statutes, and ordinances." In other words, Québec was to be the same as Massachusetts. To be sure, the Proclamation of 1763 was more a statement of principles than a colonial charter; Whitehall was not eager to extend equal representation to Francophone Catholics, and so it delayed the establishment of colonial assemblies. Nevertheless, the king's actions changed the status of the new territories. They were no longer foreign lands held by force, but civilian provinces whose inhabitants had the same rights as American colonists. The Americans insisted that these rights included protections against billeting in their houses, but the British army was unable to recognize such rights in Canada, Florida, or the backcountry.[92]

Of course, the British government had never accepted Americans' arguments that the English constitution protected their houses from quartering. The Earl of Loudoun had sidestepped the issue by insisting that war trumped place, and he had not stayed long enough to wrestle with the implications of his dictum once peace returned. In truth, the Americans had claimed their rights by building barracks, and the British army had not challenged this for the most part. However, this solution was not possible elsewhere in British North America. Colonists in Canada, Florida, and the backcountry had no ability to build barracks, so they were placed at the mercy of the British army, and their constitutional rights were left unclear. Loudoun had paid to build barracks in Albany out of his budget, and the British army could have done so in the new colonies. However, Whitehall was looking to cut costs, and it had no money for barracks.[93]

Before Thomas Gage could grapple with the implications of the inequity between the old and new colonies, Pontiac's War broke out in the Ohio Country. The Proclamation of 1763 had not transformed the land west of the Appalachian Mountains into colonies, but left the region to Native Americans. However, British traders quickly disappointed the inhabitants with the cost and quality of their goods, so the Odawa (Ottawa) chief Pontiac built a coalition to strike British soldiers in the region. In May and June 1763, Pontiac's forces destroyed eight forts and laid siege to Detroit, Niagara, and Fort Pitt. General Amherst proved unable to quash the revolt quickly, so Whitehall recalled him and named Thomas Gage commander in chief. In November 1763, Gage headed for New York City to take command of the North American Establishment. Although his immediate concern was defeating Pontiac, the unanswered questions of billets and barracks in Canada would continue to demand his attention.[94]

The Ordeal of Thomas Walker

On the evening of December 6, 1764, Thomas Walker sat down to dinner. He was not feeling well, so his wife Martha served the meal in the parlor. The Walkers resided in Montréal in a stone house in one of the city's better neighborhoods, a fitting situation, given Walker's position as justice of the peace. About fifteen minutes into their dinner, the Walkers heard someone rattling at the door. Thinking it was a Montréaler seeking justice, Martha Walker called out "Entrez!" Suddenly, a dozen men with blackened faces entered the house and set upon Thomas. "Good God! What is this? This is murder!" Martha cried out as a melee ensued. The intruders struck Thomas repeatedly with their swords, drawing blood as they bludgeoned him. He attempted to crawl to his bedroom, but the repeated blows caused him to lose consciousness. Martha escaped through the kitchen and ran down the street. Believing him to be dead, the assailants sliced off the magistrate's ear and fled into the night. However, Thomas Walker did not die that fateful night in December 1764. Instead, he survived to tell his story and became living proof of the dire consequences of Canada's shortage of barracks.[95]

News of Walker's attack set Montréal on edge, especially once it was revealed that his assailants were British soldiers. For four years, a thousand British regulars had been stationed in Montréal. Although the city contained "barracks for a few men" inside a small fort, most soldiers were spread across the city of five thousand, billeting in many if not most of Montréal's six or seven hundred houses. They did so without the permission of the householders or compensation from military or civilian leaders. Thomas Walker was a particularly vocal critic of quartering in Montréal. His assault drew attention to the constitutional inconsistencies of billeting in North America once Québec became a civilian colony. It also highlighted the limitations of barracks as a solution for preventing billeting in houses across the new colonies.[96]

Thomas Walker first came to Montréal in August 1763 when Canada was under military rule. A native of England, Walker had spent a decade in Boston before setting himself up as a merchant in Montréal. The year before Walker arrived, General Gage had abolished the French trading monopolies in and around Montréal, thus enticing entrepreneurs to profit from the region's lucrative fur trade. Walker was happy to benefit from the economic opportunities that the army afforded him, but he found other aspects of the martial regime less salutary. When a military court ruled against him in a civil suit, he ignored the judgment. Neither a conqueror nor conquered, Walker felt that the army's purview did not include him. He was a British subject, and as such he was entitled to his constitutional rights. It made little difference to him if such protections did not apply to British soldiers and Catholic Québécois.[97]

Billeting was Walker's chief complaint against military rule. It does not appear that Walker ever quartered troops in his stone mansion, but his fellow merchants did, and Walker took up their cause. Having troops in one's home was objectionable because it interfered with the ability to make money. One merchant declared that billeting was "a detriment to his business, as a customer might be affronted if indulgence was not shown to himself."[98] In other words, the constitutional protection of the house extended beyond one's residence to one's business. The military commander of Québec, General James Murray, rejected such claims, while British soldiers ridiculed the merchants. The Québécois took no position in the growing rift between the merchants and the army. Although Murray opined that "the genteel people of the colony despise merchants, and of course esteem the officers," in truth, they had little affection for any of the British invaders.[99]

The situation became considerably more complicated in September 1764 when military rule ended and a civilian government was established in Québec. Formally, the transition took power away from the British army. Matters of justice were transferred from courts-martial to a new system of civilian courts where Québécois were allowed to serve on juries. Practically, however, the army remained in charge. General Murray became Governor Murray, and a thousand British troops continued to billet in Montréal houses without gaining the permission of householders or providing compensation. The transition also delayed the king's promise of an elected assembly. The British government was unwilling to enfranchise Catholics or allow Québécois to hold elective office. Instead, the government of Québec consisted of Governor Murray and an appointed provincial council of Protestant elites.

Soon after Québec became a civilian colony, Murray and the council attempted to regularize billeting. Concerned that forced and free quartering were legally dubious, the council issued An Ordinance for Billeting His Majesty's Troops on Private Housekeepers in This Province, which legalized it. Murray, who had grown tired of Walker's complaints, hoped that the provincial law would quiet the critics of quartering. The governor also named Walker and several other merchants justices of the peace. Not coincidentally, the billeting ordinance exempted "all people in public employments" from housing soldiers, thus absolving Walker and the other newly named magistrates from such responsibilities. The law also allowed "merchants and other inhabitants" to hire houses for troops as a means of protecting their domiciles. In effect, Québec's billeting ordinance carved out sufficient exemptions for Protestant householders such that only the Québécois would have to billet troops in their houses.[100]

None of these concessions satisfied Thomas Walker. Although allowing merchants to pay for quarters let them keep troops out of their houses, Walker claimed that this led to extortion. "Three or four of the most drunken and riotous of the soldiers would be sent to take up their quarters at the house of a substantial citizen," he insisted, which would compel the householder to pay an exorbitant amount "rather than see his house taken up, his furniture broken and spoiled, his provisions wasted, and sometimes his wife and daughters insulted." Once again, Walker used claims of domestic privacy to defend merchants' businesses. He also found his elevation to justice of the peace to be insufficient. In Britain and the American colonies, local magistrates determined where soldiers were housed, but Murray had no intention of giving Walker or the other merchants control over billeting; free and forced quartering remained the order of the day. As a result, Walker insisted that billeting in Montréal houses remained unconstitutional.[101]

These issues came to a head in November 1764. Early that month, a British captain vacated the home of a Québécois colonist where he had billeted for some time. The householder then rented the room to Francis Knipe, an English merchant who recently had been appointed justice of the peace. Before Knipe could move in, however, the captain returned and informed the householder that another officer would be taking the room. Outraged, Knipe appealed to his fellow magistrates, who ordered the officer to vacate the premises. A nasty exchange ensued, which resulted in the officer being jailed. Knipe cited the billeting ordinance's prohibition on quartering troops in the houses of public officials, which was somewhat dubious, as he had not yet moved into the room. But what infuriated the justices more was the army's contention that the protection against quartering extended only to the justice's *rooms within a house* instead of the entire residence. By this line of reasoning, some places in a house were more private than others, and it was up to the army to decide which was which.[102]

While British officers and the merchant magistrates bickered, British soldiers took matters into their own hands. Members of the 28th Regiment of Foot were incensed by Walker's disparagement of the army and were perhaps fearful that his efforts would turn them out of their houses; accordingly, they plotted against him. Initially, the conspirators planned to attack Walker in public, but after two failed attempts to accost the magistrate in the street, they invaded his home, beating him within an inch of his life. Had the soldiers attacked Walker in the open, outrage would have followed, but it certainly would have been less severe. By assaulting him in his residence with his family around him, the men of the 28th confirmed Walker's charge that billeting troops destroyed domestic privacy and threatened the lives of civilians.[103]

Montréalers flew into a rage once news of Walker's attack got out. Commanding officer General Ralph Burton quickly arrested a suspected sergeant and offered a £200 reward for his accomplices. Governor Murray and the provincial council demanded that the 28th Regiment be removed to the suburbs, but Burton preferred to exchange the regiment with another one in North America. As Murray and Burton tried to figure out what to do, "several noncommissioned officers and soldiers" were arrested without warrants and "thrown into a jail, on a vague suspicion, and even committed to dungeons without a fire" in the dead of winter. Because of this, one officer feared that his soldiers might mutiny at any moment.[104]

Walker's assault had a profound effect on the Québécois population of Montréal. Although they had accommodated British soldiers for four years without incident, the soldiers' actions against a magistrate politicized them. A month after the attack, General Burton reported "a jealousy between the troops, and the people," including an incident in which an officer "knocking for admittance into his quarters" was greeted with abusive language and "fired upon, by some people of the house."[105] A letter from Québec that appeared in several New England newspapers suggested that such actions had become widespread. Whenever the Québécois dealt with a soldier, they "present a pistol to him to prevent his committing any outrage." Billeting likewise became increasingly tense as "the inhabitants never dine nor even sit in their own houses, without pistols before them." Violence seemed imminent, causing the author to note that Montréal was in "the greatest confusion, and may probably end, not in an Indian war, but a provincial one." Although denied a legislature, the Québécois nonetheless found a political voice on quarters. By their actions, Canadians signaled that they expected the same right as Britons and Americans to keep soldiers out of their houses.[106]

Montréal remained on edge for the remainder of the winter of 1764–1765. If Walker and his associates had planned to become heroes of the Québécois, these hopes were quickly dashed. An investigation by two provincial councilors discovered that the merchant magistrates had "sunk into so much contempt and hatred" that they no longer commanded any respect in Montréal.

Walker discredited himself in the eyes of the Québécois when he demanded that his case be heard by a jury of Protestants. He also publicly attacked Murray, who removed him as justice of the peace. Eventually, Walker departed to seek redress in London. In the meantime, a thousand troops remained billeted in Montréal houses. Then, in May 1765, a fire broke out in the rue Saint-Paul, destroying one-fourth of the city and leaving 215 families homeless. The fire combined with the memory of Walker's assault to force the army to finally address the problem of quarters in the city. Shortly after the soldiers were "burnt out of their lodgings," General Gage ordered several companies of the 28th Regiment to a fort on Lake Champlain, reducing the number of regulars in Montréal and the suburbs to 322.[107]

Not surprisingly, the favored solution was barracks. In a parallel to events in the old colonies a decade earlier, billeting in private houses in Montréal created such rancor among the local population that the colonial government sought to build permanent quarters. In June 1765, Québec's provincial council concluded that the only way to solve the "daily disputes between the civil and military" caused by billeting troops in Montréal was "by building barracks," insisting that "nothing will contribute so much to the public tranquility."[108] Unlike in the old colonies, however, the construction of barracks was opposed in Québec by the governor. The financial and legislative limitations of the new colony had not changed, and Murray had neither the money nor the authority to finance something like Québec's Nouvelles-Casernes for Montréal. Instead, he insisted that all matters of quartering, including barracks and supplies, were the responsibility of the army. As a result, billeting in domiciles continued in Québec as Governor Murray and General Burton waited for either money or clarification of policy from the commander in chief.

The ordeal of Thomas Walker had broad ramifications. The American colonists followed the story closely, fearful that the violent consequences of perpetual billeting in private houses portended a loss of liberty. They worried that the army's disregard for the English constitution might travel from the new colonies to the old, and that Britain might circumscribe their rights, reducing them to the inferior status of Canadians.[109] For the Québécois, Walker's ordeal confirmed their helplessness in the face of the British army. Although the incident gave them an opportunity to assert a right to domestic privacy, their inability to build barracks meant that they could not execute such rights. For the British army, it was another reminder that it was dependent on the will of local populations to quarter troops. Québec's provincial council could just as well have not legalized billeting in private houses, leaving the soldiers homeless. As General Gage pondered the consequences of

Walker's attack, he began to favor an act of Parliament to regularize the obligations of the colonists to quarter the North American Establishment.

Ironic Quarters

By the time Thomas Gage became commander in chief in November 1763, the military geography of the American colonies had changed dramatically. Since the capture of Montréal three years earlier, the size and strength of the British army in the thirteen colonies had atrophied, as most regulars departed for battle elsewhere. When Gage arrived at the headquarters of the North American Establishment in New York City, he entered the only city in the old colonies with an entire regiment of British regulars; the army had abandoned New Jersey and cut forces in Albany, Philadelphia, and Charleston to one company of fifty men each. Instead, the army's attention was solidly focused on new colonies like Québec and the Floridas where non-English populations dominated, and the backcountry where Pontiac's War raged.[110] The arrival of General Gage in New York prompted merchant and provincial councilor John Watts to record the momentous change at hand. "We have quite a new scene opening here," Watts wrote; "a new war, a new general, new enemies and, of course, a new system of operations."[111]

For many Americans, the new reality of 1763 was best symbolized by empty barracks. With the army gone, British military power in the thirteen colonies shrank. Except for New York's Upper Barracks, the permanent quarters that had invaded the public spaces of the capital cities, New Jersey, and Albany were either vacated or minimally occupied. As a result, the barracks that had once been testaments to Americans' constitutional freedom against billeting became ironic symbols of war in a time of peace. Beyond their symbolism, the empty barracks raised practical questions. The massive structures needed constant repair, but this seemed pointless if they held no troops. Some cities repurposed their barracks for civilian uses, effectively minimizing the army's footprint to practically nothing. However, as long as the barracks remained, they invited the British army to revert the structures to their original purpose. Time and again, the American barracks were reopened for troops. This too seemed ironic now that the colonists' enemies were vanquished, and it was alarming to some Americans when barracked soldiers actively supported the colonists' antagonists.

The transition to empty barracks was gradual. When the British regulars first departed, the structures played a supporting role in the military objectives of the growing empire. Britain's siege of Havana was a bloody affair that left thousands of soldiers wounded and diseased, many of whom were sent to recuperate on the mainland. In response, New York City turned the Lower Barracks into a military hospital, which quickly overflowed with "weak and feeble" troops, as did the army hospital in Albany.[112] By December 1762, the number of convalescing soldiers was so great that New York's General Assembly revived the province's 1756 quartering law allowing troops to be billeted in public and private houses should barracks prove inadequate. Quarters inside New York City's Fort George held French prisoners of war, while on Castle Island, Massachusetts quartered sick and wounded provincials who had helped reduce Louisbourg.[113]

After the last wounded soldiers and prisoners of war departed, the colonists sought civilian uses for the barracks. Given the configuration of the structures, it occurred to some to put the disciplinary spaces to use controlling nonmilitary personnel. In South Carolina, the emptied quarters housed Acadians. Francophone colonists from Nova Scotia, the Acadians had been forcibly evicted from their homeland in 1755 by the British army and distributed among the American colonies. Five years later, 340 Acadians were still crowded into a handful of Charleston houses. Fearing that the refugees might produce "contagious and malignant distempers," the Commons House appropriated £2,000 so that "part of the New Barracks may be allotted for the reception of as many of the said Acadians as they will conveniently hold."[114] Across town, a group of "poor distressed people" who "could give no good account of themselves" took up residence in Charleston's Brick Barracks. When South Carolina legislators looked to evict the squatters, the wardens of St. Philip's Church pleaded for mercy, ultimately persuading the lawmakers not "to turn out such poor people at this season of the year."[115] In New York, the city council likewise opened the Upper Barracks to charity, granting one room to a weaver named Hill, "he having lately come from Europe, and being unable at present to provide for himself and family elsewhere."[116]

Letting barracks serve the public good appealed to many colonists, as it reflected a benevolent and paternalistic ethos. The barracks were, in this light, no different from an almshouse or a hospital. Moreover, the charitable use of the structures also helped to justify the cost of maintaining them. In contrast to New York and Charleston, the five New Jersey towns could find little use for their barracks, thus the repairs to the buildings felt exorbitant. In 1762 alone, New Jersey spent £94 on the barracks in Perth Amboy and £148 on those in Elizabeth. Without a need for disciplinary space even for civilians, the New Jersey legislature in June 1765 approved a law appointing commissioners to "rent the said barracks with the lands thereunto appertaining" and sell off the contents.[117]

Regardless of the barracks' use, local civilian authorities continued to control them. The colonists had paid for the structures out of their taxes, and the barracks remained public buildings in service to the common good. But not all barracks had emptied of British soldiers. New York housed a regiment in the Upper Barracks, while additional regiments progressed through the city on their way to and from the hinterlands. These troops continued to tax the colonists for supplies, although at least these soldiers were defending the colonists from their enemies. By contrast, Pennsylvanians came to question the very existence of the Philadelphia Barracks when the structures housed British soldiers in defense of Native Americans. In a foreshadowing of events that followed a decade later, the army's use of the Philadelphia Barracks in 1763 raised the possibility that Americans did not control their own cities.

In late 1763, the barracks in the Philadelphia suburb of Northern Liberties were occupied by a company of regulars. There was nothing to defend in Philadelphia per se; instead, the barracks were a point of entry for troops heading west to forts on the borderland. That November, however, the soldiers and barracks were called upon to render service to the province. A few months earlier, white settlers had begun killing Native Americans with disturbing frequency, causing the Pennsylvania General Assembly to worry for the safety of 140 or so Indians who resided in the missionary town of Wechquetank. Known colloquially as Moravian Indians, the residents of Wechquetank were Lenape (Delaware) people who had been converted to Christianity by a pietistic sect of German Protestants. Sympathetic Quaker legislators knew that white settlers could not or would not tell the difference between hostile tribes and peaceful ones, and so they recommended that the Indians relocate to the Philadelphia Barracks.[118] Led by missionary Bernhard Adam Grube, the Moravian Indians marched seventy-five miles to the Northern Liberties. When they arrived, however, neither soldiers nor civilians welcomed the proselytes. "The rage of the people in Philadelphia is indescribable," reported Grube: "we had to stand five hours before the barracks and be insulted." The Indians were then denied entrance to the barracks by the regulars, so they encamped at Province Island in the Delaware River.[119]

Confining the Wechquetank Indians to the Philadelphia Barracks was not dissimilar to sending the Acadians to Charleston's New Barracks. In both cases, the structures afforded a way of dealing with groups that most colonists viewed as outsiders. Like Acadian refugees, Christianized Native Americans were helpless dependents who required the paternalistic care lest they fall victim to violence. Pennsylvania lawmakers also looked to keep the cost of charity low, and the largely unoccupied barracks afforded an inexpensive solution. The barracks also provided a mechanism for the Philadelphians to control their guests. Culturally distinct and deserving of pity, the Wechqu-etank Indians had to be monitored, something that barracks made possible. As in Charleston, Philadelphia used the disciplinary space to control non-English civilians.

At the same time, there was something new about Pennsylvania's deci-sion to barrack Native Americans. As the hostility expressed by the soldiers and civilians suggests, the white inhabitants saw something incongruous about placing Indians in military quarters. The colonists had built the bar-racks to accommodate soldiers who fought *against* Native Americans, thus the colony's repurposing of the barracks was an inversion of their purpose. Indeed, many Philadelphians sided with the backcountry settlers who were indiscriminately killing Indians. Civilians and soldiers of Philadelphia were united in their hostility toward the Indians and were, for a time, united in keeping the Wechquetank Indians out of the barracks.

This consensus proved lasting as the attacks on Native Americans grew increasingly gruesome. In December 1763, a group of vigilantes known to history as the Paxton Boys killed six Susquehannock (Conestoga) Indians and destroyed their homes. Attempting to protect these Christian Indians from further violence, local authorities confined sixteen Susquehannocks to a workhouse in Lancaster. Much like the Wechquetank Indians, the Susque-hannocks were placed in a centrally located public building to be simultane-ously protected and controlled. Concentrating the Indians, however, proved a fatal mistake, as vigilantes broke into the workhouse and butchered the Susquehannocks. In response, Pennsylvania's Governor John Penn took action. Unnerved by rumors that two hundred Paxton Boys were headed for Philadelphia to finish off the Indians, Penn ordered the Wechquetanks to New York. In January 1764, a group of regulars marching to New York City agreed to escort the Native Americans out of town. However, their march was soon halted by the governors of New Jersey and New York, who worried that violence would follow the refugees. Three weeks after they had departed Philadelphia, the Wechquetank Indians were back at Province Island.[120]

This time, however, the Native Americans would be protected by the British army. Following the Lancaster murders, Governor Penn requested the assistance of British regulars. Penn had considered raising provincial forces but worried that they "could not be brought to act vigorously against their friends, neighbors, and relations." In response to Penn's request, Gen-eral Thomas Gage dispatched three companies of the 60th from Albany, although Gage was insistent that any order to fire on civilians had to come from the governor. As the soldiers escorted the Wechquetank Indians to the

Philadelphia Barracks, some legislators worried that Gage and Penn were conspiring to use "regular troops to make use of force and violence against His Majesty's subjects." Before they could rebuke the army, however, reports reached Philadelphia that 250 Paxton Boys were headed to the capital intent on attacking not only the Wechquetank Indians but the colonial government as well. This changed lawmakers' minds in a hurry. The provincial council hired carpenters "to erect some works at the barracks to make them more defensible" and ordered inhabitants to "turn out with their arms and repair to the barracks" should the city be attacked. In two months, British regulars had gone from being defenders of colonists against the Indians to protectors of Indians against colonists.[121]

Trapped together in the barracks, soldiers and Indians made difficult housemates. According to the communal diary of the Indian *gemeine* (community), Brother Grube warned the Wechquetank Indians that they "should in no way get involved with the soldiers." The Native Americans accordingly went about their business, conducting daily prayer services in the kitchen and occasionally attracting a few soldiers to worship. However, as the Paxton Boys neared Philadelphia, emotions ran high. When Captain Schlosser ordered the Indians to room with the soldiers on the second story, "a great confusion arose," and "everyone got alarmed and made ready to fight." On February 6, the Paxton Boys reached Germantown, only seven miles from the Northern Liberties. While "everyone took up arms" in Philadelphia, assemblyman Benjamin Franklin negotiated with the rebel leaders on the outskirts of town.[122] He convinced the Paxton Boys to disband and return home, although they did not go quietly. Instead, they petitioned against the "oppressive, unequal, and unjust" government of Pennsylvania, by which they meant the continued practice of protecting the Indians, including Christian ones.[123]

The Paxton Boys dramatically transformed the meaning of the Philadelphia Barracks, making it a symbol of the alliance between city dwellers, British soldiers, and Indians against rural colonists. The first Sunday after the vigilantes departed, the barracks became a communal space. In the morning, "many people from the city and soldiers were at the sermon," and after noon, many more came to visit "because the soldiers talk much about how prettily our Indians can sing." Although life at the barracks was a voyeuristic curiosity, it was also a testament to the city's values of charity and order. The British regulars and Wechquetank Indians barracked together until the troops departed in May 1764, leaving the Native Americans alone in the structure for another eleven months. Waiting for permission to depart for friendlier surroundings, the Indians grew bored and frustrated with their confinement.

Barrack life proved especially intolerable for the young, who wandered "too far from the barracks" like errant soldiers. The similarity was not lost on those outside the city who viewed the Philadelphia Barracks with hostility.[124]

The Barracks

Historians largely have been uninterested in barracks as a place. Perhaps because the purpose of the structures has been unchanged since ancient times, we have assumed that the meaning of permanent military quarters is unchanged as well. But barracks had a profound significance for eighteenth-century Americans that was not shared by Britons or other colonists. In the 1750s, American colonists built barracks to effect constitutional liberties, specifically the right to protect one's house from billeting troops. They were not indifferent to the structures, but embraced them as public buildings that they viewed as literally central to their communities much like churches, workhouses, and jails. To maintain quarters, the colonists appropriated large sums of money at a time when war already had driven up their taxes. But the meaning that Americans invested in barracks claimed rights that London was not willing to recognize and proffered a solution that was impractical in Canada. Accordingly, it was unclear how the hopeful vision of barracks would fare in a growing British Empire in need of unification.

Barracks also profoundly changed the military geography of North America. While they protected New York City and Charleston from billeting troops in homes, they also made these places a legitimate part of the North American Establishment, as barracks were an open invitation to British soldiers. Although the colonists in 1764 did not perceive the British army to be a threat per se, Philadelphia's experience with the Wechquetank Indians left unsolved the problem of what local inhabitants should do if they did not want British troops in their midst. Barracks created a permanent space for British military power in American cities and towns, although the consequences of this decision would take another decade to work out.

Eighteenth-century barracks also held significance for the people who lived in them. For thousands of British soldiers, as well as many women and children, barracks were home. At a time when domiciles were increasingly being defined by privacy and refinement, barracks offered neither. Although British officers like Thomas Gage rarely worried about the complaints of soldiers, they did expect troops to have the basic necessities for survival. The provisioning of blankets, firewood, and alcohol fell entirely to the local civilian population, and as long as the colonists had a positive view of the barracks, the supplies were satisfactory. But events in Philadelphia suggested that Americans' view of quarters was easily changeable, with troubling implications for barrack supplies. By late 1764, General Gage had concluded that parliamentary intervention was needed to keep barracks habitable regardless of fluctuating colonial opinion. In short, the unique meaning that eighteenth-century Americans attached to barracks was extremely important and would prove the basis for the Quartering Act.

CHAPTER 3

Empire

Drafting and Implementing the Quartering Act

Benjamin Franklin was at home in London. In early 1765, the Philadelphia printer, scientist, and politician was living at the epicenter of the British Empire, greedily consuming the culture and power of one of the world's great cities. He found accommodations on Craven Street near Charing Cross and the shops in the Strand. From there, Franklin was less than a fifteen-minute walk from the cabinet offices at Whitehall and Parliament at the Palace of Westminster. Nearby were taverns, ideal for the conviviality of club life and debating politics over pints of ale. Franklin's location also made it possible for him to patronize the arts and learn the latest scientific discoveries at the Royal Society. The city quenched his thirst for urbanity and led Franklin to muse that he would remain "a Londoner for the rest of my days."[1]

Franklin's affection for London reflected an imperial perspective. Born in Boston in 1706, Franklin had long had cosmopolitan ambitions. At sixteen, he ran away to Philadelphia to become a printer, making him a conduit for a transatlantic information network. During the French and Indian War, Franklin was a proponent of British military power, arguing that a strong empire benefited the colonies; thus he supplied Braddock's troops and subverted the Paxton Boys' raid on the Philadelphia Barracks. An imperial outlook continued to inform Franklin's ideas when he departed for London to become an agent for the Pennsylvania assembly, basically a lobbyist. Indeed, when news of quartering disputes in the colonies reached London in 1765, Franklin advocated an imperial solution: the Quartering Act.

Since 1755, quarters had been a contentious issue in the American colonies. The North American Establishment created a demand for military accommodations, but the Earl of Loudoun had angered colonists by billeting troops in private houses. Barracks addressed this problem, but new challenges had arisen since then. As the army worked contrary to colonial interests, as it had in Philadelphia in 1763–1764, Americans became reluctant to supply soldiers. Moreover, the presence of barracks did not necessarily keep troops out of colonists' homes, as the inhabitants of Albany could attest. As a result, Commander in Chief Thomas Gage requested that Parliament take action. Heretofore quarters had been a local issue, but Gage envisioned a Mutiny Act for America that would regularize soldiers' accommodations and end colonial resistance. As a bill moved through Parliament, Benjamin Franklin and others became involved, insisting that any law for quartering in North America also protect Americans' homes. The Quartering Act accomplished both: it stipulated the colonists' right to keep soldiers out of their private houses, as well as their responsibility to pay for the troops' accommodations. Both Gage and Franklin hoped that an imperial solution had solved the eternal struggle of quarters in North America.

The history of quarters in North America after 1765 is dominated by the Quartering Act, alternately known as the Mutiny Act for America or the American Mutiny Act. Accordingly, the narrative shifts from houses and barracks to legislative chambers. Although social interactions continued to inform legislation, the process of writing and enforcing the Quartering Act is a more traditionally political story. The main actors are colonial agents like Franklin and army officers like Gage, Britain's Parliament and cabinet members at Whitehall, royal governors and colonial assemblies. The records left by these political actors reveal a detailed discussion of military power. Lawmakers on both sides of the Atlantic used quartering to ask broader questions about constitutional rights and the bonds between metropole and periphery. In effect, the Quartering Act invited a discussion of the empire as a place.

Historians have thoroughly investigated the British Empire, especially London's effort to assert greater control over North America in the 1760s. Fearful of growing colonial autonomy, the British government sought to replace the empire's loose and unwieldy structure with one that tightly bound the colonies to the mother country, creating what one historian terms a "unitary empire."[2] Many historians have focused on the role that taxes and trade regulations played in these efforts, and thus we know a great deal about the Stamp Act and the Tea Act.[3] However, the colonists quickly opposed both laws not only because they saw them as evidence of taxation without representation, but because they offered Americans nothing in return for their taxes. The Mutiny Act for America more completely embodied the spirit of the unitary empire as it was an attempt to spread English rights and responsibilities to the colonies. Consequently, American resistance to the Quartering Act was slower and more uneven than with other parliamentary laws. It also had more dramatic consequences, as enforcement of the law undermined the empire in ways that the Stamp Act never did.

When General Gage first proposed the Quartering Act, he asked that it be part of the English Mutiny Act; this would have extended English rights and responsibilities to the colonists. Although Parliament passed a separate law for America, it nonetheless protected the colonists' domestic privacy and required them to provide the same barrack supplies as Britons. Moreover, the statute originally encompassed all of British North America, not just the thirteen colonies. In 1765, Americans like Franklin welcomed the statute because it signaled that imperial unity meant equity. But the implementation of the Mutiny Act for America demonstrated that British North America was not one place but many places. The law proved unworkable in Canada, while it evoked a diversity of responses in the old colonies. New York's colonial assembly resisted the enumeration of supplies as a usurpation of its prerogative. In response, Whitehall singled out New York for punishment, while Gage discovered that compliance required acknowledging the colonies' individual circumstances. In 1768, the Quartering Act promised colonial inequality, prompting Americans like Franklin to turn against the law and the unitary empire.

The Quartering Act also reshaped the military geography of British North America. On one hand, the statute offered a definitive response to the question of where soldiers belonged by confirming that homes were civilian spaces. The law also declared barracks constitutional and provided alternatives when barracks were not available. On the other hand, the Quartering Act reflected that all of British North America shared the same military geography. Following the conquest of Canada, the American colonies disbanded their provincial armies, leaving the defense of the continent to fifteen regiments of British regulars. This granted the army access to all corners of Britain's North American empire and erased local control of military power. The American Mutiny Act confirmed this by prescribing the same accommodations for troops in New York and Philadelphia as for those in Montréal and Detroit. As regiments marched into the middle colonies and demanded supplies under the statute, it occurred to the Americans that they had no more control over British military power than did Canadians or Indians. Eventually, this would cause them to challenge the presence of British regulars anywhere in North America, but they were too disunited in 1768 to think beyond the empire.

In sum, the Quartering Act suggests how the spatial discourse of houses and barracks expanded into a contest over the meaning of empire. What had begun as an attempt to quarter soldiers became a debate about the relationship between Britain and the American colonies. Imperialists like Benjamin Franklin hoped that a unitary empire would solve the problem of quarters and protect colonial rights, but this proved not to be the case. Instead, the Quartering Act created new tensions that destabilized Britain's North American empire.

The Ideal of Imperial Unity

The immediate impetus for the Quartering Act came from New York. In the winter of 1764–1765, nearly all of the North American Establishment had been relocated to the new colonies in order to patrol non-English colonists in Québec and the Floridas, or to fight Pontiac's forces in the Ohio Country. The one exception was New York. Located in the middle of the Atlantic coast with unimpeded routes to Canada and the Great Lakes, New York was the keystone of the British army in North America. Commander in Chief Thomas Gage maintained headquarters in New York City along with a company of the 60th, while a second company was stationed in Albany. Although both cities possessed ample barracks to keep the troops out of private houses, New York City and Albany had begun to bridle at the imposition of quarters. Regulars in New York aroused animosity among the colonists, who wanted them out.[4]

The calls for removal were loudest in Albany. After 150 years of vulnerable existence on the "great warpath," the Hudson Valley and Albany welcomed peace and intended to make the most of their strategic location. Situated halfway between New York City and Montréal, Albany was poised to become a great commercial entrepôt, and it saw British troops as an impediment to this. The city council turned a covetous eye toward the military buildings that populated the town. As figure 3.1 reveals, Fort Frederick, a parallel row of barracks, and an H-shaped military hospital bounded the city's western edge, while a magazine clogged a main street at the center of town. The council was shameless about its appropriation of military property, allowing inhabitants to cut down a fence that enclosed the army's pasture and fielding a request from the local Anglican church "for the ground on which the old barrack stands."[5]

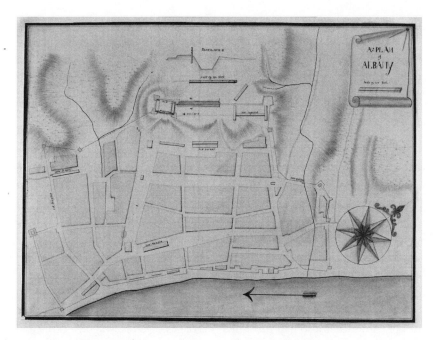

FIGURE 3.1. Albany in 1757. Abercrombie, *A Plan of Albany* (ca. 1757). Watercolor and ink on paper, Albany Institute of History and Art Library.

In January 1764, civilians scuffled with soldiers when a British colonel tried to billet provincial recruits in private houses. Albany thought little better of barracked troops, and in March, two hundred men attacked a dozen grenadiers after a couple of drunken lieutenants harassed a local woman.[6] The following June, the colonists redirected their anger toward military buildings when a group assembled "to pull down His Majesty's stables."[7] Although regulars were able to prevent this, a crowd returned a few days later and "entirely stripped the guardhouse of every board."[8] The quartermaster appealed to magistrates for help, but Albany's civilian leaders ignored the call. Three months later, two men returning home from a tavern decided to break into the army's storehouse. When a private tried to stop them, they "fell upon him and beat him much, so that the sentinel called out murder."[9] In response, the city council took action but not against the vandals. Instead, it petitioned the commander in chief "to have the buildings and other nuisance in the public streets removed."[10]

General Gage was not surprised by Albany's actions. Having spent five winters in the city, he knew that Albany had suffered more than most places when it came to quarters. But Gage had no intention of removing the army, as the city's location meant that troops "should constantly pass and repass" through it. Instead, he made a veiled threat of forced quartering, informing Albany mayor Volckert Douw that if the barracks "were pulled down," then he would "require an act to quarter the troops."[11] Had Albany been alone in its defiance, Gage probably would have ignored it, but in late 1764, such rebelliousness seemed to be contagious. When the 55th Regiment headed to New York City, Mayor John Cruger Jr. refused to provide firewood because "there is no law to quarter soldiers."[12] In Montréal, Lieutenant Colonel Gabriel Christie warned that the Québécois were becoming as uncooperative as Americans. The people of Albany, Christie opined, "are more licentious, than they yet have had time to be in Canada," but he predicted that "the same will come to pass here in time."[13]

Having pondered the need for a thorough reformation of quarters nine years earlier, Gage took steps in late 1764 to achieve it. He dispatched Deputy Quartermaster General James Robertson to survey quartering in the colonies, and on January 2, 1765, Robertson reported his findings. During the war, a general shortage of public houses had led "several of the large towns" to build "barracks for the soldiers," and the colonists had supplied the barracked troops. Americans also had furnished "carriages," that is, wagons, carts, and other vehicles to transport army supplies. "But since the peace," Robertson continued, "some of the inhabitants have been taught to think, that the law for punishing mutiny, etc., does not extend to them." Officers were jailed for billeting troops in public houses, barracks went unsupplied, and cartage was exorbitantly expensive when available at all. Factious local leaders made writing a series of colonial quartering statutes impractical, so Robertson recommended that Parliament "have the next Mutiny Act extended to America."[14]

Three weeks later, Gage dispatched a letter to London detailing his plan. Like other imperial planners at the time, Gage sought to foster a unitary empire, and therefore he advised adding lines to the English Mutiny Act to extend it to the colonies. There would not be separate laws for each colony, or even a unique law for America; rather, there would be one law for the empire. Gage advised adding, "after the 23rd clause" of the Mutiny Act, "that this, and all the clauses of this act herein before mentioned, shall extend to all the dominions belonging to His Majesty in North America." To make the English Mutiny Act applicable in the colonies, Gage suggested setting the official conversion rate of "a Spanish milled dollar" to pound sterling, and he included a provision adjudicating cases "committed at any of the posts not in the inhabited parts of the country."[15]

But there was one stipulation that set America apart from England: Gage insisted that if soldiers "cannot otherwise be sheltered and accommodated," then they should "be quartered upon private houses."[16] The provision was a curious one. Robertson's report had not suggested billeting troops in homes, indicating that Gage himself added it. But why? The commander in chief had lived among the colonists long enough to know how poorly they would receive the idea. Moreover, Gage's biographers paint him as a moderate Whig who believed that all the king's subjects had inviolable rights.[17] The problem was most likely the new colonies. In 1765, there were not enough forts, barracks, or public houses in Canada, Florida, and the backcountry to accommodate the thousands of British troops stationed there. It was neither in Gage's budget to build quarters nor in his conscience to winter men in tents. As a result, his vision of a unitary empire did not mean that Americans would have the same rights as Britons.

Gage's recommendations arrived in London in March 1765, but White-hall was occupied by more pressing matters. The cabinet of Prime Minister George Grenville was focused on tackling the massive national debt that Britain had incurred during the Seven Years' War. As the ministry put the finishing touches on the Stamp Act, the king's confidence in Grenville was waning, and Whitehall was uneasy. Gage's letter made its way into the hands of Secretary at War Welbore Ellis and Secretary of State for the Southern Department George Montagu-Dunk, the second Earl of Halifax, but neither paid it much attention. Indeed, the only observation that either Ellis or Halifax made was that Parliament had already approved the annual English Mutiny Act, so a separate law for America would have to be written. The task of doing so was delegated to Deputy Secretary at War Christopher D'Oyly, who hastily assembled a bill with consultations from the Treasury and the attorney general. The resulting legislation included many of Gage's recommendations, including quartering in private houses.[18]

Perhaps surprising, given the eventual course of the American Revolution, it was King George III who first raised questions about violating the colonists' privacy. The king closely monitored the inner workings of his government, a tendency that increased as he lost patience with his prime minister. King George informed George Grenville that he was disturbed by the cabinet's decision "to disregard the noise that may be made here in Parliament by extending the quartering [of] soldiers in private houses in America."[19] Grenville dismissed the king's concerns, but as was true of the Stamp Act, he misread the situation. On March 29, Secretary Ellis introduced a "new mutiny bill for the American army" to the House of Commons. It was immediately apparent that the king had been correct. Members objected to billeting in private homes, citing "Magna Carta, dragoons, liberty, etc." As a result, the bill failed its first reading by a vote of fifty-three to nineteen, and Ellis quickly withdrew it.[20]

At this point, the American agents got involved. Benjamin Franklin was not the only lobbyist in London advocating on behalf of an American colony. Edward Montagu and Charles Garth, agents for Virginia and South Carolina, respectively, were the first to act, denouncing the bill in a petition that they presented to the House of Commons in early April.[21] Once Ellis pulled the bill, the agents worked behind the scenes, narrowing their criticism to the billeting clause. "We do not object to every part of the bill," noted Connecticut agent Richard Jackson, who elaborated on the merits of the potential law. It was only the clause that "empowers the civil magistrate to quarter soldiers in private houses" which they sought to remove.[22] Faced with such opposition, Grenville called on former Massachusetts governor Thomas Pownall to rewrite the bill. Pownall reached out to Franklin, and the two drafted a law that did not allow quartering in American homes.[23]

As Pownall and Franklin set to work, the debate shifted to the press. On April 11, a letter from "Civis" appeared in London's *Gazetteer and New Daily Advertiser* bemoaning a bill to quarter soldiers "in private as well as public houses" in America. "Good God! Are there no watchful guardians of our liberties left?" Civis asked, answering that "every Englishman must shudder at the thoughts of so unconstitutional a design." Civis employed Coke's metaphor of the home as a protected space, arguing that "the laws of England call every man's house, *his castle*; but surely they never meant it should be garrisoned by hireling soldiers." This invariably would lead soldiers to "ransack a man's private papers" before claiming "his wife or daughter's bed."[24] In response, the bill's principal author defended the provision and the law as a whole. Using the pseudonym "C.D.," Deputy Secretary at War Christopher D'Oyly charged that the hysteria of the "angry gentleman" ignored the pertinent question of "whether troops are not necessary for the protection of our colonies?" British regulars had to be quartered, and if public houses and barracks were insufficient, then they had to go into homes. Otherwise, the colonists would be left "to defend themselves without any military aid."[25]

However, in the spring of 1765, there was considerable support for imperial equity, such that D'Oyly's rebuke of Civis was out of keeping with the times. Writing in the *London Evening Post*, "Libertas" drew America and England together by suggesting that Parliament's actions in the colonies could set a tyrannical precedent for the mother country. He asked rhetorically "whether the passing a law for quartering soldiers on private families in our plantations abroad, will not be a large stride toward enslaving us in the same manner at home?"[26] Franklin made a similar point, only more wryly, suggesting that Parliament billet soldiers in private houses in England before exporting the practice to the colonies, as "parental example may produce

Figure 3.2. Benjamin Franklin. Mason Chamberlain, *Dr. Franklin* (London: Fielding and Walker, 1778). Library of Congress, Prints and Photographs Division, LC-USZ62–45259 (b&w film copy neg.).

filial obedience." "The people of England and America are the same," Franklin concluded; "one king, and one law; and those who endeavor to promote a distinction, are truly enemies to both."[27]

Having been embarrassed by its first attempt to pass a quartering bill for America, the Grenville administration took advantage of the spirit of imperial unity for a second try. Franklin and Pownall were so committed to the colonists' protections against billeting that they were willing to concede that such rights came with commensurate obligations. "An American" made this point in London's *Public Advertiser*. He deplored the "intended project of quartering soldiers in private houses" because it "is in fact making slaves of them." However, he acknowledged that "if the Americans enjoy the privileges of Englishmen, and the protection of this island, that they should bear some proportion of the expense."[28] Having struggled for months to get the American agents to accept Parliament's prerogative to tax the colonists, Whitehall crafted a compromise. The British government would recognize the Americans' right to keep soldiers out of their homes, but in exchange, the Americans would shoulder the costs of quarters. It was an effective solution. Although rumors circulated that the bill was so unpopular that it would be delayed until the following year, on April 30 the "American mutiny bill" returned to the House of Commons "totally disarmed of its offensive clause, the quartering soldiers, in marches and in cases of necessity, upon private houses." Without the offending passage, the bill stirred little controversy. Commons approved the bill and sent it to the House of Lords, who promptly gave their concurrence. On May 15, 1765, King George III granted his assent to the Quartering Act.[29]

Although the rules for billeting troops in America did not become part of the English Mutiny Act, the American Mutiny Act nonetheless suggested greater imperial unity, perhaps even that the British Empire would be treated as a single place. Thanks to the diligence of Benjamin Franklin and others, Parliament affirmed that the colonists had the same right as English men and women to keep soldiers out of their homes. In exchange, Americans were compelled to maintain barracks and supply troops. In early 1765, this did not seem controversial; the colonies had provided quarters during the war, and since then only local officials in New York had objected. Finally, the Quartering Act encompassed all of British North America, subjecting the continent to the same military geography. The law included provisions for troops billeted on the borderland, and it made no distinction between old and new colonies. Instead, the rights of householders and the obligations of taxpayers extended across the continent.

Stamp Act Delays Implementation

In late July 1765, Thomas Gage received the Quartering Act, and his initial reaction was mixed. On the one hand, he welcomed the regularization of quarters, as an imperial approach had obviated the need for a series of individual laws authorizing billets. Gage was particularly optimistic about how the Mutiny Act for America would help him in New York. He now had parliamentary authority to halt Albany's destruction of military buildings, and he assured the mayor that the new law "would fix matters in Albany so that the soldiers may be as little troublesome to the town's people as possible."[30] On the other hand, Gage worried about the law's shortcomings. Although the Quartering Act required the colonists to provide quarters, the American assemblies still had to appropriate the funds to pay for them. Moreover, the removal of the passage allowing billeting in private houses left the garrisoning of Canada and Florida up in the air. Although Gage dispatched copies of the law to officers in Montréal and Pensacola, he made no predictions of the law's effectiveness. Uncertain how to proceed, the commander in chief delayed implementation of the Quartering Act.[31]

The law that Gage received essentially codified what was standard practice in the American colonies. Like the English Mutiny Act, the American version put local civilian officials in charge of locating quarters for British regulars, thus prohibiting forced quartering. The law ensured that "if any military officer shall take upon himself to quarter soldiers," he would be "ipso facto cashiered," that is, relieved of duty. Unlike England's Mutiny Act, however, the Quartering Act accepted the spatial lessons of the French and Indian War. Specifically, the statute featured a tripartite approach. When troops arrived in a town, they were to go into barracks, but if there was not "sufficient room in the said barracks," then the troops would be placed in public houses. If both of these proved insufficient, then soldiers could be placed in "uninhabited houses, outhouses, barns, or other buildings." The law thus affirmed the constitutionality of barracks and provided alternatives other than domiciles should barracks be unavailable.[32]

The Quartering Act also codified the colonists' obligation to provision barracked troops. The law listed the supplies the colonists were to provide: "fire, candles, vinegar, and salt, bedding, utensils for dressing victuals, and small beer, cider, or rum." This copied the English Mutiny Act, as did a provision that required the colonists "to make such provision for carriages." When moving within a colony, officers would produce warrants for carts or wagons as well as horses or oxen to pull them. Regular troop rotations were common for the North American Establishment, and the carriage provision made such movement possible. The law also copied the language of England's Mutiny Act regarding deserters and their punishment.[33]

It is clear that the authors of the American Mutiny Act sought to protect the colonists' private houses but not their private property. The statute lacked a recitation of the Petition of Right, and it omitted the English version's allowance of quartering "in no private houses whatsoever."[34] Indeed, nowhere in the Quartering Act was billeting in the colonists' homes explicitly prohibited. Nevertheless, several of the law's provisions did this implicitly. Troops were to be quartered in "houses," but the fact that the houses had to be *uninhabited* indicates that the colonists' domiciles were not to be disturbed. It also suggests that privacy was interpreted as a conditional state that did not exist without inhabitants. Similarly, when the army pursued deserters, the Quartering Act provided that any officer who forcibly entered "the dwelling house, or outhouses of any person" would face a fine of twenty pounds. By contrast, the law empowered the British army to make use of public spaces such as barracks and forts. Although these were property of the city or colony, they were not protected like homes. Likewise, the law made no promises about moveable property: colonists' wagons and horses could be seized by the British army.[35]

The Americans were initially suspicious of the Quartering Act as rumors of the billeting provision preceded the law. In the spring of 1765, New York merchant John Watts heard about a quartering bill through his business contacts in London. In a letter to a trading partner, Watts deplored the attempt to "put the troops by Act of Parliament into private houses," predicting that the measure would cause the colonists to either love or hate the British, "but not both surely." In a second letter, Watts claimed that fears of billeting eclipsed worries of parliamentary taxation: "People say they had rather part with their money, though rather unconstitutionally than to have a parcel of military masters put by Act of Parliament [into] a bed to their wives and daughters.[36] Similar sentiments made their way from the London press to American newspapers. In May 1765, the *Connecticut Courant* reported that Parliament was drafting a law "to quarter soldiers in private houses."[37] Outrage traveled quickly, and soon the *Georgia Gazette* bemoaned how "this intended project of quartering soldiers in private houses is in fact making slaves of them."[38]

American opinion of the Quartering Act worsened once the Stamp Act appeared. The Grenville administration's quest for new revenue had led Parliament to approve a tax on nearly every type of paper in America, including newspapers, playing cards, and court documents. Incensed by the Stamp Act's taxation without representation, Bostonians rioted in August 1765, and violence followed in several colonial capitals, orchestrated by a network of colonial protesters known as the Sons of Liberty.[39] The Mutiny Act for America arrived in the middle of the unrest, leading colonists to connect the two laws. "The Stamp Act and billeting act were hatched at once, and God grant they may be both repealed at once," wailed one New Yorker.[40] Others saw the Quartering Act as part of a conspiracy to collect taxes, ignoring the law's prohibition of billeting in residences. A colonist from Plymouth argued that the reason why "the colonies have of late been threatened by wicked and designed parasites with having soldiers quartered upon them, even in their private houses," was that the troops were there "to enforce obedience to the detestable Stamp Act."[41] Although this was a misreading of the two laws, by linking them the colonists thwarted the promulgation of both. When popular violence rendered the Stamp Act unenforceable by persuading the stamp distributors to resign their commissions, General Gage pocketed the Quartering Act until tensions cooled. "We can't yet put the Act of Parliament in execution," Gage informed officers in Albany. "We must in the meantime go on as usual."[42]

The Americans' opposition to the Quartering Act raised serious questions about the prospect of a unitary empire. Viewing the law through the lens of the Stamp Act, the colonists could see only the obligations imposed on them without their consent and not the protections that the act afforded. In time, the hatred of parliamentary taxation became contagious, spreading to British military power. In the fall of 1765, a few hundred British regulars sat nervously in New York and Charleston. The Stamp Act was to go into effect on November 1, and as that date approached, protests encircled the troops. On October 19, two thousand Charlestonians gathered to protest the law by hanging effigies of the stamp distributors. The demonstration culminated in a march "to the green, back of the brick barracks, where the effigies were committed to the flames, amidst the loud and repeated shouts of an increasing multitude."[43] In New York City, Acting Governor Cadwallader Colden ordered the stamped paper stored at Fort George, where he resided with two hundred British regulars. On November 1, thousands of colonists pelted the fort with stones and burned the "governor's effigy with the devil's on a gallows."[44] According to Captain John Montresor, "three hundred carpenters belonging to the mob were collected and prepared to attempt to cut down the fort gate on the first shot fired from thence."[45] Colden demanded that Gage order British troops into the breach, but Gage demurred. "Though a fire from the fort might disperse the mob, it would not quell it," he replied.[46] Before the colonists could force down the gate, Colden turned the stamped papers over to the mayor and city council. This ended the standoff, and the crowd went home.[47]

American hostility to the Quartering Act caught many people by surprise, including Benjamin Franklin. In a letter to London's *Gazetteer*, Franklin touted the fairness of the law. The French and Indian War had produced "dispute between the inhabitants of New York and the soldiery, concerning the quartering of troops by force on private houses," but the American

Mutiny Act's protection of domiciles had put an end to these types of conflicts. Franklin did not understand that such concessions did not satisfy a colonial public outraged by parliamentary overreach. However, he believed that Americans had not rejected their obligation to provide quarters, insisting that "where a real necessity appears, no good man would refuse to shelter and entertain a soldier." Nevertheless, Franklin remained peevish that no one gave him credit for "opposing and preventing the quartering clause" that would have put soldiers in the colonists' homes.[48]

The experience shook Franklin's faith in imperial unity. As he sought to retain American support, he turned against the Quartering Act. Nowhere was this clearer than in February 1766 when Franklin was called before the House of Commons to explain Americans' resistance to the Stamp Act. Taking a page from the colonial press, he conflated the Stamp Act and the American Mutiny Act to discredit both. During the questioning, one member asked if the colonists would submit to the tax "if it was moderated." Franklin responded: "No, never, unless compelled by force of arms." Other members asked if "anything less than a military force [could] carry the Stamp Act into execution?" and what he thought would be "a sufficient military force to protect the distribution of the stamps in every part of America?" Franklin's marginalia indicates that these questions were posed "by friends." Both queries set him up to rebuke the very thought of using soldiers to promulgate the law, and thus he shamed the House for even considering the use of force. The administration made no such connections. Indeed, the Quartering Act was mentioned only once during the day's questioning, and it was Franklin who brought it up. When paymaster of the forces Charles Townshend attempted to discern the colonists' objections to "imposition as distinct from taxes," Franklin responded duplicitously that the colonists meant "impressing of men, or of carriages, quartering troops on private houses, and the like."[49] By citing billeting in homes, Franklin embarrassed Townshend, who moved on to other topics. Franklin's performance won him the respect of Parliament, but more important, it restored his reputation in America.[50]

By February 1766, it was clear to everyone that the Stamp Act had failed. King George III had grown weary of George Grenville and replaced him with Charles Watson-Wentworth, the second Marquess of Rockingham, and a month after Franklin's examination, Parliament repealed the Stamp Act. But the American resistance had changed Westminster's view of the British Empire. The colonists had challenged Parliament's right to legislate for the entire empire, and this could not be countenanced. The same day that Parliament repealed the Stamp Act, it approved the Declaratory Act, announcing that the "colonies and plantations in America have been, are, and of right ought to be, subordinate unto, and dependent upon the Imperial Crown and Parliament of Great Britain."[51] Henceforth the relationship between Britain and the colonies would be devoid of any discussion of constitutional liberties. The British government intended to maintain its pursuit of a unitary empire, but this no longer meant imperial equity.

Failure in Canada

As Thomas Gage waited for the Stamp Act riots to end in the old colonies, he turned his attention to the new. While Massachusetts, South Carolina, and New York protested parliamentary taxation, Gage collected reports from Nova Scotia, Québec, and East Florida, where "the Stamp Act has taken place without any tumults." It thus seemed reasonable for these places to contribute to their defense by paying for the quarters, supplies, and transport of British regulars. Gage had to wait before he could implement parliamentary law in the thirteen colonies, but he figured that Québec might be ready for the Quartering Act now. However, the commander in chief was mistaken. Canada did not have the same military geography as the old colonies, and the statute proved unenforceable.[52]

Gage did not expect to promulgate the Quartering Act in all the new colonies. He sent copies to Nova Scotia, East Florida, and West Florida, but this was pro forma. These colonies were not self-supporting but received annual appropriations from Parliament; thus any payment for quarters would have transferred money from one branch of the British government to another. The absence of a provision allowing billeting in private houses also may have hindered the implementation of the Mutiny Act for America in Nova Scotia and the Floridas. Although Halifax contained barracks, the same was not true of Nova Scotia's outlying towns, St. Augustine, or Pensacola, where billeting in homes continued unimpeded. The general did implement certain provisions of the statute in the backcountry, but these had to do with the transportation of supplies and administration of justice. In terms of restrictions on where soldiers could billet or local funding of quarters, the Quartering Act was inapplicable in the West. Instead, Gage was left to accommodate troops at Detroit, Michilimackinac, and Fort de Chartres out of his own budget. Finally, Gage failed to dispatch copies of the Quartering Act to the Caribbean. Troops in Barbados, Jamaica, the Leeward Islands, and the Windward Islands were not part of the North American Establishment but fell outside of Gage's jurisdiction.[53]

In fact, the Quartering Act could cause real harm in the new colonies. In West Florida, a prickly governor and an obtuse officer misused the law to carry out a personal feud. Problems began in late 1765 when the abrupt death of the commanding officer in Pensacola gave Governor George Johnstone an excuse to seize the small huts the soldiers used as barracks. When Lieutenant Colonel Ralph Walsh arrived a few weeks later to take control of the troops, he ordered the men back into the huts. However, Governor Johnstone had rented out the buildings in the meantime, so the soldiers displaced several colonists, including the son of a provincial councilor. Consequently, Johnstone arrested Walsh for "tending to intimidate the civil magistrates from performing their duty, in quartering His Majesty's troops, agreeably to an Act of Parliament."[54] In other words, the governor arrested the commanding officer for violating the Quartering Act. Things rapidly deteriorated after that. Johnstone had two justices of the peace cashier Walsh for violating parliamentary law, then stripped him of the perks of his position, including fifty acres of land. Forced to scrap for his reputation, Walsh sought to prove his obedience to the Quartering Act. Insisting that his men had not terrorized a washerwoman living in one of the huts as Johnstone claimed, Walsh attested to his respect for the privacy of the home and the gender of the person inside it. As Gage sorted out events in Pensacola, he grumbled how "the Mutiny Act made for America has been twisted and perverted to serve private revenge." The Quartering Act was not meant to apply to West Florida.[55]

Québec, however, was different. Alone among the new colonies, Québec had a military infrastructure, a functioning albeit limited civilian government, and money. Since taking control of the colony in 1759, James Murray had tried to squeeze taxes out of the Québécois, and although this had been largely unsuccessful, imperial planners continued to seek money from the province.[56] In late 1765, the British Board of Trade ordered that the duties on alcohol and dry goods that had been "payable to the French king before the conquest and cession" resume in order "to defray the expenses of the civil government of the said colony."[57] If the Québécois could afford a colonial government, then they could pay for accommodations and supplies. Gage carefully pursued this possibility, dispatching a copy of the Quartering Act to the military commander in Canada, Major General Ralph Burton, asking him to "give me your opinion concerning it, how far it will answer the purpose of quartering the troops and providing of carriages."[58]

Gage's decision to transmit the Quartering Act to the military commander instead of the civilian governor was a poor one. When Québec received a civilian government in 1764, Governor James Murray lost control of the British regulars in the colony. Instead, all troops in North America fell under General Gage and his officer corps. Murray was deeply wounded by this loss of military power, complaining that his position as governor did not annul his thirty years as "a military man" nor alter the rule that a governor was commander in chief of his colony.[59] Gage had little sympathy for Murray's complaints, informing him that "the civil and military [have] to become separate branches."[60] Murray was still smarting from this reply when General Burton arrived to take command of the three regiments in Québec. Murray took his anger out on Burton, and Burton responded in kind. The two sniped at each other through the Thomas Walker affair, which did little to elevate British authority in the eyes of the Québécois.

When the Quartering Act arrived in Québec, both Burton and Murray employed the law to attack each other, subverting the statute's intent and doing nothing to accommodate British regulars or protect the rights of the colonists. General Burton concluded that "the act plainly shows, that the provinces are to furnish barracks and everything necessary thereto belonging."[61] Accordingly, he expected the governor to build barracks and pay for supplies out of the Québec treasury. Burton no doubt hoped that this would resolve the problem of soldiers in Montréal who were still billeted in private houses.

Governor Murray, however, reached a different conclusion. In September, he convened the provincial council to discuss billeting in light of the Quartering Act. The year before, the council had authorized quartering in domiciles, but now lawmakers concluded that "the ordinance for billeting His Majesty's troops in this province is now repealed by the late Act of Parliament for quartering the troops in America." The council then ordered Burton to remove regulars from colonists' homes and place them in uninhabited buildings hired in compliance with the American Mutiny Act. Knowing that this would be nearly impossible in war-weary Montréal, the councilors added that "if the said general will not take upon himself to comply with the said resolutions," then "the government here must provide quarters for the forces." The council had no intention of paying for the quarters, but planned on sending the bills to the British Treasury. This would not only give Burton headaches, but would also embarrass him in London.[62]

Burton responded by arguing that the Quartering Act placed the burden of quarters on civilian authorities, not the military. In a formal response to the council, Burton stated that he intended "by no means to interfere with any respect with civil matters" and that he would be pleased to remove the troops from private homes "as soon as barracks, etc., are provided and fitted up agreeable to the Act of Parliament." The council took the general's salty reply as a refusal and then relieved him of power. It appointed Captain John Carden provincial barrack master and charged him with "quartering and finding necessaries for His Majesty's troops in the districts of Montréal and Trois-Rivières." Although Carden was "to provide everything at the cheapest rate," Murray estimated that quartering a thousand soldiers for thirty weeks would cost nearly £6,000, the bill for which he promptly dispatched to the Board of Trade.[63]

In truth, neither General Burton nor Governor Murray faithfully executed the Quartering Act. Burton violated the provision of the law that stated that should barracks be unavailable, then the army was to seek accommodation in public houses or uninhabited buildings. Instead, he left the troops in private homes to spite Murray. Nor were Murray and the provincial council any more principled. In its instructions to Captain Carden, the council demanded that "if you can hire quarters for all or a part of the troops and find it will be cheaper to engage the people upon whom the soldiers are now quartered," then Carden was to choose the latter. This instruction violated the statute's ban on billeting in private houses.[64]

What the Québécois thought about all this is unclear, although their actions in the winter of 1765–1766 suggest that they were torn. Some, like René-Ovide Hertel de Rouville, tried to make the best of things. Hertel de Rouville was born in Québec and studied law there, becoming the chief judge at Trois-Rivières before the French colony fell to Britain. After a sojourn in France, Hertel de Rouville came back to Québec in 1763 to rejoin his family. Upon his return, the former judge befriended Governor Murray, who appointed him chief road commissioner for the District of Montréal. In truth, Hertel de Rouville was Murray's ambassador to the Québécois, thus it fell to him to persuade Montréalers to billet troops in their homes.[65]

In December 1765, Captain Carden came close to ending billeting in Montréal when he rented a large building in the center of the city and filled it with furniture, utensils, and fuel to accommodate the ninety-two British regulars still lingering in the city. But Montréal was perpetually unlucky when it came to quarters, and on the day before the troops moved in, the building burned down. Rumors spread that the fire had been set by haughty soldiers who laughed at the blaze, crying "now let us see if the rascals will put us into barracks."[66] Governor Murray worried that the incident would leave the soldiers homeless in the Canadian winter, so he looked to Hertel de Rouville for help. Hertel de Rouville thought that Montréalers could be persuaded to devise a solution, but at a meeting of the city's inhabitants, the "tumultuous assembly" resolved nothing. Hertel de Rouville worried about Québécois intransigence, informing Murray that there seemed "to be a lack of respect for the government."[67]

Montréalers may have lacked respect for the colonial government, but they understood the rights contained in the Quartering Act. Still in need of quarters, Hertel de Rouville and Captain Carden went door to door, asking each resident currently billeting troops to keep the soldiers until May. Most agreed to do so, but four or five homeowners refused, leading to twenty-seven "soldiers being turned into the streets, without provocation, or apology." When a sergeant major went to investigate the situation, he found "the door was purposely shut against him" and Montréalers citing the English constitution: "He was told they had no right to quarter, nor would they."[68] In effect, some Québécois used the Quartering Act to defend their domiciles. Not all Québécois embraced British rule, but those who tossed redcoats out of their homes did so because they claimed the constitutional liberties of British subjects.

The Canadian interpretation of the Quartering Act was not lost on General Gage. Instead, he charged that "if any complaints are made about their being quartered on the inhabitants," then Governor Murray was to blame.[69] Truthfully, Gage cared less about the rights of the Québécois than he did about getting Murray to pay for quarters. On this point, he was adamant, even appealing to Secretary to the Treasury Charles Lowndes for clarification. But the Treasury did not like Murray's plan of sending it the bills for quarters, so it ruled against Gage, voiding the Mutiny Act for America in Québec. Instead of the colonial government paying for quarters, "those matters are to be thrown into the same channel with all other affairs which relate to barracks," Gage conceded.[70] The army would continue paying for quarters in the new colonies. Oddly enough, although the Québécois never had to abide by the responsibilities of the Quartering Act, they were able to claim its rights. In March 1766, Burton reported that all troops were quartered in hired houses. No longer was any inhabitant forced to billet troops. By then, Gage had begun sketching plans for barracks in Montréal to be paid for by the army.[71]

With the failure of the Quartering Act in Canada, the British army abandoned the hope of a uniform military geography in North America. After 1766, Gage no longer expected anyone outside of the old colonies to pay for quarters. Once again, billeting set Québec, Florida, and Nova Scotia apart from the thirteen American colonies. Moreover, the episode undermined the ideal of a unitary empire, as the Québécois obtained the English right to keep soldiers out of their homes without facing fiscal responsibility. This no doubt helped to improve the relationship between British soldiers and the Canadians. Once the army ended forced quartering and assumed responsibility for military expenses, the Québécois began to welcome redcoats, and the type of unrest that followed Thomas Walker's assault disappeared. Over the next decade, as the American colonies soured on their place in the British Empire, Canada found it more appealing.

Redeployment to the Middle Colonies

As Benjamin Franklin turned against the Quartering Act, his son William became an ardent proponent of the law. William Franklin was the illegitimate progeny of what Benjamin termed "that hard-to-be-governed passion of youth," born around 1730 in Philadelphia when his father was still a journeyman printer.[72] As Benjamin's fortunes soared, he took William with him, often literally. The two Franklins traipsed through Maryland to meet Braddock and sailed to England to hobnob with the London elite. Like his father, William maintained an imperial perspective. He received legal training at London's Middle Temple and married the daughter of a Barbadian planter; his education and family thus touched several corners of the British Atlantic. William Franklin's place among the imperial elite was secured when the Board of Trade appointed him governor of New Jersey. In early 1763, he took up residence in Burlington, and before the year was out, Governor Franklin was raising provincial forces for Pontiac's War.[73]

Two years later, the Stamp Act riots taught William Franklin to appreciate the importance of British military power. In September 1765, ships filled with stamped papers appeared off the coast of New Jersey. As had happened in other colonial capitals, Burlington soon filled with angry colonists determined not to allow the Stamp Act to be promulgated. In response, Governor Franklin proffered an imperial solution. He suggested storing the stamped papers in the Burlington barracks and asked Gage for "about sixty men with officers" to protect them.[74] For Franklin, the North American Establishment existed to maintain order in the colonies, whether the cause of the disorder was Native Americans or colonists. Although Gage assured Franklin that troops would be available, the increasing number of Stamp Act riots changed the general's mind, and Franklin neither received soldiers nor unloaded the stamped papers. William Franklin's view of British military power was not shaken by the incident, but strengthened. When Gage dispatched troops to New Jersey the next year, Franklin welcomed the British soldiers into the colony's barracks and sought to supply them according to parliamentary law.[75]

William Franklin's support for the Quartering Act put him at odds with his father and most American colonists. Although the law had extended to America the English right against billeting troops in one's home, the colonists took no notice of this, focusing instead on the rights that the statute took away. Like the Stamp Act, the American Mutiny Act was an instance of taxation without representation. Not only had the law been written without their consent; it also voided the long-standing legislative prerogative that the colonial assemblies alone determined how they would quarter troops. These arguments came into full view in late 1766 when General Gage stationed regiments in Pennsylvania, New Jersey, and New York. When it came to quarters, the British Empire was far more fractured than unified.

In May 1766, the Quartering Act had been in effect for a year, yet it had not been implemented. The Stamp Act riots in the old colonies and the Murray-Burton feud in Québec had stymied the law, but there were also problems in London. The installation of the Marquess of Rockingham as prime minister had done little to inspire the confidence of King George III, who began casting about for a new ministry. This weakened the cabinet, especially the office of secretary of state for the southern department who was responsible for colonial affairs. As a result, many American matters went untended, including the Mutiny Act for America. With little direction from the cabinet, Secretary at War William Wildman Shute Barrington, the second Viscount Barrington, introduced a bill renewing the Quartering Act in March 1766. Parliament had approved the law for one year only, meaning that the British government had to reauthorize it again every year, much as it did the English Mutiny Act.[76]

With little direction from Whitehall, Commander in Chief Thomas Gage began to see the Quartering Act in a new light. The Americans' reaction to the Stamp Act had discouraged him, leading him to lament, "The people [are] so accustomed to excess and riot without control, that it is to be feared it would not be an easy task, to bring them back to their duty."[77] However, Pontiac's War was winding down, and this presented the general with a new opportunity to restore British authority in America. In a series of private letters with the secretary at war, Gage hatched a plan to reorder the North American Establishment. He would remove several regiments from the West and "quarter them in the great towns upon the coast," specifically New York and Philadelphia. There, they could protect "the king's magazine which lie exposed" in the event of further "tumults"; should violence accelerate, the troops could be "a support to the civil government." Yet it was not only the defensive strategy that appealed to Gage; it was the economics. "The disposition now making of the troops will procure a saving to the Crown," he told Barrington.[78] To wit, he would promulgate the Quartering Act in the middle colonies.

Viscount Barrington approved of Gage's plan, but others were not so sure. King George III once again proved more prescient about colonial sensitivities than Whitehall. "His Majesty is of opinion," Secretary of State Henry Seymour Conway informed Gage, that "bringing any considerable number of troops into the interior of those provinces, in time of peace and tranquility" might "occasion difficulties." For this reason, the king urged caution. Although Conway would not contradict the king, he thought Gage's economics made sense. It was important "to settle amicably, if possible, everything that relates to the quartering, where there is a necessity of doing it on the inhabitants."[79] Ultimately, Whitehall left it to Gage. It was up to him to administer the North American Establishment and by extension to enforce the Quartering Act.

In the summer of 1766, Gage ordered three regiments into the middle colonies and divided them among New York, Albany, Elizabeth, Perth Amboy, and Philadelphia. This was the first time since the fall of Montréal six years earlier that the thirteen colonies had accommodated so many British regulars. The redeployment signaled that Gage saw no reason why the Americans should not accommodate troops; the old colonies were part of the same military geography as the new. In fact, the American Mutiny Act prompted Gage to discount differences within the empire, as the ability of the middle colonies to pay for billets encouraged him to quarter soldiers in New York as if it were Québec. As the troops marched into cities, they entered the empty barracks. Gage promptly dispatched requests to the governors for supplies, each time citing the Quartering Act. The colonists' reactions varied widely.[80]

Pennsylvania complied fully with the Quartering Act. In June 1766, the 42nd Regiment of Foot, which had been scattered across western Pennsylvania and the Illinois Country, converged on Philadelphia and barracked in the Northern Liberties, as depicted in figure 3.3.[81] Gage then asked Pennsylvania's Governor John Penn for "provision to be made for quartering and providing them according to the Act of Parliament."[82] When the assembly convened in September, it promptly allocated £4,000 colonial currency for "quarters, firewood, candles, vinegar and salt, bedding, utensils for dressing victuals, and small beer."[83] Without controversy or even much debate, Pennsylvania had complied with the Mutiny Act for America. Nor were lawmakers out of step with public opinion. The *Pennsylvania Gazette* published the appropriations law without commentary, and no hostile letters appeared in subsequent issues. If Benjamin Franklin knew of the assembly's actions, he left no comment. The Quartering Act simply was not controversial in Pennsylvania.[84]

In New Jersey, the Quartering Act elicited considerably more disagreement. In May 1766, "some officers, and about 140 recruits" sought rooms in Elizabeth's barracks. Gage requested Governor William Franklin provide

FIGURE 3.3.   Barracks at Philadelphia. "British Barracks, Northern Liberties," in John F. Watson, *Annals of Philadelphia, in the Olden Time; Being a Collection of Memoirs, Anecdotes, and Incidents of the City and its Inhabitants, and of the Earliest Settlements of the Inland Part of Pennsylvania,* enlarged and rev. by Willis P. Hazard, 3 vols. (Philadelphia: Stuart, 1884), 1:412–13.

"sufficient quarters for them, agreeable to the Act of Parliament made in this respect." However, this was a taller order than it seemed. Empty for several years, the Elizabeth barracks were not "in a condition for the immediate reception of troops," so New Jersey had to pay not only for supplies but costly repairs as well.[85] Nevertheless, the New Jersey assembly quickly approved an act "for supplying the several barracks erected in this colony with furniture, and other necessaries for accommodating the king's troops."[86] Gage was so pleased with the results that he redeployed the 28th Regiment from Québec to New Jersey, barracking four companies in Elizabeth and five in Perth Amboy.[87]

New Jersey's acquiescence was deceiving. Details of the provincial law were missing from local newspapers, and it was not until hundreds of troops were in the colony that the truth came out. In a December 1766 letter to Whitehall, William Franklin admitted that New Jersey's law provided only "firewood, bedding, blankets and such other necessaries as have been heretofore furnished to the several barracks within this colony." Consequently, the colonial statute did not supply items explicitly mandated by the Quartering Act, including vinegar, salt, and alcohol. Franklin had tried to persuade legislators otherwise, "but it was to no purpose." Lawmakers harangued the governor, claiming they "had always furnished everything which was necessary" and dismissing the American Mutiny Act "as much an act for laying taxes on the inhabitants as the Stamp Act." Faced with the prospect of leaving the troops "unprovided with necessaries," Franklin signed the bill.[88]

Of the three colonies, New York was the most intransigent. Unlike the other colonies, New York had quartered troops since the French and Indian War and was well versed in refusing British demands for supplies. In December 1765, Gage first tried to implement the Quartering Act in New York, but the assembly cited precedent to claim that barracked troops were supplied "without any expense to the countries in which they are quartered," while a mob burned the commander in chief in effigy.[89] In May 1766, Gage tried again. Ordering the 46th Regiment from Niagara and Fort Stanwix to New York City, the general requested the colonial government "to provide sufficient quarters, bedding, etc., agreeable to the Act of Parliament."[90] However, the intervening time had not improved the legislature's opinion of the Mutiny Act for America. The House of Representatives insisted that it had "always been ready and willing to comply with every requisition made," such that the members could not "recollect one single instance wherein they have withheld the aid requested." Yet the costs of quarters were exorbitant and "would very soon exceed the ability of this colony to pay." While New Jersey had cited past practice to defy the Quartering Act, New York cited financial distress. Eventually, the House decided to furnish "barracks, bedding, utensils for dressing victuals, and firewood and candles," but it insulted Gage in the process. The legislature would not appropriate money without "a proper requisition from the Crown," so when the 46th Regiment reopened the Upper Barracks in June, there were no supplies for the men.[91]

The impasse in New York may have persisted indefinitely if violence had not broken out in Dutchess County. An old Dutch settlement, Dutchess County was controlled by a few wealthy families who leased land to farmers. Tensions between landlords and tenants had been brewing for years, although the defiance of the tenants had increased with the Stamp Act riots. In June 1766, the protests turned violent when more than six hundred vigilantes attempted to restore displaced tenants to their lands.[92] As Dutchess County dissolved into chaos, local officials turned to the colonial government for help. Fearful that the militia might prove unwilling to "fire at the mob," the provincial council unanimously voted "to apply to the commander in chief of His Majesty's force for three hundred troops to enable the civil magistrate to enforce the laws."[93] The 28th Regiment was passing through Albany on its ways to New Jersey, so Gage ordered it "to suppress some confederacies of a dangerous nature in Dutchess County" before heading south.[94]

The Dutchess County riots softened New Yorkers' opinion of supplying regulars, but not their resistance to the Quartering Act. The same day that the council requested troops, the House of Representatives resolved that there was no need to approve supplies "because the troops have hitherto subsisted very well without any such provision."[95] When Governor Sir Henry Moore objected to this duplicitous claim, the House reversed its position and voted that "provision should be made for furnishing the barracks in the cities of New York and Albany with beds, bedding, firewood, candles, and utensils for dressing of victuals for two battalions not exceeding five hundred men each." To pay for this, the House volunteered what was left of the £4,790 New York currency that it had appropriated for veterans of the Havana expedition four years earlier.[96] However, New York flagrantly defied the Quartering Act, leaving Governor Moore to despair at how lawmakers refused "to show that obedience which was due to an Act of Parliament" by ignoring the law's requirement for "salt, vinegar, and cider or beer."[97] Nevertheless, Moore signed the bill, largely at Gage's urging. "In my demand for quarters, it was necessary to manage matters," Gage informed Whitehall, and the imperfect New York law ensured that soldiers "may be hereafter comfortably lodged, instead of lying on bare board."[98]

In an ominous twist, New York's refusal to implement the Quartering Act denied the protections of the English constitution to its colonists. Upon receiving orders, Major Arthur Browne marched nearly four hundred British regulars into Dutchess County, where they exchanged fire with insurgents, drew blood, and forced most of the rioters to either surrender or flee to Connecticut. When a handful resisted capture, Browne posted "troops at the rioters' habitations, which would put them under the alternative of surrendering to justice, or losing their harvest which was ready for reaping."[99] When a second tenant riot broke out at the Massachusetts border, Captain John Clarke and a hundred troops set on the rebels' property and torched seven houses. The American Mutiny Act should have made these actions illegal. Perhaps the extenuating circumstances of insurrection changed the rules of billeting, but had the law been in place, the legality of such actions might have been questioned. For their part, the landlords of Dutchess County were happy to billet troops at their estates. Captain Clarke marveled at how cavalier they were about quarters, wondering if the landlords intended "to protect everyman's house by placing a few men in each."[100] Coming from England, where soldiers stayed out of the home, Clarke must have thought Dutchess County not very English.

Like the failure of the Quartering Act in Canada, the uneven promulgation of the law in the middle colonies was a blow to imperial unity. The

Mutiny Act for America had been designed to provide one set of rights and responsibilities, but only Pennsylvania complied with the letter of the law. By contrast, New Jersey and New York ignored the portions they did not like. Following the Declaratory Act, complying only with portions of the Quartering Act suggested sedition, and Whitehall would not let the matter go unnoticed. At the same time, William Franklin's actions in New Jersey pointed a way forward. Forced to choose between implementing part of the American Mutiny Act or none at all, Franklin opted for the former, implicitly conceding that the colonial assembly had the final say on quarters. General Gage applied the same logic in New York. In effect, both men concluded that in order to promulgate the Quartering Act, it was necessary to treat the empire as a collection of different places.

The New York Restraining Act

While the middle colonies undermined the prospect of a unitary empire, in London the idea retained currency. In July 1766, King George III prevailed upon William Pitt to form a government. The mastermind of Britain's victory in the Seven Years' War, Pitt had been out of power since his resignation as secretary of state in late 1761. However, a string of disappointing ministries and the failure of the Stamp Act had brightened Pitt's place in the imperial memory. People on both sides of the Atlantic remembered how he once had united Britons and Americans. It was under Pitt, the colonists recalled, that provincial soldiers stood equal to British regulars, and the cost of their defense was borne by English taxpayers. To Britons, Pitt evoked memories of victory over a common enemy before faction divided Parliament and the Stamp Act alienated Americans. It was a daunting feat, but Pitt agreed to form a government that would promote the rights and responsibilities of all His Majesty's subjects. He even extracted a peerage in exchange. If anyone could make the British Empire a single place, it was William Pitt, henceforth the first Earl of Chatham.[101]

However, imperial unity was always more aspirational than practical, and quartering laid bare the inherent inequality of empire. New York saw nothing particularly fair about having to quarter a regiment when other colonies either had no troops or were absolved of the expense. For this reason, the New York General Assembly challenged the Quartering Act and, by extension, Parliament's right to legislate for the colonies. The Chatham administration ignored the revolutionary potential of the colony's response, at least at first. Less than a week after Chatham became prime minister, the cabinet received reports of New York's defiance and decided that a strongly worded letter would suffice. The newly appointed secretary of state for the southern department, William Petty, the second Earl of Shelburne, wrote to New York's Governor Sir Henry Moore, instructing him to enforce the law "in the full extent and meaning of the act." Indicative of the administration's tenor of imperial unity, Shelburne insisted that New York omit any reference "to the usage of other parts of His Majesty's dominions." It was inappropriate for a colony to set itself apart from the empire, even to protest its unequal treatment.[102]

But this response only made New York more defiant. When the House of Representatives reconvened in November 1766, lawmakers brushed aside Shelburne's admonition and again bemoaned their unfair treatment. "We shall always be ready to give the amplest testimonies of our loyalty to His Majesty and submission to his government," the representatives declared. Five months earlier, they had voted supplies for quartering two regiments even though this was "a burden much greater than any of the neighboring governments lie under for that service." Some members suggested that the House interpret the Quartering Act as applying to "soldiers only on a march," thus leaving the regiment in New York City without quarters, but this was a minority view.[103] The House approved £400 New York currency for "firewood and candles for His Majesty's Fort George in the City of New York" but refused to cite the Mutiny Act for America or to provide all the supplies mandated by the law. In contrast to his actions the previous June, Governor Moore refused to sign the bill. Instead, he prorogued the assembly and sent the lawmakers home before dispatching word to Whitehall that the Quartering Act had not been implemented in New York.[104]

News of New York's disobedience reached the Earl of Chatham in February 1767, and it wounded him deeply. "America affords a gloomy prospect," he wrote to Shelburne. The prime minister feared that New York's "disobedience to the Mutiny Act will justly create a great ferment here" and "leave no room to any to say a word in their defense." Once again, Chatham drew upon a vision of the empire as a single place for direction. New York had imperiled "the whole state," and thus a solution had to come from the very center of the British Empire: New York's disobedience had "to be laid before Parliament."[105] With that, he abandoned the issue. In truth, Chatham had been suffering from violent spells of gout since becoming prime minister. Debilitated to a state that bordered on insanity, he went into seclusion in March 1767, leaving his own ministry leaderless. Shelburne managed colonial affairs, but he and the other ministers eschewed Chatham's vision for an empire of shared rights and responsibilities. Henceforth the colonists would be treated as unequal subjects of the British Empire.[106]

Charles Townshend embodied Whitehall's new direction. Appointed chancellor of the exchequer by Chatham in 1766, Townshend was a longtime member of the Board of Trade who believed that colonial obedience was preferable to imperial equity. He waxed poetic about the Petition of Right and "the blessings derived to these kingdoms by the Revolution," but Townshend did not believe that such privileges transferred to the colonies.[107] He knew the "long correspondence from General Gage" and closely followed the Stamp Act riots, especially the differences they revealed about "the mob, at Boston" and obedient Canadians.[108] Based on these experiences, Townshend sketched a new ideal of imperial unity. Like Chatham, he believed that England and America should be intimately connected, but he did not think that they had the same rights and responsibilities. Townshend argued that Americans had to be led; Parliament alone passed laws for the empire, and regardless of representation, the colonists had to obey them. For Townshend, the empire was a collection of unequal places, and he advocated treating the colonies differently based upon their value to the whole and their obedience to Parliament. Many in London found this way of thinking persuasive, especially once news arrived that New York had defied the Quartering Act.[109]

The Earl of Shelburne was receptive to Townshend's view of empire. Meeting with the king in Chatham's absence, the secretary of state "took the liberty" to hope that "both he and Parliament would distinguish between New York and America."[110] Shelburne also sought to better understand the law that New York was in defiance of, so he contacted Viscount Barrington, who recounted the history of the Quartering Act. The secretary at war explained that originally the law was "intended to give a power of billeting on private houses," but after "merchants and agents" objected to this, troops were directed to "empty houses, provincial barracks, and barns in their room, understanding that the assembly should supply them with the additional necessaries." Barrington also observed that the American statute was distinct from laws regulating quartering in England, noting that Grenville "made it a separate bill, lest it might embarrass the general Mutiny Act." This led Shelburne to speculate if quartering in America might proceed as it did in Scotland and Ireland. Those kingdoms had "no direct law whatever" but let "old prerogative or custom" determine where soldiers quartered. In effect, Shelburne wondered if the Quartering Act had been too sensitive to colonial rights.[111]

In early 1767, rewriting the Quartering Act became a popular topic in London. Unlike two years earlier, now the debate centered on how the law could be used to distance America from England. Gone were concerns about constitutional liberties and the protection of homes. Former chancellor of the exchequer William Dowdeswell demanded local leaders billet troops "in private houses, if the assembly would not make provision." Others called for eliminating the role of the colonial legislatures altogether, including former prime minister George Grenville, who advocated giving "power to the treasurer of the colony to pay the money." Others advised a local levy, a special import tax on New York, or a test act to bar Americans from holding public office unless they complied with the Quartering Act. Westminster never would have considered such draconian proposals for soldiers in England.[112]

The men who had shaped the Quartering Act objected vociferously to these ideas. In the London press, Benjamin Franklin attacked efforts to silence American assemblies, while Thomas Pownall took the fight to Parliament. The former governor of Massachusetts had won the seat for Tregony in early 1767, and he devoted his first speech in the House of Commons to quarters. Pownall recounted the history of the American Mutiny Act, acknowledging the statute's now-obvious limitations. Having been so concerned with preventing "quartering in private houses," Pownall explained, the authors had forgotten to include a mechanism for enforcement. He also conceded that it had been a mistake to ask colonial legislatures to appropriate funds annually, as this had given them repeated opportunities to refuse quarters. But Pownall dismissed the idea of silencing the colonial assemblies, arguing that the solution lay not in eliminating them, but empowering them. He observed that the Quartering Act's primary flaw was its universalism, since it "can never be applied to numberless particular cases that must arise." Instead of one law for the empire, Pownall urged Parliament to amend the Mutiny Act for America such that "both the mode of quartering, and the act of making the supply for the expense of it, may originate with the people of the colonies, and be an act of their own assemblies."[113] In other words, Pownall advocated allowing the Americans to write their own quartering laws as best suited their individual circumstances.

Pownall's recommendations fell on deaf ears, as did other efforts to revise the Quartering Act. In May 1767, Parliament voted to reauthorize the law without changes.[114] By that point, however, attention had shifted from rewriting the statute to punishing the colonies. Charles Townshend took the lead, collecting evidence from a half dozen colonies where obedience to the law was in question. As he did so, he had to decide if all the colonies should be punished or only the most egregious transgressors. The chancellor of the exchequer and his advisers studied the Stamp Act riots in Massachusetts and Rhode Island, and they investigated news that Gage had requested billets for 134 recruits in Connecticut. They pored over New Jersey's appropriations, as well as reports of difficulties in Georgia. It soon became apparent that not all colonies had defied parliamentary law. Specifically, "the ready obedience of Pennsylvania" caught Whitehall's attention and led the ministry to advocate that "a just distinction . . . be made between the different provinces according to their different behavior."[115] With that, the ministers narrowed their scope. The London papers reported that "all the southern provinces had acceded to the orders of government, for making the necessary provisions for quartering the military," while Parliament concluded that Connecticut was also in compliance.[116] It all came down to one colony. "New York had been much the most disobedient," Townshend declared, adding that he would make an example of it to show "the Americans that this country would not tamely suffer her sovereignty to be wrested out of her hands."[117]

In April and May 1767, various arms of the British government moved to punish New York. First, the Board of Trade convened with King George III in attendance and disallowed New York's July 1766 quartering act furnishing troops "with firewood and candles and other necessaries."[118] It issued a similar ruling for New Jersey's quartering law, while approving Pennsylvania's.[119] Second, either Charles Townshend or the Earl of Shelburne (or perhaps both) drafted a bill to punish New York.[120] Early drafts suggest that they initially envisioned a vague decree similar to the Declaratory Act. A version offered by Attorney General Sir William de Grey rebuked New York's assembly for acting "against the nature of their limited and subordinate constitution" and declared that the province would not be forgiven until it passed a law "which shall be a direct and explicit obedience of the said Act of Parliament."[121] However, as the ministers revised the bill, they made the provisions more particular. In the final draft, New York was cited for its defiance of the Quartering Act and instructed to pass a law "furnishing the king's troops with all the necessaries required by the said Act of Parliament." Until then, the law ordered "the governor, council, and assembly, be respectively restrained and prohibited from passing or assenting to any act of assembly, for any other purpose whatsoever."[122] In sum, the New York Restraining Act dissolved the General Assembly of New York and prohibited it from reconvening unless it did so to comply with the Mutiny Act for America.

Once the final language of the bill was settled, Townshend moved the New York Restraining Act through Parliament expeditiously. He vigorously defended the bill, basing his case on the inequality of places in the empire. "The superiority of the mother country can at no time be better exerted than now," the chancellor contended as he singled out one colony for exceptionally harsh treatment. To answer his critics, Townshend ordered the Declaratory Act read in the House of Commons and voted resolutions avowing that Parliament had "full power and authority to make laws and statutes, of sufficient force and validity to bind the colonies and people of America, subjects of the Crown of Great Britain, in all cases whatsoever."[123] Whig philosopher and member of Parliament Edmund Burke assailed the bill as unenforceable. If Parliament punished New York until the colony complied with the Quartering Act, Burke asked, then what would happen if New York continued to defy the law? Burke predicted an "endless rotation of vain and impotent efforts," which would undermine Parliament and make it "the ridicule of the world."[124] Townshend dismissed such objections and shepherded the bill through the House of Commons and then the House of Lords. The New York Restraining Act received royal assent on July 2, 1767, and was dispatched to the colonies.[125]

Both the Quartering Act and the New York Restraining Act were premised on the ideal of a unitary empire, but the two laws demonstrated how much the meaning of this notion had changed in two years. The American Mutiny Act extended English liberties to North America, while the Restraining Act reduced New York to a subordinate status, lower than not just England but the other colonies as well. Although Americans had not embraced the Quartering Act, they vehemently rejected the revised vision of imperial unity. After 1767, the colonists became increasingly skeptical of efforts to bind America more closely to England.

American Compliance and Disunity

The New York Restraining Act reached the colonies in September 1767, but by then it was a fait accompli. Rumors of a parliamentary punishment had made it to North America in April, and the most willful defiance ebbed quickly after that. Between the spring of 1767 and the fall of 1768, eight provincial assemblies appropriated money for supplies or transportation for British regulars, marking the high-water mark of the Quartering Act. Although the New York Restraining Act encouraged compliance, much of the credit was due to the diligence and practicality of Thomas Gage. The commander in chief manipulated the colonies' perception of British military power, but he also acknowledged the right of colonial assemblies to appropriate supplies. More importantly, he accepted local variation, effectively accepting Pownall's idea that decisions about quarters were best left to the Americans. Ironically, a single law for quarters was its most effective when the colonists were granted the greatest variance at interpreting it.[126]

In New England, quartering was an infrequent inconvenience. The region had mostly stayed out of the barrack-building frenzy of the 1750s, so the only permanent quarters were on Boston's Castle Island and inside a few backcountry forts. Indeed, New England celebrated its lack of barracks. In early 1767, a letter appeared in several New England newspapers that decried permanent quarters because they legitimated a standing army. "Quartering on the inhabitants is a very great evil, and barracks are terrible," the letter concluded; "may we never have occasion for either."[127] Perhaps the letter writer reflected on what was happening in New York, as New England's lack of barracks had exempted it from Gage's coastal garrison. Nevertheless, the region still had to quarter troops when British soldiers arrived by accident or traipsed through on their way somewhere else. Although Massachusetts and Connecticut chafed at acknowledging the Quartering Act, both colonies appropriated money to supply their temporary visitors.

In December 1766, two companies of Royal Artillery headed for Québec were blown off course and landed at Castle Island. It being winter, Gage asked Governor Sir Francis Bernard of Massachusetts "to provide them with quarters" until troops could resume their trek in the spring.[128] When the House of Representatives convened a month later, it demanded to know "whether any provision has been made, at the expense of this government," for the soldiers. Bernard replied that the provincial council had approved provisions "in pursuance of the late Act of Parliament." The House was outraged that the governor had usurped its control over financial matters, but found it "still more grievous" that the governor would cite the Quartering Act. However, it was a moot point: the money had been spent, and the troops departed. In response, Bernard reminded lawmakers that the colony had built the Castle Island barracks so that when soldiers appeared, "there might be no occasion for quartering them on the inhabitants." Had the council not voted supplies, the barracks would have been uninhabitable, and British soldiers may have had to billet in Boston houses. Bernard then observed that the council's appropriation "did not include several articles prescribed by the Act of Parliament," such as alcohol. Bernard's strategy of threatening to billet regulars while defying the Mutiny Act for America worked, and the House of Representatives moved on to other matters.[129]

Six months later, British troops were again in Massachusetts. In May 1767, twenty-seven recruits from Scotland landed at Boston on their way to Halifax to join the 14th Regiment. When the commanding officer appealed for quarters, Bernard "ordered that they should be received into the barracks at the Castle" and requested supplies from the House of Representatives. As before, the issue was moot; in this case, the recruits had already departed before the assembly took up the matter. The House voted to provision the soldiers "as has been heretofore usually made for His Majesty's regular troops, when occasionally in this province," and passed a law to that effect.

Although Massachusetts again failed to obey the letter of the law, this time legislators refrained from griping about parliamentary interference.[130]

In Connecticut, quartering proceeded without controversy. In January 1767, a ship containing 188 German recruits bound for Québec landed at New York. As the harsh winter prevented them from marching north, Gage dispatched fifty-four to Charleston and sent the rest to Connecticut with a request that they "may be supplied with quarters, etc., according to the Act of Parliament," in Stamford, Norwalk, and Fairfield.[131] In response, the Connecticut General Court promptly approved a law supplying troops billeted at the colony's public houses.[132] The brief sojourn of the soldiers probably softened lawmakers, as did their ability to modify Gage's request. Connecticut lawmakers asked that off-duty soldiers not carry weapons and that the troops be sent to New Haven and nearby Wallingford and Branford instead of the three towns Gage identified.[133] Gaining these concessions, Connecticut complied with the Quartering Act without the usual obfuscations; indeed, each soldier received a daily ration of "small beer or cider, not exceeding five pints, or half a pint of rum mixed with a quart of water."[134]

While British regulars were an occasional inconvenience in New England, they were a minor presence in the southern colonies. At the end of the French and Indian War, the British army had scattered troops across South Carolina, Georgia, Bermuda, and the Bahamas to occupy borderland forts and urban barracks. They were hardly garrisons. Augusta in rural Georgia boasted the largest force on the southern mainland, with thirty-three, while Bermuda and the Bahamas shared fifty troops between them. Such small concentrations of troops mostly escaped Gage's attention, and he only halfheartedly pursued supplies in the South.[135]

Before the summer of 1767, all four southern colonies refused to quarter British troops. In Bermuda, the commanding officer requested £40 for candles and firewood "conformable to the acts of Parliament relative to the quartering His Majesty's troops."[136] Although the Bermuda assembly routinely provided barrack supplies, procedural matters delayed action, prompting the governor to promise that he would personally supply "firing and oil for the soldiers."[137] Matters were not much better in South Carolina. When Gage received reports of how soldiers at the colony's borderland forts were in "want of every necessity (except barracks)," he insisted that South Carolina lawmakers appropriate money for supplies and transportation "agreeable to the Act of Parliament."[138] This reference to the Quartering Act put the assembly "so much out of humor" that lawmakers voted quarters only "as were allowed the troops which were in this province in the year 1757," meaning that South Carolina refused to provide alcohol or to transport supplies to the backcountry.[139] Still, this was better than Georgia, where the Commons House announced that it would consider funds "in lieu of a compliance with the Mutiny Act," but not before the end of the year.[140] Similarly, when Gage asked the Bahamas for "bedding, firing, candle, and other barrack utensils," the colonists ignored him.[141] The southern colonies' obstinancy so frustrated Gage that he compared them to New York.[142]

However, news that Parliament was drafting the New York Restraining Act emboldened Gage to employ more creative solutions. Although lawmakers on the islands and the southern mainland grumbled about paying for quarters, they also welcomed the British regulars. At the edge of the empire, the southern colonies feared invasion and slave insurrections, and the token detachments symbolized the empire's commitment to protecting the region. Here was leverage for Gage. In April 1767, the commander in chief wrote to Georgia's Governor James Wright, condemning the assembly's defiance of the Quartering Act before concluding that if the regulars were not supplied, then he would remove them. "The soldiers cannot be left there to perish," Gage explained.[143] A month later, he likewise informed Bermuda's Governor George James Bruere that "soldiers must have such necessaries . . . or be withdrawn" from the colony.[144]

Gage's threats proved effective. Georgia and Bermuda continued to play games, but both eventually complied with the Quartering Act. In October 1767, the Georgia Commons House approved £200 for all the supplies named in the American Mutiny Act, including alcohol and transportation costs, but adjourned before the appropriation became law. Governor Wright did not let the matter drop, but pressed the assembly until it finally approved supplies in April 1768.[145] Bermuda was even more evasive. The legislature insisted that its previous appropriations for quarters were "sufficient for that purpose" and refused to implement the Quartering Act, even after Gage rebuked the actions of "inferior legislatures presuming to interfere with laws" of Parliament.[146] In February 1768, the Bermuda assembly returned to the issue and approved funds "for defraying the further expenses of His Majesty's troops quartered in these islands" in compliance with the Mutiny Act for America, but only until the law expired on March 24. The lawmakers no doubt thought themselves quite clever, at least until they received word that Parliament had already extended the Quartering Act for another year.[147]

Yet compliance with the Quartering Act in the southern colonies was as incomplete as the British establishment in the region. Both South Carolina and Bermuda continued to evade the law after the New York Restraining Act arrived, and Gage made no effort to force their obedience. The general did not threaten South Carolina with the removal of troops, but accepted the limited supplies that lawmakers offered him. Perhaps this was because of South Carolina's outsize importance in the region, or perhaps it was because the colony had powerful friends in London, like the secretary of state, who praised the colony for its "dutiful behavior" of complying with the American Mutiny Act.[148] Gage also ignored the insolence of the Bahamas, perhaps fearful that his authority was tenuous in the Caribbean. He proved reticent about citing the Quartering Act in his correspondence with the colony, preferring instead to request that "the island should supply the troops with firewood and barrack necessaries, as at Bermuda, and other inhabited parts of North America."[149] However, lawmakers in the Bahamas ignored this appeal.[150]

Despite Gage's successes in New England and the South, the real test was the middle Atlantic, where three regiments were stationed. The troops in the middle colonies were neither temporary as in New England nor small detachments like in the South. Instead, armies of between two and five hundred men barracked in New York City, Elizabeth, Perth Amboy, and Philadelphia. Given their size and position, the middle Atlantic regiments had to be supplied by the colonial assemblies. As before, Pennsylvania faithfully complied with the Quartering Act, appropriating £8,000 in September 1767. New York and New Jersey proved more obstinate.[151]

In the spring of 1767, both New York and New Jersey were aware of their impending punishment and took preemptive action. When the New York House of Representatives convened in May 1767, Governor Sir Henry Moore promptly requested supplies for the troops "on the plan prescribed by the Act of Parliament."[152] Much as in the previous sessions, the House complained about the unequal burden faced by New York, but now legislators were more contrite. With little debate, the assembly appropriated £3,000 in New York currency "for furnishing necessaries for His Majesty's troops quartered within this colony."[153] As before, the assembly did not acknowledge the Quartering Act, although this time lawmakers did not specify how the army could spend the money. As a result, New York was no longer on record as refusing to provide soldiers with alcohol or other supplies. New Jersey followed suit a few days later, appropriating funds "for defraying the necessary expense of the troops quartered in this colony."[154] New Jersey also would not name the Mutiny Act for America, but Governor William Franklin believed that the law would supply "all the neces[saries] required by the Act of Parliament."[155]

New York and New Jersey waited nervously for London's response. When Governors Moore and Franklin received the final version of the New York Restraining Act, they dispatched letters to Whitehall certifying that their colonies were in full compliance with the Quartering Act. General Gage did likewise, despite the fact that the colonial statutes "make no mention" of the

British law.[156] But Whitehall was in no hurry to ease the colonists' anxiety. In November 1767, with still no word from London, the New York House of Representatives reconvened, not sure if in doing so the members were violating parliamentary law. Just in case, the House voted another £1,500 New York currency "for quartering His Majesty's troops in this colony."[157] In January 1768, Governor Moore finally received word from the Earl of Shelburne that "His Majesty has been graciously pleased to approve of your proceedings relative to the Mutiny Act."[158] When the Board of Trade made this decision official in May 1768, New York was finally in compliance with the Quartering Act. New Jersey was not so fortunate. The Board of Trade rejected the colony's 1767 law because it deviated from the American Mutiny Act in its procedure for appointing barrack masters, a lack of enumeration of articles to be supplied, and the statement that it would supply only one regiment. Accordingly, the New Jersey legislature wrote a new law in May 1768.[159]

By May 1768, the Quartering Act had been implemented at least partially in eight colonies. The New York Restraining Act was effective at threatening the colonial legislatures into compliance, although the real credit went to Thomas Gage. The commander in chief's practicality and flexibility extracted thousands of pounds from the colonists to support the North American Establishment. However, Gage's actions had done little to promote parliamentary supremacy, as few colonies acknowledged the Quartering Act in their appropriations laws. As a result, the financial success of the statute must be weighed against the cost of its enforcement.

As had happened with the Stamp Act, efforts to obtain quarters in 1767–1768 merged with parliamentary taxation in the American mind. Shortly after the New York Restraining Act reached the colonies came word that Parliament had passed the Townshend Acts. Another brainchild of the chancellor of the exchequer, the Townshend Acts placed duties on paper, paint, lead, glass, alcohol, and tea imported into the colonies, and created several new bureaucracies to effect their collection.[160] In response, John Dickinson combined Townshend's laws and attacked them collectively in a widely read series of newspaper articles known as "Letters from a Farmer in Pennsylvania." Dickinson tied parliamentary taxation to abuses of military power, arguing that in times of great injustice, laws like the New York Restraining Act and the Townshend duties flourished; "a standing army and excise have, from their first slender origins, though always hated, always feared, always opposed, at length swelled up to their vast present bulk." Based on this logic, Dickinson inverted Townshend's view of empire, contending that the colonists were entitled to English rights but not obligated to England's taxes. He also questioned the unitary empire, promoting instead a confederation of semiautonomous places, each of which controlled its own taxation.[161]

Empire

From London, Benjamin Franklin viewed the entire matter cynically. When Parliament first discussed quarters in early 1765, Franklin embraced the opportunity for imperial unity with equal rights and responsibilities. The Quartering Act had accomplished this by prohibiting billeting in private houses in exchange for colonial contributions. Yet in protecting domiciles, the law had charted a course that abrogated the colonists' right of representation. Franklin recounted this history in "Causes of the American Discontents before 1768," which appeared in print in January 1768. The Americans had been "put into high good humor by the repeal of the Stamp Act," Franklin argued, thus they "by various ways in different colonies, provided for the quartering of the troops." Some colonies evaded the letter of the law "by some variety or small diminution," but they had not resisted its spirit. However, the New York Restraining Act "greatly alarmed the people everywhere in America," who took the act's message as "obey implicitly laws made by the Parliament of Great Britain to raise money on you without your consent, or you shall enjoy no rights or privileges at all." For Franklin, the unitary empire had begun as a vehicle for protecting colonial rights, but three years later, it had accomplished the opposite.[162]

The passage and promulgation of the Quartering Act allow us to think about how people on both sides of the Atlantic imagined the British Empire as a place. Before the French and Indian War, the meaning of the empire was vague and open to interpretation. This variance persisted into the 1760s, as even when the ideal of the unitary empire came into vogue, there was little consensus on what this meant. It was in the attempt to secure quarters for the North American Establishment that Whitehall and the colonial legislatures came to terms with the fact that empire meant different things on opposite sides of the Atlantic. The resulting dispute drove British lawmakers like Charles Townshend to promote an empire where the colonists had responsibilities but not rights, and led Americans like John Dickinson to advocate for the opposite.

Nevertheless, the Quartering Act changed the discourse on military geography in North America. For over a decade, the colonists had fought to have the British army recognize that their homes were off-limits to soldiers, and the American Mutiny Act had confirmed this throughout British North America, even in Québec. However, the Quartering Act also capitalized on an unintended consequence of the barrack-building frenzy of the 1750s; now that the American capitals and towns had rooms for British soldiers, there was little the colonists could do to keep soldiers out. Moreover, the Mutiny Act for America obligated the colonists to supply barracked troops in ways that undermined the prerogative of the colonial assemblies and exposed the colonists to higher taxes. As the New York General Assembly learned, it was difficult to oppose the Quartering Act without challenging parliamentary supremacy and the British Empire itself. Accordingly, some colonists began to argue that troops should be removed from their cities and towns and relocated to decidedly hostile areas like the backcountry. Before the Americans could challenge the British Empire as a place, they challenged its military geography.

CHAPTER 4

Borderland

Native Americans, Soldiers, and Colonists
in the Backcountry

Pontiac understood that life on the borderland meant war. A member of the Odawa (Ottawa) people, Pontiac was born near Detroit around 1720, a place and time of intercultural conflict. For nearly a century, the Odawa had controlled the trade of furs and manufactures by warring against various groups of Native Americans and Europeans. On occasion, the Odawa fought against the French, especially when the price of trade goods went up; but as British forces pushed deeper into North America, the Odawa allied with the French against the redcoats. Pontiac grew into manhood as a warrior, possibly fighting to defend Canada in 1745, and perhaps helping to defeat General Braddock a decade later. He continued to lead Odawa warriors against British soldiers until the fall of Montréal in 1760. When the French ceded the Great Lakes, including Detroit, to the British, Pontiac refused to make peace with the redcoats or accept their trade goods. The British may have gained title to the Great Lakes, but they did not control the region. Instead, it was a borderland: a contested place where warriors fought for power.[1]

On May 9, 1763, Pontiac and hundreds of Native Americans attacked Detroit. "It is important," Pontiac reportedly told his troops, "that we exterminate from our lands this nation which seeks only to destroy us." Citing the poor quality and high cost of English goods, Pontiac called on his men to rage against British soldiers, traders, and settlers. Following a feigned peace parlay

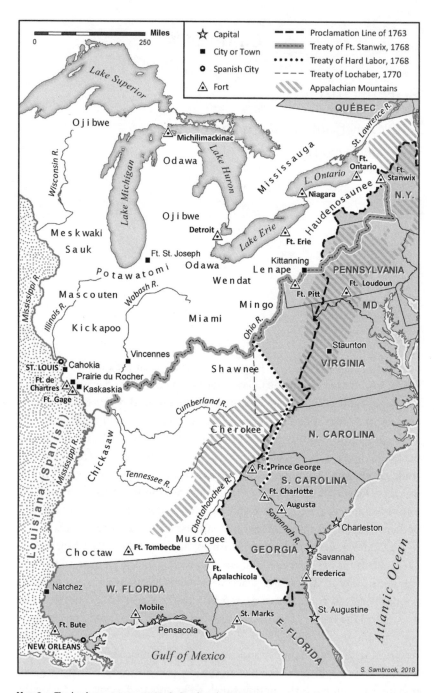

Map 3. The backcountry, ca. 1768. S. Sambrook, 2018.

FIGURE 4.1. *Chief Pontiac and Major Henry Gladwin at Detroit.* Gari Melchers, "The Conspiracy of Pontiac, 1763." Courtesy of the Burton Historical Collection, Detroit Public Library.

with commanding officer Major Henry Gladwin (depicted in figure 4.1), Pontiac and his warriors laid siege to Detroit. As weeks passed, Pontiac gathered the support of other Native Americans, building a pan-Indian alliance of Ojibwes (Chippewas), Wendats (Wyandots/Hurons), Miamis, and others, who destroyed eight British forts around the Great Lakes. He also reached out to French colonists in the region, asking them to take up arms against the British. "My brothers," he declared, "I am beginning to grow tired of seeing our lands encumbered by this carrion flesh (the English) and I hope you feel the same."[2]

Warfare on the borderland was expansive and intrusive; it ran contrary to changing notions of place elsewhere in British North America. When Pontiac's warriors proved unable to force their way into Detroit, they raided houses in the surrounding area. An observer related how "an old English woman" and her two sons "were killed, scalped, their property plundered, and their house set on fire." Such actions enraged the French inhabitants, who insisted that the home was a place of peace. Accordingly, the colonists rejected Pontiac's entreaty for a military alliance, because "when you enter our homes you enter with the tomahawk raised as if you intended to kill us." However, Pontiac's opponents also ignored domestic privacy. Before the siege began, the British army confined itself to barracks in the fort, segregating civilian and martial places in Detroit. However, when three hundred redcoats arrived in late July, the barracks overflowed with soldiers, thus "an order was issued that some should be quartered till further orders on private citizens." The reinforcements effectively halted the Indians' siege, as Pontiac withdrew to rouse support in Illinois. Although the assault on Detroit had ended, Pontiac would continue his war with Britain for another three years.[3]

In order to understand quarters and their effects on place in Revolutionary America, we must turn to the borderland. A borderland is a region around colonial settlements: a place at the periphery of European colonies where indigenous peoples also hold considerable power. Borderlands accompanied English colonization in the seventeenth century and moved west to the Appalachian Mountains in the eighteenth; Britain's victory in the French and Indian War pushed the borderland to the Mississippi River. Although King George claimed title to these interior regions, Native Americans maintained a powerful presence in the backcountry. The presence of multiple peoples in the same places made the borderland a heavily militarized place. Armies of colonists erected forts across the region, while Indian warriors violently resisted white encroachment; with the creation of the North American Establishment, British regulars entered the borderland. With so many combatants, there was little in the borderland that was not part of the military geography. As Pontiac's War demonstrated, spatial distinctions made in the American colonies by houses and barracks did not easily transfer to the borderland, thus complicating efforts to unify the British Empire.

The entrance of British soldiers onto the borderland also made quarters a priority. During the French and Indian War, the responsibility for quarters fell to the commander in chief, and the men who held this post devoted considerable attention to locating accommodations for British regulars in the backcountry. Consequently, General Thomas Gage insisted that the Quartering Act contain several passages to make the transportation of supplies and the administration of justice possible in places without colonial governance. Historians have ignored quartering on the borderland, especially how the American Mutiny Act affected the North American interior. Recovering this history helps us to understand that the struggle to accommodate British regulars reached far beyond New York and Boston. It also illustrates that despite the Quartering Act's original aim of imperial unity, its implementation required a recognition of local circumstances. Finally, billeting on the borderland presented insurmountable problems that undermined the statute. Long before the Mutiny Act for America failed in Boston, General Gage had abandoned the law in Detroit.

Quarters helped to shape British and colonial ideas about the borderland as a place. As the British army took control of the backcountry, officers had to determine whether soldiers could be placed in Native American and French colonial homes. The inconsistency with which Britons answered this question reflected the complexity of the empire's approach to the region. Following the passage of the Quartering Act, there was increased interest in deriving revenue for the army from colonial sources. Accordingly, proponents of colonizing the backcountry like Benjamin Franklin argued that allowing settlers into the region would generate taxes to quarter troops. Conversely, opponents of western colonization like Thomas Gage used the high cost of quartering troops to argue that lands west of the Appalachians should be left to the Indians. Ultimately, neither position prevailed, leaving the borderland another part of the eternal struggle of quarters in North America. As a place, the borderland has long been part of historical analysis. Quartering adds nuance to the military geography of the borderland, revealing how attempts to determine where soldiers belonged affected the British Empire's approach to its borderland and why it proved impossible to transform the region into anything else.

Expansion of the Anglo-American West

Borderlands were a familiar aspect of colonial America. Since the seventeenth century, the American colonists had dreamed of pushing colonial settlements far into the North American continent. Most colonial charters either set no western boundaries or terminated at the Pacific, thus encouraging such ambitions. Yet colonization was slowed by the presence of other peoples. Various groups of Native Americans controlled the interior of the continent, some establishing powerful empires that subjugated Europeans who ventured onto their lands. In between the American colonies and the Indian lands a buffer zone emerged, a borderland that neither colonists nor Native Americans controlled. A middle ground, the borderland was characterized by its diversity of inhabitants. Individuals from various indigenous nations and colonies ventured into the borderland to trade, hunt, or farm, carefully negotiating with others for their survival.

Beginning with the first English settlement at Jamestown in 1607, the Anglo-American frontier gradually pushed west, such that by 1754 the borderland reached the Appalachian Mountains. Approximately 1.2 million European Americans and 250,000 African Americans lived in British colonies from Nova Scotia to Georgia, but few colonial settlements ventured far from the Atlantic coast.[4] Instead, there was a vast area known as the backcountry that the colonial governments claimed title to but which they did not possess. At the northern periphery, Francophone Acadians and Mi'kmaq Indians inhabited the lands surrounding Halifax and the military outposts of Nova Scotia. In the central region, Haudenosaunees (Iroquois), Lenapes (Delawares), and Cherokees forged commercial and military alliances with American colonists, and occasionally with French traders and soldiers. On the southern periphery, colonists in Georgia struggled to maintain good relations with Muscogee (Creek) Indians in order to counter Spaniards in Florida.[5]

A chief characteristic of the borderland was its military geography. Fearful of raids by Native Americans and their French and Spanish allies, colonists built forts across the backcountry and manned them with provincial soldiers. As was generally true of military affairs before 1755, Britain left the military infrastructure of the borderland to the Americans. Massachusetts garrisoned Maine, while New York manned installations along the Great Lakes like Niagara. Farther south, South Carolina established forts and trading posts a hundred miles inland, including Fort Prince George at the Cherokee town of Keowee. Visitors to the backcountry reported a desolate land of forts and troops. In 1749, Swedish traveler Peter Kalm documented a burned-out garrison with "palisades" and "barracks, all of timber," north of Albany surrounded by a land of Indians eking out an existence, refugee colonists in shantytowns, and marauding French soldiers.[6] Similarly, when visiting Frederica in 1743, Edward Kimber found Georgia's southernmost settlement "surrounded by a rampart," with a population "in the provincial service" or serving the troops. "The civil government does not seem yet to be quite rightly settled," Kimber concluded. The same was true for much of the borderland.[7]

This militarization of the backcountry, in turn, precipitated the French and Indian War. In an attempt to dislodge French and Indian forces at Fort Duquesne, the colonial governments of Virginia and Pennsylvania erected a chain of forts along the Appalachian Mountains. New York, Maryland, and South Carolina followed suit, pushing their provincial armies farther north, south, and west. Between Washington's defeat at Fort Necessity in 1754 and the French surrender of Fort Duquesne four years later, the region was the bloodiest theater of the war. Bands of Lenapes raided colonists' homes, taking women and children captive and causing a panic that turned half the colonial population of Augusta County, Virginia, near Staunton, into refugees. In retaliation, Lieutenant Colonel John Armstrong led the Pennsylvania Regiment against the Lenape village of Kittanning, burning the town and taking eleven scalps. South Carolina used chaos in the backcountry to seize land from Cherokees, but this provoked a war that lasted for two years.[8]

The French and Indian War had profound effects on the borderland. First, it persuaded the British government to reverse its long-standing policy of leaving the region to the colonists. With the creation of the North American Establishment, Whitehall sent thousands of redcoats into the wilderness. Later, the British army constructed massive citadels such as Crown Point on Lake Champlain, Fort Ontario on Lake Ontario, and Fort Pitt at the forks of the Ohio River. Each dwarfed anything the colonists had built. Fort Pitt covered seventeen acres and was rumored to have cost £100,000. These citadels incorporated the latest innovations of military science: surrounded by bastions, ramparts, parapets, and curtain walls, and filled with massive barracks. In 1765, British colonel Lord Adam Gordon was impressed by backcountry citadels, contrasting their solid construction with the "other American forts," which were "fast verging to decay."[9]

Second, the conclusion of the war dramatically expanded the size of the borderland. The Treaty of Paris granted Great Britain title to roughly a half million square miles bounded by the Great Lakes, the Appalachian Mountains, Florida, and the Mississippi River. The region was dominated by a diverse population of Native Americans. One observer estimated "ten thousand Indian hunters throughout the Northern department," plus women, children, and the elderly; another reported the same number in the South.[10] All told, there were more than one hundred thousand Native Americans in the region, divided into dozens of villages, nations, and language groups. Mingos, Wendats, and Miami dominated the Ohio Country, with Odawas, Ojibwes, and Potawatomis along the Great Lakes. To the west, Kickapoos, Mascoutens, Meskwakis (Foxes), and Sauks populated the Illinois Country, while Chickasaws and Choctaws occupied Lower Louisiana. A small number of French colonists also resided in the region. In Illinois, two thousand whites and a thousand blacks lived along the Mississippi at Fort de Chartres and in the villages of Cahokia, Prairie du Rocher, and Kaskaskia. On the Great Lakes, six hundred colonists lived near Detroit, with more at Michilimackinac and Fort St. Joseph. A few dozen Francophone settlers farmed and traded at Vincennes on the Wabash River and at Natchez on the Mississippi. Beginning in 1760, British troops took control of the French forts, and by 1765, four regiments stretched out across Detroit, Niagara, Fort Pitt, and Fort de Chartres. Anglophone settlers and traders followed. As a result, the borderland expanded from the Appalachians to include all lands east of the Mississippi River.[11]

The enlarged Anglo-American borderland quickly came under assault. To the colonists, the removal of the French created the opportunity to exploit the region, but as American traders and farmers ventured over the mountains, they came into conflict with Native Americans. By the time Pontiac's warriors laid siege to Detroit, it was already apparent to many at Whitehall that colonists and Indians had to be separated from one another. Accordingly, the government divided British North America, leaving the backcountry to its indigenous inhabitants. With the Proclamation of 1763, King George III announced that all lands west of the Appalachians were reserved for the "nations or tribes of Indians with whom we are connected" and that the government would "strictly forbid" the colonists from "making any purchases or settlements whatever" in the region.[12]

The expansion of the borderland also meant the expansion of military geography. As the British army headed west, the American colonies withdrew militarily from the region. Eager to cut costs, the colonial assemblies disbanded the provincial armies and abandoned their backcountry forts shortly after the fall of Montréal. The Pennsylvania assembly informed Governor James Hamilton that it had no interest in paying for troops detained on Lake Erie and requested that he close two other forts "with all convenient speed."[13] Virginia, which had built seventeen forts early in the French and Indian War, vacated them all, while South Carolina and Georgia turned Fort Prince George and Frederica, respectively, over to British regulars.[14] When Pontiac's War broke out, the British army rued the new arrangement. Short on men and money, Commander in Chief Jeffrey Amherst turned to the colonists for help. However, New York, New Jersey, and Pennsylvania refused the general's request for provincial troops, leading Amherst to rebuke them for choosing to "tamely look on while their brethren are butchered by the savages."[15] Amherst's successor likewise pressed the colonies to provide troops, although he too soon grew frustrated. Eventually, Thomas Gage cajoled three colonies into raising troops, but the recruits were slow to make it to the front, and many deserted along the way. It was clear that the Americans expected the British army to maintain order in the backcountry.[16]

Perhaps predictably, the struggle between the colonists and the British army over the borderland came down to quarters. Of greater concern to Amherst and Gage than a lack of provincial troops was the colonial assemblies' refusal to supply British regulars. When Amherst approached Pennsylvania for troops, he also demanded the assembly pass "a law to compel the inhabitants to furnish carriages" to transport regulars and supplies to the front. Fearful of an Indian uprising in its backcountry, the Pennsylvania assembly fulfilled Amherst's request.[17] However, other colonies were not so accommodating. New York balked at the request for provincials unless Britain paid their billeting expenses. Although Gage was initially receptive to this request, the pressure from Whitehall to cut costs caused him to change his mind. As he informed a subordinate, "His Majesty looks on this Indian war, as a war carried on, for the interest and good of the provinces, and that they should bear the expense of it."[18]

In the South, colonists displayed even less willingness to supply British regulars. In February 1764, Gage received word that the South Carolina assembly would no longer provision British troops in the colony, nor would it pay to transport regulars from Charleston to Fort Prince George. Worse, the legislature delayed plans to repair Fort Charlotte. Georgia was even more parsimonious, shirking all responsibility for Augusta and Frederica, leaving Governor James Wright to provision troops out of his own pocket. Gage tried to reason with southern lawmakers, informing them that the borderland was a joint effort. "The king is to feed his own troops," he wrote, "but the provinces are to transport the provisions as heretofore practiced, to the forts, from the inhabited country."[19] South Carolina did finally relent, agreeing to "transport salt, military stores, and regimental clothing till the first of July" 1765, but Georgia continued to ignore Gage's requests.[20] Gage yearned for "the people called crackers" to submit, but until then, he quartered men at the southern forts out of the army's budget.[21]

In sum, the expansion of the borderland pushed issues of quartering deep into the North American interior. The question of where troops belonged was as relevant in Illinois and Detroit as it was in New York and Montréal. As British regulars became a permanent part of the backcountry, the same questions of whether troops could be quartered in a house or confined to barracks traveled west to the Mississippi. The race and the status of the inhabitants complicated matters, but these factors did not obviate British constitutional principles necessarily. Rather, the borderland remained uncertain, and it was unclear how uncolonized territories fit into the empire.

Houses and Barracks beyond the Appalachians

Sir William Johnson was a natural fit for a borderland. Born in Ireland in 1715, Johnson hailed from a family that was both old English gentry and Roman Catholic, a curious mix that made him both a leader and an outsider. When his uncle purchased land near the Mohawk River, Johnson immigrated in 1738 and built a fortune on New York's frontier. Unlike most settlers, Johnson ingratiated himself with the local Indians, becoming an honorary sachem of the Haudenosaunee and having long-term relationships with at least two Mohawk women. During the French and Indian War, he successfully led thousands of Haudenosaunee warriors against the French at Lake George and Niagara. Johnson's reputation among Native Americans made him indispensable, especially once the backcountry expanded to the Mississippi River.[22]

As the British army turned the tide in Pontiac's War, Whitehall looked to Sir William Johnson to effect a lasting peace on the borderland. Although the Proclamation of 1763 set the region west of the Appalachians aside for Native Americans, Pontiac's complaints and actions convinced the British government that it could not abandon the backcountry. Instead, the indigenous inhabitants needed traders to supply them with goods and British troops to police them. In July 1764, the Board of Trade issued the "Plan for the Future Management of Indian Affairs" creating the Indian superintendence system. The so-called Plan of 1764 codified imperial management of the borderland, repealing "all laws now in force in the several colonies for regulating Indian affairs." Instead, Native Americans became the responsibility of two Indian superintendents: Sir William Johnson in the North and John Stuart in the South. The plan tasked the superintendents and their staffs of Indian agents with appeasing the indigenous populations, primarily by regulating traders in the region. A trader had to be licensed and had to "declare the post or truck house" where he intended to conduct commerce with Native Americans. Trade was confined to "certain limits round each post," and anyone who dealt outside his area would forfeit his trade goods and be fined and imprisoned. Traders could avail themselves of western forts both as trading posts and for protection "whenever any disturbance shall arise." Should traders break these rules, the superintendents were empowered to render justice. In effect, the Plan of 1764 transformed the backcountry into a carefully regulated borderland.[23]

As Johnson assumed the office of northern superintendent, he confronted some profound questions about place in the borderland. The Plan of 1764 made it his duty to keep peace among the Native Americans, so he had to consider where traders belonged. As had been true in the old colonies, this led Johnson to contemplate houses and barracks. Was an Indian's house constitutionally protected against billeting, the same as a colonist's? Likewise, Johnson had to consider the role of martial places within the borderland, specifically forts. Did they exist to segregate civilian and martial places like urban barracks, or were they mixed-use facilities that both soldiers and civilians shared? Such questions were not unique to Johnson, but mirrored General Gage's queries about quartering British soldiers in the West. In a region in which all European Americans were armed, the distinction between soldiers and civilians was very fine indeed. Remaining at his manor house at Johnstown, Johnson studied the reports of younger and more ambitious men who headed west: reports that revealed an inconsistency of places in the empire. Houses and barracks on the borderland looked different from those in the old colonies, differences that defied Anglo-American military geography.

The Indian agents and explorers who ventured west of the Appalachians recorded detailed descriptions of Indian houses. Most found such dwellings to be simple, temporary, and lacking differentiation: qualities that made them seem devoid of privacy and domesticity. In 1766, Massachusetts native Jonathan Carver visited a number of Indian villages west of Lakes Michigan and Superior. Most contained twenty-five to fifty houses, except for a Sauk settlement on the Wisconsin River that Carver labeled "the largest and best built Indian town I ever saw." The houses of Great Lakes peoples fascinated Carver. "These cabins have neither chimneys nor windows," he noted. As depicted in figure 4.2, most were frames covered with animal skins or bark,

FIGURE 4.2. Winter House of Sauks and Meskwaki. "Winter House of Sacs and Foxes, Iowa (from Photograph)," in Frederick Starr, *American Indians* (Boston: Heath, 1899), 10.

makeshift structures that Indians situated "just as it suits their convenience." Carver also observed a lack of spatial differentiation inside the house. Everyone slept together atop bearskins on the ground, with some homes "large enough for several families."[24]

Other Britons and American colonists who traversed the backcountry confirmed Carver's findings. Hailing from places where the colonists' houses were increasingly refined, these men found the Indians' domiciles to be savage. Traveling among the Cherokees in 1761–1762, British lieutenant Henry Timberlake found the Indians' houses "tolerably well built," with some "two story high, tolerably pretty and capacious." But he also found them too primitive for a civilized people. "For want of saws," the Cherokees' houses were uneven and unremarkable; "for want of chimneys," they filled with smoke.[25] Irish immigrant James Adair was similarly disappointed by the housing of southern nations. Adair despaired that the Chickasaws would rip the bark siding from their homes every spring and abandon the structures until autumn because they claimed "building houses in the troublesome hot summer, is a needless and foolish affair, as it occasions much sweating." Adair and other explorers also disliked how the Indians carelessly combined living and working spaces in ways that recalled the colonists' seventeenth-century dwellings.[26] They also worried about the gender implications of Indians' houses. As was true in England and its coastal colonies, the indigenous home was a decidedly female space, although some wondered if it was *too* female. Adair wrote that during battle, men abandoned their houses to their wives, observing that "Indians will not cohabit with women while they are out at war." When New Jersey fur trader Alexander Henry the Elder observed an Ojibwe woman about to give birth in a village near Michilimackinac, he puzzled over how she "was immediately removed out of the common lodge; and a small one, for her separate accommodation" was built by the other women of the community. The house was supposed to be a place where a man protected his wife and children, but Indian men ceded domestic control to women, thus abdicating paternal duties and confirming their savagery in the eyes of the English.[27]

While Indians' housing signaled a lack of civilization, the dwellings of the backcountry's French colonists were little better in the eyes of Anglophone visitors. Traveling to Illinois in 1766, British captain Harry Gordon noted that Kaskaskia consisted of "eighty houses well-built mostly of stone, with gardens, and large lots to each," which allowed the inhabitants to "live generally well."[28] However, the French use of space was too mixed for English tastes. Not only did the Francophone inhabitants not segregate work from home; they failed to distinguish martial from civilian, and white from red. French homes were scattered in and around Detroit, paying little mind to military infrastructure, an arrangement that even Pontiac's siege could not disrupt. At Michilimackinac, Alexander Henry reported how Odawa warriors "billeted themselves in several houses, among the Canadian inhabitants."[29] Although parallel French and Indian towns were the norm, in some cases the two became one. In Ohio, Indian agent George Croghan stumbled upon a Miami village of "forty or fifty cabins besides nine or ten French houses" built as one community.[30]

Sir William Johnson was troubled by the reports he received of houses on the borderland. The Indian dwellings were too muddled and too multipurpose, completely disregarding the proper distance between soldier and civilian that barracks provided in coastal cities. Johnson hoped to convert Native Americans to Christianity and entertained a proposal to build towns where "sober white families" would teach the Indians husbandry and trades.[31] In the meantime, the uncertainty of Indian houses raised a pressing question: were they sufficiently private to prevent billeting? The reports that Johnson collected suggest that Indian agents avoided quartering with the Indians. When George Croghan visited a Mingo town in Ohio in 1765, he was warmly received by a chief who offered to guide him to Illinois. Although Croghan felt he could not refuse the man's generosity, that night Croghan and his men "encamped near an Indian village" but not in it.[32] Similarly, when Indian agent David Taitt traveled among Muscogee villages several years later, he noted enjoying women's singing and dancing, but at the end of the evening he always "left the house" for his own quarters.[33] By not intruding on their houses, British agents tacitly recognized an Indian right to privacy.

General Gage's soldiers followed a similar procedure with Indian villages. When Captain Gordon sailed west from Fort Pitt in 1766, he and his men passed several Indian villages but chose to camp each night in tents until they reached Fort de Chartres. However, the British army was not as respectful of French homes in the backcountry. Although the army barracked soldiers whenever possible, the French had not left the British much of a military infrastructure. Except for Fort de Chartres, the French forts were hastily built of poor materials, and most were verging on collapse. At Mobile on the Gulf Coast, poor accommodations meant that "almost everybody is ill of fevers, fluxes and agues."[34] When barracks proved insufficient, the army had no choice but to billet troops in the inhabitants' homes. Three hundred British soldiers quartered in private houses in Detroit during Pontiac's siege of 1763, and when Colonel John Bradstreet visited a year later, he found British regulars still billeted in the colonists' homes.[35]

Traders who did business with Native Americans were also supposed to stay out of Indian villages; since they were licensed representatives of the

British Crown, their actions reflected on the empire as a whole. Many followed the law and roomed at forts. In 1766, New York native Matthew Clarkson stopped at Fort Pitt on his way to Illinois. He noted that fort commander Major William Murray "was extremely polite and obliging" and "offered me a room in the barracks, which I accepted." Clarkson stayed at Fort Pitt for nearly a month, during which time he "supped with the mess" alongside soldiers as he prepared for his journey down the Ohio River. When John Jennings headed west that same year, he carefully avoided intruding on indigenous villages, noting in his journal how he "encamped about twelve miles below the Indian town" instead of residing in it. As per order of the Board of Trade, Clarkson and Jennings avoided trading with any Native Americans until they reached Fort de Chartres. Both men were licensed on behalf of Baynton, Wharton, and Morgan, a Philadelphia mercantile firm that virtually monopolized Indian trade in the West. Because Baynton, Wharton, and Morgan also looked to supply British troops, their agents carefully followed the official protocol. When the firm received word that "a person with a small assortment of goods" had ventured into a Shawnee town to trade, the directors apologized to British authorities and promised to rectify the situation immediately.[36]

But not all traders were as well behaved as Clarkson and Jennings. Despite prohibitions of the Plan of 1764, a number of western merchants did not trade at the forts but took their business to Native American towns. When Indian agent George Morgan visited "Shawnees' cabins" near Fort Pitt, he reported that several temporary trading posts had become permanent residences. Morgan discovered one man "who lived near this Indian hut" and another who was accompanied by his wife. Some traders took up residence in Indian villages and remained there through the winter. A man named Abbot, who was arrested for trading without a license in late 1766, "refused to give bond for his future behavior" and "said he would continue to trade till turned out of his house." For such men, spatial divisions meant little, and Indian privacy was irrelevant.[37]

The superintendents were acutely aware of the traders' violations of Native Americans' places. Southern superintendent John Stuart heard from the Choctaws about dishonest traders who "stole their horses and debauched their wives," while Sir William Johnson fielded similar complaints from northern Indians. Before either could rectify the situation, violence broke out in the West. News of white aggression against Indians appeared first, with reports flowing back to New York and London, including how nine Cherokees were murdered in Virginia "by the back settlers of that province." Outraged, Native Americans demanded justice from British officials.

Arriving at Fort Pitt in early 1767, George Croghan found "a great number" of Haudenosaunees, Shawnees, Lenapes, and Wendats waiting to protest "the murder of some of their people" in Ohio.[38] Johnson observed that "a universal discontent has prevailed for some time," and he feared that the Indians would take matters into their own hands.[39] His fears proved prescient in late 1767 when a report surfaced of a white trader killed inside a Shawnee village, followed by news of the murder of fourteen employees of Baynton, Wharton, and Morgan by Ojibwes near Detroit. The South also was rattled by violence as Muscogees and whites clashed across Georgia's frontier.[40]

As the borderland descended into a cycle of retaliatory violence, British troops found themselves caught in the middle. In March 1765, a group of colonial vigilantes led by James "Black Boy Jimmy" Smith attacked a train of contraband passing through Pennsylvania on its way to Indians in the West. A small force of British regulars stationed at nearby Fort Loudoun responded, but when the Black Boys fired on the soldiers, the troops retreated to the fort. Eight months later, the troops prepared to evacuate the installation, taking with them nine rifles and smooth guns they had captured from the colonists. Before they could depart, however, "the fort was surrounded by a number of the rioters, who kept firing and hooting the whole night." For two days, Smith's men besieged Fort Loudoun, until Lieutenant Charles Grant surrendered the weapons to a local gentleman. Black Boy Jimmy and his followers thought that British troops were too sympathetic to the Indians, and for this reason they were prepared to fire on His Majesty's forces.[41] British soldiers also ran afoul of the Native American population. In March 1765, Lieutenant Alexander Fraser reported from Kaskaskia how his men "were very ill treated every day by such Indians as were drunk." Two months later, a group of Potawatomis "killed two of the garrison of Detroit." In response, Detroit commander Lieutenant Colonel John Campbell prohibited trade between whites and Indians until the offending Indians delivered up the culprits. However, it soon came out that the soldiers had been killed in retaliation for raping an Indian woman. Such stories poisoned relations between regulars and Native Americans.[42]

In order to reestablish peace on the borderland, Sir William Johnson went to meet with Pontiac. Three years after the Odawa warrior had broken off his siege of Detroit, Pontiac had lost standing among the Great Lakes peoples, and his pan-Indian movement had collapsed. Some Indians had grown tired of resisting and tried to make the best of the situation. In the summer of 1765, delegations from the Ohio Lenapes, Genesee Senecas, and Shawnees concluded peace with the British, thus splintering Pontiac's support. In the face of defections, Shawnee war chief Charlot Kaské sought to supplant

Pontiac and resume the fight, while St. Joseph Potawatomis harshly criticized Pontiac for emboldening the Cherokees in the South. Indian commissary Benjamin Roberts reported that "the Indians are very jealous of Pontiac and want to choose another chief," explaining to Johnson, "They think we make too much of him." In response, Pontiac tried to reassert himself as an Indian leader by making an alliance with the British. He turned to the one Briton whom Indians universally admired and made a treaty with him.[43]

In July 1766, Pontiac and Johnson met face to face at Fort Ontario. "The affairs of the Indians are in as bad a situation as possible," Johnson wrote Gage as he made his way from Johnstown to Fort Ontario, adding that the way "to make them easy" was to allow Pontiac and his compatriots to "obtain some satisfaction."[44] When they sat down to talk, "Sir William Johnson caused Pontiac's pipe to be lighted," then they exchanged wampum belts and official proclamations. The two men quickly found common ground. Pontiac took Johnson "by the hand in the name of all the nations" and promised "as long as I live no ill shall ever happen about Detroit, if in my power to prevent it." In return, Johnson assured Pontiac that the British would respect Indians' places by keeping white settlers out of the region and traders confined to the forts. Pontiac was pleased with these assurances, telling Johnson that "we likewise heartily thank you for letting the traders to straggle through the woods to our villages, but to trade only at the posts under the inspection of the commissaries." After a few days, the two men departed in peace, hopeful that they had found a way to share the borderland.[45]

The Quartering Act in the Backcountry

Major General Thomas Gage took a special interest in the borderland. He owed his position as commander in chief to his predecessor's inability to put down Pontiac's War, and this may have made him fearful that a similar fate would befall him. Gage accordingly exercised a gentle paternalism over the western reaches of Britain's North American empire. Although he never ventured west of the Appalachians, it was Gage's words that British officers read to the French inhabitants of Illinois when the army arrived. Like a good father, Gage promised peace to those who remained to become faithful British subjects, saving them from "the scourge of a bloody war, and of all the evils which the march of an army into their country would draw after it."[46] Gage's name was also printed on the borderland through the work of his officers. Commodore Alexander Grant launched the brig General Gage onto the Detroit River in 1772, while on the Mississippi a new fort near Kaskaskia was christened Fort Gage.[47]

While the Plan of 1764 made Sir William Johnson responsible for civilians on the borderland, Gage was responsible for the soldiers. With four regiments scattered from Fort Pitt to Fort de Chartres, Gage had to figure out where to quarter them and how to supply them. While deciding such matters was difficult under normal circumstances, the region's remote location and escalating violence intensified the challenge. Nevertheless, Gage saw the backcountry as part of a unitary British Empire, much as he did the old and new colonies, and he sought to extend the same constitutional protections and financial obligations practiced on the Atlantic coast west to the Mississippi River. For this reason, he advised Parliament to include the borderland in the Quartering Act. However, the commander in chief also accepted that quartering had to be modified to suit a place without organized colonies, so he included provisions in the law unique to the region.

The borderland was a financial headache for the British military, as the army alone was responsible for providing barracks, supplies, and transport. None of these were cheap. The barracks left behind by the French needed constant repair. In 1766, Captain Harry Gordon calculated it would cost £1,666 to make Michilimackinac, Detroit, Fort Erie, Niagara, Oswegatchie, and Fort Pitt habitable, an amount comparable to building new barracks in New Jersey. Then there were the supplies. In late 1766, barrack master general James Robertson determined that he needed nearly £1,500 to buy firewood, candles, bowls, utensils, and bedding for troops in Illinois, South Carolina, Georgia, and around the Great Lakes. This was roughly the same amount that New York appropriated for a year's supplies and three times what New Jersey spent. The remote location and poor roads added to the cost. Gage estimated it cost £315 each year to transport provisions from Charleston to the four southern forts. Water routes made it easier to move provisions across the Great Lakes, but it still cost £23 to ship supplies for four men for one year at Niagara, £59 at Detroit, and £67 at Michilimackinac.[48] Transport meant greater risk, so the army also had to appropriate funds for "unavoidable losses in transportation" as well as barrels, storage, and "salt for repacking."[49]

To offset these costs, Gage followed the long-standing policy of placing the financial burden for quarters on the local population. However, this proved impractical. Much as Gage did not billet soldiers in Native American villages, he ignored a suggestion from Sir William Johnson that borderland troops be "left at the discretion of the Indians for supplies." Indeed, the flow of supplies usually went in the opposite direction. Indian agent George Croghan worried about the army's duty to supply Native Americans with gifts, fretting that "maintaining the Indians . . . could not be supported by the garrison without distressing the troops."[50] Gage did not show the same respect for French settlers, routinely billeting troops in colonial houses and seizing supplies. When Major Robert Farmar took command in Illinois, he supplied his troops by taking "materials from several houses in the village, which were pulled down by his orders for this purpose and to make cord wood of."[51] However, Gage did make an exception for Detroit because of its outsize importance to the region. In August 1764, he dispatched engineer John Montresor to build barracks in Detroit, thus removing troops from the homes where they had resided since Pontiac's siege a year earlier. In return for the barracks, however, Gage insisted that the residents supply the soldiers. He instructed the local commander to investigate "the tax formerly paid by the inhabitants to the French king" and how the army might collect it.[52] Dutifully, Lieutenant Colonel John Campbell imposed a tax on Detroiters comparable to their former obligation, although this failed. "The people in general are so wretchedly poor, that they have not been able hitherto to pay the one half of this," Campbell noted, so he took firewood in lieu of money.[53]

Both the struggle to supply western troops and escalating violence on the borderland were on Gage's mind when he asked Parliament to add North America to the English Mutiny Act. Specifically, the commander in chief included two provisions that applied exclusively to the western region. The first had to do with supplies. Experience had persuaded Gage to abandon efforts to have the French colonists supply British soldiers. Not only were most western settlements impoverished like Detroit; the Proclamation of 1763's prohibition of civil governments meant that there were no colonial assemblies to appropriate funds. The British army would have to supply the troops. However, because such supplies invariably passed through places that had colonial governments, Gage recommended that the old colonies cover transportation costs. The second provision stemmed from the constant stream of illicit traders and settlers to the backcountry who angered Native Americans and elicited violence. Without civil governments in the region, there were no local courts to try miscreants, so Gage recommended giving criminal jurisdiction to the British army. "If such crime or trespass be committed at any of the posts not in the inhabited parts of the country," then the accused was to be "tried and convicted by a regimental or general court martial according to the degree of the offense." Although Parliament revised the specifics of Gage's proposals, the British government nonetheless ensured that the Quartering Act would be promulgated in the borderland.[54]

The requirement that colonists provide transportation costs was not unique to the Quartering Act, having previously appeared in the England's Mutiny Act. Like the English law, the American version made local civilian officials responsible for locating a "wagon, cart, or carriage" and animals to pull them. The Mutiny Act for America detailed how far such transports would travel, compensation rates for owners, and procedures for when vehicles or animals were damaged. The transportation provision rankled American colonists, who saw it as a covert attempt to make them pay for the western forts. Such a burden ran contrary to the rest of the Quartering Act, which made the colonies responsible only for troops within their territory. It also contravened the Plan of 1764, which had severed all forts west of the Appalachians from colonial governance. Moreover, the transportation provision perpetuated the American Mutiny Act's uneven application by burdening some colonies but not others; only South Carolina and Pennsylvania were ordered to provide wagons and horses for moving supplies.[55]

Gage had struggled to compel South Carolina to transport military supplies to Forts Prince George and Charlotte since he became commander in chief in 1763. When he received the Quartering Act in July 1765, he did not immediately invoke the transportation provision, but delayed its implementation along with the rest of the law for the first year. "The assembly of South Carolina has refused making any further provision for the transportation of military stores of any kind to the upper posts in that province," Gage informed Whitehall in October 1765, concluding that "the expense therefore of said transportation will for the future fall upon the Crown."[56] Yet South Carolina's defiance grew bolder in time. In the summer of 1766, the Commons House appropriated £6,733 South Carolina money for repairs to Fort Prince George and promised another £5,000 for Fort Charlotte. It also voted £162 "for firewood delivered at Fort Prince George" and nearly £26 "for carriage" to the outpost.[57] However, the legislature would only pay to move military stores that were not provisions, leaving the British army to cover the rest. The colony's willingness to approve tens of thousands of pounds for forts and carriage while refusing a few hundred for transporting provisions baffled the general.[58]

Finally, Gage invoked the Quartering Act. In December 1766, the commander in chief informed South Carolina lawmakers that he expected them to cover the whole bill. "At the request of General Gage," Governor Lord Charles Montagu asked the Commons House to defray "the expense of transporting provisions and military stores to His Majesty's troops, which garrison the frontier posts of this province." Despite news that Parliament was at work on the New York Restraining Act, South Carolina remained defiant. In April 1767, when the Commons House agreed to supply British troops in Charleston, it also announced that it would not cover transportation costs to the western forts. Constitutional arguments against the American

Mutiny Act were unpopular in anticipation of New York's punishment, so the House cited financial reasons instead. It supposed that "the contractors for the provisions are obliged to supply them at those posts" in the backcountry. It then observed that the revenue collected under the Townshend Acts was sufficient for "defending, protecting, and securing the British colonies." Finally, the House cited equity: transportation had "never been borne by any of the northern colonies."[59] Gage excoriated South Carolinians' lack of "obedience they owe to the legislative acts of Great Britain," but he let the decision stand.[60] Once again afraid to challenge the colony's defiance of the Quartering Act, Gage allowed South Carolina to evade transportation costs, much as he had allowed the colony to supply British troops with the articles it provided in 1757. When Captain Lewis Valentine Füser took command of the British troops in South Carolina in August 1767, he paid out of his own pocket to ship supplies.[61]

Gage also struggled to acquire transports in Pennsylvania. Although the colonial legislature dutifully appropriated money for supplies, the Quartering Act's provision for transportation rankled Pennsylvanians. In June 1768, Lieutenant Colonel John Wilkins was leading seven companies of the 18th Regiment through the colony on the way to Fort de Chartres when he discovered that "not a horse or wagon could be found in or about Carlisle." All horses had been "concealed in the woods and the wagons taken to pieces," indicating the colonists' open defiance of the British army and parliamentary law. For two days, Wilkins waited for locals to produce transportation, amusing himself with "their humdrum meetings" until he was "obliged at last to quarter five of our companies on the farmers" and send the other two "through the woods, etc., to search for what we want." In so doing, Wilkins violated the Quartering Act's protection of domiciles in order to enforce the law's transport provision.[62] The experience left a sour taste in the mouths of Pennsylvanians that persisted for years. In January 1772, Gage was still trying to soothe the outraged townspeople of Carlisle, ordering that they be compensated at "the sum directed to be paid them by Act of Parliament." Presumably, he paid them out of the funds appropriated by the Pennsylvania assembly under the Mutiny Act for America.[63]

The second provision of the Quartering Act that pertained to the borderland had nothing to do with money. Instead, it set the rules for the administration of justice where civilian courts did not exist. Although Gage had requested that the army be empowered to adjudicate cases for civilians accused of crimes, when this suggestion came before Parliament, too many in the House of Commons found it to be "anti-constitutional," so they modified it.[64] The final text of the law ordered that if anyone "commit any crime" at a place "not within the limits or jurisdiction of any civil government," then he or she would be delivered by the commanding officer "to the civil magistrate of the next adjoining province" for trial. It was not a minor change, and Gage's efforts to promulgate the provision quickly convinced him of its injudiciousness.[65]

The first time the army removed a criminal from the backcountry for trial in a civilian court elsewhere, the racial animosity of the borderland came to the fore. In May 1766, Detroit commander John Campbell reported that "an English Negro belong to Mr. Sterling merchant of this place" had attempted to rape a Native American woman, but the man ended up killing her and another woman. Upon learning of the incident from an Indian woman and a French boy, Colonel Campbell interrogated the accused and discovered "the Negro's shirt sleeves all stained with blood." This convinced Campbell of the man's guilt, so the colonel prepared to send him to Albany for trial in accordance with the Quartering Act. But this caused him to regret the law's directive. "I wish with all my heart he could be tried here," Campbell opined, believing that it would be a good example for the local Indians and "convince them that we never screen bad people from justice."[66] General Gage agreed with Campbell, but his hands were also tied by the American Mutiny Act. "I cannot order him to be tried at . . . Detroit," Gage explained, because the law insisted that the trial "must be in the inhabited country, by a civil court."[67] However, Gage did reach out to Sir William Johnson, fretting that "the affair of the Negro puzzles me a good deal," as trying the accused elsewhere "will never answer our purposes in giving satisfaction to the Indians." With violence sparking between white traders and Native Americans, Gage feared that the murders in Detroit would escalate matters. Accordingly, he encouraged Johnson to send some Indians east to witness the trial and "convince them of our desire to do them justice." Gage worried that he had only narrowly avoided an Indian uprising at Detroit and laid the blame with the "clause in the late mutiny acts."[68]

After that, Gage began to dread the justice portion of the Quartering Act. When, in 1769, two Potawatomis were delivered up "by their nation" for murdering a white man, he despaired that the army's inability to either try or execute the culprits would sour the Indians' "desire to live amicably with us."[69] That same year, Gage predicted "Indian commotions" when the army arrested a white murderer of Native Americans at Fort Pitt and sent him eastward for trial.[70] Without local justice, British authority in the borderland was undermined and the region's racial unrest exacerbated. In 1771, German sutler Tobias Isenhout was murdered by his French clerk Michael Dué, and the Quartering Act invoked again. Although the details of Isenhout's murder are unclear, they resulted in a manhunt throughout the backcountry that eventually found Dué in Kaskaskia. He was brought back to Detroit, where, once again, the commanding officer lamented the message that a remote trial would send to Native Americans. Nevertheless, Captain James Stevenson "proceeded in this business in the manner directed by a clause in the Mutiny Act, passed for North America," and sent Dué to Montréal.[71] For his part, Gage consoled himself with the hope that executing Dué "at Montréal, in the sight of so many voyageurs to the upper country, may have nearly the same effect, as his being sent to suffer at Detroit."[72] However, Gage made sure to communicate his distaste of this aspect of the Mutiny Act for America to Whitehall.[73]

Although Gage and the British cabinet ministers worried about New York's defiance of the Quartering Act, the statute was a much greater failure on the borderland. Through Gage's liberal interpretation of the law, the American Mutiny Act was promulgated in seven American colonies plus Bermuda, where lawmakers appropriated funds for barracks supplies. By contrast, South Carolina never approved money for transport costs, while Pennsylvanians provided wagons only when confronted with illegal billeting. The administration of justice portion of the Quartering Act did at least provide the accused a civilian trial, although this threatened the stability of the region by aggravating racial tensions. Tellingly, Gage ceased invoking the transportation provision long before he abandoned other sections of the Mutiny Act for America, and he was far more critical of the justice portion than any other clause. In some ways, the statute's failure in the backcountry mirrored its failure in Canada, where a lack of taxation and representation made the law unworkable. But whereas Gage accepted that Québec and the other new colonies would have British troops barracked at British expense, he refused to tolerate the same situation in the backcountry. Instead, he and other imperial planners looked for a way to change the status of the region by abolishing the borderland. In the debate that followed, quartering was never far from the designs for the western regions of British North America.

Plans to Colonize the West

In the summer of 1766, Benjamin Franklin began to wonder if London was truly his home. Although he still enjoyed the urbanity of the imperial capital, his forceful rebuke of the Stamp Act before Parliament had diminished his reputation at Whitehall. Meanwhile, life in America was proceeding without him; his last brother died, his daughter got married, and his wife managed his affairs. Yet rather than abandoning his dream of a unitary British Empire where the colonies played an important role and the inhabitants maintained constitutional rights, Franklin expanded it. As reports of borderland violence reached London, Franklin refocused his energies on the North American interior. For too long, he reasoned, British soldiers had protected Native Americans while preventing the American colonists from enjoying the spoils of war. It was time to push the English constitution into the backcountry and fully incorporate the West into the empire by colonizing the region with white settlers. It was time to end the borderland.[74]

Franklin's colonization schemes implicitly addressed quarters. Since helping to draft the Quartering Act, Franklin had turned away from matters of accommodating soldiers, especially once it proved unpopular in the colonies. Nevertheless, his plan for creating new colonies west of the Appalachians offered a better solution than the transportation and justice portions of the American Mutiny Act. South Carolina had balked at transporting supplies, but if white settlers erected a western colony, then they could have their own assembly to vote taxes for supplies. Adjudicating crimes would also be easier, as the creation of new western colonies would establish civilian courts to ensure that all cases were tried near the scene of the crime. Colonization thus would render the borderland portions of the Quartering Act moot, while the law's requirements for colonists to quarter troops could come into effect.

The inspiration for Franklin's interest in colonizing the West was Indian agent George Croghan. In June 1764, Croghan urged the Board of Trade to "plant a respectable colony" along the Mississippi River, but the board ignored his suggestion.[75] Two years later, Croghan wrote to Franklin, seeking redress for traders who had been robbed and killed by bands of Indians since Pontiac's War. Franklin considered Croghan's letter carefully, underlining one line in particular: some Native Americans observed that peace would not come to the backcountry "except by a *surrender of a part of their country*, which they would *most cheerfully* do." Franklin found this point interesting and pressed Croghan for more information.[76]

In response, Croghan reached out to Franklin's son, New Jersey Governor William Franklin, asking him to recruit investors to buy up land in Illinois. Both father and son saw the advantages of such a plan, understanding that western colonies would not only promote the security of the British Empire, but generate profits for them through land speculation. Soon, the two Franklins were hard at work selling their colonization scheme to investors and policy makers on both sides of the Atlantic. From Burlington, William Franklin organized the Illinois Company "to apply to the Crown for a grant of twelve hundred thousand acres or more" bounded by the Wisconsin, Mississippi, Ohio, and Wabash Rivers (effectively, the present State of Illinois) and "for the settlement of an English colony there."[77] For charter members of the Illinois Company, Governor Franklin recruited the three partners of the Philadelphia mercantile firm Baynton, Wharton, and Morgan, as well as George Croghan and, most impressively, Sir William Johnson. He even sought General Gage's support, but the commander in chief demurred. In London, Benjamin Franklin began lobbying at Whitehall and Westminster for support. Father and son corresponded faithfully during the negotiations, forging a juggernaut poised to rip up the borderland.[78]

In the summer of 1766, the Franklins and their allies began circulating "Reasons for Establishing a British Colony at the Illinois." The proposal began by arguing that the region's French and Indian inhabitants had squandered the economic possibilities of the land. "But were the lands on the Mississippi well settled," then tobacco, rice, indigo, hemp, flax, and silk could be grown there. "Reasons" added that a western colony would allow for "a more extensive and advantageous fur trade, with the numerous Indian nations," and create new markets for British manufactures. For these reasons, the Illinois Company requested that the British government purchase land from the Indians and erect a civil government "agreeable to the principles of an English constitution." The first settlements would need the protection of "two or three companies of light infantry, and one of light horse," but unlike troops currently on the borderland, British regulars in the Illinois colony would be supported by the inhabitants. The company reasoned that a western colony would obviate the expense of sending supplies over a long distance, claiming that locals would man militias, as generous land allotments to soldiers and veterans would be "a great encouragement to the colonists to enter into the military service on any future occasion." Without mentioning quarters, the Franklins' proposal for an Illinois colony solved the financial dilemma of defending the backcountry.[79]

The Illinois Company was not the only group to propose settling the borderland. Phineas Lyman, a Connecticut native who led provincial forces in the 1762 assault on Havana, also called for a western colony. Lyman spoke for thousands of veterans like himself who had "left very profitable professions, and other beneficial branches of business" to fight for king and country but now were destitute. Accordingly, Lyman proposed a colony at Natchez on the Mississippi River for veterans. The details of Lyman's plan were not much different from those of the Franklins', although Lyman's plan was more explicit about the colony's military advantages. Lyman observed that a western colony would alleviate the financial pressures of defense, predicting that should interracial violence escalate in Lower Louisiana, the Natchez colonists would join the army and supply the troops. Consequently, "a war on our part might from such settlement be carried on with a quarter part of the cost and expense, as from the English colonies already settled." Ever the clever politician, Benjamin Franklin did not fret about Lyman's proposal, but allied with his fellow colonist. Soon, both men were lobbying for colonies at Illinois and Natchez.[80]

Indeed, Franklin's challenge was not competitors, but disorder at Whitehall. The western proposals coincided with the formation of the Chatham ministry, which meant a shuffling of cabinet positions and uncertainty over leadership for American affairs. In July 1766, Sir William Johnson dispatched a letter to Secretary of State for the Southern Department Henry Seymour Conway advocating for a colony in Illinois. "The scheme appears to me so reasonable and so well calculated for the mutual interests of Great Britain and its colonies," Johnson informed Conway, that he fully supported the plan to "tend to the security of our southern frontiers, and enhance the public revenue."[81] By the time Johnson's letter made it to London, however, William Petty, the second Earl of Shelburne, had replaced Conway as secretary of state. Fortunately, Benjamin Franklin was on hand to guide Johnson's letter to Shelburne and lobby the new secretary on the benefits of an Illinois colony. At first, Shelburne offered a tepid response. The secretary "said it appeared to him a reasonable scheme," Franklin informed his son, "but he found it did not quadrate with the sentiments of the people here" and set it aside. In response, Franklin flooded Shelburne with letters and maps to prove the wisdom of colonizing the backcountry. Although Shelburne found such evidence persuasive, he "intimated that every new proposed expense for America would meet with great difficulty here." In late 1766, Chancellor of the Exchequer Charles Townshend was pushing Parliament for new colonial taxes. With a consensus that America should generate revenue, London had little interest in funding western colonies.[82]

While Franklin and Lyman prepared their responses, including how new colonies would actually save Britain money by shifting quartering expenses to the colonists, some traders put forth an even more radical plan for ending the borderland. A group of Canadians who styled themselves the Committee of Merchants for American Affairs requested that "trade with the Indians, should be free and open to all His Majesty's subjects without exception." The committee argued that Whitehall's previous efforts to restrict trade west of the Appalachians to licensed traders had stalled commerce with Native Americans. As a result, foreign traders from St. Louis and New Orleans had begun to encroach on British territory. To remedy the situation, the merchants advocated allowing any trader to venture into the region and winter in Indian villages. The scheme had the advantage of being cheap, as it privatized the region's defense. The committee made no appeal for soldiers, leaving it to traders who entered the backcountry to defend themselves.[83]

For the next year, all proposals for new colonies stalled as Charles Townshend finalized the Townshend Acts and pushed the New York Restraining Act through Parliament. Nevertheless, Benjamin Franklin continued to lobby the cabinet. In August 1767, Franklin informed his son that "the secretaries appeared finally to be fully convinced" of his plan for Illinois.[84] Sure enough, when Charles Townshend died the following month, the Earl of Shelburne introduced a plan for planting western colonies.[85] The secretary of state's plan combined many of the ideas proposed by the Franklins, Phineas Lyman, and the Committee of Merchants. In a series of presentations to the cabinet and the Board of Trade, Shelburne rejected the notion that the North American interior should be a borderland. He called for canceling the Plan of 1764 and returning control of Indian commerce to the American colonies. The secretary also dismissed the Proclamation of 1763 as "little less than an attempt to set limits on the increase of our people and the extension of our dominions," and called for the creation of colonies at Detroit and in Illinois. Rather than provoking violence, Shelburne predicted that settlements would lead to peace through the submission of the Native Americans. "It is well known that Indians do not like to be surrounded by Europeans," he opined, concluding that colonies would induce the tribes "to retire westward" or to "become what the Americans term domestic, and consequently dependent."[86]

Shelburne's plan reduced costs by shifting quartering costs onto the western colonists. He claimed that the Indian superintendence system had placed heavy burdens on British taxpayers in the form "of the army as well as the keeping up of the forts," but the settlements would have their own militias and provincial armies, thus reducing the need for regulars. British troops would continue to maintain order in the region from forts at Niagara, Michilimackinac, Pittsburgh, and Natchez. However, the cost of "raising provisions of all sorts to supply such interior garrisons" would fall on the new colonies, and their proximity to the forts would lessen the price "of transporting provisions as well as stores to supply the garrisons." Shelburne never mentioned the Quartering Act, but his plan acknowledged the failure of the law in the borderland and suggested that the law could work if the backcountry was settled like the old colonies.[87]

Shelburne's proposal immediately attracted a number of supporters. A group of North American merchants in London praised the idea of returning the Indian trade to the colonies, advising the Board of Trade that such a measure would "tend greatly to secure the British dominions" and "increase the consumption of British manufactures."[88] In late November 1767, Benjamin Franklin informed his son that an Illinois colony was imminent. Shelburne had laid his plan "before the king in council," informing His Majesty that it had the backing of "the best authorities for anything that related to America," including Franklin.[89] As the proponents waited anxiously, King George III referred plans for "the establishment of new governments on the Ohio, Mississippi, and at Detroit" to the Board of Trade. The board took no immediate action, but Franklin's conversations with its members made him cautiously optimistic. Meanwhile, Shelburne ordered General Gage to prepare to redeploy the North American Establishment to the new western colonies.[90]

But the secretary of state had gotten ahead of himself. As the Board of Trade weighed Shelburne's plans, disorder once again overtook Whitehall. Into a new power vacuum, voices opposed to western colonies emerged and soon became dominant. When Shelburne lost control of the American colonies in early 1768, he was replaced by new ministers who sought to remove the British army and convert the backcountry from a borderland into an Indian country.

Plans to Create an Indian Country

Back in New York, Sir William Johnson began to get cold feet about colonizing the North American interior. When the northern superintendent negotiated a treaty with Pontiac at Fort Ontario in the summer of 1766, he believed that white colonists and Native Americans could share the borderland. Like other imperial planners, Johnson sought to Christianize the Indians and to profit from the sale of western lands; for both reasons, he had signed onto the Illinois Company. But escalating violence in the backcountry had turned Johnson against maintaining a borderland. In June 1767, George Croghan reported a meeting at Fort Pitt in which Shawnee delegates complained of the invasion of their homeland. The Shawnees asserted "that the country westward of the Allegany Mountains was their property" and appealed to Johnson to remove "the white people" who "had settled on it and drove the wild game out of that part of their country."[91] Stories like these deeply troubled Johnson, who believed that the indigenous peoples were entitled to their lands and should be free from colonial exploitation. Accordingly, Johnson began promoting the idea that the lands west of the Appalachians should be left to Native Americans alone.[92]

Sir William Johnson's opposition to colonization was shared by British military leaders. The War Department worried that new colonies would increase violence in the West, and it rejected any plan that might trap British soldiers in the crossfire. General Gage agreed, urging caution at Whitehall, even as the calls for colonization grew louder. Once again, the approach to the backcountry centered on quarters. Although creating new colonies would generate revenue to support the British regulars, advocates for devolving control of the interior to Native Americans argued that removing all troops from the region would be even cheaper. These men agreed with Franklin that the borderland was not working, but they promoted the opposite solution: an Indian country.

In September 1767, Sir William Johnson dispatched a lengthy "Review of the Progressive State of the Trade, Politics, and Proceedings of the Indians in the Northern Department" to Whitehall. A personal as much as a professional statement, the "Review" reflected on his thirty years on the borderland, including how relations between American colonists and Indians had changed since the fall of Montréal. Johnson lambasted the colonies and their "frontier inhabitants" who "attacked, robbed, and murdered sundry Indians of good character." He also assailed traders who entered Indian villages, and blamed them for the "loss of trade, robbery, murder of traders, and frequent general ruptures." Ultimately, Johnson turned to the spatial division that had given rise to these conditions, excoriating the Proclamation of 1763 and the Plan of 1764. A porous border had permitted white traders to invade Indian villages and white settlers to bring war to the region. A firm boundary was needed to separate British North America into two places: a European American coast and a Native American interior.[93]

The idea of a border line was not new. The Proclamation of 1763 had proposed a western boundary, and the Plan of 1764 had assumed it. But actually marking such a line across North America was a daunting project that required negotiating treaties with dozens of indigenous nations, the expense and complexity of which led Whitehall to put it off. As violence escalated, the boundary line increased in popularity, especially with Native Americans. But colonizers like Benjamin Franklin and the Earl of Shelburne worked to avoid a permanent boundary, knowing that it would complicate their plans for western colonies. Shelburne insisted that it was the colonists' responsibility to pay for the border, perhaps hoping that American parsimony would stymie the project. However, South Carolina proved Shelburne wrong by negotiating a boundary line with the Cherokees, and the other southern colonies followed suit.[94]

Long before Johnson's "Review" arrived in London, Viscount Barrington, the secretary at war, had advocated leaving the backcountry to the Indians. In October 1765, Barrington concluded that if the Proclamation of 1763 was right, then "the maintenance of forts to the westward of the line must be wrong." Barrington cared little for the fate of Native Americans; rather, he worried about the cost of the North American Establishment, opining that the need to provide quarters would "no longer exist, if the forts were demolished." Accordingly, the secretary at war advocated withdrawing all British troops from the interior and concentrating them "in any convenient place near the sea."[95] Barrington elaborated on these observations in a report to the king and cabinet in which he argued that an extensive network of western forts was unnecessary for either Indian trade or security, claiming that the presence of British soldiers only enraged Native Americans. Barrington then repeated an argument that London found particularly galling: the colonists benefited from the presence of British regulars, but made no effort to supply them. Drawing attention to the defiance of the Quartering Act in regard to the "forts in the province of South Carolina," Barrington noted that "since we have garrisoned them, the assembly has refused to pay even the expense of transporting provisions thither." He concluded that the only solution was to pull regulars from the backcountry and separate Indian lands from the American colonies.[96]

Barrington's idea of leaving the West to Native Americans was warmly received by Commander in Chief Thomas Gage. Like Johnson, Gage initially had been attracted to the backcountry as an opportunity to build a patrimony for his growing family. He even sought Johnson's advice "about purchasing of the Indians" lands in the West, "perhaps on the Ohio," but he rejected Franklin's Illinois scheme and later secured lands in Nova Scotia and on the Caribbean island of Montserrat.[97] Gage's unending quest for quarters also changed his opinion of western colonies. He welcomed Barrington's idea of removing troops to the coast and recommended that they be barracked at New York, Philadelphia, and Boston's Castle Island. As Barrington made his case to the cabinet, Gage became increasingly strident in his communications with Shelburne. In April 1767, the general sharply criticized the secretary's decision to station troops in western forts by citing South Carolina's refusal to defray "the expense of the transportation of provisions and stores to the forts." It was much wiser to relocate all regulars to the old colonies, Gage argued, adding that "the Crown will save the expense of quartering" by removing troops from the backcountry.[98]

As long as the Earl of Shelburne retained his grip on the cabinet, the hope of western colonies remained alive. Then the British government shuffled again. As the Chatham ministry entered its second year without a prime minister, power passed to the first lord of the treasury and leader of the House of Lords, Augustus FitzRoy, the third Duke of Grafton. Grafton brought energy and a new direction to the cabinet, becoming the de facto prime minister in late 1767, although the Earl of Chatham formally retained the position for another year. Inheriting a chorus of complaints about the Townshend Acts and violence on the borderland, Grafton made colonial affairs a top priority. In a rebuke of Shelburne, he transferred control of America from the secretary of state for the southern department to a new cabinet member: the secretary of state for the colonies. Consequently the fate of the borderland fell to a man firmly opposed to western colonies: Will Hills, the first Earl of Hillsborough.[99]

In January 1768, King George III named the Earl of Hillsborough secretary of state for the colonies and first lord of trade. The import of Hillsborough's ascent was immediately apparent to all. Benjamin Franklin greeted the change grimly. "The purpose of settling the new colonies seems at present to be dropped," he lamented to his son, explaining that "there seems rather to be an inclination to abandon the posts in the backcountry as more expensive than useful."[100] Viscount Barrington was far more optimistic, informing Gage that "we shall soon have that decision concerning the disposition of the troops under your command, which I have long wished, and began to despair of."[101] Two months later, Hillsborough dispatched his first orders to Gage, commenting on the finer points of Bermuda's interpretation of the Quartering Act. It was clear that the new secretary intended to take a more active role in American affairs than Shelburne had.[102]

In March 1768, the Board of Trade under Hillsborough's direction voted to transform the borderland into an Indian country. The board reiterated its commitment to the Indian superintendence system of the Plan of 1764 and ordered that the border line be completed. It voted to close all forts west of the Appalachian Mountains, except Niagara, Detroit, and Michilimackinac, retained primarily to aid the Royal Navy on the Great Lakes. "We trust that the expense of the present disposition of troops for Indian purposes, may be reduced," the board announced, effectively repeating Gage's earlier observation that the best way to enforce the Quartering Act was to station the troops in places where it could be implemented. Hillsborough's board extinguished the last hopes for western colonies, announcing that it would maintain the long-standing "policy of this kingdom to confine her settlements as much as possible to the sea coast." The board even dismissed the arguments that colonies could be useful for supplying western forts, concluding that "French inhabitants in the neighborhood of the [Great] Lakes" were "sufficient to furnish with provisions whatever posts may be necessary."[103]

News of the Board of Trade's decision reached New York in early June 1768, and before the end of the month Gage had sent orders to governors and commanding officers to prepare for redeployment. The Hudson River Valley and Lake Champlain were to be emptied of troops, leaving the nearly four hundred miles between New York City and Montréal undefended for the first time in over a century. In Pennsylvania, all forts west of the Susquehanna River were to be closed, as were the installations in Illinois.[104] Gage ordered Captain Füser "to withdraw the garrisons in South Carolina and Georgia," thus vacating Forts Prince George and Charlotte, as well as Charleston, Augusta, and Frederica.[105] No longer would General Gage need to pressure the colonies to provide transportation costs. The creation of Indian territory must have given Gage a sense of relief, as violence in the backcountry seemed to be increasing in the spring of 1768. The general's letters to Whitehall contained new stories of colonists murdering Indians and vice versa, while Fort de Chartres had become a target amid simmering interracial tensions.[106]

Without British regulars, the inhabitants of the borderland were left to their own devices. Although Hillsborough had advocated retaining the Indian superintendence system in its entirety, the prospect of cutting costs won out, and the Board of Trade opted to devolve the Indian trade to the American colonies. Gage carried out these orders by informing governors that it was their responsibility to take over abandoned forts and to appoint new "officers to superintend the trade."[107] Without British soldiers, the colonies were now responsible for the safety of traders who ventured into Indian country. Likewise, French settlers at Detroit, Cahokia, and Kaskaskia were left to defend themselves, although the practicality of this was uncertain. Colonists in Illinois refused to take up arms against Native Americans, while the Detroit militia removed "vagabond French settlers from among the Indians."[108] The defenselessness of the white inhabitants even led Sir William Johnson to ponder employing friendly Indians for colonial security. "Should the service require the attendance of the Indians at any place on the continent," Johnson suggested the commissioning of Native American armies, provided "that the province will defray their expenses." This curious proposal mimicked the Quartering Act, although no one took it seriously.[109]

The final step toward decolonizing the borderland was the completion of a boundary line. Hillsborough made this a top priority, and the Indian superintendents set to work finishing what the colonists had begun. In the fall of 1768, Johnson hosted a massive conference at Fort Stanwix, an obscure outpost midway between Johnstown and Lake Ontario. Three thousand Native Americans attended, led by at least twenty-seven chiefs of the Haudenosaunees, Shawnees, Lenapes, and Mingos. The colonies of New York, New Jersey, Pennsylvania, and Virginia sent delegates, including Governor William Franklin; George Croghan also attended, as did Samuel Wharton of Baynton, Wharton, and Morgan. For two weeks, the emissaries exchanged wampum belts and made official proclamations while they sought to repair the damage caused by bad-faith treaties and war. Negotiations continued in public and private, with Johnson at the center of it all. On November 5, 1768, the attendees inked the Treaty of Fort Stanwix, drawing a line between the colonial coast and the Indian interior.[110]

Yet defining the borderland was never a simple matter. At Fort Stanwix, the powerful Haudenosaunee ceded lands in western Pennsylvania and south of the Ohio River in exchange for £10,000 in cash and goods. However, as the French had done in the Treaty of Paris three years earlier, the Haudenosaunee issued a title to lands they did not control. The inhabitants of the region were outraged. The Shawnees refused to accept the loss of their lands in present-day Kentucky, while the Cherokees noted that they had negotiated a less-expansive boundary with Southern superintendent John Stuart in the Treaty of Hard Labor a month earlier. Additional negotiations proceeded two years later with the Treaty of Lochaber, although contradictory borders left it unclear whether the region between the Ohio and Cumberland Rivers was open to white settlement. Around the same time, the boundary of West Florida pushed north, increasing the importance of Forts Tombecbe, Apalachicola, and Bute. Even when creating an Indian country, the borderland proved remarkably persistent.[111]

Persistence of the Borderland

In December 1768, General Gage dispatched a letter to Sir William Johnson, acknowledging the successful conclusion of the Treaty of Fort Stanwix. The commander in chief had been occupied with events in Boston, but he could not let the moment pass by without sending felicitations to the northern superintendent. "I congratulate you very sincerely," Gage wrote, that "you have at length settled" the border in a manner "to your satisfaction and I doubt not equally satisfactory to the Indians." With the North American interior now officially Indian territory, both Gage and Johnson believed that peace would follow. But it was not so easy to erase a borderland. Just because representatives of the Crown and delegates from Native American nations had drawn a boundary did not mean that the American colonists were going to respect it. White traders and settlers continued to pour across the Appalachian Mountains, some peaceful and some not. The backcountry remained a borderland.[112]

The persistence of the borderland meant a persistence of military geography. As had been true before 1754, the fear of continued conflict discouraged the removal of forts and soldiers. However, in the intervening fifteen years, the responsibility for the backcountry had shifted from provincial forces to

British regulars; thus as long as the borderland persisted, the white inhabitants of the region demanded redcoats. This complicated and ultimately
blocked the army's plan to evacuate the region. It also meant that quarters
remained a continued challenge. Having forbidden western colonies, Britain
could not expect backcountry settlers to supply troops, while the consolidation of the North American Establishment ended efforts to elicit funds for
transportation. The effect was the weakening of the Quartering Act and
greater conflict between the British army and American colonists.

In 1767, parts of six regiments were scattered across the backcountry,
stationed at Forts Pitt and de Chartres as well as a number of small installations around the Great Lakes and across the southeastern interior. As Gage
prepared to remove nearly all these troops, Secretary at War Barrington
complicated matters by insisting on the demilitarization of the northern and
southern peripheries as well. The North American interior was not the only
region dotted with British soldiers: three regiments occupied eight outposts
in Newfoundland and Nova Scotia, and another three were stationed at cities
and coastal forts in South Carolina, Georgia, the Floridas, Bermuda, and the
Bahamas. Like the western troops, these peripheral forces invited conflict
with indigenous people and cost the British treasury large sums for quarters.
Accordingly, Barrington called for not only the removal of troops from the
West, but the consolidation of all northern troops at Halifax and all southern forces at St. Augustine. The Earl of Hillsborough endorsed Barrington's
plan, and soon Gage prepared for a colossal reordering of the North American Establishment.[113]

Expanding the number of places affected by the removal of troops only
increased the number of opponents. Complaints poured in from the northern and southern peripheries, with civilian leaders claiming that Whitehall's
plan threatened to turn their colonies into an Indian territory like the region
west of the Appalachians. The assembly and council of West Florida took
its case directly to the monarch. "We had the most promising prospect of
becoming a happy and flourishing province," the lawmakers informed King
George III, but with the loss of the regulars, "our lives and properties will be
exposed to the ravages and insults of the Indians who surround us." Nova
Scotia governor Lord William Campbell made a similar appeal to Hillsborough: "The outposts of this province" were "fixed as a shelter and retreat for
the inhabitants settled upon the frontiers," but if the troops were withdrawn
from the forts, then the settlements "may be either destroyed or possessed
by the savages."[114] Gage dismissed such complaints as hyperbole, especially
those coming from Nova Scotia. "There is nothing now for them to fear
but from Indians," he informed Hillsborough, adding that the Mi'kmaq "are

quiet and will remain so, if not provoked by bad usage to be otherwise." From Gage's perspective, all of North America should be left to the Native Americans except for the settlements along the Atlantic coast.[115]

In the summer of 1768, British troops across North America packed up and marched east. The colonists greeted the news with astonishment. South Carolina's Governor William Bull II expressed disbelief to Hillsborough as the troops withdrew from the southern colonies, especially since "Fort Charlotte had so lately [been] built of stone, and Fort Prince George lately repaired at the expense of this province."[116] In New England, colonists connected the demilitarization of the borderland with the recent deployment of four regiments to Boston. Claiming that the movement of troops had led to the loss of human life and cattle across the continent's periphery, Boston newspapers expressed bewilderment that Whitehall would remove "troops from a frontier province" and station them in the East. Some Americans viewed the removal of troops as imperial mismanagement, but others suspected more sinister motives. As long as four-fifths of the North American Establishment remained in the new colonies and the backcountry, the American colonists supported the British army as an effective tool to keep the Québécois and Indians in line. However, as nine regiments amassed at Halifax, St. Augustine, and the cities of the middle colonies, some Americans began to wonder if they were the ones being policed.[117]

There were other problems as well. As Gage prepared to consolidate the northern troops, he worried "that all the old barracks at Halifax must not only be repaired, but that new one[s] must be built."[118] His insight proved correct, as the removal of troops from rural Nova Scotia crammed a thousand men into the existing quarters in Halifax.[119] The situation in St. Augustine was worse. Since the British army first occupied East Florida in 1764, insufficient barracks had led to quartering "in huts, or in old houses upon sufferance."[120] Four years later, billeting persisted, such that when Gage placed two regiments in St. Augustine, the soldiers had to be "encamped in very old and much wore out tents" on the edge of town.[121] The result was delays to removal and the persistent suffering of soldiers. A plan to convert an abandoned Franciscan monastery into barracks in St. Augustine did not begin until January 1769 (figure 4.3), while new barracks in Halifax were not completed until the following Christmas. The army also had to contend with a lack of supplies. In a replay of events in Québec in 1765, a storekeeper in St. Augustine refused to provide the troops with "firing, candles, and quarters" because he claimed the "Act of Parliament for quartering the troops in America" made such matters Gage's responsibility.[122] As a result, troops in Halifax and St. Augustine faced substandard living conditions. Although

FIGURE 4.3. St. Francis Barracks at St. Augustine. William Henry Jackson, photographer, *United States Marine Barracks* (Detroit: Detroit Publishing Co., ca. 1880–1897). Library of Congress, Prints and Photographs Division, LC-DIG-det-4a26953 (digital file from original).

the consolidation of the British army should have promoted discipline and military readiness, in fact it achieved the opposite.

In effect, Whitehall made a decision for the army on the basis of saving money, without realizing that this would produce new expenses. The removal of troops from the periphery required the construction of new barracks in Halifax and St. Augustine. Moreover, the reordering of the North American Establishment closed several forts that the colonists had supported. South Carolina may have stubbornly refused to transport supplies, but it had kept its backcountry forts in good repair. Once British soldiers withdrew from Forts Charlotte and Prince George, the colony left the posts to molder. Similarly, South Carolina, Georgia, and Bermuda had all funded supplies for troops stationed in settled areas, but the removal of regulars from Charleston, Frederica, and the islands meant that even these small remittances disappeared. The result was the denigration of British authority. For the better part of two years, Gage had tussled with Georgia and Bermuda to supply regulars, ultimately threatening to remove the troops if the legislatures would not comply with the Quartering Act. It was poor coincidence that the month that this threat produced results was the very same month that Hillsborough ordered forts in Georgia and Bermuda shuttered.[123]

It also proved impossible to demilitarize the continent as drastically as Barrington had hoped. Although Gage could dismiss complaints from Nova Scotia, it was harder to ignore West Florida. The nascent colony attracted many well-connected investors who cited a growing number of "French and Spaniards on the Mississippi" as a cause for retaining at least one regiment at Pensacola. This appeal for continental security, along with the high status of the petitioners, forced Hillsborough to change his mind and Gage to agree.[124] However, this meant the retention of an installation unprepared to accommodate soldiers. According to West Florida's Governor Elias Durnford, Pensacola provided "miserable accommodations for brave men": no proper quarters, only small structures that Durnford dismissed as "Negro huts."[125] Again, it was up to the army to build barracks, something that Gage estimated would cost more than £13,000 New York currency.[126]

When combined, the lack of barracks along with complaints from powerful men postponed indefinitely the creation of Indian country. In July 1769, the Earl of Hillsborough effectively admitted defeat. Many at Whitehall and Westminster had a change of heart about abandoning the region to Native Americans, so the secretary of state ordered the commander in chief to suspend removal. "I wish it was in my power," Hillsborough wrote Gage, "to transmit to you His Majesty's final commands, in respect to the posts in the Illinois Country and upon the Ohio," but it was not.[127] Instead, Fort de Chartres was retained, and soon Gage was negotiating contracts with trading firms to supply troops stationed there. Retaining Fort de Chartres forced Gage to keep open Fort Pitt and Vincennes to maintain communication and supply lines to it. Ultimately, the British army ended up closing more forts in the East than the West, and the ones that remained were starved for funds and began to decompose. "The works and barracks are all gone to wreck," reported one observer of Fort Pitt, who could have said the same thing about the other outposts.[128]

As a result, the backcountry remained a borderland. In addition to British soldiers, white settlers and traders continued to traipse west. Although the colonies took control of the Indian trade, their governments proved no more able at regulating commerce than Sir William Johnson and his agents had been. Johnson heard from Detroit "that the English and the French go trading wherever they please." Some continued to request a license, but if "it is refused, they proceed just the same and do a good business." Increasingly, the traders settled on the borderland, with even licensed traders demanding to bring their wives. This enraged Native Americans, and the violence continued.[129] In October 1768, Gage reported that a group of white hunters "had been attacked by a party of Indians of the Wabash, who killed most of them" and scalped at least nine. Upon investigation, Gage learned that "the Indians were not so much to blame, as the hunters" who were seeking "bear, beaver, deer, and other skins" on Indian lands. Retaliations by settlers and traders followed.[130] As the competition for trade intensified, Native Americans began to fight among themselves and catch innocents in their crossfire. "The western Indians going to war against the Cherokees, seem to spare neither white nor red people who fall in their way," Gage lamented to Johnson. But the northern superintendent had no solutions. By late 1769, Johnson had begun to fear that an all-out war in the West was imminent.[131]

The persistence of the borderland confused other senses of place as well. The desire to treat the British Empire as one place had informed both proponents of colonizing the backcountry and advocates for leaving it all to the Native Americans, the former wanting to include the region in a unitary empire and the latter wanting to exclude it. But the retention of a nebulous borderland left it unclear if the British constitution applied west of the Appalachians. Similarly, the distinction between civilian and martial was murky on the borderland. As interracial violence increased, Gage confined British regulars to barracks, refusing to allow them to protect either settlers or Native Americans. Instead, he encouraged locals to remove "vagabond French and Canadians settled in the Indian nations," although this only encouraged militias to destroy the homes of white settlers and resulted in retaliatory violence.[132] Even the status of the house was unclear. In June 1769, an ensign at Fort de Chartres reported how "a party of the Kickapoos broke into a house in this village; surprised a soldier and his wife in bed, scalped both and got off without the least hurt." In sum, the Quartering Act's original principles of protecting domestic privacy, isolating military power, and uniting the empire failed in the borderland.[133]

The Borderland

The growing violence on the borderland ultimately consumed Pontiac as well. After he made peace with Sir William Johnson in the summer of 1766, the Odawa warrior's reputation among Native Americans declined sharply. Two years later, Pontiac's standing approached ignominy as he was turned out of his village in Ohio and had to join a hunting party on the Wabash River to pay off his debts. After a scuffle with some Illinois Indians, during which he stabbed Chief Makachinga, Pontiac was a marked man. In April 1769, a young warrior clubbed the once great leader and left him to die in the streets of Cahokia. Thomas Gage greeted the news of Pontiac's death somberly. Writing to Johnson, Gage reflected on the growing violence in the backcountry, which had resulted in "several murders committed on Indians as well as white people, among others the famous Pontiac was killed." Unlike before, however, the commander in chief had no solution for the problem. Despite the best efforts of Benjamin Franklin, the Earl of Shelburne, Sir

William Johnson, and the Earl of Hillsborough, the North American interior would be neither colonized nor left to indigenous populations. It was a borderland and would remain so.[134]

The persistence of the borderland meant the persistence of an expansive military geography in the backcountry. Six years after Pontiac's War, the segregation of civilian and martial places continued to elude soldiers, settlers, and indigenous peoples of the Appalachian Mountains and beyond. The constitutional principles of the Quartering Act should have rectified this, but General Gage's decision to forgo the law in the West impeded this possibility. Likewise, plans to colonize the backcountry or leave it to the Indians would have offered a definitive response to the question of where do soldiers belong, but the failure of both plans prevented this. By 1769, however, British military power on the borderland had become a rhetorical devise used by Americans to protest the presence of British soldiers in the coastal cities like Boston. If the interracial violence of the backcountry required the presence of the British army, then the civilized tranquility of the old colonies made the redcoats unwelcome. As Americans saw the borderland as a place of war, they began to reimagine their cities and towns as places of peace.

As a place, the borderland has long fascinated historians, although the framing devices have changed with the times. For most of the nineteenth century, the region was labeled a "frontier," as historians focused on how interactions with rugged nature and savage inhabitants affected European Americans. By the 1930s, historians introduced the term "borderland" to counter such an ethnocentric view, and the similar "middle ground" emerged in the 1990s. Instead of only seeing places like the backcountry for their effects on white colonists, historians asked how natives and newcomers shared the place. Within the last generation, historians have begun exploring "Indian empires," insisting that in places like the Great Lakes in the eighteenth century, it was indigenous groups like the Odawa that held the reins of power, subjugating Europeans and other Indians. Quartering on the borderland in the 1760s suggests that these different framing devices are not mutually exclusive but existed as a series of options for imperial planners, colonial invaders, and Native American warriors.[135]

CHAPTER 5

Cities and Towns

Accommodation and Eviction of the British Army

Joseph Fox made quartering possible in Philadelphia. Born in 1709 to modest means, he apprenticed to a wealthy carpenter who died a bachelor and left him his estate. Fox went on to become a member of the Carpenters' Company and was chosen master of the company in 1763, later directing the construction of Carpenters' Hall. Fox was also a notable politician, serving as city commissioner, assemblyman, and Speaker of the Pennsylvania House of Representatives. Such positions put him at the center of Philadelphia politics. In 1765, the Pennsylvania assembly voted to send Fox to the Stamp Act Congress, and five years later he chaired the meeting that declared "the claim of Parliament to tax the colonies . . . is subversive of the constitutional rights of the colonies." In effect, Fox was a town father.[1]

Joseph Fox was also Philadelphia's barrack master. During the French and Indian War, Fox oversaw the construction of permanent quarters in the Northern Liberties, no doubt because of his carpentry expertise. For the next twenty years, Fox maintained the structure, collecting £60 a year "to do and perform every matter and thing which may be requisite to the comfortable accommodation of His Majesty's troops." When the Wechquetank Indians sought shelter in the Philadelphia Barracks, Fox procured blankets for them, and when the Quartering Act made the colonists responsible for supplying soldiers, he provided "firewood, candles, vinegar, small beer, bedding, etc."

Fox's diligence earned the praise of Major Isaac Hamilton, who asserted that "no troops have been better supplied, nor any applications from command-ing officers more politely attended to, than here."[2]

As both town father and barrack master, Fox bridged the civilian and martial demands of Philadelphia. He quartered the troops not out of finan-cial desperation or blind allegiance to British authority, but civic duty. In so doing, he made it possible for soldiers and colonists to share the city. Nor was he alone. In New York, Elizabeth, Perth Amboy, New Brunswick, and Charleston, local barrack masters successfully accommodated and supplied regulars.[3] The experience of Fox speaks to a larger truth often lost in histories of the American Revolution: before the war, most Americans had learned to live with British troops. This was made possible by barrack masters who procured supplies, night watchmen who corralled disorderly soldiers, and judges who meted out punishment. These local leaders mitigated the worst excesses of errant soldiers and helped integrate the British regulars into the city. Some cities even came to look on the troops as a positive good. Between 1766 and 1768, British soldiers were such an unremarkable part of American cities that few anticipated how poorly things would go when British troops garrisoned Boston.

The history of quarters is an urban history. The majority of the North American Establishment was concentrated in the cities and towns. In the old colonies, troops abided by the Quartering Act. In New York, Philadel-phia, Charleston, and the towns of New Jersey, soldiers respected domestic privacy, colonists provided supplies, and civilian authorities retained control. In the new colonies, the American Mutiny Act had no effect, so the army dominated. In Québec, Montréal, Halifax, St. Augustine, and Pensacola, the soldiers became integral to life, even policing civilians. Until 1768, Brit-ish regulars were tolerated if not welcomed in the communities of British North America. However, when four regiments landed in Boston, the army was marked as a hostile invader. Soldiers in Boston poisoned the colonists against British military power, which in turn led New York and South Caro-lina to question the presence of troops in their cities. Once violence broke out between soldiers and civilians, the Quartering Act crumbled as the law became a hated symbol of British tyranny.

Quartering British troops in American cities and towns reveals a discourse of military geography. In the old colonies before 1768, soldiers and civil-ians shared cities because civic leaders firmly segregated civilian and martial spaces. In New York, soldiers stayed out of houses, and the colonists stayed out of the barracks; conflict occurred only in the in-between places like streets and commons. By contrast, the new colonies did not sharply divide martial and civilian places; rather, a lack of barracks forced troops into houses, and the dominance of the army prevented civilian resistance. Neat divisions of civilian and martial spaces also eluded Boston, in part because of a lack of barracks in the city. As opponents of the troops publicized stories of troops invading homes and attacking women, some Bostonians began to imagine the city as a wholly civilian place completely devoid of military power.

As a place, the city has been thoroughly examined by historians and geographers. This is true even of Revolutionary America, where only four cities contained more than ten thousand people, and the largest of these (Philadelphia) had fewer than thirty thousand inhabitants.[4] Although such places do not comport with modern expectations of urban space, historians have argued persuasively that the city was key to the coming of the American Revolution. The Stamp Act riots originated in the colonial capitals, as did the nonimportation agreements, and it was in Boston, New York, Philadelphia, and Charleston that independence was nurtured. The British army plays a key role in these histories, as it was in the cities that the most violent confrontations between soldiers and civilians occurred: the so-called Battle of Golden Hill and the Boston Massacre. Regardless of size, the cities and towns of British North America were intimate places where British military power was most keenly felt. Historians have not appreciated the extent of military geography in the late colonial community or how quarters became an opportunity for the colonists to debate not only the British army but the meaning of the city as a place.[5]

Sharing Urban Spaces in the Old Colonies

In May 1766, a group of New Yorkers known as the Sons of Liberty placed a liberty pole on the city common, like the one illustrated in figure 5.1. News of Parliament's repeal of the Stamp Act recently had arrived, and the Sons celebrated the occasion by erecting a large pine mast, topped with a banner proclaiming "Liberty." Across the Fields stood New York's Upper Barracks, which was then occupied by the 28th Regiment of Foot. For three months, British soldiers drilled beneath the liberty pole without incident. But then, one day in August, some soldiers cut down the mast. The response was a series of confrontations that came to be known as the Liberty Pole Riot of 1766. Incensed colonists hurled bricks at the troops, causing the soldiers to draw their bayonets, but when the officers ordered the troops to quarters, New Yorkers "surrounded the barracks, and vented so much abuse."[6] For the next week, the people would not allow the army onto the Fields, such that when the 28th stood for review in front of the Upper Barracks, colonists were

FIGURE 5.1.   Liberty pole in the Fields. Pierre Eugene du Simitiere, *Raising the Liberty Pole in New York City* (ca. 1770). Library Company of Philadelphia.

"pushing though the line, saying that the ground was theirs." The experience was especially disquieting to Major General Thomas Gage, who resided only a few blocks away. As Gage collected reports of "soldiers daily insulted in the streets" and handbills advocating the forcible removal of troops, he ordered the regiment out of the city. When the departing soldiers chopped down a second liberty pole, Gage had "two light field six pounders planted at each entrance of the barrack yard." It seemed that soldiers and civilians could not share New York City.[7]

The summer of 1766 was a particularly low point for martial-civilian relations in the old colonies. While colonists and regulars sparred over the liberty pole, the General Assembly of New York refused to comply with the Quartering Act. Yet even as General Gage worked to promulgate the statute, civilian and military officials sought to peacefully accommodate the presence of British regulars in American cities. In May and June 1766, the commander in chief moved three regiments of redcoats into the middle colonies, quartering them in the capital cities of New York and Philadelphia, as well as the New Jersey towns of Elizabeth, Perth Amboy, and New Brunswick; a company also barracked in Charleston. Although the specter of the Liberty Pole Riot never completely disappeared, from 1766 to 1768 British regulars became a part of the American urban landscape. City councils, night watchmen, and army officers, through the careful negotiation of urban spaces, achieved a

degree of harmony by segregating civilian from martial places and by policing the in-between areas. This peace complemented Gage's implementation
of the Quartering Act, as the ability of soldiers and colonists to share American cities and towns made supplying the British army more tolerable to the
inhabitants of the old colonies.

The cornerstone of peaceful urban quartering was good barracks. Barracks effectively kept troops out of the colonists' houses, and for this reason
the colonists paid handsomely to keep the permanent quarters habitable.
While the colonial assemblies bemoaned the cost of supplies required by
the Mutiny Act for America, they said little about the repairs to the barracks. New Jersey found £80 to add "weather-boarding" and windows to
the barracks in Perth Amboy; New York, Pennsylvania, and South Carolina
made similar improvements.[8] The urban barracks may even have been points
of pride for the colonists. Lawmakers in South Carolina listed repairs to
Charleston's barracks under charges "for the public buildings" alongside the
statehouse and a new exchange building—a telling choice, since they could
have classified them under "forts and garrisons."[9] Physically, the massive barracks were dominant features of the urban landscape like steepled churches,
colleges, and capitols. On a walk to the north side of Philadelphia, Sarah Eve
was stunned by the size of the city's "much better built" barracks. Tellingly,
she compared the Philadelphia Barracks favorably to "an ill-looking" hospital
nearby, suggesting that not only did she perceive the barracks to be a public
building, but she found it superior to others.[10]

While the barracks' exteriors were comparable to civilian edifices, the
interior was a decidedly martial place. Barracked at Philadelphia, Alexander
Mackraby observed that "the mess rooms at the barracks are something like
Circe's cave," a reference to a mythological dark place "out of which no
man ever returned upon two pegs."[11] Similarly, General Gage's orderly books
reveal the barracks to be the site of severe discipline. Inside New York's Upper
Barracks, court-martials for "disrespectful and opprobrious language" convened in the officers' guardroom; another room held privates awaiting trial.
Colonists rarely interfered with events inside the barracks, leaving it to the
army to police its own personnel without question.[12]

Around the barracks, a middle ground formed that soldiers and colonists
shared. Following the Liberty Pole Riot of August 1766, New York's Fields
became a liminal zone, neither wholly civilian nor martial. In July 1767, the
17th and 46th Regiments mustered across the Fields as they prepared to
return to England, sorting invalids and veterans, and seeking volunteers to
remain in America as part of the 31st. Five months later, the army marched
onto the Fields to auction off a dead captain's effects. Neither assemblage

provoked a reaction from the Sons of Liberty. The colonists also said nothing about the punishments that took place outside the barracks. When Private Richard Smith was found guilty at a court-martial, Gage ordered fifty lashes "to be inflicted by the drummers of this garrison on the parade at the Upper Barracks." New Yorkers also had no comment when the army executed Private Arthur Rogers on a beach just north of the city.[13]

But it was impossible to confine soldiers to barracks. The neighborhoods around the barracks were colored by the heavy presence of young and single uniformed men. Prostitution and hard drinking were rampant in the Northern Liberties, where the Philadelphia Barracks was a magnet for runaway servant women intent on selling their bodies in nearby public houses. In New York, the rapid development of the area around the Fields, including the construction of King's College and two glistening new churches, did little to discourage brothels and taverns serving the men of the Upper Barracks. Nor were the troops confined to nearby neighborhoods. Broadway in New York City was often thronged with troops marching from the Upper Barracks to Fort George and the Lower Barracks. In all the cities, idle troops wandered in search of entertainment. Like the area around barracks, streets and taverns generally were shared by soldiers and colonists.[14]

At times, the in-between spaces became the sites of soldier-civilian conflict. Typically, these skirmishes were fueled by alcohol. Alexander Mackraby remembered how he and four or five other "young officers of the regiment in barracks" would "drink as hard as we can" and then "sally forth" with a band of musicians to serenade the women of Philadelphia.[15] Similarly, the *New York Journal* reported nighttime noises at the Exchange on lower Broad Street. "It was soon discovered," the paper explained, "that the disturbance was made by two soldiers and two lewd women, who seemed to be much intoxicated with liquor."[16] Alcohol emboldened the soldiers and could fuel vandalism and violence. In July 1767, the men of the troublesome 28th Regiment wreaked havoc in Elizabeth, New Jersey, the night before they were due to ship out. "They first broke a window in the meeting house," reported the *New York Mercury*, and then "attacked the court house and jail." In response, the jailer rang the town bell, awakening the townspeople in the middle of the night. The inhabitants of Elizabeth faced off against "a body of soldiers, some with bayonets fixed," and "a fray ensued."[17]

In response to such incidents, civilian officials took action. As American cities lacked formal police companies in the 1760s, drunk and disorderly soldiers became the responsibility of the night watch, a civic body on which most male inhabitants were compelled to serve.[18] In New York in June 1766, the night watch intervened when a group of inebriated officers smashed streetlights and slashed an innkeeper. Overtaking the officers, the watchmen attempted to arrest the offending parties, and a melee ensued. When the watchmen detained one officer, another raised a force of a dozen privates to stage a jailbreak. City officials also intervened. Following an attempt to pull down a third liberty pole, New York mayor Whitehead Hicks implored General Gage to keep the troops barracked. "The inhabitants complain that the soldiers are out of their barracks in large numbers at unseasonable times of the night," the mayor informed the commander in chief, adding his dismay at how "last evening a number collected together with their arms, and many guns were discharged."[19] In an attempt to limit the influence of alcohol, several cities made it illegal for publicans to serve troops "between setting and rising of the sun," and most colonial legislatures ignored the Quartering Act's demand for alcohol.[20] Nocturnal carousing in Charleston prompted the South Carolina Commons House to order "a fence built in front of the barracks to prevent the soldiers from straggling at night."[21]

The army also policed the regulars as a means of maintaining placid relations with civilians. Officers countered inebriation by sanctioning the consumption of small beer, a concoction with so little alcohol that colonists routinely served it to their children. The 16th Regiment in New York ordered enough small beer to supply each man with half a gallon per day, while in Charleston, Captain Lewis Valentine Füser "established a brewhouse in the barracks."[22] The army also took steps to limit the movement of soldiers at delicate moments like elections. In March 1768, General Gage ordered "all the troops in garrison to keep close in their different quarters" when New Yorkers went to the polls, and forbade the soldiers "entirely any intercourse with the inhabitants during the said election."[23] The army also took responsibility when the troops turned violent against civilians. Following scuffles in New York, Gage sent patrols "to take up all drunken or disorderly soldiers" scattered about the city.[24]

At times, military and civilian authorities worked together to keep the peace. The Quartering Act empowered local justices of the peace to hear "every bill, plaint, action, or suit, against any person or persons, for any act, matter, or thing, to be acted or done in pursuance of this act."[25] Accordingly, when members of the 28th Regiment wrecked the jail in Elizabeth and induced a riot, local magistrates sought justice in New Jersey courts. Once an arrest warrant was issued, the commanding officer turned the suspects over to judges in Elizabeth, who tried the men and found them guilty. After paying damages of £25 and "asking pardon of the jail keeper," the men were allowed to return to their unit.[26]

While soldiers and colonists shared public spaces, civilian control of the home was unbreached. The Quartering Act prohibited British regulars from entering private houses without the owner's permission, and all evidence indicates that the army obeyed the law in the cities of the old colonies. To be sure, housekeepers could choose to billet soldiers, and some took in officers for cash. When the 26th Regiment marched into New Brunswick in July 1767, enlisted men were quartered in the town's barracks, while officers rented "private lodgings" upon paying "a shilling or eighteen pence a week over and above what the province allows them."[27] Alexander Graydon spent his youth living among officers billeted at his mother's Philadelphia boardinghouse. Graydon had a poor opinion of the officers, especially a pair of "gay rakes" and their drunken antics. However, the two confined their disruptions to the street and coffeehouse, respecting the privacy of the home. When "a diminutive Maryland parson" was assaulted by the officers and "kicked from the street door to the kitchen," the pair made amends by treating their victim to a drink.[28]

In compliance with the American Mutiny Act, some officers billeted in public houses. Although publicans happily sold food and drink to soldiers, they were hostile to providing quarters. When Captain Thomas Sterling arrived in Philadelphia with the 42nd Regiment in October 1766, the sorry state of the barracks caused him to billet the officers in taverns across the city. In response, publicans petitioned the Pennsylvania assembly, claiming that "the officers have no right to billets," so the House of Representatives ordered the city's barrack master to prepare rooms in the barracks for the officers. A year later, Joseph Fox recommended that Pennsylvania construct officers' quarters in the Northern Liberties. Fox subsequently built a house between the parallel rows of soldiers' barracks, thus forming the Philadelphia Barracks into a U-shaped structure.[29] Struggles between officers and tavern keepers followed in New Jersey, while the Liberty Pole Riot prompted the Sons of Liberty to advise innkeepers "not to have any intercourse with the military or even to admit them in their houses." Public houses were complex places, as it was not entirely clear whether they were part of the city's military geography or not.[30]

Deserters could also threaten domestic privacy. "Desertion is very frequent in all the regiments," General Gage noted in September 1766, concluding, "The whole country is full of deserters from the regiments."[31] Gage and the local commanding officers typically blamed colonists for the problem. According to Captain Füser, "one Doctor Simon, a German," lured men away from Charleston's barracks by offering them ten shillings per day to work on his plantation.[32] Similarly, when one-eighth of the recruits raised in Connecticut in the winter of 1766–1767 absconded, Gage claimed that they were "seduced to desert, and secreted by the inhabitants of the places adjacent."[33] American officials denied complicity in desertion; rather, they worried about how runaway soldiers contravened the separation of civilian and martial places. In July 1768, the *Boston Chronicle* reported that "several robberies have been lately committed" in houses north of New York City "by some deserters from the regulars." When the army sent patrols to collect deserters, this could cause problems as well, for although the Quartering Act forbade search parties from entering houses, some disguised themselves to cross the threshold.[34]

Despite the sporadic confrontations between soldiers and civilians, martial-civilian relations also exhibited concord and peace. When the 26th Regiment was quartered at Perth Amboy, local leaders requested that its chaplain minister to the city's Anglican church. Some cities cared for wounded troops. In 1767, the South Carolina legislature appropriated funds for "invalid soldiers, soldiers' widows and orphans" who sought charity at St. Philip's Church in Charleston.[35] As troops left the service, the cities welcomed them as civilians. Gage learned that many veterans "have for the most part crowded into the towns to work at trades."[36] At times that the regiments departed, the cities gushed with praise. When the 42nd Regiment withdrew from Philadelphia, the *Pennsylvania Gazette* offered its "thanks for that decorum in behavior" that the soldiers "kept up during their stay in the barracks of this city." The troops had set a good example, the paper noted, by demonstrating "that the most amiable behavior in civil life, is not inconsistent with the character of the good soldier."[37]

Some cities even employed the troops to keep the peace among civilians. When "some riotous fellows" attempted arson in Charleston in February 1767, South Carolina governor Lord Charles Montagu requested "day and night sentinels" from the Royal American Regiment. Füser was happy to oblige, granting the governor four soldiers for the day watch and five for the night.[38] British troops also helped to protect Manhattan's nascent theater district. At the opening of a theater on John Street, just off Broadway, in December 1767, a letter appeared in the *New York Mercury* denouncing "the dangers youth are exposed [to], from a public theater."[39] Eighteen months earlier, a mob of evangelicals and radical Whigs had pulled down a playhouse and burned it in the Fields, so this time, General Gage offered military protection. He dispatched a sergeant, a corporal, and twelve men from the 16th Regiment "to mount guard at five this evening at the playhouse" and ordered that "this guard to be continued as often as necessary till further orders." The troops proved effective, and the performance proceeded without incident.[40]

At times, relations between the army and the city could be quite harmonious, such as when soldiers and civilians joined together to celebrate the king's birthday. June 4, 1766, began in New York with the peal of bells from every church in the city. At 7 a.m., cooks began "to roast two large fat oxen, on the common," and spectators soon assembled. At noon, soldiers fired guns at the Battery, while at the other end of Broadway, soldiers in the Fields fired in response, "and the air resounded with the joyful acclamations of, *Long live the king, the darling of his people.*" Governor Sir Henry Moore, General Gage, the provincial council, the city council, and "all the gentlemen" of the city toasted the king's health at Fort George. Then, to the sound of cannon fire from naval ships and merchant vessels, they paraded up Broadway to the Fields, where they found "twenty-five barrels of strong beer, a hogshead of rum, sugar and water, to make punch, bread, etc." Atop the liberty pole, the royal colors fluttered. After "the guns in the common" blasted twenty-eight times, beer and grog were distributed to the crowd and forty-one toasts drunk. The toasts intermingled civilian and martial ideals. After honoring the king and the royal family, celebrants drank to Moore and Gage, repeal of the Stamp Act, the Earl of Chatham, and "English laws to American subjects." A great feast followed, with everyone invited to dine, including those confined to "the new jail, and poorhouse." After nightfall, "the town was illuminated in the grandest manner that was seen here." Parties continued late into the night at the homes of Moore and Gage, while colonists and soldiers made merry in the streets without "any disputes, quarrelling, or accident."[41]

The comity of the king's birthday contrasts sharply with the Liberty Pole Riot. Although historians often have focused on the acrimony between soldiers and colonists, harmony was far more common. The clear division of spaces made cities and towns places that could be shared by troops and civilians, while the liminal areas they shared were patrolled jointly by local and army officials. This carefully negotiated military geography allowed the spirit if not the letter of the Quartering Act to prevail. From 1766 to 1768, New York, Elizabeth, Perth Amboy, New Brunswick, Philadelphia, and Charleston peacefully quartered hundreds of troops.

Dominating Urban Spaces in the New Colonies

The British army was a constant presence in the cities and towns of the new colonies. Since before the French and Indian War, several regiments had quartered in Nova Scotia, primarily in Halifax, and with victory over the French, the British army garrisoned the urban areas of Canada and Florida. The concentration of regulars was greater in the new colonies than in the old, which led the British army to dominate their cities and towns. Moreover, Halifax, St. Augustine, and Québec lacked the civilian infrastructure of New York, Philadelphia, and Charleston, and thus there were fewer opportunities for local inhabitants to negotiate martial and civilian places. Instead, soldiers invaded houses, while policing drunk and deserting troops fell to the army alone. The army's domination in the new colonies reflected the failure of the Quartering Act in Nova Scotia, Québec, and the Floridas. The army alone provided barracks and supplies, and although this spared the colonists from quartering costs, it also meant that they had little ability to curtail the British army's expansive urban military geography.

The army dominated the new colonies' cities demographically. In February 1767, parts of nine regiments, numbering approximately twenty-five hundred British regulars, were stationed in Québec, Nova Scotia, and the Floridas. Some 70 percent of troops in the new colonies and 40 percent of all British regulars in North America resided in five cities: Québec, Montréal, Halifax, St. Augustine, and Pensacola. Given the small size of the communities, soldiers overwhelmed the civilian populations. Nearly eight hundred British officers and enlisted men quartered in Halifax, a city of fewer than two thousand colonists. Even in Québec, the largest city in the new colonies, regulars constituted a fifth of the population. Only the small towns of New Jersey had ratios similar to Québec City; in New York, colonists outnumbered soldiers twenty to one.[42]

If barracks were a point of civic pride in the old colonies, they were embarrassing, uncomfortable, and inadequate in the new. Because the Quartering Act was not promulgated in the new colonies, the British army bore sole responsibility for acquiring quarters, and it did so mostly on the cheap. Only Québec City possessed barracks sufficient to house a regiment, although the army did not adequately maintain the Nouvelles-Casernes, leading officers to eye the Jesuits' college for quarters. The barracks in Halifax and Pensacola were insufficient to quarter all the troops they received; Montréal and St. Augustine had no barracks at all before 1768.[43] General Gage repeatedly pressed Whitehall to build and repair barracks in the new colonies, although such pleas often fell on deaf ears. "None of the new provinces, Nova Scotia excepted, have proper or sufficient lodgment for the forces now in them," Gage informed the secretary of state in April 1767. "Canada is distressed in this respect, St. Augustine but ill provided, and the miserable huts in West Florida scarcely keep the soldiers from the weather."[44]

Without barracks, the cities suffered billeting in private and public houses. In Montréal, the army continued to rent houses from the Québécois four years after the brutal attack on Thomas Walker. Each year, British officers renegotiated rental agreements, and each year Montréalers threatened not to renew their leases. Gage advised the governor to make "use of the billeting act, where publicans are capacitated to furnish quarters," but this was aspirational, as Whitehall had ruled that the Mutiny Act for America did not apply in Québec.[45] Matters were worse in St. Augustine. When British forces took control of East Florida in 1763, the army billeted troops in the capital city's houses. According to one observer, the Spanish colonists disliked "to have strangers in their families" and "generally quitted the houses where officers were quartered."[46] For the next five years, British troops billeted in St. Augustine "in old houses upon sufferance."[47] Even cities with barracks faced billeting. In 1767, the army granted "an allowance to officers in lieu of lodgings," as neither Québec nor Halifax contained officers' quarters.[48]

Throughout the new colonies, local barrack masters kept quarters supplied and habitable. In contrast to the old colonies, in the new colonies barrack masters answered to the British army, rather than serving as intermediaries between civilian and military authorities. While the Pennsylvania assembly selected Joseph Fox, the British Board of Ordnance commissioned "William O'Brien, gentleman," barrack master for Québec City, and tasked active members of the Royal Artillery with quartering soldiers in Montréal and St. Augustine.[49] Overseeing O'Brien and other barrack masters was the barrack master general, a position created by the Quartering Act. Fittingly, the position was held by the man who had been instrumental to drafting the law, Lieutenant Colonel James Robertson. Although he oversaw all colonial barrack masters, Robertson limited his interest to the new colonies. In early 1767, Robertson calculated that it would cost nearly £7,000 to provide barrack supplies like candles, bowls, and bedding for soldiers quartered in the five cities of the new colonies for one year. This was about six times as much as New York contributed annually for quartering and nearly as much as Pennsylvania appropriated for five years of barrack supplies.[50]

Given their numbers and quarters, British regulars overwhelmed the capitals of the new colonies and Montréal. This was most evident when troops engaged in drunkenness, disorderliness, and desertion. Two regulars broke into a warehouse in Québec City in 1765; two years later, two others were tried for burglary, "found guilty, and sentenced to be hanged."[51] Such crimes were fueled by alcohol. "The rage of drinking" was so strong in St. Augustine that Colonel William Tayler reported it led to "pilfering to supply them with rum," while one soldier "nearly drank himself to death."[52] Desertion was rampant. Newspapers carried the story of how Daniel Burns spent six months in the Canadian wilderness before he "surrendered himself to the Reverend Dr. Brooke, chaplain to the garrison." Burns received a pardon, but the paper hoped his story would make others aware that "accumulated misery must be the inevitable, and only fruit of desertion."[53] Nine months later, Gage was disappointed that "the spirit of desertion still subsists" in Québec.[54]

In each case, it was the army that meted out punishment, not civilian officials. With only rudimentary night watches and courts, the new colonies' urban dwellers relied on the army to administer justice. When George Allsopp found two soldiers breaking into his warehouse in Québec City, he chased after the men and accosted one of them, only to have a detachment of soldiers arrive and take the perpetrators into custody. The army even intervened in crimes that did not involve soldiers. "The only policemen during my childhood were the soldiers on duty who happened to be within call," recalled Philippe-Joseph Aubert de Gaspé in his memoir of growing up in late eighteenth-century Québec. The army also dominated those moments when soldiers and civilians came together in the new colonies. When Quebecers celebrated the king's birthday in 1767, "all persons regardless of social standing joined in," but it was soldiers who organized the celebration.[55] When troops departed, the colonists praised the redcoats' heroism rather than their restrained behavior. In July 1768, Quebecers thanked the departing 15th Regiment, noting they were "particularly beloved" by "the inhabitants where they have been quartered."[56]

In sum, Quebecers, Haligonians, and Floridians lost control of their cities' public and private spaces. One Saturday night in February 1767, Lieutenant James Burns stopped a carriole carrying John Malcolm and his two children on the outskirts of Québec City. A colonial newspaper reported that Lieutenant Burns upset the coach and proceeded to thrash Malcolm with a large club, vowing "that he would finish him."[57] A year later, Burns explained his actions to General Gage. When the lieutenant arrived with the 52nd Regiment, he brought a family with him and rented a house outside town. "I lodged in the country near Québec," Burns explained, "as lodgings were at that time dear in the town, and as a subaltern, [I] could not bear too heavy an expense." In time, however, the property was sold to Malcolm, who demanded that Burns "should quit the house within three days or become tenant to him." Although Burns would have vacated the premises, his wife was "confined to her bed, having had both her breasts laid open" and thus could not leave. It was at this point that the soldier assaulted the civilian.[58]

The Burns-Malcolm dispute in Québec stands in sharp contrast to New York's Liberty Pole Riot of 1766. Instead of a public fight on the city common between groups of soldiers and civilians, the Québec incident was a brawl conducted in the privacy of the home and the seclusion of the urban periphery. This was indicative of the army's overwhelming power in the new colonies and the lack of spatial divisions within their cities and towns. By contrast, Americans kept the army in check through prohibitions on billeting, local provisioning of supplies, and the authority of civilian officials, all of which were guaranteed by the Quartering Act. Without such a law to regulate accommodations, the new colonies were at the mercy of the British army. However, the inhabitants of the new colonies generally did not protest expansive military geography. In time, this acquiescence to British military power would further separate the new colonies from the old.

Garrisoning Boston

Boston was the exception. Between 1766 and 1768, every major city and several towns in British North America quartered regular soldiers except for Boston. During the French and Indian War, the city refused to billet British soldiers in houses and resisted building barracks in the center of town. Instead, the Massachusetts General Court placed the Long Barracks on Castle Island, and since 1755, the Boston Harbor quarters had kept British recruiting parties and the occasional regiment isolated from the city. Castle Island's remoteness even may have softened colonial opposition to the Quartering Act, as twice, in 1766 and 1767, Massachusetts provided supplies to British troops at the Long Barracks. But Boston's unique urban military geography was seen as problematic by British leaders, especially as the local inhabitants repeatedly protested parliamentary taxes. It also meant that Boston was unprepared to quarter troops when Whitehall dispatched four regiments to enforce British law in the city. Instead of sharing its urban spaces, as had New York and Québec, Boston remained the exception, criticizing British military power and resisting the American Mutiny Act. Garrisoning Boston had profound implications for the empire, yet it began as a debate over whether or not soldiers belonged in the city.

Appropriately, Boston's assault on the Quartering Act stemmed from Britain's attempt to enforce the statute. Although Bostonians had long been suspicious of the billeting statute, the Sons of Liberty ignored the law when protesting the Stamp Act. However, the New York Restraining Act ignited popular opposition to the Mutiny Act for America, especially once John Dickinson's "Letters from a Farmer in Pennsylvania" tied it to the Townshend Acts. In January 1768, the Massachusetts House of Representatives dispatched a letter to its agent in London denouncing both quarters and taxes. The letter questioned the need for the North American Establishment, claiming that Americans were able to defend themselves and labeling "a standing army in the colonies a needless expense." It also attacked the

Quartering Act as dangerous to colonial liberties, observing that should a colony not "provide certain enumerated articles," it faced "the pains and penalties" as "evident in the precedent of New York." A month later, radicals in the House of Representatives dispatched the Massachusetts Circular Letter to the other colonial legislatures, decrying the unconstitutionality of taxation without representation and citing "the hardship of the act for preventing mutiny and desertion" as proof.[59]

When the Sons of Liberty followed up the Circular Letter with violence and protests, some imperial officials began to lament the lack of British regulars in Boston. As part of the Townshend Acts, Parliament created the American Board of Customs Commissioners to better collect import duties. Centered in Boston, the commissioners became an easy target for urban dwellers who resented parliamentary taxation. Claiming that an insurrection was imminent, the commissioners pressed Governor Sir Francis Bernard to ask General Gage for troops. Bernard, however, refused, because his instructions obliged him "to consult the council about requiring troops; and they will never advise it."[60] Nevertheless, the governor relayed stories of lawlessness to Whitehall, as did the commissioners themselves.[61] These letters ended up on the desk of the recently appointed secretary of state for the colonies the Earl of Hillsborough, who took the issue to the king and solicited the orders he wanted. In June 1768, Hillsborough informed Gage of "His Majesty's pleasure that you do forthwith order, one regiment or such force as you shall think necessary to Boston, to be quartered in that town."[62]

Over the summer of 1768, tensions mounted in Boston. While merchants framed a nonimportation agreement, the Sons of Liberty hanged effigies of the customs commissioners, and conspicuous smuggling proceeded unabated. The arrival of HMS *Romney* emboldened the commissioners, who impounded John Hancock's sloop *Liberty* for contraband wine. A riot ensued, and the British officials fled to Castle Island. As the commissioners quartered in buildings intended for soldiers, they implored the commander in chief to send British regulars to rescue them. Governor Bernard joined the chorus, informing Gage that "the state of affairs in Boston is full as bad as the reports you have received can make it." It was no use asking the provincial council to consent to soldiers, Bernard insisted, as Boston had dissolved into anarchy. Besides, it was within Gage's purview to redeploy the North American Establishment as he saw fit: "It should seem that the same power which enables the general to send a regiment to Philadelphia or to New Jersey would authorize him to send one or more to Boston."[63]

Gage was unmoved—although, as he collected letters from Boston and Whitehall, he ordered a regiment in Nova Scotia to ready for Boston.

However, he refused to move a single soldier until he heard from the Massachusetts council. Bernard's equation of Boston with Philadelphia and New Jersey was a false one: whereas the other old colonies only lodged soldiers, the Massachusetts governor wanted regulars to crush an incipient revolt. "It is contrary to the laws and constitution," Gage explained to Bernard, "for troops to quell tumults and riots, unless military aid is required for those purposes by the civil power." Gage could have cited the example of the Dutchess County riots, where the army was "under the command of the civil power" and acted "solely in obedience thereto." But Governor Bernard wanted the army to act independently of the civilian authority.[64]

However, Whitehall agreed with Bernard and the commissioners. A recent incident in which British soldiers had quelled a riot in London by firing into a crowd emboldened Secretary at War Viscount Barrington, who opined that "riotous Englishmen in New England must be treated as their fellows in old England; they must be compelled to obey the law, and the civil magistrate must have troops to enforce that obedience."[65] In late July, Hillsborough overruled Bernard's instructions and Gage's reluctance to contradict colonial lawmakers. The secretary of state informed the commander in chief that the king was sending two regiments from the Irish Establishment to Boston. In the meantime, Gage was to assemble soldiers recently removed from the backcountry and the new colonies' rural forts for redeployment to Boston. Gage complied, ordering two regiments in Halifax to prepare to ship out.[66]

News of the impending army reached Boston at the beginning of September 1768. Within days, rumors circulated that the Sons of Liberty were planning to destroy the Long Barracks on Castle Island. But this response missed the point. Hillsborough had no intention of barracking the soldiers in Boston Harbor; he wanted them "in that town."[67] Gage relayed the secretary's orders to Bernard, along with a request that the troops be "provided with quarters, on their arrival in your government, as by law directed." The governor proposed quartering the four regiments in the Manufactory House, the remnant of a failed antipoverty program located at the edge of Boston Common. As this would place regulars in the city center, the provincial council rejected Bernard's suggestion and reevaluated its notion of urban space. The council declared "that the barracks at the Castle were in the town of Boston," thus all soldiers should be quartered there.[68]

To bolster their argument, civilian officials cited the Quartering Act. Boston's selectmen quoted the provision that "when any barracks are provided by any of the colonies where troops shall be sent, that such troops shall be quartered in those barracks." Massachusetts had barracks on Castle Island,

and these were "fully sufficient to receive the said troops."[69] The provincial council concurred, adding that the Mutiny Act for America allowed for cashiering officers who acted "otherwise than is limited and allowed by this act."[70]

But the Quartering Act was ill suited to handle the garrisoning of Boston. Although Boston officials were correct that troops had to be barracked, the statute also allowed for alternative housing when the barracks were full. Bostonians insisted that all four regiments could reside on Castle Island, but Captain John Montresor observed that the island's Long Barracks and casemates contained enough room for only four hundred soldiers: about one regiment. The American Mutiny Act contained no means for determining when barracks were at capacity or who decided this, so the impasse between civilian and military officials went unresolved. More important, the Quartering Act protected private houses from quartering, not entire cities. Written in the heady days of imperial unity, the law treated all cities and towns the same. But this presumed comity between the army and the community, something that Whitehall precluded by sending soldiers to enforce parliamentary law and undermine rebellion. As a result, the garrisoning of Boston revealed the inherent limitations of the Mutiny Act for America.[71]

On September 29, 1768, a flotilla of British warships containing the 14th and 29th Regiments of Foot arrived in Boston Harbor. With the governor and the council still in stalemate, commanding officer Lieutenant Colonel William Dalrymple took matters into his own hands. "Determined to land the troops and take quarters . . . until some provision should be made for us," Dalrymple encamped the 29th Regiment on Boston Common.[72] However, he still needed quarters for the 14th, so he turned to Boston's selectmen. Sympathetic to the homeless soldiers and perhaps fearful of forced quartering, the city allowed troops to billet in Faneuil Hall and the Massachusetts statehouse. The speed at which the British army took control of Boston's communal land, central market, and capital was breathtaking. "In short the town is now a perfect garrison," reported one newspaper.[73]

Perfect perhaps, but temporary. The oncoming New England winter meant that the men of the 29th could not remain on Boston Common for long, while merchants and assemblymen soon would need the buildings. Accordingly, General Gage dispatched army engineer Captain John Montresor to Boston to construct barracks "on some advantageous spot for defense or offense."[74] However, Gage recognized that tensions were so high that Montresor would bring "the barracks at Castle William into Boston as Birnamwood was brought to Dunsinane": a reference to Shakespeare's *Macbeth* that suggested the plan's portent for tragedy.[75] So Montresor and

Dalrymple began renting rooms and seizing abandoned buildings. Montresor also sketched plans for a large guardhouse at Boston Neck and hired carpenters to frame the accompanying quarters. Even this was inadequate. Traveling to Boston in early October, Gage informed the council that additional accommodations were needed for the two Irish regiments still to come. Sharply divided, the councilors surrendered the Manufactory House for barracks.[76]

However, there were people living in the Manufactory House, and they refused to vacate the building. For two weeks, the Boston sheriff tried to evict the tenants, even entering the cellar, only to be captured and shackled. John Brown, a weaver renting rooms at the Manufactory, then sued the sheriff, contending that he "unlawfully and injuriously did break and enter into the dwelling house."[77] In effect, Brown claimed domestic privacy in a space he rented from the government. This was a far more expansive definition of privacy than anyone had claimed in the 1750s, but it seemed reasonable to many Bostonians. In a letter to the *Boston Gazette*, "Legipotens" made Brown's case the cause of all Bostonians. "The Manufactory House was built by a tax laid by the General Court," thus it was the "property of the province" and "cannot be disposed of without the consent of the inhabitants, either by themselves or their representatives." Notions of place were converging: home had become a metaphor for country. To invade one was to violate the sanctity of the other.[78]

As the separation of civilian and martial places broke down in Boston, the Quartering Act failed. Having billeted his troops, Colonel Dalrymple appeared before the provincial council and "demanded barrack provisions accordingly, agreeable to Act of Parliament." Duplicitously, the council agreed to comply with the law, so long as the suppliers "will take the risk" of the province reimbursing them.[79] When Dalrymple reported the council's "poor and paltry evasion" to Gage, the commander in chief conceded that the army would supply Boston troops and ceased attempts to enforce the American Mutiny Act in Massachusetts.[80] Indeed, the more that Bostonians cited the statute to argue that quartering troops anywhere other than Castle Island was illegal, the less the general wanted to hear about the law. In a letter to Hillsborough, Gage lamented how the colony's "absurdity of a construction of the Act of Parliament" had "annihilated the act."[81]

In early November 1768, the 64th and 65th Regiments arrived from Ireland. Dalrymple barracked some of the troops at Castle Island and quartered the rest in warehouses along Boston's eastern shore. But not all soldiers were relegated to the periphery; married officers rented rooms in private homes, while sentries were posted throughout the city. With nearly two thousand

British regulars in and around a city of fifteen thousand colonists, Boston had been transformed into a martial space. An eerie peace followed, and soon the American Board of Commissioners was prosecuting smugglers again. The city had been profoundly transformed.[82]

No Sharing in Boston

Leading Bostonians' opposition to the British army was Samuel Adams. A descendant of the Puritan founders of Massachusetts, Adams was raised to distrust the king and standing armies. In 1747, Adams observed British military power firsthand when Commodore Charles Knowles sent a press gang into Boston to recruit sailors. As rumors spread that "persons had been hauled out of their beds," Adams published the *Independent Advertiser*, a newspaper in which he and other authors cataloged the navy's abuse of colonists.[83] In 1765, Adams joined the Sons of Liberty and led the charge against the Stamp Act on the streets of Boston and at the town meetings. Three years later, he sat in the House of Representatives, where he wrote the Massachusetts Circular Letter. When the British army garrisoned Boston, Adams again took the lead, citing "the Act of Parliament providing for the quartering and billeting of His Majesty's troops" to argue that all regulars had to be barracked at Castle Island. When the troops entered the city, Adams's ideas if not his actual words appeared in a series of newspaper articles known collectively as the "Journal of the Times." The "Journal" illustrates how Bostonians like Samuel Adams refused to share their city with British regulars.[84]

Although propaganda, the "Journal of the Times" is the best source for understanding interactions between soldiers and civilians in Boston. The articles' tenor contrasts sharply with media from other colonial cities. Written with a high degree of detail in almost daily stories, the "Journal" depicted the British army as an invading force rather than as a population integrated into the urban landscape. Accordingly, soldiers' actions that were dismissed in New York and Philadelphia were dissected for their tyrannical implications in Boston. Significantly, the "Journal of the Times" reflected a new view of military geography. In New York and the other cities of the old colonies, British regulars were tolerable because they were spatially and constitutionally limited, and were policed by military and civilian officials. By contrast, the "Journal" portrayed Boston as if it were Québec, with soldiers unrestrained in their movements around the city and uncontrolled by any authority. Much as Samuel Adams had long suspected, the "Journal" confirmed that it was impossible to quarter troops in a city without terrible consequences.

FIGURE 5.2. Samuel Adams. Charles Goodman and Robert Piggot, engravers, *Samuel Adams / Painted by Copley* (1810–1835). Library of Congress, Prints and Photographs Division, LC-USZ62–102271 (b&w film copy neg.).

Like troops elsewhere, the regulars in Boston partook of drunken antics. The "Journal" reported how an enlisted man made "too free a use of spirituous liquors" and was "found dead in his barracks." Other stories documented the how "the insults and outrages of the drunken soldiery" fueled property destruction and robberies throughout the city. But while papers in New York depicted inebriated soldiers as something to be controlled, reports from Boston focused on the darker motives revealed by spirited indulgences. The articles lamented the redcoats' Sabbath breaking and their familiarity with the city's African American population. Indeed, the very presence of British soldiers threatened to corrupt Boston's inhabitants. "One great objection to the quartering of troops in the body of a town," the "Journal" proclaimed, "is the danger the inhabitants will be in, of having their morals debauched."[85]

Reports of desertion also took on a more sinister tone. Desertion was probably about as common in Boston as it was elsewhere, but the "Journal of the Times" treated runaway soldiers as proof that regulars should not be quartered in the city. Shortly after the first troops arrived, the "Journal" touted "reports of great desertions and a general disposition to desert from the regiments here" and gleefully claimed that twenty-one men had already left their regiments. Such actions were not surprising, the authors reasoned, because New England was a thoroughly civilian space. The region's pleasant environs, godly people, and plentiful markets made it hard to keep any man in the military and proved "that Boston is a very unsuitable place for quartering of soldiers." The "Journal" then reminded everyone that had the troops been confined to Castle Island, it "would have prevented any desertion, and many other evils and disorders, which are daily taking place."[86]

Misbehavior and desertion were not the only ills documented. The "Journal" also decried noises that were innocuous in Philadelphia and celebrations that evoked unity in New York. The heart of the city beat with the rhythm of a martial leviathan. On Boston Common, soldiers marched every day of the week, leaving the authors to despair how "serious people at public worship were greatly disturbed with drums beating and fifes playing, unheard of before in this land." Other sounds emanating from the Common were likewise discordant to Puritan ears. Faithful members of Old South Meetinghouse like Samuel Adams deplored the sermons of the army's Anglican clergyman. Although the "Journal" did not mind soldiers celebrating the king's birthday, it had little appetite for other royal holidays such as King George's coronation, Queen Charlotte's birthday, and "the preservation of King Charles" against his Puritan enemies.[87]

The "Journal" also confirmed the worst fears of the Sons of Liberty that the regulars had come to suppress not only smuggling, but the colonists' constitutional rights as well. Shortly after its arrival, the army placed cannons outside the Massachusetts statehouse and pointed them at the front door. When Bostonians went to the polls in May 1769, the selectmen asked the commanding officer to remove troops so that the inhabitants "should be in the full enjoyment of their rights of British subjects upon this important occasion, agreeable to the Bill of Rights."[88] However, Major General Alexander Mackay would only restrict his men to barracks, much to the displeasure of the "Journal of the Times." Confining troops had been sufficient in New York on election day a year earlier, while Gage explained that troops were withdrawn from English cities during elections because they "are quartered in public houses, and it's necessary they should evacuate those houses to make room for the voters."[89] Such assurances were dismissed by the "Journal," which countered with reports of how "armed men, sent under the pretense indeed of aiding the civil authority," disrupted the election of the Speaker of the House of Representatives.[90]

The arguments of the "Journal of the Times" were inherently spatial. The stories insisted that British regulars did not belong in the city, that civilian and martial places could not be separated, and in-between spaces could not be shared. "A physician of the town walking the streets the other evening, was jostled by an officer, when a scuffle ensued," reported the "Journal" in October 1768. Yet whereas civilian and military authorities shared the responsibility for keeping the peace in New York, in Boston they fought with one another. Some altercations were harmless, such as when a drunken soldier harangued a watchman, but others were more serious. When a watchmen came upon a pair of sergeants quarreling with townsmen, "they were answered with, drawn bayonets" and threats against their lives. Another night, a soldier struck a watchman who "returned the blow, which laid him in the gutter." At Boston Neck, the army supplanted civilian authority, seizing a public space and policing it. As a result, "an honorable gentleman of His Majesty's council, lately riding over Boston Neck in his coach" was threatened with violence when he refused to halt for a sentry. Due to such clashes, the "Journal" repeatedly asserted the colonists' right to bear arms against "Lord Hillsborough's military peace preservers."[91]

Violence in the streets of Boston was more dramatic because it victimized women. Reports from New York and Philadelphia characterized women as contributors to the troops' debauchery, with no accusations of sexual violence, but the "Journal of the Times" depicted women as passive objects of soldiers' brutality. "A married woman living in Long Lane, returning home in the night, was seized by the neck and almost strangled," the "Journal" reported in November 1768. Four months later, a woman was "much abused and wounded by a soldier," while another "was served in the same brutal manner, and then robbed of a bundle of linen she had under her arm." Sexual violence underlay these assaults. Sometimes women were subjected to unwanted advances or catcalls. Other times, they were nearly raped. An elderly woman in the North End was assaulted when she attempted to help a wounded soldier, while another filed charges against a regular "for a violent attempt upon her, but a rape was prevented." Sexual assault even could lead to death. When Sarah Johnson suddenly died on her way to market, an inquest determined that "she had been recently ravished" by "soldiers unknown." Tellingly, stories from the "Journal" include a variety of women, suggesting that in Boston all women were potential victims of redcoats.[92]

Once the British soldiers started raping and killing women in the streets, there was little to keep them from invading the home. One evening in February 1769, two women received the "solicitations and insults of a soldier" in the street, but when they ducked into a house, "the soldier was so audacious, as to enter with them." Surprised by the commotion, the master of the house came to investigate, but he was knocked senseless by the soldier. To the "Journal," this verified "the unhappy effects of quartering troops in this town." Additional invasions of domestic privacy followed, most of which emphasized the helplessness of the homes' inhabitants and the carnal lust of the troops. A corporal who had been carrying on an affair with a woman while her husband was at sea entered the couple's house and assaulted the husband upon his return. Later, an ensign, who lusted after a married woman, attempted to break down the door of her home, shouting "by God I'll have her in spite of all the men in the country."[93]

Ultimately, the "Journal of the Times" connected places. Once soldiers started invading the home, it was impossible to constitutionally or physically segregate troops in a way to keep civilians safe. Moreover, the "Journal" contrasted the garrisoning of Boston with the recent withdrawal of regulars from the backcountry and the new colonies' peripheral forts. While Massachusetts suffered from troops it did not want, the removal of regulars left colonists in West Florida "surrounded by savages" and prompted Mi'kmaq to murder settlers in Nova Scotia. The "Journal" even claimed that Nova Scotians were so desperate for soldiers that some were "erecting a liberty pole, and employing some boys to sing the liberty song through the streets" in hope that Britain would send troops to crush the fictitious revolt. The problem was not just regulars in Boston but the military geography of all British North America.[94]

In time, tensions cooled. Although Bostonians never accepted the British troops, a year passed without a major revolt. "Everything here remains quiet," reported General Joseph Pomeroy, who also observed that even the annual celebration of the Stamp Act's repeal in March 1769 failed to produce "anything tending to the least disturbance."[95] Such reports comforted General Gage, especially when the 64th and 65th Regiments returned to Ireland in June 1769, reducing the number of troops in the city by half. Even the "Journal of the Times" expired with its last article on August 1, 1769. But Samuel Adams and the Sons of Liberty had not been persuaded that soldiers and civilians could share the city. Rather, Boston's actions had changed many Americans' minds about the city and the Quartering Act.[96]

Boston's Effect on the Quartering Act

From London, Benjamin Franklin closely followed reports of Boston. "It seems like setting up a smith's forge in a magazine of gunpowder," Franklin wrote to the great evangelist George Whitefield. The problem was spatial, the Boston native reasoned: placing soldiers and colonists "too near each other" would "occasion some mischief." Before violence consumed the city, Franklin suggested that the British government "recall the troops, refund the money, and return to the old method of requisition."[97] Franklin's sentiments matched those of many Americans in 1769. Whitehall's decision to use regulars to enforce parliamentary taxation soured many on British military power and disrupted the peaceful sharing of cities and towns. Seeing the soldiers as a threat to their constitutional liberties, the colonists asked why British troops belonged in their communities instead of Canada or the borderland. As discontent spread from Boston to New York and Charleston, an aggressive new opposition to the Quartering Act appeared. With the comity of troops and civilians in question, colonies renewed their obfuscation of the law. Although Whitehall attempted to address these issues, instability in the British government prevented a workable solution. Not only did garrisoning Boston halt the American Mutiny Act in Massachusetts; it permanently damaged the law throughout the American colonies.

While Benjamin Franklin worried about the constitutional implications of quarters, it was the financial consequences that concerned Whitehall. Garrisoning Boston was not cheap. Massachusetts's refusal to abide by the Quartering Act meant that the soldiers' rent, candles, fuel, and incidentals came out of the budget of barrack master general James Robertson. A 1791 audit of Robertson's accounts reveals that it cost £2,500 to quarter troops in Boston for the last three months of 1768, which was the same amount spent quartering four regiments in Québec, Montréal, and Trois-Rivières for an entire year. Thereafter, the cost fell to about £100 per regiment per month, although this was still twice the price of garrisoning Québec. The high cost of quartering in Boston came from renting warehouses instead of using barracks. Poor relations with civilians also added to the bottom line. Doubtful that the troops would be well served by Bostonians, the army paid extra to import beef and other foodstuffs to feed the troops rather than giving the men cash to buy their own meals, which was typical elsewhere.[98]

As bills from Boston mounted, the Earl of Hillsborough sought to revive the Quartering Act in Massachusetts. In March 1769, the secretary of state instructed General Gage to calculate the cost of quartering troops "in order to be laid before the assembly of that province when it meets."[99] However, at the convocation of the Massachusetts General Court in May, several representatives arrived with instructions "by no means to comply with such a requisition."[100] Accordingly, when Governor Bernard formally requested that the House of Representatives supply troops "as are directed by Act of Parliament," lawmakers received the request with incredulity. The House of Representatives not only refused to consider a bill provisioning the troops; it issued a lengthy diatribe denouncing the American Mutiny Act as an unconstitutional violation of the colonists' liberties. Because the law required colonies to compensate the army at levels Britain deemed appropriate, the Quartering Act meant that "we can no longer be free representatives, nor our constituents free subjects." Then the House adjourned, not to meet again for another eight months.[101]

Massachusetts's defiance reverberated throughout North America. Benjamin Franklin reported that the colonies were "universally irritated by our sending troops to Boston, and by their behavior there," while newspapers in Connecticut and Pennsylvania applauded Massachusetts's refusal to comply with the Quartering Act.[102] The defiance even spread outside the old colonies. The commanding officer in Newfoundland thought that "the troubles at Boston" had "inspired people here with a frumpish sort of air," while Gage believed that Massachusetts's "spirit of insurrection" led to unrest in New Orleans.[103] From Boston, General Alexander Mackay saw matters more clearly than most; provisioning troops "at His Majesty's expense" had set "a bad precedent" for the other colonies.[104]

Massachusetts's bad precedent soon appeared in New York. In response to the garrisoning of Boston, a riot broke out in New York City in November 1768, during which the governor of Massachusetts and sheriff of Boston were hanged in effigy. A month later, this defiance spread to the New York General Assembly when representatives arrived with instructions to "pay not the least regard to the acts" of Parliament.[105] Although the Restraining Act prevented the legislature from openly defying Parliament, public opinion was more extreme. As the assembly appropriated £1,800 for barrack supplies in December 1768, and the same amount in May 1769, local papers carried sentiments more characteristic of Boston than New York. "A standing army is dangerous to liberty," proclaimed a letter in the *New York Journal* that challenged the ability of soldiers and colonists to share the city. Claiming that regulars were "kept here to overawe" the colonists "into a tame and blind submission," the letter insisted that the assembly reject any future requests for military requisitions.[106] The House of Representatives could not comply with this demand, but it did insist its agent in London "endeavor to prevent the clause for billeting soldiers in America from being inserted in the next Mutiny Act."[107]

Events in Boston also echoed across South Carolina. As in New York, the colony's Commons House instructed its London agent to advocate against the renewal of the Quartering Act. But South Carolina was always more brazen than the rest of the colonies. In October 1768, as troops marched into Boston, the 21st Regiment arrived in South Carolina, requesting "quarters in the barracks of Charleston, until next spring."[108] The regiment was supposed to be in St. Augustine, but the delayed construction of barracks in the East Florida capital had forced Gage to divert the troops to South Carolina instead. In the autumn of suspicion, some Charlestonians wondered aloud about imperial duplicity: "that this place will be further strengthened by another regiment from Florida."[109] Privately, Gage noted that South Carolinians had become "troublesome" and hoped "the troops may prevent riots," but he had no intention of turning Charleston into Boston.[110] The Quartering Act became inoperable in South Carolina nonetheless. The Commons House adjourned when the 21st arrived, and Gage knew that "when that assembly meets, they will not be very ready to provide the troops according to the Act of Parliament."[111]

Hillsborough took a dim view of American intransigence. The transfer of control of the British government from the Earl to Chatham to the Duke of Grafton that had begun in late 1767 finally concluded two weeks after British regulars arrived in Boston. However, Grafton and the cabinet soon were distracted by France's invasion of Corsica and charges that they should have done more to prevent it. In this vacuum, the Earl of Hillsborough's determination to punish the colonies went unchecked, and before the end of 1768, South Carolina agent Charles Garth sent word that the House of Commons "would not listen to a proposition for a repeal of the billeting clause."[112] Not only did Hillsborough want to retain the Quartering Act; he wanted to use it to effect colonial submission. In February 1769, Hillsborough presented a plan to the cabinet to amend the four-year-old law. The proposed revision penalized civilian officials who refused to locate quarters for regulars and empowered governors to appoint commissaries in their stead. It added that if barracks, public houses, and uninhabited buildings "are not sufficient to accommodate them, then" British soldiers would billet "in private houses."[113]

Viscount Barrington shared Hillsborough's opinion, so the secretary at war presented a bill to the House of Commons revising the Quartering Act such that if "magistrates [be] remiss in quartering" troops, then "commanders should have orders to quarter them in private houses."[114] But the proposal was roundly rejected by Parliament, including those sympathetic to the American cause, like Isaac Barré, and those who were not, like Lord North. "I am as little desirous as any man that troops should be quartered in private houses; nor was that the intention of my clause," Barrington later explained to Gage. He only wanted to show the Americans that there were worse things "than hiring empty houses and furnishing bedding." Both Hillsborough and Barrington saw the Mutiny Act for America as an instrument to use against the colonists, thus reneging on Parliament's promise that the British army would *never* quarter regulars in private houses.[115]

After Hillsborough's revisions to the Quartering Act collapsed, the House of Commons adopted a more conciliatory approach. "To show a kind of seeming lenity toward the colonies," reported an American agent, "they have adopted a clause providing that, when the several assemblies shall make billeting acts of their own," such laws "shall take place of the Act of Parliament."[116] As Commons resurrected Thomas Pownall's recommendation that the colonies be allowed to write their own quartering laws, dreams of imperial equity faded away. Realistically, British lawmakers simply codified General Gage's practice of allowing the Americans considerable latitude over how they accommodated, supplied, and transported British soldiers. Parliament quickly approved the revised statute in March 1769, no doubt hoping the changes would de-escalate tensions and encourage colonial compliance.[117]

It seemed at first as if the revised Quartering Act of 1769 might reverse American defiance. Benjamin Franklin hailed the alteration as a triumph. Not only had Parliament fended off a second attempt to force troops in the colonists' homes; the deference to American legislatures made the law "rather more favorable than it was."[118] His son, New Jersey's Governor William Franklin, also welcomed the revision, as it legalized what his colony was already doing. When New Jersey approved a new quartering bill in December 1769, Gage was hopeful that "all of the provinces do not follow the example of the Massachusetts Bay."[119] But he was wrong. Newspapers in Boston and New York reported the amended American Mutiny Act unenthusiastically, focusing on how Parliament had almost added a clause "of the most offensive nature."[120] Soon Gage reported to Barrington "that the Americans will not, as the act stands, trouble you with any laws of their own making for quartering of troops."[121]

South Carolina was unimpressed by the revisions to the Quartering Act of 1769. When Governor Lord Charles Montagu asked the colony's Commons

House to provision the 21st Regiment, the assembly refused to appropriate any money "during the existence of those acts, acts which strike at the very root of our constitution." Yet South Carolina's objection was as spatial as it was constitutional. Upon receiving the governor's request for supplies, the Commons House demanded to know "whether His Majesty's troops now in the province, are to garrison the frontier forts." In other words, South Carolina lawmakers wanted to know why British troops were barracked in Charleston instead of Forts Prince George and Charlotte. Like Bostonians, Charlestonians were connecting places. They could not comprehend why British regulars were garrisoning cities instead of the borderland. The Commons House then contrasted the obligations of old and new colonies. By August, the 21st Regiment had departed for East Florida, where the British army "could not expect to be supplied with any barrack necessaries at the expense of the province." As a result, the South Carolina legislature refused to appropriate any money for quarters.[122]

The 1769 amendment also did little to endear the Quartering Act to New Yorkers. In November 1769, as the New York General Assembly convened to appropriate money for barrack supplies, a letter appeared in the *New York Journal* lamenting how the colony had "given away several thousands already for the troops," while "Boston has refused any contribution to this unnatural tax" and "[South] Carolina has followed." New York should join the other colonies, the letter urged.[123] Although the shadow of the New York Restraining Act still hung over lawmakers, they did use popular distaste for the American Mutiny Act to push through a currency bill. Since 1764, Parliament had forbidden the American colonies from issuing paper money to be used for public and private debts. New Yorkers, especially merchants in the capital, were "chagrined" by this restriction because it removed the colony's principal medium of exchange and made commerce difficult. As calls grew louder for New York to defy the Quartering Act, the leaders of the House of Representatives decided to marry the two issues; the House would appropriate barrack supplies if Parliament would allow the colony to buy those supplies with New York currency. The assembly passed the law, and on January 5, 1770, the acting governor, Cadwallader Colden, signed a law appropriating £2,000 for quartering troops, half of which would be paid in colonial currency.[124]

Gage watched the proceedings in New York with frustration. Although he had no instructions regarding paper money, the commander in chief certified the law as compliant with the Quartering Act. He then itemized how the £2,000 would pay for beds and blankets, firewood and candles, utensils, and supplies for a spruce brewery. Gage claimed that the 1769 amendment made New York's quartering law legal and hoped it was proof that New Yorkers had "abandoned their Boston friends."[125] Privately, however, Gage was far more pessimistic. His own house stood on Broad Street near Marketfield, and like other regulars, Gage long had shared New York with the colonists. With defiance spreading across the colonies, however, the general had begun to agree with Hillsborough and Barrington that stricter measures were needed "that shall render the disobedience of the Mutiny Act inconvenient to the Americans." He suggested allowing governors to quarter troops without consulting magistrates, billeting soldiers at businesses, and forcing colonies to pay for supplies without their consent. Gage even speculated that "if private houses were inserted also it might facilitate the business of quartering." Garrisoning Boston not only hobbled the Quartering Act; it had ended the promise that colonists and soldiers could live together peacefully in American cities and towns.[126]

The Battle of Golden Hill and the Boston Massacre

In the winter of 1769–1770, tensions that had been simmering since Whitehall garrisoned Boston came to a head in two major confrontations between soldiers and civilians: New York's Battle of Golden Hill and the Boston Massacre. Although historians have long understood these events as integral to sparking the American Revolution, they were also moments of spatial discourse when the colonists challenged the prevailing military geography. Before 1768, many colonial cities and towns made room for British regulars, but once Massachusetts refused to abide by either the spirit or the letter of the Quartering Act, South Carolina and New York turned against the idea that soldiers could be accommodated in their communities. In this climate, Parliament's law became a hated symbol of British tyranny and a target for the Sons of Liberty. Although the American Mutiny Act had been made possible by civilians willing to share their places with soldiers, in 1770 the law led to violence that drove British regulars from American cities.

In New York City, unrest began in December 1769 when the assembly was debating how to supply British regulars in accordance with the Quartering Act. As the House of Representatives approved £2,000 for the regiment in the colony, a member of the New York Sons of Liberty named Alexander McDougall published a broadside and posted it throughout the city. Titled "To the Betrayed Inhabitants of the City and Colony of New York," the broadside denounced the Mutiny Act for America as expensive and unconstitutional, and called on New York to follow "the laudable example of the colonies of Massachusetts Bay and South Carolina." It also repeated spatial arguments that had become popular in Boston and Charleston: "What makes the assembly's granting this money the more grievous, is, that it goes to the support of troops kept here, not to protect, but to enslave us." Overnight, McDougall's broadside popularized the idea that New York was a civilian space that could not be shared with soldiers.[127]

Events accelerated quickly after the posting of McDougall's broadside. One day later, a second broadside appeared that called for "the inhabitants of this city" to convene and discuss the assembly's decision "to vote supplies to the troops." Moving politics out of the House of Representatives into the city's public spaces, the broadside invited all to the Fields.[128] The meeting that followed was spirited but nonviolent, as were several subsequent assemblages, which Acting Governor Colden dismissed as "too small and inconsiderable to have any weight."[129] Yet they took place in the city common underneath a fourth liberty pole. This latest iteration dwarfed its predecessors: at fifty-eight feet, it stood taller than most of the city's church steeples. It was encased in earth and stone, and wrapped in iron. Much as the first liberty pole had been a symbol of colonial resistance to the Stamp Act, the more imposing fourth version was the apotheosis the colonists' hatred for the Quartering Act.[130]

As the colonists asserted their control over the Fields through meetings and symbols, the British soldiers in the city grew irritated. In the winter of 1769–1770, the 16th Regiment of Foot was quartered in New York. The troops occupied not only the Upper Barracks but spread across the city. Some quartered at the Lower Barracks near Fort George, and others inhabited an abandoned house that had once belonged to John Harris near the Fields (see figure 5.1). Although the dispersal of troops had not disrupted placid soldier-civilian relations, the protests against the Quartering Act angered the troops. On Saturday night, January 13, 1770, forty British regulars devised a plan to bring down the liberty pole. Because the pole's encasement protected it, the soldiers loaded the base with explosives to blow it up. The noisy doings soon were discovered by colonists, who gathered to mock the redcoats. In response, members of the 16th Regiment marched across Broadway to Abraham de la Montayne's tavern and "entered it with drawn swords and bayonets, insulted the company and beat the waiter." The soldiers sacked the house, breaking "eighty-four panes of glass, two lamps and two bowls." Montayne's tavern was a known meeting place for the Sons of Liberty, so the attack carried the same meaning as if the troops had taken down the liberty pole.[131]

Both military and civilian authorities acted quickly to address the dispute. British officers confined three suspected soldiers to the Upper Barracks and placed a sentry at the liberty pole to prevent another attack. The colonists also investigated the pole to ensure that it was secure and monitored the situation. All seemed calm, but the battle for control of the city had begun. On January 15, soldiers were back at work attempting to topple the pole. In response, Son of Liberty John Lamb published a broadside decrying the cost of quartering the soldiers. New Yorkers were paying to accommodate the troops and their "whores and bastards" with "such necessaries which many of the good burghers want." The billeting charges had poisoned the soldiers, Lamb argued, such that "all the money that you have hitherto given them, has only taught them to despise and insult you." To protest New York's compliance with the Quartering Act, Lamb called for a meeting at the liberty pole.[132] Early the next morning, some determined members of the 16th Regiment finally downed the pole, chopping it into fifty-eight foot-long pieces and depositing them in front of Montayne's tavern. When three thousand New Yorkers assembled in the Fields a few hours later, they dispensed with their protest of the American Mutiny Act and turned on the regulars instead. The crowd demanded the city pull down the Harris house and confine all troops to quarters. If any regular was found "out of the barracks after the roll is called" and armed, then the colonists would take action.[133]

To refute the charges of the Sons of Liberty, some soldiers printed a broadside of their own. It claimed that the troops had suffered from the colonists' parsimony, as they had "wives and children, and not whores and bastards" to support. The broadside also rejected the colonists' exclusive claim to public spaces, insisting that the troops "have watched night and day, for the safety and protection of the city and its inhabitants."[134] On January 19, two colonists discovered seven regulars posting their broadside near the Fly Market, a half mile from either the Upper or the Lower Barracks, and set upon them, dragging them before Mayor Whitehead Hicks for punishment. Before Hicks could decide what to do, twenty soldiers from the Lower Barracks appeared. Although the mayor tried to order the troops to quarters, the soldiers marched north toward John and William Streets. Followed by a growing crowd of civilians, the regulars halted at Golden Hill, an area so named as it had once been the site of rich wheat fields. Forty troops rushed down from the Upper Barracks and joined the other regulars in attacking the colonists. A bloody battle ensued, with soldiers and civilians fighting each other with clubs and bayonets, leaving it "evident that there has been blood spilled on both sides." Before anyone was killed, Mayor Hicks, Colonel James Robertson, and others dispersed the combatants. But the fighting was not over. The next day, Nassau Street erupted as a group of sailors set upon soldiers from the Lower Barracks. Once again, civilian and military leaders interceded to prevent fatalities.[135]

To avert further violence, New York officials reordered the city. On January 22, the mayor proclaimed that owing to the recent "unhappy differences," General Gage had ordered "that no soldiers are to go out of their barracks, off duty, unless under the command of a non-commissioned officer."[136] Confinement to barracks was actually a concession by the colonists, as some demanded "that the general should be applied to for a removal of the regiment as the only means to preserve the peace."[137] In return, provincial leaders imprisoned Alexander McDougall, although this did not stop him from publishing attacks on the Quartering Act. A request from the Sons of Liberty to erect a new liberty pole "in the Fields (the most public place)" was rejected by the city council, but the group simply purchased land north of the common and erected a fifth post even closer to the Upper Barracks.[138] General Gage was dismayed by how quickly New York City had ceased to be a place shared by soldiers and civilians. "Endeavors were not only used to set the people against the bill for quartering, but also against the soldiers," the commander in chief lamented, such that "the minds of the soldiers were at length so soured, as to become alarming." A month later, Gage redeployed the 16th Regiment to Pensacola.[139]

The Battle of Golden Hill was a preview for what would come a month and a half later in Boston. Since their arrival in October 1768, the troops had spread across Boston. Some of the 14th Regiment resided at Murray's sugar house three blocks northwest of Faneuil Hall, while most of the 29th occupied warehouses along the waterfront. Such an expansive military geography encouraged conflict between soldiers and civilians. In October 1769, actions of the Sons of Liberty seemed to grow bolder, prompting the commanding officer, Lieutenant Colonel Dalrymple, to opine that "I am sure something very unpleasant is at hand." Accordingly, the army conceded greater swaths of the city to civilian control, even confining the troops to quarters during the sitting of the General Court. When Ebenezer Richardson, a notorious critic of the Sons of Liberty, fired into an angry crowd and killed eleven-year-old Christopher Seider in late February 1770, Dalrymple's troops were far from the action.[140]

Nevertheless, civilians and soldiers in Boston continued to taunt one another, including during the highly orchestrated funeral for young Seider. Soon, the verbal exchanges turned into physical altercations. On March 2, Private Patrick Walker, an off-duty member of the 29th Regiment, inquired about work at the city's massive ropewalks near his quarters in southeastern Boston. When rope maker William Green told the soldier to "go and clean my shithouse," Walker and Green began to spar. Although the initial confrontation proved inconclusive, Walker returned with forty comrades, who faced off against a growing crowd of rope makers and bystanders. A skirmish ensued, although the intervention of a local magistrate prevented casualties. As in New York, heightened emotions could not be easily contained, and further scuffles between soldiers and civilians followed the next day.[141]

Late on Monday, March 5, 1770, the bloody confrontation that everyone had been predicting for the past year and a half finally occurred. Events began near the main guardhouse, a small building that served as British army headquarters, and which was located across the street from the Massachusetts statehouse. From his sentry box outside the guardhouse, Private Hugh White of the 29th Regiment began a verbal exchange with an apprentice that quickly escalated into a physical altercation. Soon, other apprentices and boys appeared to heckle White, while another group headed to Murray's sugar house to confront soldiers billeted there. Although an officer was able to disperse the growing crowd and return the soldiers to their quarters, the tolling of the city's bells brought colonists back to King Street in front of the statehouse. As hundreds surrounded Private White, Captain Thomas Preston attempted to rescue the sentry from the growing crowd. Soldiers and civilians jostled each other, and some colonists began hurling objects at the redcoats, one of which struck a soldier's musket, causing him to fire. Other soldiers then joined in, opening a volley into the crowd that killed three, mortally wounded two, and injured six people.[142]

Appropriately, the incident that would go down in history as the Boston Massacre took place in the center of town amid a series of civilian spaces that had been repurposed for martial use. Son of Liberty Paul Revere made this point exceptionally clear in his sensationalized engraving of the event (figure 5.3). Not only does Revere depict Captain Preston ordering his men to fire on the unarmed crowd; he carefully avoids depicting any martial places like the warehouses that quartered the soldiers, the main guardhouse, and White's sentry box. Instead, the picture is dominated by civilian structures: the statehouse, Boston First Church, and a line of shops—symbols of representative government, Puritan religion, and peaceful commerce, respectively.

The Boston Massacre initiated the process of expunging of military geography from the city. Minutes after the smoke cleared, Captain Preston ordered the troops to the main guardhouse. The next day, Acting Governor Thomas Hutchinson pressed Colonel Dalrymple to remove the 29th Regiment to Castle Island and confine the 14th to their houses. But this was not enough. According to one observer, "Sam Adams told Colonel Dalrymple in public" that if he kept either regiment in town "it must be at his own peril."[143] Likewise, an assembly of Bostonians informed Governor Hutchinson "that the inhabitants and soldiery can no longer live together in safety," concluding

FIGURE 5.3. The Boston Massacre. Paul Revere, engraver, *The Bloody Massacre Perpetrated in King Street Boston on March 5th 1770 by a Party of the 29th Regt.* (Boston: Revere, 1770). Library of Congress, Prints and Photographs Division, LC-USZ62–35522 (b&w film copy neg.).

that nothing could "prevent further blood and carnage, but the immediate removal of the troops."[144] When Hutchinson and Dalrymple responded that they did not have the authority to redeploy troops, colonists informed the two that they "would infallibly unite and, at all events, drive the troops from the town."[145] This threat persuaded Dalrymple to dispatch the 29th Regiment to Castle Island's Long Barracks, while he awaited instructions about the 14th.[146]

As the withdrawal of troops began, General Gage returned, almost comically, to the Quartering Act. When he retroactively approved Dalrymple's removal of the 29th Regiment to the harbor island, Gage instructed the commanding officer "to incur as little expense as possible for the accommodation of the regiments."[147] Then, when it became clear that Hutchinson would not advocate keeping troops in Boston, Gage ordered Dalrymple "to prevail on government to provide the 14th with proper quarters in some other place."[148] But the colonists were outraged by the suggestion that they should supply soldiers who had fired on them. "It is in vain to expect any quarters or any other provision for the troops," Dalrymple informed Gage. "The assembly will do nothing of the kind," and the governor refused to "even propose it to them." The Quartering Act would not be implemented in Massachusetts because the Boston Massacre had snuffed out the spirit of the law. The colonists refused to share their places with British troops.[149]

Throughout the spring of 1770, Colonel Dalrymple emptied the city of soldiers. A week after the Boston Massacre, all of the 29th Regiment had removed to Castle Island, while the 14th Regiment had "never left our barracks since" the fatal confrontation.[150] Dalrymple then proceeded to extract the remaining soldiers house by house as he terminated leases throughout the city. On April 15, the colonel reported that "all the houses lately occupied as barracks are given up, one excepted": a building that served as an army hospital.[151] As six hundred soldiers occupied the Long Barracks, the poor living conditions became apparent, including "crowding thirty or forty men in a room eighteen feet square during the hot weather."[152] But Governor Hutchinson observed that any crowding was the army's fault, as "the greatest difficulty is caused by the multitude of women and children belonging to the 29th."[153] Finally, Gage conceded that Boston would never be reconciled to British regulars. "Experience has fully shown us the inutility of quartering troops in Boston, either for the support of government, or the preservation of the public tranquility," he informed Dalrymple in early April 1770. Thereafter, Gage sought new quarters for the troops.[154]

Cities and Towns

Five years after the Boston Massacre, Dr. Joseph Warren delivered an oration in commemoration of the bloodshed of March 1770. A member of the Sons of Liberty like Samuel Adams and Alexander McDougall, Warren was highly critical of British military power, especially in places like Boston. "Martial law and the government of a well regulated city are so entirely different," Warren expounded, "that it has always been considered improper to quarter troops in populous cities." Although Warren's speech reflected contemporary events, it revealed a surprising lack of memory. Before the garrisoning of Boston, soldiers and civilians had lived in harmony in many cities and towns of British North America. However, after the Battle of Golden Hill and the Boston Massacre, the idea of soldiers in the city was simply unimaginable.[155]

The military geography of cities and towns underwent a tremendous transformation between 1766 and 1770, although the change remained incomplete. Events in Boston and New York had little effect on the new colonies, where regulars continued to dominate Québec, Halifax, and St. Augustine. Likewise, the Battle of Golden Hill and the Boston Massacre did not preempt the Quartering Act in New Jersey or Philadelphia; rather, British troops continued to share public spaces, and colonists supplied barracked troops. Like the empire, communities had fragmented based on their experience with British military power. The Revolutionary War was not inevitable in 1770; instead, further events would intervene to change the focus of the question of where soldiers belonged from the city to the nation as a whole.

Urban historians often point to industrialization and immigration as moments when the villages of our colonial past became the modern cities we recognize. Often forgotten in their analyses is how quartering soldiers transformed the American metropolis. Ever since Colonel Richard Nicolls landed in New Amsterdam in 1664, soldiers had been a part of the urban American experience. Later, the Seven Years' War and the Quartering Act noticeably increased the urban presence of British regulars. All of this had happened without a debate over whether or not soldiers belonged in the city. Although most cities simply made room for the redcoats, by 1770 the idea of cities without soldiers had been firmly articulated. It would prove an extremely durable one. With the withdrawal of troops from Boston, Americans began to connect urban life with the absence of military power. Shortly after the Revolution, soldiers were removed from the American cities, to return only at moments of mass mobilization like the Civil War. The city as a place free of military geography had been crafted by soldier-civilian interactions of the late 1760s.

CHAPTER 6

Nation

American Armies and the March toward Independence

Edward Long was never really at home in Jamaica. In 1655, his great-grandfather helped snatch the island from the Spanish, and since then, three generations of Longs had profited from sugar plantations worked by African slaves. But like most West Indian elites, the Longs were absentee planters. Edward Long was born and educated in England. He was in his twenties before he traveled to Jamaica to take control of his father's estates and marry a wealthy heiress. Long assumed several offices in the colony, serving as governor's secretary and judge of the vice admiralty court. He also became a careful observer of colonial life, publishing his three-volume *History of Jamaica* in 1774. Yet life in the colonies was temporary for Edward Long. Five years before he published his *History*, he returned to England, never to see Jamaica again.[1]

Edward Long's distance from Jamaica shaped his views of quarters. In 1760, a Coromantee chief named Tacky launched a bloody slave revolt that lasted six months and killed ninety white and four hundred black Jamaicans. Although Long did not participate in Tacky's War, the experience led him to conclude that Jamaica's thirteen thousand white colonists could never by themselves control the nearly two hundred thousand Africans: they needed British regulars to do so. In his *History*, Long recounted how Jamaicans spent £100,000 building twenty-six barracks to welcome the 36th and 66th Regiments of Foot shortly after Tacky's War. The barracks were scattered across sixteen of the colony's eighteen parishes because, as Long wrote, it was "in the internal parts, where the greatest danger lies." This placed British soldiers among the plantations and empowered them to police slaves. Troops in Clarendon Parish monitored a site where "a small market is held occasionally by the Negroes of the neighborhood," while in Westmoreland Parish, slaves were "kept in awe by these barracks." It was a very different military geography from that of New York or Québec. In Jamaica, barracks did not serve to contain regulars—they were a dominant presence throughout the colony.[2]

Jamaica's embrace of British military power was remarkable for how much it differed from the situation in North America. Edward Long's praise for regulars barracked throughout Jamaica stood in sharp contrast to Samuel Adams's denunciations of British troops and Boston's refusal to billet troops. For Long, the availability of troops was an attribute of empire; thus he saw nothing wrong with spending two-thirds of Jamaica's annual budget quartering soldiers. Jamaica was in fact what Benjamin Franklin wished for the backcountry and the Earl of Hillsborough wanted for Massachusetts: a place where British soldiers restrained the local population. But Jamaica's military geography made no sense to colonists who saw British troops as an inconvenience to be tolerated as cheaply as possible. Moreover, the violence in New York and Boston in 1770 led many Americans to wonder if British regulars were necessary at all. Even southerners who lived amid large populations of African Americans could not fathom Long's solution. Slaveholders like George Washington built barracks to house slaves, not to give Britain an opportunity to police their property. While Jamaica was dependent on British military power for its survival, the thirteen American colonies were not. They were becoming a nation.[3]

There were many reasons why the American colonies became the United States, but a central cause was British military power. The old colonies had been skeptical of redcoats since they arrived in large numbers in 1755, but they made room for them in their houses, barracks, and cities until the Battle of Golden Hill and the Boston Massacre. Although the removal of troops from Boston and a threat of international war quelled an immediate rebellion, the lessons of 1770 could not be unlearned. As Americans grew doubtful that British soldiers would treat them any better than Jamaican slaves, they began building their own armies. Meanwhile, British military leaders grew overly cautious in their deployment of regulars. Although the army continued to dominate the new colonies, Commander in Chief Thomas Gage abandoned the borderland and failed to send troops to mediate intercolonial conflicts. The Americans filled this void with provincial troops and continental cooperation, further marginalizing the British army. From 1770 to 1775, American military power became the primary means by which the colonists began to imagine their own nation.

As had been true since 1755, Americans after 1770 experienced British military power through quarters. Events in Boston and New York did not end Whitehall's efforts to render the colonists financially responsible for British regulars. More importantly, British soldiers remained barracked in New York, New Jersey, and Philadelphia, leading to continued requests for the Americans to accommodate and supply the troops. But the Quartering Act was a shadow of its former self, ebbing along with the civilian-martial sharing that had once made the law effective. The British government made several attempts to improve the law, including as part of the Coercive Acts of 1774, but these corrections were too little, too late. As Whitehall tried a second time to use regulars to suppress rebellion in Boston, the last support for the American Mutiny Act evaporated. Yet before the colonists abandoned the law, the British army rendered it moot by withdrawing from friendly locales and creating a state of war in Massachusetts. As the Revolutionary War began, British troops invaded colonial homes while Americans eagerly billeted provincials.

As a place, the nation was in its infancy during the American Revolution. In Europe, the doctrine that the collective passion of nationalism should result in a sovereign state did not emerge until the nineteenth century. However, a proto-nationalism was evident much earlier in British North America, as the thirteen colonies coalesced around a common history and identity, setting themselves apart from the empire and neighboring peoples. It was not inevitable that this would happen. The Canadian colonies did not become a nation in the eighteenth century, but remained a diverse set of peoples within the British Empire. Key to the different trajectories of Canada and the United States, and at the heart of the rise of the nation, was war. War was a unifying experience that brought the American colonies together into a nation, giving them a common cause. In order to fight Britain, the Americans had to create a central government and a continental military. Through battle, the United States tested its boundaries, claiming territories that ultimately gave shape to the nation as a place.[4]

The discourse of military geography was also key to shaping the United States as a nation. Unlike for the house or the city, for the nation the dominant question was not whether soldiers belonged there but *which* soldiers. Since the French and Indian War, the North American Establishment had been the sinews of empire, holding together the old colonies, new colonies, and the backcountry. However, the garrisoning of Boston had initiated the debate of how much control local inhabitants had over British soldiers, including the ability to prohibit them altogether. Between 1770 and 1775, the colonists came to see British regulars as a foreign presence out of place in America. The rise of provincial armies further crafted America as distinct from the rest of the British Empire. By the Revolutionary War, the Americans had thoroughly rejected the vision of military geography that men like Edward Long accepted.

The Quartering Acts of 1770–1773

While the Battle of Golden Hill and the Boston Massacre riled the American colonists, change was afoot on the other side of the Atlantic. In January 1770, the Grafton ministry collapsed, and the king turned to Frederick, Lord North, to form a government. The eldest son of the Earl of Guilford, Lord North had served at Westminster and Whitehall since 1754, most recently as chancellor of the exchequer. In that time, he had acquired the reputation as a competent leader who was neither a radical Whig nor an unrepentant Tory. Upon becoming prime minister, North built a cabinet of men from various factions that was far more capable than any of the ministries previously formed under King George III.[5]

North applied this spirit of conciliation to American affairs. Seeking to end the impasse between colonial sympathizers like former Massachusetts governor Thomas Pownall and hard-liners like Secretary at War Viscount Barrington, North turned first to the Townshend Acts of 1767. He pushed Parliament to repeal the duties on glass, paint, and paper imported by the colonies while retaining the American Board of Custom Commissioners and the tax on tea. North dealt with the Mutiny Act for America in much the same way. With the statute scheduled for renewal in March 1770, the cabinet instructed Barrington to introduce a bill renewing the law without alteration. "I obeyed them, though unwillingly," the secretary explained privately, "for I want to make it effectual." The last five years had taught him that the Quartering Act had to be strengthened to be fully implemented in America, but the North ministry did not want to hear this. Parliament reauthorized the law as it was and moved on to more pressing issues.[6]

News of the Boston Massacre momentarily put quartering back into the House of Commons. As sketchy reports hit the London papers, Thomas Pownall offered his explanation for what had just transpired in Boston: Britain's exclusive control of military power. When he had been governor of Massachusetts, Pownall had authority over British regulars, but since then, the commander in chief had usurped the governor's prerogative. It was unconstitutional to have troops where the civilian authorities could not control them; consequently, it was no surprise that in Massachusetts "the

magistrates will not quarter them." "Whatever was the particular provocation of the late catastrophe," Pownall concluded, "the real cause is, you have
separated your people, the civil and military." Former West Florida governor
and now member of Parliament George Johnstone concurred. Five years earlier, Johnstone had used the Quartering Act to seize military buildings, and
the resulting tussle with General Gage had soured the governor's opinion
of the present organization of the North American Establishment. "Gentlemen who have not thought very deeply upon this subject, easily think the
civil, and military power can be separated," Johnstone told Commons. As
more members began to agree, it fell to the secretary at war to defend the
status quo. Still thinking imperially, Barrington explained that troops had to
be independent of colonial governments so they could move about North
America and lodge wherever they were needed. But Barrington was once
again out of step with Parliament and was savaged for being "inclined to
quarter troops in the private houses of America."[7]

There the matter stood for the next four years. In 1771, 1772, and 1773, Parliament renewed the Quartering Act without comment or change. Colonial
agents like Benjamin Franklin and Charles Garth took little notice of the renew-
als, while even Barrington moved on to other matters. Commander in Chief
Thomas Gage became a lone voice crying out for reforming the Mutiny Act for
America in order to save it. In November 1771, Gage informed Barrington that
"there appears to be only three ways of acting with respect to the quartering
of troops stationed in the colonies." First, Parliament could enforce the law,
presumably through another measure like the New York Restraining Act. Second, the government could revise the law by not requiring the army to barrack
troops before commanders sought alternative housing, and by placing heavy
penalties on magistrates who defied the law. Both remedies recalled Gage's
struggle with Boston three years earlier. Third, if Westminster was unwilling to
either enforce or change the law, then Gage insisted that Whitehall "remove the
troops into those provinces where barracks are supported at the expense of the
Crown." In other words, if the old colonies would not pay for quarters, then
the regulars should be redeployed to the new colonies and the Americans left
to defend themselves. However, no one at Whitehall wanted to deal with the
Quartering Act, so the law remained unchanged until it was too late.[8]

American Military Power in the Old Colonies

The North ministry might have ignored Gage's ideas regarding the Quartering Act, but it was not unappreciative of the general's seven years as commander in chief of all His Majesty's forces in North America. In April 1770,

King George III promoted Thomas Gage to lieutenant general, making him the one of the highest-ranking officers anywhere in the British Empire. By the time Gage received word of his promotion, however, British military power had lost some of its prestige in America. The garrisoning of Boston and the deaths of five Americans had taught the colonists to be suspicious of British troops. Although the regulars continued to barrack in several old colonies, Americans began to organize their own defense by rebuilding militias and provincial armies. From his headquarters on Broad Street in New York City, General Gage watched the emergence of American military power.[9]

For most of 1770, the lieutenant general's most pressing concern was Massachusetts. In late April, Gage ordered the 29th Regiment out of the province, although the civil authorities detained Captain Thomas Preston and eight regulars once a grand jury indicted them for murder in what was already being called the Boston Massacre. As the soldiers marched overland to Providence, Gage invoked the Quartering Act, asking the colonists to billet men along the way. Massachusetts magistrates ignored the request, but Rhode Island permitted the troops to "shift for a night, in barns" and other outbuildings.[10] Once the 29th departed, the 14th Regiment settled into the Long Barracks on Castle Island. But this did not sit well with many people in Massachusetts. In May, the town of Boxford voted not to import any goods from Britain in order to protest "quartering troops in this province in a time of profound peace." It was a bold statement that had never been uttered before: British soldiers did not belong in America. The reference to "peace" was also novel, as it revived a temporal understanding of British military power that had been muted since the passage of the American Mutiny Act.[11] Two months later, the Massachusetts House of Representatives adopted Boxford's position, denouncing "armies stationed here without our consent." General Gage ignored these complaints and left the 14th Regiment on Castle Island.[12]

As autumn approached, commanding officer Lieutenant Colonel William Dalrymple began to worry about the quarters on Castle Island (figure 6.1). Since the garrisoning of Boston, the government of Massachusetts had made little effort to maintain the Long Barracks, so two years later, the structures were "in a most dismal state and almost unfit for quartering troops."[13] Soon after, Gage received orders from Whitehall to seize Castle Island; if the colony would not quarter British soldiers, then Britain would. As Gage ordered repairs to the Long Barracks, he toyed with the idea of transforming Castle William into a massive citadel. He even sent military engineer Captain John Montresor to draw up plans, but such designs proved financially unfeasible. The Massachusetts House of Representatives was outraged when it learned

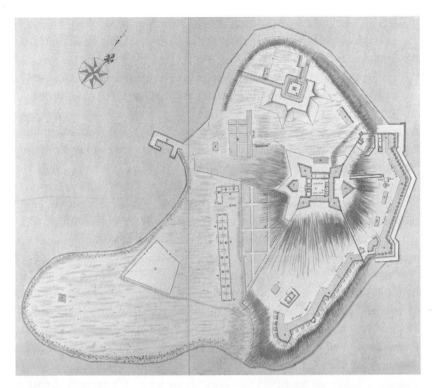

Figure 6.1. Barracks and casemates at Castle Island. *A general and particular plan of the island of Castle William near Boston. Shewing the works in their original and present state, together with sections through the same. Carried on and survey'd under the direction of, and by Iohn Montrésor, Esqr:, engineer extraordinary and Capt. Lieut:; by order of the Honble. Thomas Gage, Esqr:, Lieut: General and Commander in Chief of His Majesty's forces in North America &c. New York, 16th Jany: 1771.* Library of Congress, Geography and Map Division, gm71000937.

of the theft of provincial property, and it instructed its agent in London (a position now held by Benjamin Franklin) to lobby Parliament for redress. However, there was nothing Massachusetts could do to evict the troops, as the colony had no means of taking on four hundred regulars, so it dropped the matter. Oddly enough, by seizing Castle Island, the British army gave Massachusetts exactly what it wanted: the removal of regulars from the province. With the harbor installation no longer under colonial control, British troops no longer garrisoned Massachusetts.[14]

In October 1770, the trials of the soldiers involved in the Boston Massacre began. For the next two months, newspapers throughout the colonies carried the trials in great detail, although the verdicts were disappointing to many Americans. Captain Preston and six of the eight soldiers were acquitted; the other two were branded on the thumb and released.[15] By then, however, an international crisis in the South Atlantic had supplanted the trials in the papers. In June, Don Juan Ignacio de Madariaga and fourteen hundred Spanish troops landed at Port Egmont on a rough outcropping off the coast of Argentina known as the Falkland Islands to the British and the Islas Malvinas to the Spanish. Both Britain and Spain had been trying to colonize the islands for several years, although the arrival of a Spanish army convinced the British soldiers and colonists to evacuate. This flash of Spanish bravado enraged Britons, who demanded vengeance. Soon, Whitehall was ordering North America to prepare for war. Secretary of State for the Colonies the Earl of Hillsborough advised the colonial governors to make arrangements "in case matters should, contrary to His Majesty's just expectations, come to extremities," and in December 1770 he announced that recruiting parties would descend on North America. The Americans took this quite seriously and momentarily forgot about the Boston Massacre.[16]

The Falklands crisis had two important effects on American opinions of British military power. First, it revived the Quartering Act. The garrisoning of Boston had turned most colonies against the statute or produced dubious schemes like New York's plan to print money, such that by 1770 only Pennsylvania and New Jersey were in compliance with the law. Because the American Mutiny Act made billeting for recruiters and recruits legal, General Gage began to predict "great difficulties, when the recruiting parties are spread over the colonies."[17] But the commander in chief's pessimism was unfounded. Within six weeks of requesting billets for recruiting parties, Gage received positive responses from nine colonies, including Massachusetts and South Carolina. New Englanders even proved receptive when Gage informed them that the 64th and 65th Regiments were returning and would need quarters on their march to New York. Massachusetts's Acting Governor Thomas Hutchinson reported "no complaint anywhere else from the recruiting parties," while Rhode Island politely considered the request and Connecticut reauthorized a law allowing billeting in public houses. It was an international crisis, and the Americans wanted a powerful British army, even if it meant abiding by the Quartering Act.[18]

Second, the Falklands crisis encouraged American military power. With the "prospect of war with Spain," Governor Hutchinson invited the Massachusetts House of Representatives to revive the colony's militia. The assembly agreed, citing "the deplorable state of the militia of this province," and it began to write a new military law. Son of Liberty Samuel Adams took the lead on militia reform, informing the House of Representatives that he would "cheerfully do all" he could to support the cause. Reviving the Massachusetts militia coincided with a point that men like Adams had made in the "Journal of the Times": the colonists should take up arms in self-defense.[19] From London, Benjamin Franklin applauded the assembly's actions, arguing that in a world war, the colonists might have to defend themselves. "If we once lose our military spirit," Franklin continued, "we shall become contemptible."[20]

Massachusetts was not alone. Since the fall of Montréal, most colonies had abandoned their local defenses. New York's militia had not exercised in years, while South Carolina's militia was reduced to slave patrols. Despite their complaints about quarters, the Americans had come to depend on British regulars to defend them from foreign invasion or Indian attack. With the Falklands crisis, however, they rethought the situation. By January 1773, "several regiments of the militia" in Massachusetts were complete, while in New York, "the revival of a militia law" aroused "the desire of acquiring a knowledge in the art military."[21] Some colonies also renewed their provincial armies. Following the removal of British regulars in 1768, Georgia created the Light Infantry Company to defend Savannah. The Philadelphia Artillery patrolled the capital of Pennsylvania, while New York City raised seven hundred provincials for its defense. For the first time in a decade, the Americans devised their own defensive forces instead of relying on British troops.[22]

In the end, the preparations were unnecessary. As Britain and the colonies recruited soldiers, Lord North pursued a diplomatic course that resolved the matter peacefully. In January 1771, British and Spanish negotiators agreed to restore Port Egmont to Britain. However, six months passed before General Gage received orders to cease mobilization. By then, the Falklands crisis had changed the tone of military affairs in the old colonies. The Americans made their peace with the Quartering Act, but they also built their own armies.[23]

Once the threat of war passed, Gage returned to seeking quartering expenses from New York, New Jersey, and Pennsylvania for the three regiments barracked in the middle colonies. Of the three, New York proved the hardest to corral. The Board of Trade thought little of New York's plan to pay for military supplies by printing its own currency, and so it disallowed the law. In the wake of the Battle of Golden Hill, New Yorkers received this news poorly. Acting Governor Cadwallader Colden observed that "the grant of money for the troops is unpopular" and doubted that the House of Representatives would appropriate anything for the 26th Regiment in the Upper Barracks.[24] As a stalemate ensued, Gage resisted using army funds to supply the troops, as he worried it would cause New York to abandon the Quartering Act forever. So he ordered the officers to provision the men out of their own pockets until a solution could be found. Ultimately, the North ministry proffered a compromise: Parliament would allow New York to print £120,000 in paper currency to be legal tender for public transactions only. In other words, New York could raise revenue through the emission of its own currency, but this currency could only be used to pay taxes. New Yorkers panned the proposal, because it deprived them of a legal medium of exchange, and for six months the legislature took no action on quarters. However, the Falklands crisis and merchants' demand for any type of currency changed lawmakers' minds. In February 1771, the assembly approved a law printing £120,000 in New York currency, out of which up to £2,000 could be drawn "for quartering His Majesty's troops in this colony." But New York remained piqued. When Gage delivered the bill for quartering expenses incurred during the stalemate, the provincial council refused to pay it.[25]

New Jersey and Pennsylvania were more compliant. The former attempted to tie quartering expenses to its own currency bill, but when the Board of Trade disallowed this, the legislature approved £500 for supplies. Six months later, the money ran out, and Governor William Franklin asked the assembly for more. This elicited a nasty feud between the governor and legislators, during which representatives from Hunterdon County were instructed to ask the governor "whether to have the king's troops stationed among us in time of peace is constitutional and agreeable to our rights and privileges?"[26] But Gage had little patience for such intransigence; he evacuated the 29th Regiment from New Jersey and sent Franklin the bill. The colony had been slow to revive its militia, thus Gage reported "one half of New Jersey is now complaining that they have not troops." Indeed, lawmakers were more willing to abide by the Quartering Act when part of the Royal American Regiment arrived in August 1772.[27] Pennsylvania also bridled under the burden of quarters, if only momentarily. In 1766 and 1767, the assembly appropriated £12,000 for quartering expenses, but this fund was exhausted by 1772 when Major Nicholas Sutherland reported that the Philadelphia Barracks had fallen into disrepair. Although the House of Representatives approved another £4,000, it wanted answers on wagons the army had impressed five years earlier and insisted that all monies for quartering come from excise taxes on alcohol. By March 1772, positive responses from the three colonies led Barrington to conclude that "Americans are quiet in general, and growing reasonable with respect to the Mutiny Act."[28]

To some extent, the secretary at war was correct. In New York, Elizabeth, Perth Amboy, New Brunswick, and Philadelphia, British regulars slowly emerged from their barracks and began interacting with colonists again. On August 16, 1770, "most of the gentlemen of the city and army" in New York came together to dedicate a large, gilded statue of King George III near Fort George.[29] Cities also came together to remember the victory over the French. In 1773, the producers of *The Conquest of Canada; or the Siege of*

Québec recruited actual soldiers from the Philadelphia Barracks to enhance a theatrical performance, while troops in Perth Amboy invited "most of the principal gentlemen of the city" to celebrate with them at the barracks.[30]

But this was only half the story. American cities and towns were no longer shared spaces. A month after they venerated King George, New Yorkers erected a statue of the Earl of Chatham on Wall Street. Although many people gathered for the dedication, neither General Gage nor any British soldier attended to celebrate the man who had promoted the repeal of the Stamp Act. Royal holidays also divided communities, as festivities took on a martial cast. In 1771, Philadelphians commemorated the accession of King George III "especially in the barracks of this city," while in New York "the principal gentlemen assembled at the fort" for the king's birthday.[31] As American armies grew, competing events appeared. On June 4, 1773, New York's Governor William Tryon marked the king's birthday by reviewing seven companies of provincials and three militias in the Fields. The New York soldiers then "marched to the Bowling Green opposite Fort George," where local leaders "drank His Majesty's health." Simultaneously, the Royal Artillery fired guns in the Fields, and General Gage entertained "military gentlemen of this city" at his house. Unlike before, Britons and Americans now celebrated the monarch separately.[32]

While British and American soldiers competed for public space in New York City, militias and provincials had celebrations to themselves in Boston and Charleston. According to merchant and selectman John Rowe, Boston had long made the king's birthday "a great holiday," which often coincided with the militia's "high training day." Boston abandoned most royal celebrations when British troops arrived in 1768, but after the regulars departed, local forces reclaimed the day. On June 4, 1773, a company of cadets, the artillery, a regiment of provincials, and the city's militia "all made their appearance in the Common."[33] The scene was much the same in Charleston, where the colonists erected a statue of Chatham but not one of the king. In 1770, when a company of the Royal Artillery in the New Barracks launched fireworks for the king's birthday, the townspeople looked askance, announcing that "they will not dissemble joy, while they feel themselves unkindly treated, and oppressed." Thereafter, the Charleston militia organized its own celebrations of the monarch.[34]

The displays of militias and provincial forces in the cities were more theater than proof of prowess, but they spoke to a larger truth: Americans were replacing British regulars with their own soldiers. This was especially true in Georgia and South Carolina, where the removal of regulars left the borderland undefended. In response, Georgia raised twenty-nine companies of militia, consisting of nearly three thousand men, by December 1773. The prowess of these soldiers impressed German engineer and former architect of Charleston's defenses William De Brahm, who praised the colony's defense force as "all better trained" than any "militia in Europe." Out of the militia, the government raised a provincial army to expand the colony's frontier. After Georgia's Governor James Wright purchased two million acres from the Muscogees (Creeks) and Cherokees, he dispatched rangers to remove any Indians reluctant to depart the ceded lands.[35] South Carolina also took responsibility for the backcountry. Following the withdrawal of British troops, the Commons House abandoned Forts Prince George and Charlotte. Indeed, South Carolina needed neither regulars nor provincials to guard its backcountry; it had an aggressive backwoods population to do so instead. When the acting governor, William Bull II, toured "some of our western settlements," he observed several militia bands. "Every man is expert in the use of a gun," Bull noted.[36]

British regulars also withdrew from the northern borderland. Although the British army maintained installations along Lakes Ontario and Champlain, an explosion at Crown Point in April 1773 leveled the largest fort in the region and left only a skeleton crew between New York and Montréal. The army also failed to intervene when it may have proved constructive. In 1770, competing land claims brought settlers from Connecticut and Pennsylvanians to blows in the Wyoming Valley a hundred miles west of New York City. In response, Pennsylvania's Governor John Penn asked General Gage for "the aid of the military, to support the civil power" to settle the dispute.[37] But the commander in chief refused, informing Penn that "the affair in question seems to be a dispute concerning property."[38] Perhaps the Boston Massacre made Gage skittish, but the lack of British military power in the Wyoming Valley allowed armed colonists to make war on each other. Thereafter, the North American Establishment ceased to intervene in colonial disputes. Three years later, settlers from New York and New Hampshire fought over Vermont, but when Governor Tryon asked for help, Gage replied that he thought it "a dangerous tendency to employ regular troops, where there are militia laws." The Americans were on their own.[39]

In effect, the British army forfeited large portions of the borderland. From the Green Mountains to the Georgia Piedmont, colonists built an American military power that was separate and independent from Britain. This had two effects. First, as provincial armies ventured into the backcountry, they seized large amounts of land and pushed the colonial frontiers west. When this provoked conflicts with Native Americans, such as Georgia's war against the Muscogees and Lord Dunmore's War against the Shawnees, colonial

governments assumed exclusive control over interior lands and their inhabitants.[40] Second, with the British army unwilling to broker disputes, some
Americans called for intercolonial cooperation. In *Common Sense*, Thomas
Paine would invoke "the difference between Pennsylvania and Connecticut"
to argue for American independence, adding that "nothing but continental
authority can regulate continental matters." By determining its own borders
and seeking intercolonial unity, American military power was setting the
foundations for a nation.[41]

On December 29, 1773, New York's Government House, inside Fort
George, burned down. Governor William Tryon and his wife Margaret Wake
escaped with their lives, but they lost £6,000 worth of belongings and had
to find a new place to live. Since Richard Nicolls arrived in 1664, every New
York governor had resided inside Fort George alongside barracked soldiers,
and it was inside the fort that the provincial council met. The loss of Government House literally evicted the civilian government from Fort George. The
century-long marriage of American colonial governance and British military
power was permanently and spatially ruptured.[42]

British Military Power in the New Colonies, the Backcountry, and the Islands

As the American colonies began to establish their own defenses, the rest
of British North America continued to be subject to redcoats. The Boston
Massacre did little to turn people outside the old colonies against the British
army, and the Falklands crisis was not a cause for mobilization. As a result,
British military power remained important in Nova Scotia, Québec, and the
Floridas, as well as in the backcountry, Bermuda, and the West Indies. However, not all places in British North America were protected by regulars. The
concentration of the North American Establishment that had begun in 1768
continued apace; thus while the British army became more powerful in the
new colonies' capital cities and the Caribbean, it vanished in the backcountry
and Bermuda. Yet the loss of regulars did not stimulate militias and provincial armies in these places; rather, the inhabitants pleaded for more British
troops. Ultimately, the divergent views of British military power widened the
rift between the colonies, ensuring that when Americans declared independence, Canada, Florida, and the islands did not follow.

Numerically, the concentration of troops was greater in the new colonies, the backcountry, and the islands than in the old colonies. Five regiments were stationed in the British West Indies, although these fell outside
the North American Establishment. Among the fifteen regiments under the

purview of the commander in chief, twelve garrisoned the new colonies and the borderland. In September 1771, Thomas Gage reported four regiments in Québec, three in Nova Scotia, two in East Florida, and one each in West Florida, around the Great Lakes, and "at Fort [de] Chartres, Pitt, etc." A few companies from these regiments quartered in the Bahamas and Newfoundland. General Gage and barrack master general James Robertson constantly worried about the cost of quartering three thousand soldiers in a dozen forts and barracks scattered across a continent, so they looked for ways to reduce costs by concentrating forces.[43]

By 1770, five cities had emerged as the centers of British military power in North America: Québec, Montréal, Halifax, St. Augustine, and Pensacola. It was these cities that Gage consistently focused on, approving exorbitant amounts to maintain their barracks. Québec City held the largest number of troops, and thus it received the most attention. In 1771, military engineer Lieutenant John Marr produced an elaborate plan for the city's defenses, including new barracks estimated to cost £85,000.[44] Halifax and Montréal also received thousands of pounds for barrack repairs, although the poor state of quarters made Florida a top priority.[45] In St. Augustine, the British army converted an abandoned Franciscan monastery into officers' quarters and built new barracks for the men complete with "a large iron weathercock, which is to be placed upon a cupula in the center of the building."[46] However, bricks and building materials had to be imported from distant places, increasing the cost and delaying construction, such that billeting did not end in St. Augustine until the summer of 1771.[47]

With or without barracks, the British army dominated the new colonies' cities. Visiting Halifax in September 1774, Patrick McRobert contrasted the city's vast military infrastructure with its paucity of civilian buildings. A "large and convenient barracks for above a thousand men" towered over a city of unpaved streets and wooden buildings, many of which "seem to be going to decay."[48] Nor were the troops confined to martial spaces. When the 7th Regiment arrived in Québec in June 1773, the city's barracks were not prepared, and so the soldiers were "marched into quarters of cantonment in the environs of this city" and billeted in private houses.[49] Regulars also went into homes for nefarious reasons. In Halifax, a soldier from the 65th Regiment "entered the dwelling house of William Mott" and robbed it, although the army later detained the culprit.[50] However, there was little agitation against the regulars in the new colonies. While Americans grew suspicious of British soldiers, Canadians and Floridians celebrated them. When the 21st Regiment appeared in St. Augustine in February 1771, East Florida's Governor James Grant praised the soldiers, especially those capable of playing music. "This has become the gayest place in America," Grant contended, adding that numerous "balls, assembly, and concerts" made the colonists unwilling "to enter into politics and faction" like Americans.[51]

The cost of barracking the cities was the desertion of the outlying forts. Although Whitehall shuttered most installations in the northern and southern peripheries in 1768, a number persisted across Canada and Florida, most of which were garrisoned by a company of soldiers eking out an existence. When Lieutenant Governor Joseph Gorham arrived at Placentia, Newfoundland, in 1771, he found "most everything of that kind out of repair" and the soldiers "obliged to purchase their cooking utensils."[52] But Newfoundland long had been ignored by the British army; more novel was the ill treatment of troops along the St. Lawrence River and on the Gulf Coast. When a military engineer delivered a report of the dire condition of Trois-Rivières and Chambly, Gage made the two forts split £500 with Montréal to waterproof the barracks, but no more. Barracks in Mobile received less than one-sixth as much as Pensacola, while Oswegatchie relied on the generosity of the commanding officer at Niagara to keep the soldiers' wives and children from starving. As the Earl of Hillsborough dryly observed, "All the king's troops in America are not as well accommodated with barracks as those at St. Augustine."[53]

A similar dynamic emerged on the borderland. Consistent with Hillsborough's plan for evacuating the backcountry, the British army maintained garrisons at Niagara and Detroit at considerable expense. The soldiers helped to preserve placid relations between colonists and Native Americans even as the number of white settlers in the region increased. In part, they did so by policing the borderland. When a white settler named Ramsay murdered Native Americans near Niagara in early 1773, British soldiers apprehended the perpetrator and transported him to Albany for trial. Although General Gage had once rued the provision of the Quartering Act that made this possible, by 1773 he no longer worried about its effects on British-Indian relations. Similarly, British soldiers at Fort Pitt may have forestalled growing tensions between settlers and Shawnee Indians in the Ohio Country. However, the smaller forts on the borderland were forgotten. The commander at Michilimackinac complained the barracks were "so rotten as to render it dangerous to the troops." Forts Pitt and de Chartres went untended, while the commander in chief even left his namesake, Fort Gage, to rot.[54]

In addition to concentrating troops, General Gage tried to cut costs by transferring the cost of quarters onto the colonists. In a reversal of events in 1765–1766, now Gage used the breakdown of the American Mutiny Act in the old colonies to push for its implementation in the new. In 1771, Gage reduced billeting costs in Halifax by ordering the officers of the 59th Regiment to be quartered in the city's barracks. A year later, a shortage of supplies and transportation for troops traveling from New York to Montréal prompted Gage to invoke the Quartering Act in Québec. "When regiments march through the inhabited country they must supply themselves," Gage instructed, or they could "do as they do in this part of America, make their landlords furnish their diet, paying for the same as directed in the Mutiny Act."[55] However, officers in Halifax refused to barrack with their men, and Quebecers would not provision troops, so Gage's efforts failed. Frustrated with Canadians' parsimony, perhaps the general appreciated the old colonies. When Walter Patterson requested regulars to help settle St. John's Island (later Prince Edward Island), Gage refused, tartly informing Patterson that the island would be settled "as most of the other colonies have been established; without putting the mother country to the expense of troops."[56]

While Gage's attempt to enforce the Quartering Act in Canada proved futile, he faced continued pressure from Whitehall to reduce the cost of the North American Establishment. As New York resorted to paper currency schemes and Massachusetts abandoned Castle Island, the cost of quartering troops weighed more heavily on the British Treasury. Accordingly, Whitehall finally agreed to remove regulars from the backcountry. In late 1771, the Earl of Hillsborough convinced the cabinet that to pay for new barracks at Pensacola and St. Augustine, it had to eliminate costs in Ohio. The secretary of state ordered Fort de Chartres closed in May 1772, leaving only a skeleton crew at Fort Gage. Gage subsequently closed Fort Pitt, effectively emptying the Illinois and Ohio Country of British military power, and leaving the borderland to Native Americans and white settlers. As usual, Pennsylvania was out of step with military matters. When the colonists at Pittsburgh heard that the nearby citadel would be closing, they proposed that the province support it with "a small number of troops to garrison the fort, in place of the king's forces." Gage was sympathetic, but a military engineer determined that there was nothing worth saving at Fort Pitt, so the departing troops demolished it before anyone could stop them.[57]

The removal of troops from the backcountry turned out to be Hillsborough's last major act as secretary of state for the colonies. There was mounting pressure to abolish the borderland and open the West to white settlement. Trader James Sterling claimed that merchants and colonists at Detroit were "begging for a government," opining that "the settlement is really becoming too powerful" to continue under martial rule. Like colonizers before him, Sterling argued that a western colony could revive the Quartering Act, as the settlers would be able to supply the troops in forts on the Great Lakes.[58] By

August 1772, this view had captivated the cabinet, and Lord North forced out Hillsborough, according to Barrington, "because he did not choose to carry into execution a measure tending to settle the interior parts of America."[59] His replacement was an enthusiastic colonizer, William Legge, the second Earl of Dartmouth. In his first letter to Gage, Dartmouth declared the king's intent that "a settlement should be formed upon the lands" acquired from the Haudenosaunee (Iroquois) in the Treaty of Fort Stanwix. Thereafter, former West Florida governor Montfort Browne resumed lobbying for a colony near Natchez, while in Illinois, speculators purchased land directly from the Indians.[60]

Gage thought little of the change in policy. "I cannot see any good" in Dartmouth's plan, he confided to Barrington, "though I think I perceive much evil to arise from it."[61] Consequently, Gage refused to deploy any troops to the West. Like his refusal to send soldiers into the Wyoming Valley, this decision left the borderland to the Americans. Without the British army to block their movement, white settlers pushed into Kentucky and the Ohio Country, and the American frontier moved west. The most that Parliament did to protect the French and Native American inhabitants of the borderland was pass the Québec Act in 1774. In addition to restoring French civil law and allowing Roman Catholics to hold office in the Canadian colony, the law surrendered all lands between the Great Lakes and the Ohio River to the provincial government of Québec. This increased the uncertainty of the region and ended the Quartering Act west of the Appalachians. By extending the boundaries of a colony where the statute had never been in force, the Québec Act ensured that Ohio and Illinois did not have to pay for quarters either.[62]

Britain's island colonies also relied on British regulars for their defense, although they willingly provided accommodations, supplies, and transport. Since the end of the Seven Years' War, the Bahamas, Barbados, Bermuda, Jamaica, the Leeward Islands, and the Windward Islands had prospered from slavery and sugar. Most had large black majorities, such that the white colonists lived in constant fear of slave revolt. Following Tacky's War in Jamaica, Grenada faced rebellion in 1767, as did Tobago in 1771 and St. Vincent in 1772. In response, Edward Long's solution for Jamaica was applied throughout the region: the white colonists demanded British regulars to defend them from their slaves. Britain obliged with five regiments to protect its most lucrative colonies. In return, the islanders paid for quarters. Nearly all the islands had elected assemblies that lavishly funded barracks and supplies. Except for Barbados, which bolstered its militia, the spirit of the Quartering Act thrived in the West Indies.[63]

Of the islands, only Bermuda and the Bahamas were part of the North American Establishment. Whiter and less profitable than their neighbors, the two shared fifty soldiers between them until 1768, when General Gage evacuated regulars from the southern periphery. Until 1768, the two island colonies had responded to the Mutiny Act for America in much the same way as the old colonies: Bermuda delayed implementation of the law for several years, while the Bahamas disregarded it altogether. Four years later, however, the two were more in line with the Caribbean colonies. Both responded poorly to the loss of troops and pleaded with Gage for regulars. Although Bermuda reformed its militia law, and the Bahamas proposed a civilian night watch, neither viewed self-defense as adequate. Bermuda's pleas went unanswered until 1778, but the Bahamas received a company of the 31st Regiment during the Falklands crisis. The troops arrived with a request that the assembly provide bedding, furniture, and fuel to the barracked troops. At first, the Bahamian assembly repeated its intransigence, but its defiance softened in time. In April 1772, the assembly agreed to provide "oil and candles for the troops," finally implementing the Quartering Act in the Bahamas six years after Gage's initial request.[64]

The Coercive Acts

By 1772, Lieutenant General Thomas Gage had become deeply suspicious of Americans. In June, the British customs schooner HMS *Gaspee* ran aground in Rhode Island, and the Sons of Liberty torched it. Incensed, Whitehall dispatched a commission to investigate and bring the culprits to justice. Although Gage offered to send British regulars to protect the commissioners, he knew "that no magistrate will ask their assistance; nor do I believe they will give them quarters."[65] British military power had become ineffectual in the old colonies, and the commander in chief despaired that Whitehall was doing nothing to stem the growing American violence. In a series of private letters to Secretary at War Barrington, Gage relayed rumors from Boston of obstinate colonists, unchecked smuggling, even talk of independence. "Something is generally out of order in this part of the world," he griped. Although he had been ambivalent about the use of British military power to enforce parliamentary law in 1768, now Gage called on Britain to "support that supremacy which she claims over the members of the empire," or else "we shall become a vast empire composed of many parts, disjoined and independent of each other." It was a prescient warning that Gage ultimately took to England. In late 1772, the general requested leave from his post to deal with affairs at home, placing him in London when events in the colonies pushed Whitehall to take a firmer hand against the Americans.[66]

Shortly before Gage departed for England, Parliament passed the Tea Act. As prime minister, Lord North had yet to abandon his conciliatory approach to the colonies. Although the middle colonies complied with the Quartering Act, smugglers continued to defy the last vestige of the Townshend Acts: a three pence per pound duty on tea. This annoyed North, who calculated that the average American paid one-fiftieth the taxes of a Briton. When the empire's exclusive purveyor of tea, the East India Company, teetered on bankruptcy, North decided to nudge the colonists toward compliance with the Tea Act of 1773. The statute reduced the cost of shipping tea to the New World and, therefore, the price of tea. Even with new tax, it was now cheaper for Americans to purchase tea legally than to smuggle it.[67]

The Tea Act outraged Americans, especially the Sons of Liberty. As Samuel Adams and Alexander McDougall organized protests in Boston and New York, respectively, incendiary broadsides appeared. Some connected the Tea Act to previous injustices. A letter in the *Boston Evening Post* condemned the law for "raising a revenue in America, which in some future time might afford quartering."[68] As ships laden with six hundred thousand pounds of tea headed to America, nervous customs officials wondered if British troops might provide protection when the tea was unloaded. However, acting commander in chief Frederick Haldimand informed officials that should they "require the aid of His Majesty's troops," then he expected them to be "accompanied by a civil magistrate."[69] In New York and Philadelphia, the merchants who had agreed to sell the tea on consignment resigned, but in Boston, the consignees refused to back down. When four ships appeared in Boston Harbor in late November, some wondered if the soldiers of the 64th Regiment stationed on Castle Island might intervene, while rumors circulated that the tea would be "deposited in the lower barracks" on the island. But this never happened. On December 16, 1773, the Sons of Liberty dumped the tea into Boston Harbor while British regulars were stranded three miles away.[70]

The Boston Tea Party extinguished Lord North's conciliatory policy. News of the colonists' actions outraged London, as seemingly everyone at Whitehall and Westminster called for action against Massachusetts. As North sought a punishment to fit the crime, he consulted with former Massachusetts governors Thomas Pownall and Sir Francis Bernard, as well as General Gage. Since arriving in London in July 1773, Gage had been feted, and he and his wife Margaret attended a royal levee. He also reconnected with his brother William, Viscount Gage, a member of Parliament and paymaster of pensions, and discussed military affairs with the cabinet. When news of the

Boston Tea Party arrived, Gage had an audience with King George III, who was impressed by the general's analysis of American affairs. It soon became clear that Gage was the one indispensable part of any plan to bring the colonies to heel. In April 1774, Thomas Gage was named governor of Massachusetts. He retained his position as commander in chief, and the cabinet voted to send four new regiments to Massachusetts. For the first time since the end of the French and Indian War, military and civil power was bestowed on one man.[71]

Before Gage departed for Boston, Lord North led Parliament in approving three Coercive Acts: the Boston Port Act, which closed Boston Harbor until Massachusetts made restitution for the lost tea; the Administration of Justice Act, which allowed British soldiers to be tried in courts outside the old colonies; and the Massachusetts Government Act, which gave the governor wide-ranging powers. Deemed the Intolerable Acts by the Americans, these laws escalated matters considerably. In September 1774, representatives from twelve of the colonies convened the First Continental Congress in Philadelphia. The delegates debated how best to confront the Coercive Acts, ultimately opting for another boycott on British trade and a petition to the king.[72]

There was a fourth Coercive Act: the Quartering Act. In March 1774, Parliament renewed the Mutiny Act for America of 1765 and its 1769 amendment without comment, but when the idea of taking a hard line on the colonies gained popularity, Barrington introduced a second quartering bill to Commons. The secretary at war no doubt had consulted with Gage, as the new law repeated an idea Gage had proposed three years earlier: the army should not be required to fill a colony's barracks before it could rent houses. The bill moved quickly through Commons and was stymied only temporarily in the House of Lords by the Earl of Chatham. On June 2, King George III assented to the second Quartering Act of 1774. Henceforth, should a colony's barracks not be located where British regulars were "necessary and required," then the army could direct troops to "be quartered and billeted in such manner as is now directed by law, where no barracks are provided by the colonies." Should local magistrates delay appointing quarters for more than twenty-four hours, then the governor was empowered to select houses for the troops.[73]

The Americans largely ignored the Quartering Act of 1774, focusing on the other Coercive Acts instead. Rumors spread through London that New York and Connecticut had joined Massachusetts in a nonimportation agreement "on hearing of the bill being brought in for quartering soldiers in America," but this was hyperbole.[74] The text of the law was printed in Boston and Philadelphia, but it barely made an appearance at the Continental

Congress. Although delegates decried the four regiments Gage brought to Boston, the American Mutiny Act appeared as only one of thirteen "acts of Parliament" Congress demanded be repealed.[75]

Nevertheless, some historians have misunderstood the law, equating the loosening of restrictions on when soldiers could billet in houses with forcing troops into private homes. But the 1774 revision did not invalidate the law's directive that soldiers could be quartered only in barracks, public houses, or uninhabited buildings, not private homes. Gage had toyed with billeting in homes in the past, but he had no taste for attempting this in Massachusetts. In retrospect, the revision should be critiqued for its timidity, not its tyranny. Either Gage or Barrington should have added a solution for when the Americans refused to pay for supplies or transportation. But Gage had abandoned the Quartering Act by this point; he no longer expected soldiers and civilians to share places peacefully.[76]

Occupying Boston

Back in Massachusetts, Abigail Adams waited for the British invasion. The future founding mother began life as the daughter of a Weymouth parson and absorbed much of the colony's Puritan past. Home-schooled in religion and politics, Abigail (née Smith) was as righteous as Samuel Adams; indeed, she married his cousin John. In April 1768, the Adamses moved to Boston, only to be joined by British regulars six months later. Abigail Adams bore and buried a daughter during the garrisoning of Boston, and remained in the city with her husband and remaining children after the troops departed. On the eve of the Boston Tea Party, Adams corresponded with Mercy Otis Warren, keeping her Plymouth friend apprised of the situation in Boston because she was "so sincere a lover of your country." As she waited for news of Boston's punishment, the Boston woman quoted *Paradise Lost* to Warren: "What though the place be lost?" As Parliament passed the Coercive Acts, Abigail Adams rallied her "courage never to submit or yield."[77]

On May 13, 1774, Thomas Gage landed in Massachusetts to take control of the colony's civil and military operations. Much had changed since Gage had visited Boston six years earlier. In 1768, the army came to enforce parliamentary law, but in 1774, soldiers arrived to punish the city. However, American military power had become greater and more confrontational in the meantime. Upon entering Boston, Gage was greeted by a regiment of provincials, companies of grenadiers and artillery, the Boston militia, and John Hancock's "company of cadets." Such forces represented colonists like Abigail Adams who saw British troops as hostile invaders.[78]

FIGURE 6.2. Abigail Adams. Harris and Ewing, photographer, *Portrait of Abigail Adams by Benjamin Blyth* (1910–20). Library of Congress, Prints and Photographs Division, LC-DIG-hec-13515 (digital file from original negative).

Soon after his arrival, Gage set about reorganizing civilian and military affairs in Massachusetts. As governor, he removed the General Court to Salem and sacked members of the provincial council suspected of disloyalty. Even so, he had to listen to members of the House of Representatives do nothing "but harangue" until the Massachusetts Government Act arrived in June and he could dissolve the assembly.[79] These actions made Gage an enemy of Abigail Adams, especially since one of the dismissed councilors was her husband. As general, Gage established British military power in the heart of Boston. When the 4th and 43rd Regiments arrived from England in the middle of June, and the 5th and 38th from Ireland two weeks later, Gage ordered the troops to encamp on Boston Common. The general did not press the legislature to comply with the Quartering Act, but paid for supplies out of the army's budget. Gage also ordered the two thousand soldiers to avoid "all intercourse with the inhabitants," thus sealing off the Common from Bostonians.[80] Brigadier General Earl Percy subsequently increased the segregation of soldiers from civilians by placing pickets around the Common "to prevent people coming into the camp who have no business there." Percy also monitored soldiers who left the Common, requiring that each one carry a pass and commanding them to avoid a baker named Stephen Harris who was known for "deceiving and abusing the soldiers."[81]

Nevertheless, conflicts soon arose. In early August, "several persons" appeared before the Boston selectmen to complain about the "ill treatment from some officers."[82] Desertion also plagued the regiments. At first, Gage issued pardons to entice the deserters to return, but then turned to harsher measures. He ordered Valentine Ducket "shot in the rear of the camp in the Common, pursuant to the sentence of a court martial," and instructed the province's attorney general to file suits against colonists for "seducing" soldiers to desert.[83] Attempts by British soldiers to regulate the flow of people through Boston Neck also aroused the ire of the colonists. In mid-July, troops at the Neck reported being fired on, and two months later, delegates to a convention meeting to denounce the Coercive Acts listed "the repeated insults offered by the soldiery, to persons passing and repassing into that town" as part of the Suffolk Resolves.[84]

As fall approached, General Gage worried a rebellion was imminent. Believing that Boston "will keep quiet, as long as the troops are there, but no longer," he ordered portions of the North American Establishment to Boston.[85] In early August, the 59th Regiment arrived from Halifax, joined two days later by the 23rd Regiment from New York, driving the total number of British regulars in the city to nearly three thousand.[86] The new arrivals joined the soldiers on Boston Common or encamped at Fort Hill, but a tent city was not a permanent solution. As the weather grew colder, Gage sought more substantial quarters. The Quartering Act of 1774 granted the army the right to billet troops in uninhabited houses, but Gage ignored the law. Cost may have motivated this decision, especially since Massachusetts was not paying for billets. An officer insisted that it was "difficult to find houses for quartering," and what there was cost "one thousand pounds a regiment." Instead, he concluded "that barracks can be built on a more thrifty footing than they can be hired, and fitted up." Gage agreed and invited military engineer Captain

John Montresor to design the structure. As had been the case in other American cities years before, the only place to build massive barracks was on the city's common. Like New York, Boston would have a central citadel with "a view of commanding the obedience of the town."[87]

By early September 1774, work had begun on a barracks on Boston Common. Outraged, the Sons of Liberty and other Bostonians sought to halt construction. The city selectmen declared those who worked on the barracks "enemies to the rights and liberties of America," and in response "two hundred artificers employed on the barracks" walked off the job.[88] Others sought to deprive the army of the means to build by destroying construction materials. Merchant Richard Lechmere reported how "the populace" destroyed the four thousand feet of plank boards such that "the barracks that were begun, now stand still."[89] Gage thought he smelled a conspiracy, informing the Earl of Dartmouth that Bostonians' opposition to barracks was "to oblige the troops to force their quarters upon the inhabitants," thus escalating matters.[90] Bereft of Boston laborers, Gage sought tradesmen from surrounding colonies. In a test of intercolonial unity, Portsmouth, New Hampshire, instructed its artificers not to build the Boston barracks, but the allure of employment was too great. Soon workers from New Hampshire, New York, and Nova Scotia headed to Boston. It is unclear if barracks ever arose on Boston Common. Although the newspapers reported completion, maps of the city like figure 6.3 depict tents, not barracks.[91]

It was at this point that Abigail Adams fled Boston. Fearful for their safety, she and her family moved to suburban Braintree, where they watched military geography envelop the capital. "The governor is making all kinds of warlike preparations," Adams observed. In addition to its work on the Common, the army was "mounting cannon upon Beacon Hill, digging entrenchments upon the Neck, placing cannon there, encamping a regiment there, throwing up breastworks, etc." She also monitored Governor Gage's undermining of American military power as he seized the colony's gunpowder supply and persuaded General William Brattle of the Massachusetts militia to ally with the British army.[92] For his part, Gage continued to fear rebellion. "Affairs here are worse than even in the time of the Stamp Act," the general informed Barrington; "no people are more determined for a civil war."[93] When Whitehall brushed off his request for another twenty thousand soldiers, Gage ordered the 10th and 52nd Regiments from Québec, the 18th from Philadelphia, the 47th from New Jersey, and two companies of the 65th from Newfoundland to Boston.[94] As five thousand British regulars occupied a city of only sixteen thousand civilians, Boston's selectmen condemned the governor for "reducing this metropolis in other respects to the state of a

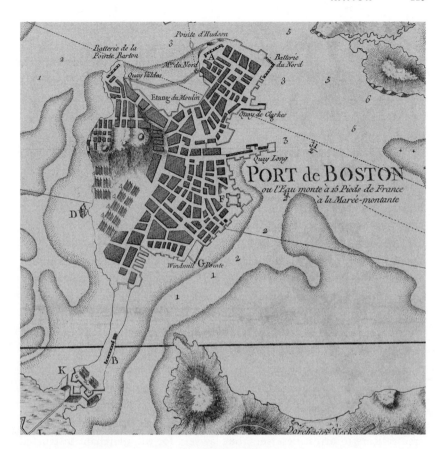

FIGURE 6.3. Boston in 1775. Chevalier de Beaurain, *Carte du port et havre de Boston* (Paris, 1776). Courtesy of the Massachusetts Historical Society.

garrison."[95] The same point was made by the Massachusetts Provincial Congress, an extralegal body that convened in place of the prorogued House of Representatives. The Congress denounced Gage's "unusual and warlike preparations," including "keeping a standing army in the province, in time of peace, without the consent of the representatives."[96]

The growing number of soldiers in Boston forced Gage to find more quarters. Although troops billeted in tents and buildings, rumors spread that redcoats were invading private homes. A letter in the *New London Gazette* expected Boston's "townhouses to be converted into barracks, and the soldiery empowered to regulate, preside over, and direct all our affairs, public, as well as private."[97] Such stories aroused sympathy outside New England as well. The *Virginia Gazette* ran a letter that labeled "quartering troops on the town of Boston" a "hostile invasion," and reprinted an article from a London paper decrying "quartering soldiers at pleasure upon private houses, so that nothing was any longer their own."[98] Although such stories were hyperbole, they matched the thoughts of General Gage. "From the situation of this country," he wrote on Christmas 1774, "I should be justified in quartering His Majesty's troops in any shape." Once the financial aspect of the American Mutiny Act collapsed, there was little reason to preserve the law's protection of domestic privacy.[99]

As Massachusetts deserted the Quartering Act, the other colonies followed suit. When the occupation of Boston began, the three middle colonies that barracked British troops were in compliance with the statute. Pennsylvania's 1772 appropriation of £4,000 was not yet depleted, while the assemblies of New York and New Jersey approved barrack supplies in March 1774.[100] Once the Coercive Acts arrived, however, all three turned against quartering. New Yorkers rioted, while Philadelphians insisted that the Continental Congress pursue the "repeal of all statutes for quartering troops in the colonies, or subjecting them to any expense on account of such troops."[101] As the occupation of Boston wore on, opposition grew personal. In July 1774, a Philadelphia jury heard a case against Major Isaac Hamilton brought by a local merchant. Hamilton had discovered a deserter from the 46th Regiment working for the merchant and sought his return, but the merchant objected to losing his employee, so he sued the major. At trial, Hamilton produced the deserter's confession and corroborating evidence, but the jury found for the merchant anyway, awarding him £13 in damages. The Mutiny Act for America empowered officers to arrest deserters, but lawyers for the merchant instructed jurors "not to pay the least attention to any of the English acts of Parliament." With that, the one colony that had always been fully compliant with the Quartering Act brushed the law aside.[102]

The Quartering Act also failed because it became moot. As the occupation of Boston grew more extreme, General Gage drained nearly all British regulars from New York City, New Jersey, and Philadelphia. By the fall of 1774, the middle colonies ceased to host the North American Establishment for the first time in a decade. New York's Governor Colden complained to Whitehall about the loss of troops, asserting that there were "only half a dozen officers, and about one hundred men" left in the Upper Barracks.[103] Colden insisted that "the moderate inhabitants have constantly expressed a wish that we had a more formidable power," as they feared that "a neglect of proper precautions" might embolden radicals to commence hostilities in New York.[104] But the British army departed the middle colonies and took the justification for the Quartering Act with it. In February 1775, New York ignored a request for supplies, while the New Jersey assembly duplicitously dismissed a call for quartering expenses incurred the previous year as "new, uncommon, and never allowed of by this colony."[105]

With the British army gone, the military geography in American cities and towns collapsed. Soon after the 18th Regiment departed Pennsylvania, barrack master Joseph Fox requested funds to repair the Philadelphia Barracks. The Pennsylvania House of Representatives pondered the matter for a few days before replying that "they do not think it expedient at this time to repair the barracks in the Northern Liberties, or to provide furniture or utensils for the same."[106] The New Jersey legislature likewise dismissed warnings that the province's barracks needed attention, voting down a bill for repairs. Even New York's martial space shrank. As the number of soldiers dwindled, civilians seized control of the Fields, using the common to advocate for boycotts against Great Britain. Meanwhile, the city plunked Bridewell, a prison, in front of the barracks. Later, when a fire broke out "behind the Upper Barracks, in a house that had some time been occupied as a military hospital," the city refused to replace it.[107]

By 1775, General Gage had concentrated British military power in America. Except for a few soldiers at New York City and Ticonderoga, the only regulars in the old colonies were in Boston. Local militias and provincial soldiers filled the void left by the redcoats, creating a shadow American army ready to oppose Great Britain. Accordingly, as Gage tightened his grip on Boston, the rest of America slipped through his fingers. In retrospect, it was probably a mistake to let Thomas Gage continue as commander in chief while tasking him with governing Massachusetts. With his singular focus on Boston, Gage forgot about the rest of the colonies. Not only did the loss of troops allow New York and other places to revolt; it permitted Massachusetts to determine the fate of British military power in America. Once New Englanders took up arms against British regulars, there was little to stop other Americans from following them.

Toward Independence

In May 1775, Benjamin Franklin returned to Philadelphia. The once vocal proponent of empire was now an advocate for American independence. Since contributing to the Quartering Act in 1765, Franklin had grown increasingly critical of British military power. When he learned of the Boston Massacre, he cast British regulars as foreign invaders, wondering how Britons would like it if American legislatures allowed the king to "raise an army and bring it into England, quartering it here in time of peace without the consent of the Parliament." In time, Franklin began to write of the American colonies as "distinct states, as I conceive they really are." In December 1774, Franklin believed the only hope of reconciliation lay in "a durable union between Britain and the colonies," including a stipulation that "no troops [be allowed] to enter and quarter in any colony but with the consent of its legislature." By the time Franklin joined the Second Continental Congress, war had commenced between Great Britain and the united American states. As Congress created the Continental army in order to coordinate the many American militaries, the ejection of British regulars became the first act of nationhood.[108]

Back in Braintree, Abigail Adams watched events in Boston escalate. By January 1775, there were twelve regiments of soldiers and two regiments of marines in the city, bringing the total number of troops to six thousand. Desperate for quarters, Captain Montresor rented houses, and the troops spread across the city. With Massachusetts refusing to provide barrack supplies, Commander in Chief and Massachusetts governor Thomas Gage contracted with merchants in New York.[109] However, in February, the Massachusetts Provincial Congress declared that anyone who supplied the troops would be "deemed inveterate enemies to America."[110] As New York, Pennsylvania, and Maryland refused requests for "provisions to be shipped for the troops at Boston," Gage had to look to Québec for supplies.[111]

As the occupation of Boston intensified, repercussions spread across New England. In January 1775, Abigail Adams received a letter from Mercy Otis Warren, informing her of "a detachment from headquarters stationed in the neighborhood of Plymouth."[112] General Gage had deployed a hundred men from the 4th Regiment to Marshfield when inhabitants clamored for "seasonable assistance and protection." In sending regulars to "defend the loyal people of this town, from the threats and violence of an infatuated and misguided people," Gage was testing to see if outlying towns were more loyal than the capital.[113] The initial results seemed promising. Marshfield willingly billeted troops in White's Tavern and in the home of a prominent landowner whom Gage had recently appointed to the provincial council. More important, there was little effort to halt the troops.[114] Instead, a Boston newspaper joked that although "the troops at Marshfield do not pay barrack money for the houses they occupy there," the redcoats would nevertheless save a man money "where they fright a wife and children from home into a neighbor's house."[115]

As Gage spread troops across New England, he invoked the Quartering Act for the last time. In late January, New Hampshire's Governor John Wentworth requested military aid. The month before, a failed attempt to seize gunpowder in Portsmouth had incited the inhabitants to chase the governor and his pregnant wife Frances to Fort William and Mary in the Piscataqua

River. Displeased with losing New Hampshire, Gage agreed to send troops, but he worried about where they would be quartered. Fort William and Mary was in a pathetic state, so alternative accommodations were necessary. However, Gage refused to pay for houses, referring the governor "to the Act of Parliament made for quartering His Majesty's forces in North America."[116] Wentworth found this response bizarre, as royal authority had collapsed in New Hampshire. But Gage never dispatched any troops to Portsmouth, preferring to entrench in Massachusetts instead. On March 31, 1775, the governor instructed magistrates in Bristol County, south of Boston, to "inform me of the proper places to quarter two hundred of His Majesty's troops."[117]

March 1775 also brought criticism of Gage's strategy from England. For eleven months, the British government had given him a free hand to bring Massachusetts to heel, but the colony remained defiant. Viscount Barrington informed Gage that the king wanted a detailed accounting of the troops and "the quarters of each regiment," suggesting that even the monarch had begun to question Gage's Boston-only strategy.[118] Moreover, concentrating the North American Establishment had created problems elsewhere. Troops were needed in New York to protect trade, in Georgia to fight the Muscogees, and in Vermont to quell an intercolonial war. Under pressure from Whitehall, Gage ordered fifty marines to New York City, a hundred regulars to Georgia, and the 7th Regiment to Vermont. However, he refused to deplete Boston: the troops for Georgia came from St. Augustine, and the 7th Regiment from Québec.[119]

While Gage kept his sights trained on Boston, the Massachusetts Provincial Congress met in various locations around the colony. Led by John Hancock, the Massachusetts Congress included Samuel Adams, John Adams, Dr. Joseph Warren, and other men who viewed Gage's government as illegitimate. At an April 5 meeting in Concord, the extralegal body approved rules "for raising and keeping an army of observation and defense."[120] Gage observed such proceedings through his network of spies, but he made no move against the assembly until he received orders from Dartmouth "to arrest and imprison the principal actors and abettors in the Provincial Congress."[121] On April 18, the general dispatched six hundred to nine hundred British regulars to march to Concord to seize colonial weapons, and if they caught congressional leaders in the process, all the better. The troops quickly discovered colonists ready for battle. At Lexington, early on the morning of April 19, British soldiers faced a band of local militiamen and exchanged fire on the village green. When they reached Concord a few hours later, a second violent confrontation ensued at North Bridge. Finding neither weapons nor leaders, the regulars retreated to Boston. But the countryside was wise to the redcoats and rallied against them. By the time they got back to Boston, between a third and a half of the expedition had been killed, wounded, or was missing.[122] "Hostilities are now commenced in this province," Gage informed Québec's Governor Guy Carleton two days later. The Revolutionary War had begun.[123]

The first priority was to secure Boston. The Royal Navy surrounded the city with ships to prevent the provincial army from laying siege. Gage then negotiated with city leaders to ensure that the residents would not launch an insurrection. In exchange for the surrender of the Bostonians' weapons, Gage agreed "that the women and children with all their effects shall have safe conduct without the garrison." Men who remained in the city were required to swear that they would not take up arms against the king's soldiers. As Gage imposed martial law, every place in Boston became part of the military geography.[124] Abigail Adams lamented the plight of Bostonians "imprisoned with their enemies, suffering hunger and famine, obliged to endure insults and abuses." She denigrated "the troops of Britain, once the pride and glory of Europe," who "have descended to become a mob."[125] From inside the city, merchant John Rowe observed chaos: "A terrible fire broke out in the barracks on Treat's Wharf," leaving the 65th Regiment homeless and the 47th without clothing.[126] Rev. Andrew Eliot noted "the greater part of the inhabitants gone out of this town" such that he could see "grass growing in the public walks of this once populous and flourishing place."[127]

Having made Boston a fortress, Gage was confronted with the problem of supplies. If acquiring enough food and fuel for six thousand soldiers had been a challenge before Lexington and Concord, then the commencement of hostilities made it nearly impossible. To make matters worse, the general ordered more regulars into the city. He recalled troops from Newfoundland and Marshfield, and diverted four regiments bound for New York, bringing the starving number of redcoats to eight thousand. Soon, the army turned to scavenging. In May, three hundred soldiers went to Grape Island in Hingham Bay ten miles southeast of Boston to collect hay. "An alarm flew," Abigail Adams recounted for her husband, "and men from all parts came flocking down till two thousand were collected." The militia fired on the troops, wounding a marine and preventing the others from collecting more than three tons of hay.[128] As the old colonies boycotted the troops in Boston, General Gage turned to the new colonies for help, but this proved futile. Nova Scotia's Governor Francis Legge claimed that "this province has till the last year depended in some measure on New England," thus he was only able to supply some coal mined at Cape Breton. Efforts to acquire flour from Québec failed when the Americans cut off Gage's communication with Canada, while supplies from Britain were intercepted by provincial ships.[129]

Military geography spread out of Boston to the surrounding area. A few days after Lexington and Concord, Gage reported to Dartmouth that "the whole country was assembled in arms, with surprising expedition, and several thousand are now assembled about this town, threatening an attack."[130] Although Gage's spies estimated six thousand Americans had armed against the British, Abigail Adams may have been closer to the truth with her estimate of thirty thousand.[131] Overnight, the provincial forces turned the countryside into a martial place. The general collected intelligence that "the colleges at Cambridge" were "occupied as barracks."[132] More dramatically, private homes opened to American troops. At her farm in Braintree, Adams reported "soldiers coming in for lodging," some billeting with the family for a day and others longer. She maintained her good humor as her home was "made use of as a barrack," believing it her patriotic duty to accommodate "the houseless child of want."[133] However, other women were terrified by American troops invading their homes. From Cambridge, Elizabeth Inman wrote of how provincials took over her kitchen, leaving her and a female friend to barricade themselves in a parlor "with a board nailed across the door to protect them from harm." In war, the rules of quartering ended and domestic privacy disappeared.[134]

As word of events in Massachusetts spread throughout the colonies, Americans took up arms. New York received the news by April 23, and according to Governor Colden, "the town was immediately in an uproar." The inhabitants seized a shipment of flour destined for regulars in Boston; then they emptied the city armory, using the confiscated weapons to march "with drums and arms through the streets." Colden worried about the one hundred British regulars at the Upper Barracks, especially as rumors swirled that New Yorkers were planning on rushing the Fields and massacring the troops.[135] Before bloodshed occurred, however, the Second Continental Congress intervened. On May 15, Samuel Adams, Benjamin Franklin, and the other delegates resolved "that the troops be permitted to remain in the barracks, so long as they behave themselves peaceably and quietly."[136] But this did not stop New Yorkers from tempting the soldiers to renounce their king. "We are losing our men very fast from the large premiums and encouragement that is publicly given them to desert," wrote commanding officer Major Isaac Hamilton.[137] In response, Hamilton decided to evacuate the regulars to a British warship in the harbor, while he remained in the Upper Barracks with a few sick men and a cache of weapons. Once the troops departed, "several hundred forced the barrack gates, and broke into the room where they were lodged."[138] At this point, the Upper Barracks fell to the province. As Gage lamented "the revolution that has happened in that town," New York City became a place of unchallenged American military power.[139]

Events in New York were replicated throughout America. In Philadelphia, eight thousand men began drilling behind the statehouse, and John Adams reported "three large regiments raised, formed, armed, trained, and uniformed." Out these regiments rose the Committee of Privates, a representative body that began legislating in place of the proprietary government.[140] The provincial congress in South Carolina raised two regiments of infantry and a regiment of cavalry, while in North Carolina, Governor Josiah Martin fled to Fort Johnson once the inhabitants had "formed themselves into companies, and taken up arms."[141] New Jersey was slower than other colonies to reconstitute its militia, although the body ultimately arrested Governor William Franklin when he refused to join the American cause with his father. Some provincial armies even took the offensive. On May 10, a hundred Green Mountain Boys led by Ethan Allen and Benedict Arnold captured Ticonderoga, easily defeating the tiny British garrison. As royal authority collapsed across the old colonies, several governors pleaded for military aid, but only Virginia's governor, the Earl of Dunmore, received a response. General Gage ordered companies from St. Augustine and the Bahamas to Virginia, although when a lack of infrastructure meant there was "no probability of landing the men," Dunmore was left to recruit an army of slaves instead. By September 1775, Boston was the only place in the old colonies quartering British soldiers.[142]

While British military power evaporated in the old colonies, it remained powerful in Canada, Florida, the backcountry, and the islands. The occupation of Boston had drawn down the North American Establishment in the new colonies, such that by April 1775 there was less than a regiment in Halifax, while troops from Québec had to patrol the Great Lakes. Yet the events at Lexington and Concord had little effect on the rest of British North America. "At present everything in this place carries a face of tranquility," wrote Captain Arendt Schuyler DePeyster from Michilimackinac.[143] Reports from Québec and St. Augustine likewise indicated no uprisings, while in Halifax, Captain Francis Marsh saw nothing "factious in the inhabitants."[144] Indeed, only Bermuda was affected by the American rebellion. Governor George James Bruere noted that "the country has been long divided into two parties," and events in Massachusetts aggravated this division. But the Bermudians organized neither an extralegal congress nor an army.[145]

Instead of rebelling, the inhabitants of the new colonies and the islands demanded the British army defend them against the Americans. In July 1775, East Florida's Governor Patrick Tonyn expressed "great apprehensions for the safety of St. Augustine" and requested reinforcements from Gage. Tonyn feared that the city's military supplies would make St. Augustine a target, as "the rebels have seized one ship with ammunition bound" for the city already.[146] Similarly, ordnance officer James Morden worried that military stores in Halifax would "be a temptation to the emissaries of the rebels," while Governor Legge reported that Americans were eyeing two forts, each "without cannon for defense, and without troops."[147] Ultimately, the fears of East Florida and Nova Scotia were realized in Bermuda. On August 14, a group sympathetic to the American cause "most audaciously and daringly forced open" the door to Bermuda's provincial powder supply and stole a hundred barrels. However, an armed uprising did not ensue.[148]

Instead of deploying regulars, however, General Gage instructed the loyal parts of British North America to raise armies of locals to defend themselves. But the new colonies and the islands had relied on the British army so completely for so long that this order struck many as counterintuitive. When officers in Nova Scotia had difficulty raising men for service, Gage pressed the legislature to offer generous bounties to recruits, assuring them that London "will reimburse you with pleasure."[149] Few Nova Scotians joined the provincials, however, as they feared being impressed by the British army and sent to Boston. More significantly, Gage called for the enlistment of Francophone colonists and Native Americans. "If you can fall upon means to secure the Indians to our side, it will also be of great use," Gage informed Governor Legge, adding that he might "try the temper of the Acadians" to see if any "may be tempted to rise for the king." The general even recommended paying such troops the same as white Protestants.[150] A similar appeal to Québec led Governor Carleton to warn that "the Canadians are not now what they were at the conquest, [when] they had been long trained to obedience, and inured to war."[151] Nevertheless, provincial forces proved critical to the retention of British military power in Canada. Although Carleton's mixed force of British regulars, Québécois militiamen, and Native Americans was unable to defend Montréal against a force of Americans in November 1775, an equally diverse group defended Québec City a month later. Unlike Americans who took up arms for independence, the Canadians mobilized so that they might remain in the British Empire.[152]

Nation

In March 1775, Parliament renewed the Quartering Act. Much as he had every spring since 1765, Secretary at War Viscount Barrington presented a bill to the House of Commons, and the members approved it without opposition. Like the year before, the cabinet tinkered with the statute, this time responding to the advice of Boston commander General Percy about problems with desertion. The American Mutiny Act of 1775 punished anyone who did "persuade or procure any soldier" to desert with a fine of £40 or six months in prison, plus an hour in the pillory. Parliament also added a provision clarifying that the law applied to "His Majesty's marine forces while on shore, in any of His Majesty's dominions in America," recognizing that not all troops quartered in Boston were infantrymen.[153] However, by the time Commander in Chief Gage received the law in May, the situation in America had changed markedly. "Things are now come to that crisis" such that he only acknowledged his receipt of the Quartering Act in a postscript. "The new clause will be useful, when acts of Parliament come to be more respected," Gage concluded understatedly.[154]

In the meantime, the war in Massachusetts continued to escalate. On June 17, the British army launched an offensive against a redoubt and breastworks built by the provincial army in nearby Charlestown. Although the redcoats prevailed, the Battle of Bunker Hill resulted in over a thousand British casualties, a fifth of whom were killed, and left Charlestown in ashes. Again, civilians streamed out of the city; by August, Boston contained fewer than seven thousand civilians, but nearly fourteen thousand British regulars, along with their wives and children.[155] Although Gage forbade any "person whatever to go into any house in town without leave from the proprietor," practically the Quartering Act had no effect.[156] Instead, British soldiers availed themselves of abandoned houses. When General John Burgoyne took up residence in a house, he treated it with little respect: "raw meat cut and hacked" on a mahogany table and "superb damask curtain and cushions exposed to the rain as if they were of no value," noted Abigail Adams.[157] Meanwhile, supplies remained scarce even for civilians, who were disproportionately women, children, and the elderly. When these Bostonians looked to the British army for food and fuel, Gage tried to alleviate the situation by sending the poorest residents to Salem and others to Britain. But in August, he conceded that it was the British army's responsibility to supply the "remaining inhabitants in the town of Boston." In so doing, Gage inverted the Mutiny Act for America; instead of civilians provisioning soldiers, now soldiers were provisioning civilians. A month later, Gage received orders from Whitehall recalling him as both governor of Massachusetts and commander in chief of all His Majesty's forces in North America.[158]

In March 1776, Parliament renewed the Quartering Act for the last time. But it was a moot point by then. The laws of Great Britain were no longer recognized by the old colonies, which now styled themselves the United States of America. Three months later, the Second Continental Congress declared independence, formally creating the American nation. But the Revolutionary War had only begun; it would take a long, bloody conflict to effect independence. With George Washington as commander in chief of the Continental army, Americans used violence to distance themselves from the British Empire and to create the United States as a place.[159]

Epilogue

The Third Amendment
and the Shadow of Quartering

Elizabeth Drinker found it difficult to keep soldiers out of her home. Living in Philadelphia on the eve of the American Revolutionary War, Drinker tried to ignore the impending conflict. As a member of the Society of Friends, she professed pacifism and paid little mind to the British soldiers quartered in the Philadelphia Barracks. However, when the Revolution began, Drinker found that war impinged on all aspects of her life. In July 1776, she noted in her diary that a Friends' meetinghouse was "broke open by the American soldiers, where they have taken up their abode." Six months later, local authorities required Drinker to billet five Continental regulars in her house. Although the Americans soon departed, in October 1777 the British army captured Philadelphia, and Drinker was pressed to billet redcoats. She initially demurred, citing the poor behavior of soldiers at neighbors' houses, like one who "drew his sword, used very abusive language, and had the front door split in pieces." Nevertheless, on December 31, 1777, Drinker recorded that Major General John Crammond "is now become one of our family." Crammond quartered with Drinker for several months; although he irritated his hostess, no abuses followed.[1]

Elizabeth Drinker was not alone. The American Revolution was a long and brutal war that forced soldiers into barracks, taverns, and homes across North America. Nor were all troops well behaved; many householders struggled with soldiers who destroyed their property or sexually violated the inhabitants.[2] As billeting in private houses became rampant, a constitutional liberty that had once been protected by the Quartering Act fell by the way-side. We are thus left to ask: What was the legacy of Americans' twenty-year struggle with quarters? Many people like Drinker had long ago determined that troops belonged in barracks, not the home, and while soldiers might be tolerable in the city, their proper place was on the borderland. If all this could be brushed away by war, even a war to defend Americans' liberties, then what is the relevance of the Quartering Act to ideas of military power in the coun-try that followed?

Historical Amnesia and the US Constitution

During the Revolutionary War, the American approach to quarters was con-flicted. In practice, lawmakers gave the Continental army broad discretion in matters of quartering. In October 1775, a committee of the Second Con-tinental Congress recommended the amount to be paid for billeting, but set no parameters on where soldiers could be quartered. Five years later, Congress elaborated on this point, recommending that states require local magistrates provide the army with "necessary quarters" and supplies as "circumstances shall require"; again, there were no limits on where soldiers could go.[3] The individual states likewise set few restrictions on billeting. Mas-sachusetts, which quartered provincials in public houses during the French and Indian War, expanded the practice into private homes until the British evacuated Boston in March 1776.[4]

Philosophically, however, Revolutionary Americans took a strong stand against quarters. In the Declaration of Independence, the Second Continental Congress included among its charges against King George III: "For quarter-ing large bodies of armed troops among us." With this succinct accusation, Congress did not denounce billeting in private houses, but *all* types of quar-tering.[5] This point became clearer in the bill of rights appended to the Mary-land Constitution of 1776, which announced "that no soldier ought to be quartered in any house in time of peace without the consent of the owner, and in time of war in such manner only as the legislature shall direct." Like the Declaration of Independence, the Maryland Constitution protected "any house," although it limited this right to peacetime.[6] Both aspects deviated from the English Bill of Rights and the Quartering Act. Only Delaware joined Maryland in prohibiting quartering. Pennsylvania made no mention of the practice in its bill of rights, while New York, New Jersey, and South Carolina were taciturn with respect to all rights. Perhaps because these states saw sig-nificant fighting early in the war, any restriction on quarters was impractical.[7]

As the war wound down, Maryland's prohibition on all quartering in peacetime gained popularity throughout the nation. Massachusetts included a similar statement in its Constitution of 1780, adding that "such quarters ought not to be made but by the civil magistrate." New Hampshire included nearly identical language in its constitution four years later.[8] By the time the Constitutional Convention met in Philadelphia in the summer of 1787, a prohibition against quarters had become de rigueur. In enumerating congressional powers, several delegates urged a quartering prohibition, but the Committee of Detail ultimately excluded one from the US Constitution. This omission, along with the absence of protections for other civil rights, slowed ratification, especially in Virginia, where Patrick Henry worried that Congress could billet troops "on the people at pleasure" and "in any manner—to tyrannize, oppress, and crush us." James Madison dismissed Henry's claim, explaining that "at the beginning of the Revolution" people objected to quartering troops, but "this was not the whole complaint." Rather, "it was done without the local authority of the country—without the consent of the people of America": problems that had been solved by creating a republic.[9] Although Madison persuaded Virginians to ratify the Constitution, he also conceded that changes had to be made. Subsequently, he proposed adding to article 1, section 9: "No soldier shall in time of peace be quartered in any house, without consent of the owner; nor at any time, but in a manner warranted by law."[10]

On August 17, 1789, the US House of Representatives took up Madison's quartering amendment. The debate was brief. South Carolina representative Thomas Sumter moved that the distinction between wartime and peace be omitted, as he "hoped soldiers would never be quartered on the inhabitants, either in time of peace or war." This was a curiously detached position for a man who had been a general in the South Carolina militia ten years earlier. Connecticut representative Roger Sherman spoke against Sumter's motion, and he too demonstrated a surprising lack of memory. Although Sherman likely encountered soldiers quartered in taverns when he lived in New Haven in the 1760s, he sounded like a British politician when he argued that "whether in peace or war," an individual should not be able "to obstruct the public service." Sherman cited the example of England, where, he claimed, troops were billeted at "public houses, and upon private houses also, with the consent of the magistracy." This inaccuracy swayed the House, and Sumter's motion failed by a wide margin. Massachusetts representative Elbridge Gerry then moved that all quartering be directed "by a civil magistrate," but this was defeated when Thomas Hartley of Pennsylvania argued that "the public safety would be endangered" if one person could keep "troops standing in the inclemency of the weather for many hours." With that, the House moved on to the next amendment.[11]

Little in the debate of the US House of Representatives suggests that the Quartering Act or billeting in the Revolutionary War weighed heavily on anyone's mind. Quartering was an abstract concept for the American lawmakers: something that England provided an example for, not America. As with the Maryland Constitution, the spatial division of the American Mutiny Act had been replaced with a temporal one. Everyone agreed that it was unconstitutional to quarter troops in any house whether public or private, but this right could be dispensed with in wartime, so long as Congress made a law. Nor did the states challenge the quartering provision when Congress sent them the Bill of Rights for ratification. It was approved effortlessly, becoming the Third Amendment to the US Constitution: "No soldier shall, in time of peace be quartered in any house, without the consent of the owner, nor in time of war, but in a manner to be prescribed by law."[12]

If the origin, passage, and ratification of the Third Amendment make a poor case for the relevance of late colonial quartering, then the judicial history of the amendment is equally bleak. Famously, the Third Amendment has never been the subject of explication by the US Supreme Court, unlike the rest of the Constitution and its amendments. The closest any case has come is *Engblom v. Carey* (1982), which was decided by the Second Circuit of the US Court of Appeals, not the highest court in the land. In 1979, New York's Governor Hugh L. Carey forced striking prison guards out of staff housing in order to make room for their replacements, who happened to be members of the National Guard. When two striking guards, Marianne E. Engblom and Charles E. Palmer, sued the governor for violating their Third Amendment rights, the appellate court rejected the claim in part because there was no previous case law to draw on. In his decision, Judge Irving R. Kaufman concluded: "The Founding Fathers, I am certain, could not have imagined with this history that the Third Amendment could be used to prevent prison officials from affording necessary housing on their own property to those who were taking the place of striking guards." Perhaps we might celebrate that the will of the founders has been so well ingrained that in two hundred years, the US government has never quartered soldiers in houses during peacetime. But it also suggests that any lessons learned from drafting, executing, and resisting the Quartering Act has had little direct impact on two centuries of American jurisprudence.[13]

Quarters since the American Revolution

While the Quartering Act lacks immediate relevance to the Third Amendment, the experience of quartering British soldiers reshaped American ideas of military geography. Before 1750, most colonies allowed troops to go anywhere they were needed; thus nearly all buildings, cities, and regions were subject to military control. The creation of the North American Establishment changed the spatial organization of the country with respect to where soldiers belonged. As the colonists were pressed to quarter British regulars, they marked the house as a civilian space and built barracks. Although the Mutiny Act for America attempted to legalize this distinction, the law's demand for supplies, as well as Britain's aggressive use of the army, prompted Americans to see cities as civilian places. As they demanded that soldiers be removed to the borderland and territories with hostile populations, they rethought the empire and imagined a nation without British soldiers. Not only did quartering lead to independence; it definitively answered the question of where soldiers belonged.

As a result, the Revolutionary experience with quarters has lived on and continues to shape our views of military power. The effects of the eighteenth-century debate can be seen in the history of the United States and other former British possessions. Since independence, Americans have continued to ask: Where do soldiers belong? As people like Benjamin Franklin and Abigail Adams built a new country, they decided that soldiers belonged as far away from civilians as possible. This view was already out of step with the British Empire; thus Edward Long and Guy Carleton maintained that soldiers belong anywhere they were needed. But quartering left a legacy for civilian places as well as for martial ones. Shadows of the Revolutionary experience touch our daily lives in ways that have little to do with soldiers' accommodations. Since 1775, the meanings of the house, barracks, empire, borderland, cities and towns, and nation have continued to be debated in ways that recall the history of quarters.

The house as a place of domestic privacy has remained steadfast since the French and Indian War. The emergence of the cult of true womanhood promoted the home as the woman's separate sphere where she raised virtuous children and provided respite for a husband wearied by the marketplace. In the nineteenth century, women were celebrated for their work as part of the domestic economy, elevating their roles within the home and, counterintuitively, broadening their situation in the private sphere into an opportunity to enter public life. Ideas of privacy have strengthened over time, emanating from the home to the body. Two hundred years after the passage of the Quartering Act, the US Supreme Court recognized a right to privacy connected to issues of gender and sexuality. In *Griswold v. Connecticut* (1965), the high court granted married couples access to birth control on the grounds that the Third Amendment and other parts of the Constitution provide "a penumbra where privacy is protected from governmental intrusion." The court subsequently cited *Griswold* in *Roe v. Wade* (1973) to recognize a women's right to an abortion, and in *Lawrence v. Texas* (2003) to decriminalize homosexuality. In drawing on the Third Amendment, these decisions have enlarged the identity of the soldier to any agent of the state. Likewise, the penumbra of privacy has expanded from the home to the body.[14]

Conversely, houses that are not homes have become subject to more governmental oversight. Equal access to businesses was a primary objective of Martin Luther King Jr. and African American activists, and was enshrined in the Civil Rights Act of 1964. Specifically, the law requires any hotel or restaurant (successors to the public house) be open to all "without discrimination or segregation on the ground of race, color, religion, or national origin." While the law makes no mention of troops, it repeats Parliament's logic from two centuries earlier. The reason why colonial tavern keepers could not refuse to billet soldiers is the same reason why a present-day business cannot refuse to serve African Americans: being a *public* business renders the place not private. However, with the advent of the share economy and businesses like Airbnb, as well as business owners' legal challenges to serving LGBTQ people, perhaps we are seeing a renewed blurring of private and public spaces. In the United Kingdom and Canada, a similar commitment to domestic privacy and public accommodations has persisted.[15]

Ideas about barracks have changed dramatically. The massive structures built in the 1750s were used by American and British armies during the Revolutionary War and then demolished. The challenge of maintenance doomed some; British soldiers destroyed the Elizabeth Barracks, while quarters in Perth Amboy were in such poor shape that one man found it more profitable to sell the bricks than to repair the buildings.[16] Elsewhere, some efforts were made to repurpose the better structures. Philadelphia transformed its officers' quarters into a community center that stood until 1880, while Charleston's New Barracks became the College of Charleston.[17] After the British army withdrew from New York in 1783, the city rented out the Upper Barracks as apartments, although by the time George Washington arrived as the first president of the United States, the buildings were "going to ruin for want of repair," so the city demolished them.[18] As New Brunswick changed Barracks Street to Paterson Street, urban dwellers scrubbed away any hint that barracks had ever been there. Today, only Trenton's barracks remain, as a museum of the Revolutionary War.[19]

In contrast to their status in the US, barracks have remained instrumental to Britain and the British Empire. Permanent military quarters arose in London and across England because of the Napoleonic Wars. In Canada, the American Revolutionary War prompted the British army to build a new massive fortress in Halifax, which was enlarged in the 1790s and 1820s. British soldiers barracked at the Halifax Citadel until 1906, and Canadian forces used the installation in both world wars. Québec similarly retained its military infrastructure, in part to discourage an attack by the US. The persistence of barracks in Canadian cities stands in sharp contrast to the demolition of barracks in American cities. Instead of stationing troops among major centers of population, the US Army barracked soldiers in rural areas or on the periphery. In addition to maintaining forts at Niagara, Detroit, and Michilimackinac long after their transfer from Britain, the US government built armories at Springfield, Massachusetts, and in Harpers Ferry, Virginia. Placing soldiers among civilians proved to be an aberration in American history, and the existence of barracks in cities was one of the clearest differences between the colonies that became the United States and those that became Canada. The St. Francis Barracks in St. Augustine (figure 4.3) bridge the distance between the old and new colonies. Acquired by the British in the 1760s, the barracks filled with Spanish troops when Spain recaptured Florida during the Revolutionary War. Forty years later, Spain sold Florida to the US, and American soldiers moved in. Then, in the early twentieth century, the United States donated the St. Francis Barracks to the State of Florida, whose National Guard continues to use at least part of the original British structure.[20]

Although the Revolutionary War removed the US from the British Empire, Americans occasionally have replayed the lessons of their former colonial masters in building their own empire. The enterprise of forging disparate territories into a unitary polity has certainly been more of a success in the US than what England was ever able to effect with North America or even in the British Isles. The US Constitution gives each state representation in Congress, thus allowing the constituent parts a voice in military matters. However, the US government retained exclusive control over the military, especially once the state militias petered out after the War of 1812. America never repeated Britain's mistake with the Quartering Act; Congress never left it to the states to appropriate funds to pay for the US Army, but collected taxes directly from the people. This deprived opponents of a forum in the state legislatures. Interestingly, Great Britain made the same change at the same time. In the Constitutional Act of 1791, Parliament stated that Canadians would not be required to pay for their defense, but neither would they control it. Instead, Britain had exclusive control over Canada's military until the 1930s. In this respect, neither the letter nor the spirit of the Quartering Act survived the Revolution in either Canada or the US.[21]

Funded and controlled exclusively by Washington, the military has allowed America to realize its imperial ambitions. Since the Revolution, the movement of the US Army has been centrifugal: the War of 1812 pushed troops into Canada, the US-Mexican War sent them to the Pacific, and the Spanish-American War sent soldiers off the continent. World Wars I and II saw the former colonists marching on Europe and Asia, while the War on Terror deposited troops on the other side of the planet in Afghanistan and Iraq. As an army of conquest, US soldiers have repeated the practices of British regulars. Like the troops that garrisoned Boston in 1768, the US Army has avoided billeting soldiers in private houses while ignoring local input on military occupation. Constitutional concerns are less important in places outside the United States, and we are left to wonder if Americans today would be as supportive of a massive US Army if it were quartered in Boston instead of Kabul.

The borderland has come to an end, and yet it has not. The American victory in the Revolutionary War put to rest to the notion that the backcountry should be left to Native Americans. Instead, the US took a hard line against Indians, treating Cherokees, Mohawks, and Shawnees as enemies to be removed for white settlement. Benjamin and William Franklin had predicted Americans' demand for land and the importance of using the army to secure it. At times, the United States designated places where Indians were safe from white encroachment, like Kansas and Oklahoma, only to break treaties and demand more land. The US Army made this possible, facilitating the removal of Native Americans, from the Trail of Tears to Wounded Knee. Yet borderlands have remained. The presence of nonwhite populations delayed statehood for western territories like New Mexico, while people in Puerto Rico still enjoy fewer rights than citizens in the fifty states. In both cases, military power has remained intrinsic to the borderland. Indeed, the clearest display of the standing army and citizen militias in the past few decades has been on the US-Mexico border.[22]

Cities and towns certainly have changed; above all, they have grown. In 1790, some 5 percent of Americans lived in a city; today, it is closer to 80 percent. Although populations have grown up around military installations, the largest cities continue to be devoid of military infrastructure and soldiers. Appropriately, most of the land vacated by colonial barracks has filled with public buildings. In New York, City Hall took the place of the Upper Barracks, and the National Museum of the American Indian stands on the remains of Fort George; in Albany, Fort Frederick was replaced by the New York State Capitol. Boston's Castle Island was rebuilt several times, although by the time urban expansion connected the island to the city, the fort had become a park. The Civil War temporarily brought military geography back into American communities, as barracks were once again thrown up on New York's common, its name by then changed from the Fields to City Hall Park. Many cities and towns across the country emulated this, engaging in the largest barrack-building frenzy in America since the 1750s. However, these were temporary structures, pulled down or repurposed after Appomattox. War memorials appeared in city parks soon after, such that statues of soldiers displaced actual troops.[23]

Nevertheless, the same dynamics of the 1760s remain in American cities and towns. In the early nineteenth century, the police replaced the night watch, effecting a greater control over communities than the British army ever attempted, even in Québec. Like the redcoats of 250 years ago, the men and women in blue are mostly at one with civilians, although the two occasionally spar, such as in the Rodney King beating in 1992 and the riots that followed. Moreover, fears that the city will return to its previous existence reappear every time the country decries urban "war zones," or when it watches nervously as National Guard troops confront violent protesters, such as in Chicago in 1968 and Ferguson in 2014. Still, Americans continue to insist that the city, as much as the home, should be a place devoid of military power.[24]

Certainly, the nation has changed. Forged in a common military enterprise, the United States is at its most unified and most divided when it comes to war. Disagreements about the War of 1812 and the US-Mexican War exposed deep divisions in the country that reappeared for the Vietnam and Iraq Wars. But the military also retains a great deal of popularity. Americans see the desegregation of their armed forces in the 1940s as part of the civil rights movement, and that optimism underscores the recent admission of gay and transgender citizens to open service. Although there have been moments when Americans have questioned what troops have done in their name, such as Sand Creek, My Lai, and Abu Ghraib, these have not weakened the faith in the nation's army as a force of good. The careful deployment of troops no doubt has helped this cause, suggesting that the US Army has thought carefully about where soldiers belong. By keeping troops out of houses and cities, the American military has kept the nation united.

In the end, the struggle over quarters was far more important in the twenty years before the American Revolution than it has been at any time since. Perhaps this can be attributed to the rarity of land wars on American soil, constitutional constraints on the military, and technological innovations, but such explanations ignore the importance of place to the coming of the American Revolution. The arrival of British soldiers in 1755 forced Americans to rethink their military geography, and the conclusions they reached by 1775 have proven surprisingly resilient since then.

NOTES

The following abbreviations are used in the notes:

ABF   *The Autobiography of Benjamin Franklin.* Edited by Leonard
        W. Labaree et al. New Haven, Conn.: Yale University Press, 1964.
AFC   *Adams Family Correspondence.* Edited by L. H. Butterfield. 2 vols.
        Cambridge, Mass.: Harvard University Press, 1963.
AHR   *American Historical Review.* 1895–present.
AMD   *Archives of Maryland.* Edited by W. H. Browne et al. 72 vols. Bal-
        timore: Maryland Historical Society, 1883–1972.
AO   Auditors of the Imprest and Commissioners of Audit. NAK.
APS   American Philosophical Society. Philadelphia.
ARMA   *Acts and Resolves, Public and Private, of the Province of Massachu-
        setts Bay: To Which Are Prefixed the Charters of the Province, with
        Historical and Explanatory Notes, and an Appendix.* 21 vols. Boston:
        Wright and Potter, 1869–1922.
BMR   *Boston under Military Rule, 1768–1769, as Revealed in "A Journal
        of the Times."* Compiled by Oliver Morton Dickerson. Boston:
        Chapman & Grimes, 1936.
BTNA   *Burnaby's Travels through North America: Reprinted from the Third
        Edition of 1798.* Edited by Rufus Rockwell Wilson. New York:
        Wessels, 1904.
CCL   Commissioners of Customs Letters [typescripts], 1764–1774.
        MHS.
CGC   "Garth Correspondence." Edited by Joseph W. Barnwell and The-
        odore D. Jervey. *South Carolina Historical and Genealogical Magazine*
        28 (1927): 226–35; 29 (1928): 41–48, 115–32, 212–30, 295–305; 30
        (1929): 27–49, 105–16, 168–84, 215–35; 31 (1930): 46–62, 124–53,
        228–55, 283–91; 33 (1932): 117–39, 228–44, 262–80.
CISHL   *Collections of the Illinois State Historical Library: British Series.*
        Edited by Clarence Walworth Alvord and Clarence Edwin
        Carter. 3 vols. Springfield: Trustees of the Illinois State Histori-
        cal Library, 1915–1921.

CKG	*The Correspondence of King George the Third, from 1760 to December 1783.* Edited by John Fortescue. 6 vols. London: Macmillan, 1927–1928.
CLB	*The Colden Letter Books.* 2 vols. *Collections of the New-York Historical Society.* New York: New-York Historical Society, 1876–1877.
CLNY	*The Colonial Laws of New York from the Year 1664 to the Revolution.* 5 vols. Albany, N.Y.: Lyon, 1894.
CO	Colonial Office. NAK.
CRA	"The City Records, 1753 to 1783." *Collections on the History of Albany, from the Discovery to the Present Time.* Vol. 1. Albany, N.Y.: Munsell, 1865.
CRGA	*The Colonial Records of the State of Georgia.* Edited by Allen D. Candler et al. 28 vols. Atlanta: Franklin et al., 1904–1971.
CRSC	*The Colonial Records of South Carolina: The Journal of the Commons House of Assembly, October 6, 1757–January 24, 1761.* Edited by Terry W. Lipscomb. Columbia, S.C.: SCDAH, 1996.
CTP	Charles Townshend Papers. WLCL.
CWP	*Correspondence of William Pitt, Earl of Chatham.* Edited by William Stanhope Taylor and John Henry Pringle. 4 vols. London: Murray, 1838–1840.
CWS	*Correspondence of William Shirley, Governor of Massachusetts and Military Commander in America, 1731–1760.* Edited by Charles Henry Lincoln. 2 vols. New York: Macmillan, 1912.
DBP	Duke of Buccleuch Papers. WLCL.
DCB	*Dictionary of Canadian Biography.* University of Toronto and Université Laval. http://www.biographi.ca/en/index.php.
DCHC	*Documents Relating to the Constitutional History of Canada, 1759–1791.* Edited by Adam Shortt and Arthur G. Doughty. 2nd and rev. ed. 2 vols. Ottawa: Taché, 1907–1918.
DCHNJ	*Documents Relating to the Colonial History of the State of New Jersey. New Jersey State Archives.* 1st series. Edited by William Whitehead et al. 42 vols. Newark, N.J.: Daily Journal et al., 1880–1949.
DCHNY	*Documents Relative to the Colonial History of the State of New-York.* Edited by Berthold Fernow and E. B. O'Callaghan. 15 vols. Albany: Weed, Parsons, 1853–1887.
DNB	*Dictionary of National Biography.* Edited by Leslie Stephen and Sidney Lee. 1st ed. 63 vols. London: Smith, Elder, 1885–1900.
EL-HJ	Edward Long. *The History of Jamaica, or, General Survey of the Antient and Modern State of That Island: With Reflections on Its*

Situation, Settlements, Inhabitants, Climate, Products, Commerce, Laws, and Government. 3 vols. London: Lowndes, 1774.

HBP   *The Papers of Henry Bouquet.* Edited by S. K. Stevens et al. 6 vols. Harrisburg: Pennsylvania Historical and Museum Commission, 1951–1994.

HMWS   *Historical Memoirs from 16 March 1763 to 25 July 1778 of William Smith.* Edited by William H. W. Sabine. 2 vols. New York: Arno, 1969.

JAH   *Journal of American History.* 1914–present.

JBT   *Journals of the Board of Trade.* Edited by K. H. Ledward. 14 vols. London, 1920–1938. http://www.british-history.ac.uk/jrnl-trade-plantations/.

JCC   *Journals of the Continental Congress, 1774–1789.* 33 vols. Washington, D.C.: Government Printing Office, 1904–1937.

JCF   "Journal of the Commissioners of Fortifications, 1755–1770." South Carolina Historical Society. Charleston.

JCHSC   *The Journal of the Commons House of Assembly.* Edited by J. H. Easterby et al. 14 vols. Columbia: University of South Carolina Press, 1951–1989.

JCHSC-M *Journals of the Commons House of Assembly* [manuscript]. SCDAH. Vols. 37–38.

JEEB   *The Journal of Esther Edwards Burr, 1754–1757.* Edited by Carol F. Karlsen and Laurie Crumpacker. New Haven, Conn.: Yale University Press, 1984.

JHRMA   *Journals of the House of Representatives of Massachusetts.* 55 vols. 1715–1779; reprint, Boston: Massachusetts Historical Society, 1919–1990.

JPC   *Journal of Pontiac's Conspiracy, 1763.* Edited by M. Agnes Burton. Translated by R. Clyde Ford. Detroit: Burton, 1912.

JPCM   *The Journals of Each Provincial Congress of Massachusetts in 1774 and 1775, and of the Committee of Safety.* Edited by William Lincoln. Boston: Dutton and Wentworth, 1838.

JSH   *Journal of Southern History.* 1935–present.

JW-OB   John Waller. Orderly Book, 1775–1776. MHS.

LBJW   *The Letter Book of John Watts, Merchant and Councillor of New York, January 1, 1762–December 1765.* New York: New-York Historical Society, 1928.

LDJR   *Letters and Diary of John Rowe, Boston Merchant, 1759–1762, 1764–1779.* Edited by Anne Rowe Cunningham. Boston: Clarke, 1903.

LNH   *Laws of New Hampshire Including Public and Private Acts and Resolves and the Royal Commissions and Instructions.* Edited by Albert Stillman Batchellor et al. 10 vols. Manchester, N.H.: Clarke et al., 1904–1922.

LO   Loudoun Papers: Americana, 1682–1780. Henry Huntington Library, San Marino, Calif.

MCCNY   *Minutes of the Common Council of the City of New York, 1675–1776.* Edited by Herbert L. Osgood et al. 8 vols. New York: Dodd, Mead, 1905.

MCCP   *Minutes of the Common Council of the City of Philadelphia, 1704 to 1776.* Philadelphia: Crissy and Markley, 1847.

MHS   Massachusetts Historical Society. Boston.

MJ   *The Montresor Journals.* Edited by G. D. Scull. *Collections of the New-York Historical Society for the Year 1881.* New York: New-York Historical Society, 1882.

MNA-LC   Maps of North America, 1750–1789. Library of Congress, Geography and Map Division. Washington, D.C.

MPCPA   *Minutes of the Provincial Council of Pennsylvania, from the Organization to the Termination of the Proprietary Government.* 10 vols. Philadelphia: Severns et al., 1838–1852.

NAK   National Archives. Kew, UK.

NJSA   New Jersey State Archives. Trenton.

NYHS   New-York Historical Society. New York.

PA   *Pennsylvania Archives.* Colonial Records and First to Ninth Series. 136 vols. Harrisburg, Pa.: Severns et al., 1838–1935.

PBF   *The Papers of Benjamin Franklin.* Edited by Leonard W. Larabee et al. 41 vols. New Haven, Conn.: Yale University Press, 1959–2011.

PDBP   *Proceedings and Debates of the British Parliaments Respecting North America, 1754–1783.* Edited by R. C. Simmons and P. D. G. Thomas. 5 vols. Millwood, N.Y.: Kraus International, 1983.

PFB   *Papers of Francis Bernard: Governor of Massachusetts.* Edited by Colin Nicolson. 5 vols. Boston: Colonial Society of Massachusetts, 2007.

PGW   *Papers of George Washington.* Various series. Edited by W. W. Abbott et al. Charlottesville: University of Virginia Press, 1987–present.

PKT   *Peter Kalm's Travels in North America.* Edited by Adolph B. Benson. New York: Wilson-Erickson, 1937.

PMHB   *Pennsylvania Magazine of History and Biography.* 1877–present.

PPOC-LC Prints and Photographs Online Catalog. Library of Congress. Washington, D.C.

PRCT   *The Public Records of the Colony of Connecticut.* Edited by J. Hammond Trumbull et al. 15 vols. Hartford, Conn.: Case, Lockwood, and Brainard et al., 1859–1890.

PSWJ   *The Papers of Sir William Johnson.* 14 vols. Albany: University of the State of New York, 1921–1965.

RCRI   *Records of the Colony of Rhode Island and Providence Plantations.* Edited by John Russell Bartlett. 10 vols. Providence: Greene, 1856–1865.

RGCMA   *Records of the Governor and Company of the Massachusetts Bay in New England.* Edited by Nathaniel Shurtleff. 5 vols. Boston: White, 1853–1854.

RNA   *The Records of New Amsterdam from 1653 to 1674 Anno Domini.* Edited by Berthold Fernow. 7 vols. New York: Knickerbocker, 1897.

RPAC   *Report of the Public Archives of Canada* (Ottawa, 1872–1949). Listed by Sessional Paper numbers.

RRCCB   *Report of the Record Commissioners of the City of Boston.* 28 vols. Boston: Rockwell and Churchill, 1876–1898.

SCDAH   South Carolina Department of Archives and History. Columbia.

SCHM   *South Carolina Historical Magazine.* 1900–present.

SLGB   *The Statutes at Large from Magna Charta to the End of the Eleventh Parliament of Great Britain, Anno 1761 [and Continued].* Edited by Danby Pickering. 46 vols. Cambridge: Bentham et al., 1762–1807.

SLPA   *The Statutes at Large of Pennsylvania from 1682 to 1801.* Edited by James T. Mitchell and Henry Flanders. 17 vols. Harrisburg, N.J.: Busch et al., 1896–1915.

SLSC   *The Statutes at Large of South Carolina; Edited, under the Authority of the Legislature.* Edited by Thomas Cooper and David J. McCord. 10 vols. Columbia, S.C.: Johnston, 1836–1841.

SLVA   *The Statutes at Large; Being a Collection of All the Laws of Virginia, from the First Session of the Legislature in the Year 1619.* Edited by William Waller Hening. New York: Bartow, 1819–1823.

SP   State Papers. NAK.

SR   *Statutes of the Realm, Printed by Command of His Majesty King George the Third, in Pursuance of an Address of the House of Commons of Great Britain; from Original Records and Authentic Manuscripts.* 9 vols. London: Eyre and Strahan, 1810–1822.

TAC   *Travels in the American Colonies.* Edited by Newton D. Mereness. New York: Macmillan, 1916.

TBRSC   *Transcripts of Records in the British Public Records Office Relating to South Carolina.* 36 vols. SCDAH.

TG-OB   Thomas Gage, Orderly Books, 1766–1774. NYHS.

TGP-AS   Thomas Gage Papers, American Series. WLCL.

TGP-ES   Thomas Gage Papers, English Series. WLCL.

VPNJ   *Votes and Proceedings of the Province of New-Jersey* (dates and publishers vary).

WHLP   William Henry Lyttelton Papers. WLCL.

WLCL   William L. Clements Library at the University of Michigan. Ann Arbor.

WMQ   *William and Mary Quarterly.* 3rd series. 1944–present.

WO   War Office and predecessors. NAK.

WSA   *The Writings of Samuel Adams.* Edited by Henry Alonzo Cushing. 4 vols. New York: Putnam's Sons, 1904–1908.

Introduction

1. "Major Thompson's Deposition," *Publications of the Brookline Historical Publication Society,* 2nd ser. (Brookline, Mass.: Riverdale, 1900), 18–19. See also *PGW,* Revolutionary ser., 3:124–26.

2. John Philip Reid, *In Defiance of the Law: The Standing Army Controversy, the Two Constitutions, and the Coming of the American Revolution* (Chapel Hill: University of North Carolina Press, 1981); Hiller B. Zobel, *The Boston Massacre* (New York: Norton, 1970); Richard Archer, *As If an Enemy's Country: The British Occupation of Boston and the Origins of Revolution* (New York: Oxford University Press, 2010); Eric Hinderaker, *Boston's Massacre* (Cambridge, Mass.: Harvard University Press, 2017).

3. James L. Roark, Michael P. Johnson, Patricia Cline Cohen, Sarah Stage, and Susan M. Hartmann, *The American Promise: A History of the United States,* 2 vols., 6th ed. (Boston: Bedford / St. Martin's, 2015), 1:156; Cokie Roberts, *Founding Mothers: The Women Who Raised Our Nation* (New York: HarperCollins, 2004), 38; Judy Baker, *The Quartering Act* (Adams Basin, N.Y.: Wild Rose, 2008); Alan Valentine, *Lord North,* 2 vols. (Norman: University of Oklahoma Press, 1967), 1:323; Mark Puls, *Samuel Adams: Father of the American Revolution* (New York: Palgrave Macmillan, 2006), 153; Brandon Christensen, "Top 10 Things That Tipped Off Revolutionary War," *Real Clear History,* April 18, 2018, https://www.realclearhistory.com/articles/2018/04/18/top_10_things_that_tipped_off_revolutionary_war_295.html. Two notable exceptions to the misinterpretation of the Quartering Act are Don R. Gerlach, "A Note on the Quartering Act of 1774," *New England Quarterly* 38 (1966): 80–88, and Woody Holton, *Abigail Adams* (New York: Free Press, 2009), 57.

4. *The Papers of Thomas Jefferson,* ed. Julian P. Boyd et al., 41 vols. (Princeton, N.J.: Princeton University Press, 1950–2014), 1:431.

5. Benjamin L. Carp, *Defiance of the Patriots: The Boston Tea Party and the Making of America* (New Haven, Conn.: Yale University Press, 2011). See also David Hancock, *Citizens of the World: London Merchants and the Integration of the British Atlantic Community, 1735–1785* (Cambridge: Cambridge University Press, 1995); David Hancock,

Oceans of Wine: Madeira and the Emergence of American Trade and Taste (New Haven, Conn.: Yale University Press, 2009); Maya Jasanoff, *Liberty's Exiles: American Loyalists in the Revolutionary World* (New York: Knopf, 2011); Kariann Akemi Yokota, *Unbecoming British: How Revolutionary America Became a Postcolonial Nation* (New York: Oxford University Press, 2011); Ann M. Little, *The Many Captivities of Esther Wheelwright* (New Haven, Conn.: Yale University Press, 2016); Alan Taylor, *American Revolutions: A Continental History, 1750–1804* (New York: Norton, 2016).

6. John Shy, *Toward Lexington: The Role of the British Army in the Coming of the American Revolution* (Princeton, N.J.: Princeton University Press, 1965); Andrew Jackson O'Shaughnessy, *An Empire Divided: The American Revolution and the British Caribbean* (Philadelphia: University of Pennsylvania Press, 2000); Elizabeth Mancke, *The Fault Lines of Empire: Political Differentiation in Massachusetts and Nova Scotia, 1760–1820* (New York: Routledge, 2004).

7. Henri Lefebvre, *The Production of Space*, trans. Donald Nicholson-Smith (Malden, Mass.: Blackwell, 1991); Tim Cresswell, *Place: An Introduction*, 2nd ed. (Malden, Mass.: Wiley Blackwell, 2015); Charles W. J. Withers, "Place and the 'Spatial Turn' in Geography and History," *Journal of the History of Ideas* 70 (2009): 637–58.

8. Rachel Woodward, *Military Geographies* (Malden, Mass.: Blackwell, 2004); Colin Flint, "Intertwined Spaces of Peace and War: The Perpetual Dynamism of Geopolitical Landscapes," in *Reconstructing Conflict: Integrating War and Post-War Geographies*, ed. Scott Kirsch and Colin Flint, 31–48 (Farnham, UK: Ashgate, 2011); Derek Gregory, "The Everywhere War," *Geographical Journal* 177 (2011): 238–50.

1. Houses

1. Robert C. Ritchie, *The Duke's Province: A Study of New York Politics and Society, 1664–1691* (Chapel Hill: University of North Carolina Press, 1977), 17–24; *DNB*, s.v. "Nicolls, Richard"; John W. Raimo, *Biographical Directory of American Colonial and Revolutionary Governors, 1607–1789* (Westport, Conn.: Meckler, 1980), 239–40; *Proceedings of the New York Historical Society for the Year 1844* (New York: Press of the Historical Society, 1845), 116–17.

2. *MCCNY* 2:50.

3. *MCCNY* 2:50.

4. Jaap Jacobs, *New Netherland: A Dutch Colony in Seventeenth-Century America* (Leiden: Brill, 2005), 192–97, 335–36, 490; *RNA* 5:219, 223, 337–38; I. N. Phelps Stokes, *The Iconography of Manhattan Island, 1498–1909*, 6 vols. (New York: Dodd, 1915–1928), 2:237–38, 402. See also Jaap Jacobs and L. H. Roper, *Worlds of the Seventeenth-Century Hudson Valley* (Albany: SUNY Press, 2014); Susanah Shaw Romney, *New Netherland Connections: Intimate Networks and Atlantic Ties in Seventeenth-Century America* (Chapel Hill: University of North Carolina Press, 2014).

5. *RNA* 5:207, 211, 213. See also *RNA* 5:196–25.

6. Jacobs, *New Netherland*, 403–21.

7. *RNA* 5:220.

8. *RNA* 5:263.

9. *RNA* 1:6, 5:338. See also Jacobs, *New Netherland*, 239–42; Sharon V. Salinger, *Taverns and Drinking in Early America* (Baltimore: Johns Hopkins University Press, 2002), 161–73.

10. *DCHNY* 13:406–14; Ritchie, *Duke's Province*, 71–73; Stanley McCrory Pargellis, "The Four Independent Companies of New York," in *Essays in Colonial History Presented to Charles McLean Andrews by His Students*, 96–123 (New Haven, Conn.: Yale University Press, 1931).

11. *CLNY* 1:114, 247. See also Ritchie, *Duke's Province*, 80–81, 167–79.

12. Gaston Bachelard, *The Poetics of Space*, trans. Maria Jolas (Boston: Beacon, 1994); Judith Flanders, *The Making of Home: The 500-Year Story of How Our Houses Became Our Homes* (New York: St. Martin's, 2014); Richard Bushman, *The Refinement of America: Persons, Houses, Cities* (New York: Knopf, 1992).

13. William S. Fields and David T. Hardy, "The Third Amendment and the Issue of the Maintenance of Standing Armies: A Legal History," *American Journal of Legal History* 35 (1991): 393–431; Robert A. Gross, "Public and Private in the Third Amendment," *Valparaiso University Law Review* 26 (1991): 215–21; B. Carmon Hardy, "A Free People's Intolerable Grievance: The Quartering of Troops and the Third Amendment," in *The Bill of Rights: A Lively Heritage*, ed. Jon Kukla, 39–58 (Richmond: Virginia State Library and Archives, 1987); William Sutton Fields, "The Third Amendment: Constitutional Protection from the Involuntary Quartering of Soldiers," *Military Law Review* 124 (1989): 195–211; Tom W. Bell, "The Third Amendment: Forgotten but Not Gone," *William and Mary Bill of Rights Journal* 2 (1993): 117–50; Frank Barlow, *The Feudal Kingdom of England, 1042–1216*, 4th ed. (London: Longman, 1988), 87–88, 111.

14. *The Book Concerning Piers the Plowman*, trans. Donald and Rachel Attwater (New York: Dutton, 1957), passus 4, lines 50, 53–54, 56.

15. *A Source Book of London History from the Earliest Times to 1800*, ed. P. Meadows (London: Bell and Sons, 1914), 9. See also John A. Lynn, "How War Fed War: The Tax of Violence and Contributions during the Grand Siècle," *Journal of Modern History* 65 (1993): 286–310.

16. Peter Clark, *The English Alehouse: A Social History, 1200–1830* (London: Longman, 1983).

17. On standing armies, see John Philip Reid, *In Defiance of the Law: The Standing Army Controversy, the Two Constitutions, and the Coming of the American Revolution* (Chapel Hill: University of North Carolina Press, 1981); Reginald C. Stuart, "'Engines of Tyranny': Recent Historiography on Standing Armies during the Era of the American Revolution," *Canadian Journal of History* 19 (1984): 183–99; Michael Roberts, *The Military Revolution, 1560–1660* (Belfast: Boyd, 1956); Geoffrey Parker, *The Military Revolution: Military Innovation and the Rise of the West, 1500–1800* (Cambridge: Cambridge University Press, 1988), 1–5; Jeremy Black, *A Military Revolution? Military Change and European Society, 1550–1800* (London: Macmillan, 1991); David Eltis, *The Military Revolution in Sixteenth-Century Europe* (New York: Barnes and Noble, 1995).

18. Bell, "Third Amendment," 122–24; Conrad Russell, *The Causes of the English Civil War* (Oxford: Clarendon, 1990), 138–39; Correlli Barnett, *Britain and Her Army, 1509–1970: A Military, Political and Social Survey* (Middlesex, UK: Penguin, 1970), 97; Lois G. Schwoerer, *"No Standing Armies!": The Antiarmy Ideology in Seventeenth-Century England* (Baltimore: Johns Hopkins University Press, 1974), 55–56.

19. *SR* 3 Car. I, c. 5. See also Schwoerer, *No Standing Armies*, 19–32, 99–101, 129; Paul Christianson, "Arguments on Billeting and Martial Law in the Parliament of 1628," *Historical Journal* 37 (1994): 539–67.

20. *SR* 31 Car. II, c. 1. See also John Childs, *The Army of Charles II* (London: Rout-ledge & Kegan Paul, 1976), 75–89.

21. John Childs, *The Army, James II, and the Glorious Revolution* (New York: St. Martin's, 1980), 84–113.

22. *SR* 1 Gul. & Mar., sess. 2, c. 2.

23. *SR* 1 Gul. & Mar., sess. 2, c. 4.

24. Quoted in David H. Flaherty, *Privacy in Colonial New England* (Charlottesville: University Press of Virginia, 1972), 85. See also Leonard W. Levy, *Origins of the Bill of Rights* (New Haven, Conn.: Yale Nota Bene, 2001), 150–54.

25. John Brewer, *The Sinews of Power: War, Money, and the English State, 1688–1783* (Cambridge, Mass.: Harvard University Press, 1988), 29–34; R. E. Scouller, *The Armies of Queen Anne* (Oxford: Clarendon, 1966), 163–72; H. C. B. Rogers, *The British Army of the Eighteenth Century* (London: Allen & Unwin, 1977), 19; Lawrence Stone, intro-duction to *An Imperial War at State: Britain from 1689–1815*, ed. Lawrence Stone, 1–32 (London: Routledge, 1994).

26. *A Proclamation, Regulating the Quartering of Soldiers, and for Preventing Abuses from Them* (Edinburgh: Anderson, 1688).

27. Magnus Magnusson, *Scotland: The Story of a Nation* (New York: Grove Press, 2000), 521–25.

28. "Representation Recommending the Building of Barracks in Scotland," SP 41/48/206. See also Victoria Henshaw, *Scotland and the British Army, 1700–1750: Defending the Union* (London: Bloomsbury, 2014), 80–84.

29. William Bradford, *Of Plymouth Plantation, 1620–1647*, ed. Samuel Eliot Morison (New York: Knopf, 1975), 97, 111. See also John Demos, *A Little Commonwealth: Family Life in Plymouth Colony* (New York: Oxford University Press, 1970); Nathaniel Philbrick, *Mayflower: A Story of Courage, Community, and War* (New York: Viking, 2006).

30. *RGCMA* 5:76. On war in colonial America see Howard H. Peckham, *The Colo-nial Wars, 1689–1762* (Chicago: University of Chicago Press, 1964); Russell F. Weigley, *The American Way of War: A History of United States Military Strategy and Policy* (New York: Macmillan, 1973); John E. Ferling, *A Wilderness of Miseries: War and Warriors in Early America* (Westport, Conn.: Greenwood, 1980); John Morgan Dederer, *War in America to 1775: Before Yankee Doodle* (New York: NYU Press, 1990); Harold E. Selesky, *War and Society in Colonial Connecticut* (New Haven, Conn.: Yale University Press, 1990); James M. Johnson, *Militiamen, Rangers, and Redcoats: The Military in Georgia, 1754–1776* (Macon, Ga.: Mercer University Press, 1992); Ian K. Steele, *Warpaths: Inva-sions of North America* (New York: Oxford University Press, 1994); Armstrong Starkey, *European and Native American Warfare, 1675–1815* (Norman: University of Oklahoma Press, 1998); Guy Chet, *Conquering the American Wilderness: The Triumph of European Warfare in the Colonial Northeast* (Amherst: University of Massachusetts Press, 2003); John Grenier, *The First Way of War: American War Making on the Frontier, 1607–1814* (New York: Cambridge University Press, 2005); Fred Anderson and Andrew Cay-ton, *The Dominion of War: Empire and Liberty in North America, 1500–2000* (New York: Viking, 2005).

31. John Shy, *Toward Lexington: The Role of the British Army in the Coming of the American Revolution* (Princeton, N.J.: Princeton University Press, 1965), 19–36; Doug-las Edward Leach, *Roots of Conflict: British Armed Forces and Colonial Americans, 1677–1763* (Chapel Hill: University of North Carolina Press, 1986).

32. *ARMA* 1:133.

33. *PRCT* 9:232.

34. *JHRMA* 23:98, 153, 24:301–3.

35. Artemas Ward, Diary and record book, 1758–1805, Ward Family Papers, MHS.

36. *PA* 8th ser., 3:2599; "Another Grievance," *New-York Weekly Journal*, November 10, 1735.

37. *JEEB* 98, 47. See also W. Jay Mills, *Historic Houses of New Jersey* (Philadelphia: Lippincott, 1902), 78–83; Joseph Atkinson, *The History of Newark, New Jersey* (Newark, N.J.: Guild, 1878), 60–86.

38. Flanders, *Making of Home*, 55–93; Bushman, *Refinement of America*, 100–138; Darrett B. Rutman and Anita H. Rutman, *A Place in Time: Middlesex County, Virginia, 1650–1750* (New York: Norton, 1984), 65–69; Bernard L. Herman, *Town House: Architecture and Material Life in the Early American City, 1780–1830* (Chapel Hill: University of North Carolina Press, 2005).

39. *JEEB* 50.

40. Mary Beth Norton, *Separated by Their Sex: Women in Public and Private in the Colonial Atlantic World* (Ithaca, N.Y.: Cornell University Press, 2011); Diana diZerega Wall, *The Archaeology of Gender: Separating the Spheres in Urban America* (New York: Plenum, 1994), 17–36; Lauren Duval, "Mastering Charleston: Property and Patriarchy in British-Occupied Charleston, 1780–82," *WMQ* 75 (2018): 589–622.

41. Fred Anderson, *Crucible of War: The Seven Years' War and the Fate of Empire in British North America, 1754–1766* (New York: Knopf, 2000), 42–65. On the French and Indian War see also William M. Fowler, *Empires at War: The French and Indian War and the Struggle for North America* (New York: Walker & Co., 2005); Warren R. Hofstra, *Cultures in Conflict: The Seven Years' War in North America* (Lanham, Md.: Rowman & Littlefield, 2007); Matt Schumann and Karl Schweizer, *The Seven Years' War: A Transatlantic History* (London: Routledge, 2008); William R. Nester, *The French and Indian War and the Conquest of New France* (Norman: University of Oklahoma Press, 2014); Patrick Spero, *Frontier Country: The Politics of War in Early Pennsylvania* (Philadelphia: University of Pennsylvania Press, 2016).

42. *JEEB* 55.

43. *JEEB* 60–61. See also George M. Marsden, *Jonathan Edwards: A Life* (New Haven, Conn.: Yale University Press, 2003), 375–431, 511–12; Ola Elizabeth Winslow, *Jonathan Edwards, 1703–1758: A Biography* (New York: Macmillan, 1940), 268–92; Patrick Frazier, *The Mohicans of Stockbridge* (Lincoln: University of Nebraska Press, 1992); Colin G. Calloway, *The American Revolution in Indian Country: Crisis and Diversity in Native American Communities* (New York: Cambridge University Press, 1995), 85–107.

44. *JEEB* 77, 217.

45. Flaherty, *Privacy in New England*, 90; Salinger, *Taverns and Drinking*, 185; David W. Conroy, *In Public Houses: Drink and the Revolution of Authority in Colonial Massachusetts* (Chapel Hill: University of North Carolina Press, 1995), 147–54; Benjamin L. Carp, *Rebels Rising: Cities and the American Revolution* (New York: Oxford University Press, 2007), 62–98.

46. *JEEB* 218–19.

47. *JEEB* 220, 223. See also Michael J. McClymond and Gerald R. McDermott, *The Theology of Jonathan Edwards* (New York: Oxford University Press, 2012), 35–37, 559–63; *Works of Jonathan Edwards*, vol. 16, *Letters and Personal Writings*, ed. George S. Claghorn (New Haven, Conn.: Yale University Press, 1998), 657–58, 664, 669–71, 681; *JHRMA* 31:101, 192, 236–37, 32:357, 33:269; Sarah Cabot Sedgwick and Christina Sedgwick Marquand, *Stockbridge, 1739–1974* (Stockbridge, Mass.: Berkshire Traveller, 1974), 1–97.

48. Although Grenville found the appellation "prime minister" to be "an odious title" and refused to refer to himself as such, for simplicity I refer to parliamentary leaders such as Grenville as prime ministers. Sidney Low, *The Governance of England* (London: Unwin, 1904), 156.

49. Anderson, *Crucible of War*, 66–73.

50. Quoted in Alan Rogers, *Empire and Liberty: American Resistance to British Authority, 1755–1763* (Berkeley: University of California Press, 1974), 12.

51. *CWS* 2:103–7.

52. *CWS* 2:97–101; *Military Affairs in North America, 1748–1765: Selected Documents from the Cumberland Papers in Windsor Castle*, ed. Stanley Pargellis (New York: Appleton-Century, 1936), 34–36; *DCHNY* 6:920–22; Lee McCardell, *Ill-Starred General: Braddock of the Coldstream Guards* (Pittsburgh: University of Pittsburgh Press, 1958), 119–34.

53. Craig Yirush, *Settlers, Liberty, and Empire: The Roots of Early American Political Theory* (New York: Cambridge University Press, 2011).

54. *CWS* 2:101. See also *MPCPA* 6:200–202; *PA* 8th ser., 5:3783–85; *DCHNJ* 8:17–20; *AMD* 52:48–50; *RCRI* 5:406–8; *JHRMA* 31:179; *CWS* 2:118–19n1.

55. Jack P. Greene, *The Quest for Power: The Lower Houses of Assembly in the Southern Royal Colonies, 1689–1776* (Chapel Hill: University of North Carolina Press, 1963); John Phillip Reid, *In a Defiant Stance: The Condition of Law in Massachusetts Bay, the Irish Comparison, and the Coming of the American Revolution* (University Park: Pennsylvania State University Press, 1977); Richard R. Beeman, *The Varieties of Political Experience in Eighteenth-Century America* (Philadelphia: University of Pennsylvania Press, 2004).

56. *AMD* 52:111.

57. *ARMA* 3:734; *JHRMA* 31:179, 186, 189, 256–58; *DCHNJ* 6:515–18; *JCHSC* 12:476–77; Larry E. Ivers, *Colonial Forts of South Carolina, 1670–1775* (Columbia: University of South Carolina Press, 1970), 70–72; Fitzhugh McMaster, *Soldiers and Uniforms: South Carolina Military Affairs, 1670–1775* (Columbia: University of South Carolina Press, 1971), 52–53.

58. Anderson, *Crucible of War*, 86–93; McCardell, *Ill-Starred General*, 164–208; *ABF* 219–20; Will H. Lowdermilk, *History of Cumberland, (Maryland)* (Washington, D.C.: Anglim, 1878), 89–132; "The Journal of a British Officer," in *Braddock's Defeat*, ed. Charles Hamilton, 39–58 (Norman: University of Oklahoma Press, 1959); Winthrop Sargent, ed., *The History of an Expedition against Fort Du Quesne, in 1755; Under Major-General Edward Braddock, Generalissimo of H. B. M. Forces in America* (Philadelphia: Lippincott, Grambo, 1855); Peter E. Russell, "Redcoats in the Wilderness: British Officers and Irregular Warfare in Europe and America, 1740 to 1760," *WMQ* 35 (1978): 629–52; Rogers, *Empire and Liberty*, 51–58.

59. *MPCPA* 6:307.

60. *JEEB* 136.

61. Paul E. Kopperman, *Braddock at the Monongahela* (Pittsburgh: University of Pittsburgh Press, 1977); David Preston, *Braddock's Defeat: The Battle of the Mononga-hela and the Road to Revolution* (New York: Oxford University Press, 2015); McCardell, *Ill-Starred General*, 240–65; Anderson, *Crucible of War*, 94–107.

62. *MPCPA* 6:519, 533. See also *PA* 8th ser., 5:3950–54; *MPCPA* 6:511–16, 535; *CWS* 2:215–16, 321–23.

63. *SLPA* 5:194–95. See also *PA* 8th ser., 5:3964–68.

64. J. Thomas Scharf and Thomas Westcott, *History of Philadelphia, 1609–1884*, 3 vols. (Philadelphia: Everts, 1884), 2:1003.

65. *The Life, Adventures, and Surprizing Deliverances, of Duncan Cameron, Private Soldier in the Regiment of Foot, Late Sir Peter Halket's*, 3rd ed. (Philadelphia: Chattin, 1756), 14–15.

66. Anderson, *Crucible of War*, 124–43; Alexander V. Campbell, *The Royal American Regiment: An Atlantic Microcosm, 1755–1772* (Norman: University of Oklahoma Press, 2010).

67. *DCHNY* 7:36n1; *DNB*, s.v., "Campbell, John, Fourth Earl of Loudoun"; Anderson, *Crucible of War*, 141–44; *SLVA* 7:61–63; Stanley McCrory Pargellis, *Lord Loudoun in North America* (New Haven, Conn.: Yale University Press, 1933); Rogers, *Empire and Liberty*, 75–89; Anderson, *Crucible of War*, 133; Leach, *Roots of Conflict*, 87–99.

68. Loudoun to Hardy, November 21, 1756, LO 2250.

69. Anderson, *Crucible of War*, 142–57; Cuyler Reynolds, *Albany Chronicles: A History of the City Arranged Chronologically from the Earliest Settlement to the Present Time* (Albany, N.Y.: Lyon, 1906), 216.

70. Pargellis, *Lord Loudoun*, 195–96; Rogers, *Empire and Liberty*, 82–84.

71. Loudoun to Cumberland, August 29, 1756, LO 1626.

72. Evarts B. Greene and Virginia D. Harrington, *American Population before the Federal Census of 1790* (New York: Columbia University Press, 1932), 102–3n; *PKT* 346; Janny Venema, *Beverwijck: A Dutch Village on the American Frontier, 1652–1664* (Hilversum, Netherlands: Verloren, 2003), 64–77, 206–14; Rogers, *Empire and Liberty*, 159n26.

73. Dean R. Snow, Charles T. Gehring, and William A. Starna, eds., *In Mohawk Country: Early Narratives about a Native People* (Syracuse, N.Y.: Syracuse University Press, 1996), 260.

74. Anne MacVicar Grant, *Memoirs of an American Lady, with Sketches of Manners and Scenery in America, as They Existed Previous to the Revolution* (New York: Appleton, 1846), 162–64.

75. Loudoun to Cumberland, November 22, 1756, LO 2262.

76. Emphasis in original. Loudoun to Fox, November 22, 1756, LO 2263.

77. Loudoun to Fox, November 22, 1756, LO 2263; Richard Trimen, *An Historical Memoir of the 35th Royal Sussex Regiment of Foot* (Southampton, UK: Southampton Times Newspaper, 1873), 25–26; Campbell, *Royal American Regiment*, 86–91.

78. Loudoun to Denny, September 22, 1756, LO 1876.

79. Yirush, *Settlers, Liberty, and Empire*, 84–90.

80. *MPCPA* 7:276. See also *MPCPA* 7:340; *SLPA* 5:532; John J. Zimmerman, "Governor Denny and the Quartering Act of 1756," *PMHB* 91 (1967): 266–81; Pargellis, *Lord Loudoun*, 191–92, 200–202; Rogers, *Empire and Liberty*, 77–82; Scharf and Westcott,

History of Philadelphia, 1003–5; John Russell Young, *Memorial History of the City of Philadelphia from Its First Settlement to the Year 1895*, 2 vols. (New York: New-York History, 1895–98), 1:283.

81. *SLPA* 5:270–71. See also *PA* 8th ser., 6:4394–4401, 4430–31.

82. *PA* 8th ser., 6:4447, 4449. See also Nicholas B. Wainwright, "Governor William Denny in Pennsylvania," *PMHB* 81 (1957): 170–98.

83. *MPCPA* 7:349–50.

84. *MCCP* 601.

85. "Notes and Queries," *PMHB* 22 (1898): 497.

86. Zimmerman, "Governor Denny," 272–73; Barry Levy, *Quakers and the American Family: British Settlement in the Delaware Valley* (New York: Oxford University Press, 1988), 182–83.

87. *MPCPA* 7:361. See also Benjamin Franklin Papers, pt. 1, no. 46, APS; *PA* 1st ser., 3:85–86; 3rd ser., 9:148–50.

88. *PA* 8th ser., 6:4469, 4463.

89. *PA* 8th ser., 6:4472–73. See also Steven C. A. Pincus, *1688: The First Modern Revolution* (New Haven, Conn.: Yale University Press, 2009), 145.

90. *MPCPA* 7:374.

91. *PA* 1st ser., 3:82, 85; *MPCPA* 7:370–79.

92. Benjamin Franklin Papers, pt. 1, no. 47, APS.

93. Loudoun to Denny, December 22, 1756, LO 2382.

94. *SLPA* 5:289–90. See also *PA* 1st ser., 3:112, 323; 8th ser., 6:4493, 4495–96, 4508, 4513–14, 4547–49; *MPCPA* 7:379, 400, 407–8, 410–12, 431, 436; *MCCP* 613–14; Pargellis, *Lord Loudoun*, 201–2.

95. *SLPA* 5:290.

96. Peter Thompson, *Rum Punch and Revolution: Taverngoing and Public Life in Eighteenth-Century Philadelphia* (Philadelphia: University of Pennsylvania Press, 1999), 26–27; Greene and Harrington, *American Population*, 118n.

97. Greene and Harrington, *American Population*, 112, 121–23, 129–33.

98. *DCHNJ* 17:68.

99. Belcher to Loudoun, November 15, 1756, LO 2224; Loudoun to Belcher, December 16, 1756, LO 2357.

100. *VPNJ* (December 1756): 7-8.

101. *VPNJ* (March 1757): 15.

102. Loudoun to Belcher, April 7, 1757, LO 3307.

103. Petition from Woodbridge, October 18, 1757, Manuscript Collection, box 1–13, item 11, NJSA.

104. *DCHNJ* 17:122.

105. Petition from Princeton, April 11, 1758, Manuscript Collection, box 1–13, item 22, NJSA. See also Petition from New Brunswick, August 23, 1757, Manuscript Collection, box 1–13, item 14, NJSA; *VPNJ* (August–September 1757): 14; Larry R. Gerlach, "Soldiers and Citizens: The British Army in New Jersey on the Eve of the Revolution," *New Jersey History* 93 (1975): 5–36.

106. Receipts for Money Paid to the Inhabitants for Trenton for Billeting Soldiers, 1757–1758, NJSA; Account of Joseph Yard for Quartering Troops, July 21, 1758, Manuscripts and Correspondence Relating to Colonial Wars, 1639–1903, MF-07-01, reel 1–006, item 79, NJSA; Israel Acrelius, *A History of New Sweden*, ed. William M.

Reynolds (Philadelphia: Historical Society of Pennsylvania, 1874), 144; Robert V. Wells, *The Population of the British Colonies in America before 1776* (Princeton, N.J.: Princeton University Press, 1975), 140.

107. *BTNA* 103.

108. John O. Raum, *History of the City of Trenton, New Jersey, Embracing a Period of Nearly Two Hundred Years* (Trenton, N.J.: Nicholson, 1871), 50–73; Brendan McConville, *These Daring Disturbers of the Public Peace: The Struggle for Property and Power in Early New Jersey* (Ithaca, N.Y.: Cornell University Press, 1999), 223–28.

109. *AMD* 6:521, 52:651

110. *AMD* 6:523.

111. Petition to Loudoun, February 26, 1757, LO 2928.

112. *AMD* 55:6.

113. Sharpe to Loudoun, December 22, 1757, LO 6868.

114. *AMD* 55:xl–xli, 212, 219, 330, 352, 386; Pargellis, *Lord Loudoun*, 204–5; Charles Albro Barker, *The Background of the Revolution in Maryland* (New Haven, Conn.: Yale University Press, 1940), 209–10.

115. Loudoun to Fox, November 22, 1756, LO 2263; *JHRMA* 33:183, 205–6, 316, 336; Pargellis, *Lord Loudoun*, 205–9; Rogers, *Empire and Liberty*, 84–87; Edward Rowe Snow, *The Islands of Boston Harbor*, updated ed. (Carlisle, Mass.: Commonwealth, 2002), 60–61.

116. *JHRMA* 33:335.

117. J. A. Houlding, *Fit for Service: The Training of the British Army, 1715–1795* (Oxford: Clarendon, 1981), 116–21.

118. *JHRMA* 34:110.

119. John A. Schutz, *Thomas Pownall, British Defender of American Liberty: A Study of Anglo-American Relations in the Eighteenth Century* (Glendale, Calif.: Clark, 1951).

120. *JHRMA* 34:111.

121. *JHRMA* 34:118, 133. See also *ARMA* 16:67, 69.

122. Pownall to Loudoun, September 2, 1757, LO 4389.

123. Cox to Forbes, November 4, 1757, LO 4760.

124. Mackinsen to Forbes, November 4, 1757, LO 4763.

125. *JHRMA* 34:148–49; *Correspondence of William Pitt*, ed. Gertrude Selwyn Kimball, 2 vols. (New York: Macmillan, 1906), 1:128–29; Schutz, *Thomas Pownall*, 110–16.

126. *ARMA* 4:47–48. See also *JHRMA* 34:153, 155, 157, 160, 162, 201–2, 208–9, 255–56, 291, 298.

127. Loudoun to Pownall, December 6, 1757, LO 4958.

128. Cosnan to Forbes, December 12, 1757, LO 5000.

129. *JHRMA* 34:385.

130. *ARMA* 4:71. See also *ARMA* 4:165–66, 175–76, 198–99, 275–76, 279. New Hampshire, Connecticut, and Rhode Island also confined recruiters to public houses. See *LNH* 3:164–65; *PRCT* 11:175–78, 215–16, 304–7; *RCRI* 6:120–21, 188–89.

131. *JHRMA* 35:34. See also *JHRMA* 32:298, 33:200, 34:299, 376, 449, 389; William Lincoln, *History of Worcester, Massachusetts, from Its Earliest Settlement to September 1836* (Worcester, Mass.: Hersey, 1862), 62; Conroy, *In Public Houses*, 192–93.

132. Hardy to Loudoun, November 11, 1756, LO 2199.

133. Loudoun to Fox, November 22, 1756, LO 2263; Loudoun to Halifax, December 26, 1756, LO 2416.

134. *CLNY* 4:124.

135. *JCHSC* 14:429. See also *JCHSC* 14:83; WHLP 4:31, March 1757, April 24, 1757, May 1757; *HBP* 1:88–90, 121; Jack P. Greene, "The South Carolina Quartering Dispute, 1757–1758," *SCHM* 60 (1959): 193–204; Salinger, *Taverns and Drinking*, 184–99.

136. *HBP* 1:170, 248, 217, 216. See also *HBP* 1:150, WHLP 6: October 10, 1757, October 11, 1757; Ian McPherson McCulloch, *Sons of the Mountains: The Highland Regiment in the French and Indian War, 1756–1767* (Fleischmanns, N.Y.: Purple Mountain, 2006).

2. Barracks

1. *De Brahm's Report of the General Survey in the Southern District of North America*, ed. Louis De Vorsey Jr. (Columbia: University of South Carolina Press, 1971), 7–13.

2. "From the South-Carolina Gazette," *New York Evening Post*, November 6, 1752. See also Walter J. Fraser Jr., *Charleston! Charleston! The History of a Southern City* (Columbia: University of South Carolina Press, 1989), 84.

3. *De Brahm's Report*, 99, 91, 12. See also 14–16; *JHCSC* 11:232–49; Emma Hart, *Building Charleston: Town and Society in the Eighteenth-Century British Atlantic World* (Charlottesville: University of Virginia Press, 2010).

4. JCF, March 15, 1756, April 17, 1756.

5. *De Brahm's Report*, 17–18.

6. B. R. Carroll, ed., *Historical Collections of South Carolina; Embracing Many Rare and Valuable Pamphlets, and Other Documents*, 2 vols. (New York: Harper & Brothers, 1836), 2:487; *Colonial South Carolina: Two Contemporary Descriptions by Governor James Glen and Doctor George Milligen-Johnston*, ed. Chapman J. Milling (Columbia: University of South Carolina Press, 1951), 109.

7. *JCHSC* 7:103–8, 232, 325–26, 393–94, 398, 8:116–17, 218–21, 9:50, 100, 272.

8. Nehemiah 3:16. See also Suetonius, *Tiberius*, 37; Tacitus, *Annals of Imperial Rome*, 4:2.

9. James Douet, *British Barracks, 1600–1914: Their Architecture and Role in Society* (London: Stationery Office Books, 1997), 2–4; M. S. Anderson, *War and Society in Europe of the Old Regime, 1618–1789* (Montréal: McGill–Queen's University Press, 1988), 172; John Childs, *Armies and Warfare in Europe, 1648–1789* (New York: Holmes and Meier, 1982), 174–200; Christopher Duffy, *The Fortress in the Age of Vauban and Frederick the Great, 1660–1789* (London: Routledge & Kegan Paul, 1985), 1–97; Paddy Griffith, *The Vauban Fortification of France* (Oxford: Osprey, 2006).

10. Michel Foucault, *Discipline and Punish*, trans. Alan Sheridan (New York: Vintage, 1995), 141–42; Anderson, *War and Society*, 173–74; Christopher Duffy, *The Military Experience in the Age of Reason* (New York: Atheneum, 1987), 14–21.

11. Joshua S. Goldstein, *War and Gender: How Gender Shapes the War System and Vice Versa* (Cambridge: Cambridge University Press, 2001); John Gilbert McCurdy, "Gentlemen and Soldiers: Competing Visions of Manhood in Early Jamestown," in *New Men: Manliness in Early America*, ed. Thomas A. Foster, 9–30 (New York: NYU Press, 2011); Ann M. Little, *Abraham in Arms: War and Gender in Colonial New England* (Philadelphia: University of Pennsylvania Press, 2007); R. Todd Romero, *Making War and Minting Christians: Masculinity, Religion, and Colonialism in Early New England* (Amherst: University of Massachusetts Press, 2011).

12. Douet, *British Barracks*, 1–2, 5–17, 37–42; Frank Barlow, *The Feudal Kingdom of England, 1042–1216*, 4th ed. (London: Longman, 1988), 87–88, 111.

13. *The Monitor: Or, British Freeholder*, 2 vols. (London: Scott, 1756–1757), 1:421. See also John Trenchard and Thomas Gordon, *Cato's Letters: Or, Essays on Liberty, Civil and Religious, and Other Important Subjects*, ed. Ronald Hamowy, 2 vols. (Indianapolis: Liberty Fund, 1995), 2:669–87.

14. "Postscript," *London Evening-Post*, January 12–15, 1760. On barracking British soldiers see H. de Watteville, *The British Soldier: His Daily Life from Tudor to Modern Times*, 2nd ed. (New York: Putnam's Sons, 1955), 6–7, 57–60; H. C. B. Rogers, *The British Army of the Eighteenth Century* (London: Allen & Unwin, 1977), 38–39, 49–51; J. A. Houdling, *Fit for Service: The Training of the British Army, 1715–1795* (Oxford: Clarendon, 1981), 39–43; Lawrence Delbert Cress, *Citizens in Arms: The Army and the Militia in America Society to 1812* (Chapel Hill: University of North Carolina Press, 1982), 15–33.

15. "Postscript," *Whitehall Evening Post or London Intelligencer*, March 9–11, 1756.

16. Petition of Innkeepers of Eastbourne to Newcastle, SP 41/48/210.

17. Douet, *British Barracks*, 16–18, 42–66; Erica Charters, "The Administration of War and French Prisoners of War in Britain, 1756–1763," in *Civilians and War in Europe, 1618–1815*, ed. Erica Charters, Eve Rosenhaft, and Hannah Smith, 87–99 (Liverpool: Liverpool University Press, 2012); Linda Colley, "The Reach of the State, the Appeal of the Nation: Mass Arming and Political Culture in the Napoleonic Wars," in *An Imperial War at State: Britain from 1689–1815*, ed. Lawrence Stone, 165–84 (London: Routledge, 1994).

18. Douet, *British Barracks*, 15, 18–23, 29–34; Plans of Cities, Castles, Forts and Barracks in North Britain, WO 78/6012; Houdling, *Fit for Service*, 34–36, 43–57; Victoria Henshaw, *Scotland and the British Army, 1700–1750: Defending the Union* (London: Bloomsbury, 2014), 82–83, 149–85; Charles Ivar McGrath, *Ireland and Empire, 1692–1770* (London: Pickering & Chatto, 2012), 69–106. The Royal Barracks have been the Collins Barracks since 1922.

19. Memorial of Brigadier General Jones to the King for Barracks for Troops in the Leeward Islands, SP 41/48/65.

20. John Shy, *Toward Lexington: The Role of the British Army in the Coming of the American Revolution* (Princeton, N.J.: Princeton University Press, 1965), 19–44; Andrew Jackson O'Shaughnessy, *An Empire Divided: The American Revolution and the British Caribbean* (Philadelphia: University of Pennsylvania Press, 2000), 43–47; Alan Burns, *History of the British West Indies* (London: Allen & Unwin, 1954); Cyril Hamshere, *The British in the Caribbean* (London: Weidenfeld & Nicolson, 1972).

21. "Boston, February 19," *Boston Weekly News-Letter*, February 19, 1756. See also René Chartrand, *The Forts of Colonial North America: British, Dutch and Swedish Colonies* (Oxford: Osprey, 2010), 54–57; J. E. Kaufmann and H. W. Kaufmann, *Fortress America: The Forts That Defended America, 1600 to the Present* (Cambridge, Mass.: Da Capo, 2004), 62–63; Lawrence E. Babits and Stephanie Gandulla, eds., *The Archaeology of French and Indian War Frontier Forts* (Gainesville: University of Florida Press, 2014); Thomas H. Raddall, *Halifax: Warden of the North*, updated ed. (Halifax, N.S.: Nimbus, 2010), 18–41; Harry Piers, *The Evolution of the Halifax Fortress, 1749–1928*, ed. G. M. Self (Halifax: Public Archives of Nova Scotia, 1947), 6–9.

22. *TAC* 394–96, 401–10; Kaufmann and Kaufmann, *Fortress America*, 38–94.

23. Kaufmann and Kaufmann, *Fortress America*, 67, 69; Chartrand, *Forts of North America*, 34.

24. *PA* 8th ser., 5:4286.

25. *JHCSC* 14:492.

26. *HBP* 1:150.

27. Petition of Trenton Inhabitants [1758], Papers Relating to the Barracks at Trenton, 1758–1793, NJSA.

28. Petition of Princeton Inhabitants, April 11, 1758, Manuscript Collection, box 1–13, item 11, NJSA.

29. *CRSC* 13.

30. "New-York, October 10," *New-York Gazette*, October 17, 1757.

31. William Smith Jr., *The History of the Province of New-York*, ed. Michael Kammen, 2 vols. (Cambridge, Mass.: Harvard University Press, 1972), 2:225. On barracks in New Jersey see Edgar Jacob Fisher, *New Jersey as a Royal Province, 1738 to 1776* (New York: Columbia University, 1911), 346–47; *VPNJ* (March–April 1758): 12, 14, 22.

32. "New York, October 27," *Pennsylvania Gazette*, November 6, 1755; William S. Stryker, *The Old Barracks at Trenton, New Jersey* (Trenton, N.J.: Naar, Day, and Naar, 1885), 12.

33. *MCCNY* 6:113, 119, 128–29; *CLNY* 4:184–85, 211–13; *DCHNY* 7:342; *PA* 1st ser., 3:62; Bouquet to Lyttelton, February 28, 1758, WHLP 6; *CRSC* 211; JCF October 27, 1757; Fisher, *New Jersey*, 347; Larry R. Gerlach, "Soldiers and Citizens: The British Army in New Jersey on the Eve of the Revolution," *New Jersey History* 93 (1975): 13; Jessica Kross, "Taxation and the Seven Years' War: A New York Test Case," *Canadian Review of American Studies* 18 (1987): 351–66.

34. John Montresor, "Estimate of the Sundry Materials Necessary to Finish and Complete the Hospital, Barracks, and Storehouse Building at Albany," February 1757, LO 6594. See also Alan Rogers, *Empire and Liberty: American Resistance to British Authority, 1755–1763* (Berkeley: University of California Press, 1974), 82; Stanley McCrory Pargellis, *Lord Loudoun in North America* (New Haven, Conn.: Yale University Press, 1933), 196–98.

35. *MCCNY* 6:108; *PA* 1st ser., 3:302; JCF July 28, 1757.

36. Accounts for Barracks, 1758–1762, Papers Relating to the Barracks at Trenton, 1758–1793, NJSA. See also Stryker, *Old Barracks at Trenton*, 13.

37. Accounts, Burlington Barracks, 1758–60, MF-07–01, reel 1–006, item 193, NJSA.

38. Josiah Quincy, *The History of Harvard*, 2 vols. (Cambridge: Mass.: Owen, 1840), 1:194; Beverly Prior Smaby, *The Transformation of Moravian Bethlehem: From Communal Mission to Family Economy* (Philadelphia: University of Pennsylvania Press, 1988); *MJ* 4–5; *PA* 1st ser., 3:278–79.

39. Stryker, *Old Barracks at Trenton*, 9.

40. William A. Whitehead, *Contributions to the Early History of Perth Amboy and the Adjoining Country* (New York: Appleton, 1856), 256–58; Edwin F. Hatfield, *History of Elizabeth, New Jersey* (New York: Carlton and Lanahan, 1868), 391–92; Stryker, *Old Barracks at Trenton*, 3; I. N. Phelps Stokes, *The Iconography of Manhattan Island, 1498–1909*, 6 vols. (New York: Dodd, 1915–28), 5: plate 46a; *MCCNY* 6:167; Pargellis, *Lord Loudoun*, 197; "From Albany We Learn," *Boston Weekly News-Letter*, October 28, 1756; *PA* 1st ser., 3:278; JCF September 15, 1757; Charles L. Fisher, "Soldiers in the City:

The Archaeology of the British Guard House," in *People, Places, and Material Things: Historical Archaeology of Albany, New York*, ed. Charles L. Fisher, 39–46 (Albany: New York State Museum, 2003).

41. Isabel M. Calder, ed., *Colonial Captivities, Marches and Journeys* (New York: Macmillan, 1938), 143.

42. *MCCNY* 6:111–12; Joseph F. W. Des Barres, *A Sketch of Operations before Charlestown* (1780), MNA-LC; *CRSC* 102–3; JCF March 3, 1758; *BTNA* 90, 103–5; Stokes, *Iconography of Manhattan Island*, 1:339–41; Pierre Nicole and John Montresor, *A Survey of the City of Philadelphia and Its Environs* (1777), MNA-LC; "New-York, October 27," *Pennsylvania Gazette*, November 6, 1755; Fisher, *New Jersey*, 346–47.

43. John Russell Young, *Memorial History of the City of Philadelphia from Its First Settlement to the Year 1895*, 2 vols. (New York: New-York History Co., 1895–98), 1:283; Pierre Eugene du Simitiere, *Raising the Liberty Pole in New York City* (1770), Library Company of Philadelphia; J. H. Easterby, *A History of the College of Charleston Founded 1770* (Charleston, S.C.: College of Charleston, 1935), 26.

44. *MCCNY* 6:140, 173–75, 179; *MJ* 64; *PA* 1st ser., 3:452–53, 559; Peter Thompson, *Rum Punch and Revolution: Taverngoing and Public Life in Eighteenth-Century Philadelphia* (Philadelphia: University of Pennsylvania Press, 1999), 59–60; Stryker, *Old Barracks at Trenton*, 12; J. Thomas Scharf and Thomas Westcott, *History of Philadelphia, 1609–1884*, 3 vols. (Philadelphia: Everts, 1884), 2:1011–12; Caroline Cox, *A Proper Sense of Honor: Service and Sacrifice in George Washington's Army* (Chapel Hill: University of North Carolina Press, 2004), 50–52.

45. *VPNJ* (July–August 1758): 34.

46. *CRSC* 13, 41. See also *CRSC* 24, 63, 65, 102, 105; JCF November 8, 1757, March 3, 1758; *HBP* 1:308–10, 327; Bouquet to Lyttelton, February 28, 1758, WHLP 6; Jack P. Greene, "The South Carolina Quartering Dispute, 1757–1758," *SCHM* 60 (1959): 193–204.

47. Bouquet to Lyttelton, February 28, 1758, WHLP 6.

48. *CRSC* 135.

49. *CRSC* 207–9.

50. JCF July 28, 1757; *CRSC* 15; Stryker, *Old Barracks at Trenton*, 10–11; Az. Dunham, *Plan of Middlesex County in the Province of East Jersey* (1766), Maps 5-A-4, Henry Clinton Papers, WLCL; Whitehead, *History of Perth Amboy*, 317.

51. Stephen Jenkins, *The Greatest Street in the World: The Story of Broadway, Old and New, from the Bowling Green to Albany* (New York: Putnam's Sons, 1911), 84–93; *Independence Day Celebration Held at City Hall in the City of New York* (New York: City of New York, 1913), 3; *PKT* 133; John Gillies, *Memoirs of Rev. George Whitefield* (New Haven, Conn.: Whitmore, Buckingham and Mansfield, 1834), 42–43; Frank Lambert, *Inventing the "Great Awakening"* (Princeton, N.J.: Princeton University Press, 1999), 112–13; Joyce Hansen and Gary McGowan, *Breaking Ground, Breaking Silence: The Story of New York's African Burial Ground* (New York: Holt, 1998).

52. *MPCPA* 7:737.

53. *PA* 1st ser., 3:278.

54. *PA* 1st ser., 3:301–2; Watson, *Annals of Philadelphia*, 3:273; Scharf and Westcott, *History of Philadelphia*, 2:987, 1005; Pargellis, *Lord Loudoun*, 202; Harry Kyriakodis, *Philadelphia's Lost Waterfront* (Charleston, S.C.: History Press, 2011), 19, 23; Steven Rosswurm, *Arms, Country, and Class: The Philadelphia Militia and the "Lower*

Sort" during the American Revolution (New Brunswick, N.J.: Rutgers University Press, 1987), 23, 38, 170–71.

55. *JHRMA* 35:87.

56. John Montresor, *A General and Particular Plan of the Island of Castle William Near Boston* (1771?), MNA-LC; MJ 399–410; Eric Hinderaker, *Boston's Massacre* (Cambridge, Mass.: Harvard University Press, 2017), 90.

57. *HBP* 1:150.

58. Pargellis, *Lord Loudoun*, 197; "State of the Quarters Provided for the First Battalion of the Royal American Regiment in Philadelphia [December 1757]," WHLP 6; Douet, *British Barracks*, 23–26; Brian Leigh Dunnigan, *The Necessity of Regularity in Quartering Soldiers: The Organization, Material Culture and Quartering of the British Soldier at Michilimackinac* (Mackinac Island, Mich.: Mackinac State Historic Parks, 1999), 17–34; "Barracks Necessaries Allowed His Majesty's Troops in 1757," enclosure in Füser to Gage, May 28, 1767, TGP-AS 65.

59. *MCCNY* 6:159. See also *MCCNY* 6:161–65. For barracks in New Jersey see Joseph Yard Accounts, 1758–1764, Papers Relating to the Barracks at Trenton, 1758–1793, NJSA; Hugh Hartshorn's Account, Burlington, 1760, MF-07–01, reel 1–006, item 185, NJSA.

60. *MCCP* 624. See also *MPCPA* 8:225; *PA* 1st ser., 3:62–63.

61. *HBP* 1:249. See also *CRSC* 13–14, 40–42; *HBP* 1:223–25, 266–69, 288–89, 326–30.

62. Correlli Barnett, *Britain and Her Army, 1509–1970: A Military, Political and Social Survey* (Middlesex, UK: Penguin, 1970), 139–40; *CRSC* 102–3; *MCCNY* 6:111–12; *MPCPA* 8:76; Douet, *British Barracks*, 27–28; Pargellis, *Lord Loudoun*, 200.

63. Stephen Brumwell, *Redcoats: The British Soldier and the War in the Americas, 1755–1763* (New York: Cambridge University Press, 2002), 122–27; Alexander V. Campbell, *The Royal American Regiment: An Atlantic Microcosm, 1755–1772* (Norman: University of Oklahoma Press, 2010), 148–50, 203–7; Dunnigan, *Necessity of Regularity*, 34–37; Paul E. Kopperman, "The British High Command and Soldiers' Wives in America, 1755–1783," *Journal of the Society for Army Historical Research* 60 (1982): 14–34; TG-OB July 10, 1767; Calder, *Colonial Captivities*, 169–98; Holly A. Mayer, *Belonging to the Army: Camp Followers and Community during the American Revolution* (Columbia: University of South Carolina Press, 1996); Myna Trustram, *Women of the Regiment: Marriage and the Victorian Army* (Cambridge: Cambridge University Press, 1984).

64. Füser to Gage, November 27, 1767, TGP-AS 72.

65. *MPCPA* 8:164.

66. *JHRMA* 35:82, 100. See also *JHRMA* 35:89, 98; Second Church (Boston) Records, 1650–1970, box 42, folder 8, MHS.

67. *PRCT* 11:304. *PRCT* 11:175–78, 190, 215–16, 243, 304–7; Pargellis, *Lord Loudoun*, 205.

68. Petition of Princeton Inhabitants, April 11, 1758, Manuscript Collection, box 1–13, item 11, NJSA.

69. Christopher French, "Journal of an Expedition to South Carolina, December 22, 1760–November 14, 1761," SCDAH.

70. Ten Broeck to Gage, February 20, 1760, TGP-AS 5.

71. Campbell to Gage, February 29, 1760, TGP-AS 5.

72. *PA* 1st ser., 3:575.

73. *MPCPA* 8:282, 330. See also *PA* 1st ser., 3:316, 480–82; *MPCPA* 8:110, 167–69, 171, 173, 224–25, 232–34, 376–78.

74. Nathaniel Fuller Journal, March 28, 1760, March 29, 1760, WLCL.

75. *CLB* 1:47.

76. Joan Pinkerton Gordon, "Barracks in Lancaster: The First Ten Years," *Journal of the Lancaster County Historical Society* 99 (1997): 80–92; Samuel M. Sener, *The Lancaster Barracks Where the British and Hessian Prisoners Were Detained during the Revolution* (Harrisburg, Pa.: Harrisburg Publishing, 1895), 3–4; I. Daniel Rupp, *History of Lancaster County, to Which Is Prefixed a Brief Sketch of the Early History of Pennsylvania* (Lancaster, Pa.: Hills, 1844), 345–46.

77. *VPNJ* (March–April 1761): 8.

78. Quoted in Thomas Keppel, *The Life of Augustus Viscount Keppel, Admiral of the White, and First Lord of the Admiralty in 1782–83*, 2 vols. (London: Colburn, 1842), 1:441–42. See also John Richard Alden, *General Gage in America: Being Principally a History of His Role in the American Revolution* (Baton Rouge: Louisiana State University Press, 1948), 32–53.

79. Alden, *General Gage in America*, 1–47; John Shy, "Thomas Gage: Weak Link of Empire," in *George Washington's Opponents: British Generals and Admirals in the American Revolution*, ed. G. A. Billias, 3–38 (New York: Morrow, 1969); John Shy, "The Empire Militant: Thomas Gage and the Coming of War," in *A People Numerous and Armed: Reflection on the Military Struggle for American Independence*, rev. ed., 81–115 (Ann Arbor: University of Michigan Press, 1990); David Hackett Fischer, *Paul Revere's Ride* (New York: Oxford University Press, 1994); Shy, *Toward Lexington*, 125–39; Hinderaker, *Boston's Massacre*, 80, 91–92.

80. Fred Anderson, *Crucible of War: The Seven Years' War and the Fate of Empire in British North America, 1754–1766* (New York: Knopf, 2000), 169–75, 208–31.

81. Anderson, *Crucible of War*, 227, 309, 325–409; Brumwell, *Redcoats*, 26–43.

82. Alden, *General Gage in America*, 14, 52–60; Shy, *Toward Lexington*, 125–39.

83. André Charbonneau, "Les Nouvelles Casernes: Haut lieu de l'histoire militaire à Québec," *Cap-aux-Diamants: La revue d'histoire du Québec* 58 (1999): 25–29; André Charbonneau, Yvon Desloges, and Marc Lafrance, *Québec, The Fortified City: From the 17th to the 19th Century* (Ottawa: Parks Canada, 1982); Serge Bernier et al., *Military History of Québec City, 1608–2008* (Montréal: Art Global, 2008); Kaufmann and Kaufmann, *Fortress America*, 12–37; René Chartrand, *French Fortresses in North America, 1535–1763* (Oxford: Osprey, 2005)

84. James Murray, *Journal of the Siege of Québec, 1759–60* (Québec: Middleton and Dawson, 1871), 16, 13.

85. *RPAC* 29a:209, 141. See also Desmond Morton, *A Military History of Canada* (Edmonton: Hurtig, 1985), 18–23; William Henry Atherton, *Montréal, 1535–1914*, 3 vols. (Montréal: Clarke, 1914), 2:11–23; *TAC* 432, 442.

86. Bradstreet to Gage, May 23, 1764, TGP-AS 19.

87. *A Collection of the Acts Passed in the Parliament of Great Britain and of Other Public Acts Relative to Canada* (Québec: Desbarats, 1824), 2.

88. *RPAC* 18:43.

89. *DCHC* 1:47–81; *RPAC* 18:50; 29a:147–51; DBP 297/4/2.

90. Gage to Halifax, November 9, 1764, TGP-ES 2; Grant to Gage, October 2, 1764, TGP-AS 25. See also Daniel L. Schafer, "'. . . Not So Gay a Town in America as

This . . .': 1763–1784," in *The Oldest City: St. Augustine Saga of Survival*, ed. Jean Parker Waterbury, 91–123 (St. Augustine, Fla.: St. Augustine Historical Society, 1983).

91. *CISHL* 1:218. See also Anderson, *Crucible of War*, 503–6; Shy, *Toward Lexington*, 45–83.

92. *CISHL* 1:41. See also Lawrence Henry Gipson, *The Great War for Empire*, 15 vols. (New York: Knopf, 1936–70), 9:41–54, 156–276; Philip Lawson, *The Imperial Challenge: Québec and Britain in the Age of the American Revolution* (Montréal: McGill-Queen's University Press, 1989), 25–41.

93. Anderson, *Crucible of War*, 518–53; John Brewer, *The Sinews of Power: War, Money, and the English State, 1688–1783* (Cambridge, Mass.: Harvard University Press, 1988), 114–26.

94. Anderson, *Crucible of War*, 476–96, 507–17, 557–71; Richard White, *The Middle Ground: Indians, Empires, and Republics in the Great Lakes Region, 1650–1815* (New York: Cambridge University Press, 1991), 269–314; Gregory Evans Dowd, *War under Heaven: Pontiac, the Indian Nations, and the British Empire* (Baltimore: Johns Hopkins University Press, 2002); Alden, *General Gage in America*, 60–64.

95. *The Trial of Daniel Disney, Esq.* (Québec: Brown and Gilmore, 1767), 12. See also George M. Wrong, *Canada and the American Revolution: The Disruption of the First British Empire* (New York: Macmillan, 1935), 62–66.

96. Gage to Burton, February 27, 1765, TGP-AS 31. On population of Montréal see *TAC* 442; Jean-Claude Marsan, *Montréal in Evolution: Historical Analysis of Montréal's Architecture and Urban Environment* (Montréal: McGill-Queen's University Press, 1990), 84–85; Gipson, *Great War for Empire*, 9:166.

97. *DCB* s.v. "Walker, Thomas"; Atherton, *Montréal*, 2:19–20; L. W. Sicotte, "The Affair Walker, Trial of Daniel Disney, Esq., An Unpublished Manuscript," *Canadian Antiquarian and Numismatic Journal*, 3rd ser., 12 (1915): 181–228.

98. Council Minutes, June 27, 1765, CO 45/1.

99. Quoted in Sicotte, "Affair Walker," 182.

100. Council Minutes, November 12, 1764, CO 45/1. See also Council Minutes, October 25, 1764, CO 45/1; Gipson, *Great War for Empire*, 9:156–76; Lawson, *Imperial Challenge*, 49–51.

101. *Trial of Daniel Disney*, 7–8.

102. Atherton, *Montréal*, 2:36; W. Stewart Wallace, ed., *The Maseres Letters, 1766–1768* (Toronto: University of Toronto Library, 1919), 47n5.

103. *Trial of Daniel Disney*, 10–12, 25–26, 31.

104. Mitchelson to Burton, December 13, 1764, enclosure in Burton to Gage, January 8, 1765, TGP-AS 30. See also Council Minutes, December 10, 1764, CO 45/1; Sicotte, "Affair Walker," 189, 194; Murray to Gage, January 10, 1765, TGP-AS 30; Gage to Halifax, February 23, 1765, TGP-ES 3; Gage to Ellis, April 13, 1765, TGP-ES 3.

105. Burton to Gage, January 8, 1765, TGP-AS 30.

106. "Extract of a letter from Québec, to a Merchant in London, dated Dec. 16," *Boston News-Letters and New-England Chronicle*, June 27, 1765. The same letter appeared in *Newport Mercury*, July 8, 1765, and *Connecticut Courant*, July 15, 1765.

107. Council Minutes, June 27, 1765, CO 45/1. See also The Deposition of Thomas Walker Esqr. of Montréal and The Deposition of Geo: Magagvoch Soldier in the 28th Regt., CO 42/86; Gage to Burton, February 27, 1765, TGP-AS 31; Walker to Gage, July 2, 1766, TGP-AS 53; Wallace, *Maseres Letters*, 40n1; *Motives for*

a Subscription towards the Relief of the Sufferers at Montréal in Canada (Montréal: n.p., 1765), 19–20.

108. Council Minutes, June 27, 1765, CO 45/1.

109. "Extracts from the Trial of Daniel Disney, Esq.," *Boston Chronicle*, March 28–April 4, 1768; "Ambe, April 24," *New-York Journal; or, the General Advertiser*, June 30, 1768; Atherton, *Montréal*, 40.

110. Shy, *Toward Lexington*, 112, 166–71.

111. *LBJW* 198.

112. *CLNY* 4:637.

113. *CLNY* 4:369, 476, 637–39; "New-York, August 20," *Boston Post Boy*, August 27, 1759; *JHRMA* 37:172, 38:47.

114. *CRSC* 460.

115. *JCHSC-M* 37, pt. 1, 252–53. See also Fraser, *Charleston! Charleston!*, 117.

116. *MCCNY* 6:412.

117. "An Act Appointing Commissioners to Take Care of, and Let the Barracks Erected in This Colony of New Jersey," Papers Relating to the Barracks at Trenton, 1758–1793, NJSA. See also Expenses for Repairing Barracks at Amboy and Elizabethtown, 1762, MF-07-01, reel 1–006, item 155, NJSA; Abraham Hunt's Account as Barrack Master, Papers Relating to the Barracks at Trenton, 1758–1793, NJSA; Gerlach, "Soldiers and Citizens," 13.

118. Peter Silver, *Our Savage Neighbors: How Indian War Transformed Early America* (New York: Norton, 2008), 137–38, 174–77; Young, *Memorial History of Philadelphia*, 1:283–84.

119. Quoted in "Biographical Sketch of Rev. Bernhard Adam Grube," *PMHB* 25 (1901): 17.

120. *MPCPA* 9:92–93, 95–97, 100–11, 118–29; Silver, *Our Savage Neighbors*, 177–85; Brooke Hindle, "The March of the Paxton Boys," *WMQ* 3 (1946): 461–86; Matthew C. Ward, *Breaking the Backcountry: The Seven Years' War in Virginia and Pennsylvania, 1754–1765* (Pittsburgh: University of Pittsburgh Press, 2003), 236–40.

121. *MPCPA* 9:105, 129, 132–33. See also Penn to Gage, December 31, 1763, TGP-AS 11; Gage to Penn, January 6, 1764, TGP-AS 12; *SLPA*, 6:325–28; Young, *Memorial History of Philadelphia*, 1:283–88; 2:144.

122. "Diary of the Indian *Gemeine* in the Barracks in Philadelphia," ed. Katherine Carté Engel, Bethlehem Digital History Project, bdhp.moravian.edu/community_records/christianindians/diaires/barracks/1764/translation64.html (accessed July 21, 2013), January 28, 1764, February 4, 1764, February 6, 1764.

123. *MPCPA* 9:138. See also *MPCPA* 9:142–45; John R. Dunbar, ed., *The Paxton Papers* (The Hague: Nijhoff, 1957); Silver, *Our Savage Neighbors*, 188–215.

124. "Diary of the Indian *Gemeine*," February 12, 1764, July 11, 1764. See also Penn to Gage, February 17, 1764, TGP-AS 14; *PA* 4th ser., 3:275–76, 291–93; *MPCPA* 9:170–71.

3. Empire

1. *PBF* 11:332. See also Carl Van Doren, *Benjamin Franklin* (New York: Penguin, 1938), 272, 317, 401–7, 419–22; Gordon Wood, *The Americanization of Benjamin Franklin* (New York: Penguin, 2004); Nathan Kozuskanich, *Benjamin Franklin: American Founder, Atlantic Citizen* (New York: Routledge, 2015).

2. Craig Yirush, *Settlers, Liberty, and Empire: The Roots of Early American Political Theory, 1675–1775* (New York: Cambridge University Press, 2011), 83–112. See also Eric Hinderaker, "The 'Four Indian Kings' and the Imaginative Construction of the First British Empire," *WMQ* 53 (1996): 487–526; David Armitage, *The Ideological Origins of the British Empire* (Cambridge: Cambridge University Press, 2000); Jon Butler, *Becoming America: The Revolution before 1776* (Cambridge, Mass.: Harvard University Press, 2000); P. J. Marshall, *The Making and Unmaking of Empires: Britain, India, and America, c. 1750–1783* (New York: Oxford University Press, 2005); Eric Hinderaker, *Boston's Massacre* (Cambridge, Mass.: Harvard University Press, 2017), 77–103.

3. For example, see Bernard Bailyn, *The Ideological Origins of the American Revolution*, enlarged ed. (Cambridge, Mass.: Harvard University Press, 1992).

4. "Distribution of Forces in America [1763]," CTP 8/22/6; *Cantonment of His Majesty's Forces in North America, 11 Octr. 1765*, MNA-LC; "Plantations (1765)," WO 24/431.

5. CRA 134. See also CRA 123, 125–26, 133, 143; Bradstreet to Gage, March 27, 1764, TGP-AS 16; Cuyler Reynolds, *Albany Chronicles: A History of the City Arranged Chronologically from the Earliest Settlement to the Present Time* (Albany, N.Y.: Lyon, 1906), 259–63; Eliot A. Cohen, *Conquered into Liberty: Two Centuries of Battles along the Great Warpath That Made the American Way of War* (New York: Free Press, 2011); James M. Johnson, Christopher Pryslopski, and Andrew Villani, eds., *Key to the Northern Country: The Hudson River Valley in the American Revolution* (Albany: SUNY Press, 2013).

6. Bradstreet to Gage, January 23, 1764, TGP-AS 12; Elliot to Gage, March 15, 1764, TGP-AS 15.

7. Schuyler to Gage, June 30, 1764, TGP-AS 20.

8. Schuyler to Gage, July 5, 1764, TGP-AS 21. See also Schuyler to Gage, July 24, 1764, TGP-AS 22.

9. Deposition of Harmanus Schuyler, enclosure in Bell to Gage, October 16, 1764, TGP-AS 25.

10. CRA 152.

11. Gage to Douw, December 16, 1764, TGP-AS 28.

12. Gage to Colden, November 27, 1764, TGP-AS 27.

13. Christie to Murray, October 10, 1764, enclosure in Burton to Gage, October 20, 1764, TGP-AS 26.

14. "The Memorial of Lt. Col. Robertson, D. Qr. Mr. Gl.," enclosure in Gage to Ellis, January 22, 1765, TGP-ES 3. See also John Shy, *Toward Lexington: The Role of the British Army in the Coming of the American Revolution* (Princeton, N.J.: Princeton University Press, 1965), 163–81; *The Twilight of British Rule in Revolutionary America: The New York Letter Book of General James Robertson, 1780–1783*, ed. Milton M. Klein and Ronald W. Howard (Cooperstown: New York State Historical Association, 1983), 25–26.

15. "Additions Proposed to Be Made to the Mutiny Act," enclosure in Gage to Ellis, January 22, 1765, TGP-ES 3.

16. "Additions Proposed to Be Made to the Mutiny Act," enclosure in Gage to Ellis, January 22, 1765, TGP-ES 3.

17. John Richard Alden, *General Gage in America: Being Principally a History of His Role in the American Revolution* (Baton Rouge: Louisiana State University Press, 1948), 65–88; John Shy, "Thomas Gage: Weak Link of Empire," in *George Washington's*

Opponents: British Generals and Admirals in the American Revolution, ed. G. A. Billias, 3–38 (New York: Morrow, 1969).

18. Ellis to Gage, March 9, 1765, TGP-ES 3; Halifax to Gage, March 9, 1765, TGP-ES 3; "The Secretary at War's Bill for Drawing and Passing the American Mutiny Bill," Treasury Papers 1–455, NAK; P. D. G. Thomas, *British Politics and the Stamp Act Crisis: The First Phase of the American Revolution, 1763–1767* (Oxford: Clarendon, 1975), 85–100; John L. Bullion, *A Great and Necessary Measure: George Grenville and the Genesis of the Stamp Act, 1763–1765* (Columbia: University of Missouri Press, 1982), 136–63; Philip Lawson, *George Grenville: A Political Life* (Oxford: Clarendon, 1984), 211–45; Allen S. Johnson, *A Prologue to Revolution: The Political Career of George Grenville (1712–1770)* (Lanham, Md.: University Press of America, 1997), 179–204.

19. *The Grenville Papers: Being the Correspondence of Richard Grenville Early Temple, K.G., and the Right Hon: George Grenville, Their Friends and Contemporaries*, ed. William James Smith, 4 vols. (London: Murray, 1852–53), 3:11. See also Jeremy Black, *George III: America's Last King* (New Haven, Conn.: Yale University Press, 2006).

20. *PDBP* 2:41–42. See also Thomas, *British Politics*, 101–8.

21. *PDBP* 2:45–46; *The Jenkinson Papers, 1760–66*, ed. Ninetta S. Jucker (London: Macmillan, 1949), 358–62; Edwin P. Tanner, "Colonial Agencies in England during the Eighteenth Century," *Political Science Quarterly* 16 (1901): 24–49; L. B. Namier, "Charles Garth, Agent for South Carolina, Part II," *English Historical Review* 54 (1939): 632–52; Ella Lonn, *The Colonial Agents of the Southern Colonies* (Chapel Hill: University of North Carolina Press, 1945); Jack M. Sosin, *Agents and Merchants: British Colonial Policy and the Origins of the American Revolution, 1763–1775* (Lincoln: University of Nebraska Press, 1965).

22. *The Fitch Papers: Correspondence and Documents during Thomas Fitch's Governorship of the Colony of Connecticut, 1754–1766* (Hartford: Connecticut Historical Society, 1918–20), 2:343–44.

23. John A. Schutz, *Thomas Pownall, British Defender of American Liberty: A Study of Anglo-American Relations in the Eighteenth Century* (Glendale, Calif.: Clark, 1951), 181–214; Shy, *Toward Lexington*, 148–49, 162–63; Stephen Conway, *War, State, and Society in Mid-Eighteenth-Century Britain and Ireland* (Oxford: Oxford University Press, 2006), 232–40.

24. Emphasis in original. "To the Printer," *Gazetteer and New Daily Advertiser*, April 11, 1765.

25. "To the Printer," *Gazetteer and New Daily Advertiser*, April 27, 1765. See also Fred Junkin Hinkhouse, *The Preliminaries of the American Revolution as Seen in the English Press, 1763–1775* (New York: Columbia University Press, 1926), 47; Eliga H. Gould, *The Persistence of Empire: British Political Culture in the Age of the American Revolution* (Chapel Hill: University of North Carolina Press, 2000).

26. "Postscript," *London Evening Post*, April 13, 1765.

27. *PBF* 12:120.

28. "To the Printer of the *Public Advertiser*," *Public Advertiser*, April 18, 1765.

29. *PDBP* 2:51. See also *PDBP* 2:52–53.

30. Gage to Douw, July 30, 1765, TGP-AS 40.

31. Gage to Burton, July 30, 1765, TGP-AS 40; Gage to Bouquet, July 31, 1765, TGP-AS 40.

32. *SLGB* 5 Geo. III, c. 33.

33. *SLGB* 5 Geo. III, c. 33.

34. *SR* 1 Gul. & Mar., sess. 2, c. 4. The English Mutiny Act was renewed every year with modifications, but each time with this passage. See *SLGB* 5 Geo. III, c. 7.

35. *SLGB* 5 Geo. III, c. 33.

36. *LBJW* 354.

37. "Extract of a Letter," *Connecticut Courant*, June 17, 1765.

38. "To the Printer," *Georgia Gazette*, August 15, 1765.

39. Sons of Liberty Records, 1766–70, MHS; Edmund S. Morgan and Helen M. Morgan, *The Stamp Act Crisis: Prologue to Revolution*, 3rd ed. (Chapel Hill: University of North Carolina Press, 1995); Pauline Maier, *From Resistance to Revolution: Colonial Radicals and the Development of American Opposition to Britain, 1765–1776* (New York: Knopf, 1972); Russell Bourne, *Cradle of Violence: How Boston's Waterfront Mobs Ignited the American Revolution* (Hoboken, N.J.: Wiley & Sons, 2006); Benjamin L. Carp, *Rebels Rising: Cities and the American Revolution* (New York: Oxford University Press, 2007); Zachary McLeod Hutchins, ed., *Community without Consent: New Perspectives on the Stamp Act* (Hanover, N.H.: Dartmouth College Press, 2016); Justin du Rivage, *Revolution against Empire: Taxes, Politics, and the Origins of American Independence* (New Haven, Conn.: Yale University Press, 2017); Jonathan Mercantini, ed., *The Stamp Act of 1765* (Peterborough, Ont.: Broadview, 2018).

40. "To the Printer in New-York," *New-London Gazette*, December 20, 1765.

41. "Plymouth, October 15, 1765," *Boston Evening Post*, October 28, 1765.

42. Gage to Bradstreet, August 12, 1765, TGP-AS 41.

43. "Charles-Town, South-Carolina, October 31," *Newport Mercury*, January 13, 1766. See also Walter J. Fraser Jr., *Charleston! Charleston! The History of a Southern City* (Columbia: University of South Carolina Press, 1989), 108–10.

44. *HMWS* 1:31. See also F. L. Engelman, "Cadwallader Colden and the New York Stamp Act Riots," *WMQ* 10 (1953): 560–78.

45. *MJ* 337.

46. Gage to Colden, November 5, 1765, TGP-AS 45.

47. Morgan and Morgan, *Stamp Act Crisis*, 165–86; Joseph S. Tiedemann, *Reluctant Revolutionaries: New York City and the Road to Independence, 1763–1776* (Ithaca, N.Y.: Cornell University Press, 1997), 62–82; Leopold S. Launitz-Shürer Jr., *Loyal Whigs and Revolutionaries: The Making of the Revolution in New York, 1765–1776* (New York: NYU Press, 1980), 22–47.

48. *PBF* 12:412, 267. See also Van Doren, *Benjamin Franklin*, 330–32.

49. *PBF* 13:134, 142, 147, 142n5, 157.

50. H. W. V. Temperley, "Debates on the Declaratory Act and the Repeal of the Stamp Act, 1766," *AHR* 17 (1912): 563–86; Lawrence Henry Gipson, "The Great Debate in the Committee of the Whole House of Commons on the Stamp Act, 1766, as Reported by Nathaniel Ryder," *PMHB* 86 (1962): 10–41; Sheila L. Skemp, *The Making of a Patriot: Benjamin Franklin at the Cockpit* (New York: Oxford University Press, 2013); Peter Charles Hoffer, *Benjamin Franklin Explains the Stamp Act Protests to Parliament* (New York: Oxford University Press, 2016).

51. *SLGB* 6 Geo. III, c. 12.

52. Tayler to Gage, December 9, 1765, TGP-AS 46. See also Wilfred Brenton Kerr, *The Maritime Provinces of British North America and the American Revolution* (New York: Russell and Russell, 1970), 53–54; Philip Lawson, *The Imperial Challenge: Quebec*

and Britain in the Age of the American Revolution (Montreal: McGill–Queen's University Press, 1989), 91–93; Grant to Conway, August 21, 1766, CTP 8/25/14.

53. Gage to Wilmot, July 31, 1765, TGP-AS 40; Gage to Grant, August 1, 1765, TGP-AS 40; Gage to Bouquet, July 31, 1765, TGP-AS 40; *PDBP*, 2:446; "Estimate of Such Services in North America," CTP 8/31/31.

54. Enclosure in Johnston to Moore, January 28, 1766, TGP-AS 48.

55. Gage to Barrington, December 18, 1766, TGP-ES 8. See also Council Minutes, February 11, 1766, CO 5/625; Hardy to Walsh, July 28, 1766, enclosure in Walsh to Tayler, August 6, 1766, TGP-AS 55; Tayler to Gage, August 8, 1766, TGP-AS 55; C. N. Howard, "Governor Johnstone in West Florida," *Florida Historical Quarterly* 17 (1939): 281–303.

56. *DCHC* 1:42–50.

57. "A Proclamation," July 5, 1766, CO 44/1.

58. Gage to Burton, July 30, 1765, TGP-AS 40.

59. Murray to Gage, August 20, 1764, TGP-AS 23.

60. Gage to Murray, August 27, 1764, TGP-AS 23.

61. Burton to Gage, August 22, 1765, TGP-AS 41.

62. Council Minutes, September 19, 1765, CO 42/5.

63. Council Minutes, September 30, 1765, CO 42/5. See also Murray to Lords of Trade, October 5, 1765, CO 42/5; "Estimate of the Expence Attending Quartering Two Battalions of Foot, and One Company of Artillery &ca in the District of Montreal and Three Rivers for Thirty Weeks or Two Hundred and Ten Days," CO 42/5.

64. Council Minutes, September 30, 1765, CO 42/5.

65. *DCB*, s.v. "Hertel de Rouville, René-Ovide."

66. "A Letter from a Gentleman in Ireland," *Newport Mercury*, June 9–16, 1766.

67. Translated from the French. Hertel de Rouville to Murray, January 22, 1766, CO 42/5. See also Carden to Murray, January 2, 1766, CO 42/5; Murray to Hertel de Rouville, January 12, 1766, CO 42/5.

68. Morris to Burton, January 29, 1766, enclosure in Burton to Murray, January 30, 1766, CO 42/5. See also Hertel de Rouville to Murray, January 30, 1766, CO 42/5; Carden to Murray, January 30, 1766, CO 42/5.

69. Gage to Burton, February 16, 1766, TGP-AS 48.

70. Gage to Murray, March 2, 1766, TGP-AS 49.

71. Gage to Lowndes, February 19, 1766, TGP-ES 6; Burton to Gage, March 19, 1766, TGP-AS 49; Gage to Burton, April 14, 1766, TGP-AS 50.

72. *ABF* 128.

73. Franklin to Gage, November 30, 1763, TGP-AS 10; Van Doren, *Benjamin Franklin*, 91, 200–201, 228–29, 272, 290–91, 300–302, 304–5, 330; Shelia Skemp, *William Franklin: Son of a Patriot, Servant of a King* (New York: Oxford University Press); Daniel Mark Epstein, *The Loyal Son: The War in Ben Franklin's House* (New York: Ballantine, 2017).

74. Franklin to Gage, September 14, 1765, TGP-AS 42.

75. Gage to Franklin, September 16, 1765, TGP-AS 42; *DCHNY* 9:499–500; Anton-Hermann Chroust, "The Lawyers of New Jersey and the Stamp Act," *American Journal of Legal History* 6 (1962): 286–97.

76. Barrington to Gage, February 8, 1766, TGP-ES 6; *PDBP* 2:356–58; *SLGB* 7 Geo. III, c. 55.

77. Gage to Conway, February 22, 1766, TGP-ES 6.

78. Gage to Barrington, May 7, 1766, TGP-ES 6. These quotes come from two different letters with the same date.

79. Conway to Gage, May 20, 1766, TGP-ES 7.

80. *Cantonment of His Majesty's Forces in North America, 11 Octr. 1765*, MNA-LC.

81. Gage to Penn, June 15, 1766, TGP-AS 52.

82. Gage to Penn, August 15, 1766, TGP-AS 56.

83. *SLPA* 7:46. See also *PA* 8th ser., 7:5897–5905; *MPCPA* 9:324.

84. "Philadelphia, September 25," *Pennsylvania Gazette*, September 25, 1766.

85. Gage to Franklin, May 28, 1766, TGP-AS 51.

86. *DCHNJ*, 17:453.

87. Gage to Barrington, October 11, 1766, TGP-ES 8; Skinner to Franklin, August 24, 1766, MF-01–07, reel 1–006, item 110, NJSA.

88. *DCHNJ* 9:577. See also Skemp, *William Franklin*, 88–92; Larry R. Gerlach, *Prologue to Independence: New Jersey in the Coming of the American Revolution* (New Brunswick, N.J.: Rutgers University Press, 1976), 65–66.

89. "Extract from the Proceedings of the General Assembly of the Colony of New York," *New-York Gazette*, December 23, 1765. See also *MJ* 344.

90. Moore to Gage, May 25, 1766, TGP-AS 51.

91. "Answer of the House of Assembly to Governor's Message of the 13th June 1766," CTP 8/28/32. See also *MJ* 373–75; Tiedemann, *Reluctant Revolutionaries*, 90–91.

92. *DCHNY* 7:825–26; Sung Bok Kim, *Landlord and Tenant in Colonial New York: Manorial Society, 1664–1775* (Chapel Hill: University of North Carolina Press, 1978), 346–94; Thomas J. Humphrey, *Land and Liberty: Hudson Valley Riots in the Age of Revolution* (DeKalb: Northern Illinois University Press, 2004), 63–81.

93. "At a Council held at Fort George in the City of New York," enclosure in Moore to Gage, June 19, 1766, TGP-AS 53.

94. Gage to Moore, June 19, 1766, TGP-AS 53.

95. "Answer to the House of Assembly to Sir Henry Moore's Message of the 13 June 1766," CTP 8/28/32.

96. "Answer to Sir Henry Moore's Second Message to the House of Assembly on 20 June 1766," CTP 8/28/34.

97. *DCHNY* 7:831. See also *CLNY* 4:901–3; Tiedemann, *Reluctant Revolutionaries*, 117–19; Launitz-Shürer, *Loyal Whigs and Revolutionaries*, 49–51.

98. Gage to Richmond, August 25, 1766, TGP-ES 7.

99. Gage to Richmond, August 26, 1766, TGP-ES 7. See also Browne to Gage, June 23, 1766, TGP-AS 53.

100. Clarke to Gage, August 1, 1766, TGP-AS 55. See also Clarke to Gage, July 29, 1766, TGP-AS 55; *DCHNY*, 7:845–46; Kim, *Landlord and Tenant*, 394–409.

101. Jeremy Black, *Pitt the Elder: The Great Commoner* (Cambridge: Cambridge University Press, 1992), 196–225; Edward Pearce, *Pitt the Elder: Man of War* (London: Pimlico, 2011); John Brooke, *The Chatham Administration, 1766–1768* (London: Macmillan, 1956).

102. Shelburne to Moore, August 9, 1766, CTP 8/28/37. See also Shelburne to Gage, December 11, 1766, TGP-ES 8; Merrill Jensen, *The Founding of a Nation: A History of the American Revolution* (New York: Oxford University Press, 1968), 227–28.

103. General Assembly to Moore, December 15, 1766, CTP 8/28/41. See also Moore to General Assembly, November 17, 1766, CTP 8/28/38; *DCHNY* 7:883–85.

104. "Resolution of the Assembly of New York," November 19, 1766, CTP 8/28/39. See also Tiedemann, *Reluctant Revolutionaries*, 118–19, 291n24.

105. *CWP* 3:188, 189, 215.

106. Black, *Pitt the Elder*, 228–38; Marie Peters, "The Myth of William Pitt, Earl of Chatham, Great Imperialist Part II: Chatham and Imperial Reorganization," *Journal of Imperial and Commonwealth History* 22 (1994): 396–99.

107. Townshend to Buccleuch, January 10, 1765; DBP 296/1/4.

108. Dowdeswell to Townshend, July 24, 1765, DBP 296/1/22; Brocklesby to Townshend, October 19, 1765, DBP 296/1/25.

109. Patrick Griffin, *The Townshend Moment: The Making of Empire and Revolution in the Eighteenth Century* (New Haven, Conn.: Yale University Press, 2017), 14–33, 42–54, 61–64, 73–98, 114–18, 132–39.

110. *CWP* 3:192.

111. *CWP* 3:208.

112. *PDBP* 2:471, 468. See also *PDBP* 464–65; CGC 29:226; "Philadelphia, August 27," *Pennsylvania Gazette*, August 27, 1767.

113. *PDBP* 2:480, 481, 485. See also *PBF* 14:66, 102–7; Schutz, *Thomas Pownall*, 200–201, 215–17.

114. *SLGB* 7 Geo. III, c. 55; *PDBP* 2:497, 501, 510.

115. "Copy of a Letter from a Gentleman of Undoubted Veracity in London," *Boston Evening Post*, June 8, 1767. See also *PDBP* 2:412–13, 431–33, 436–38, 444–45; *CWP* 3:191–93; "Philadelphia, April 23," *New-York Mercury*, April 27, 1767; "Philadelphia, April 23," *Boston Evening Post*, May 4, 1767; CGC 29:218–19, 222–24. For the papers reviewed by Whitehall, see "Connecticut Relating to Quartering Soldiers," CTP 8/28/46; "New Jersey Relating to Quartering Soldiers," CTP 8/28/44; "Abstract of the Act for Quartering Troops in America," CTP 8/28/45; "Extract of a Letter from Governor Franklin to the Earl of Shelburne," DBP 296/5/26; "New York and Georgia Minutes," DBP 296/5/9.

116. "London," *St. James's Chronicle or the British Evening Post*, May 23–26, 1767. See also *PDBP* 2:466.

117. *PDBP* 2:464. See also Griffin, *Townshend Moment*, 118–26.

118. Orders in Council, April 13, 1767, CO 5/24.

119. Orders in Council, May 13, 1767, CO 5/24; *SLPA* 7:373–74.

120. On the uncertainty over the authorship of the New York Restraining Act see Sir Lewis Namier and John Brooke, *Charles Townshend* (New York: St. Martin's, 1964), 172–79; Nicholas Varga, "The New York Restraining Act: Its Passage and Some Effects, 1766–68," *Quarterly Journal of the New York State Historical Association* 37 (1956): 245–46.

121. "Resolution from the Attorney General America," CTP 8/31/5. See also "To Read the Resolution of the Last Year," CTP 8/46/5; "A Bill for Restraining and Prohibiting the Governor Council and House of Representatives, of the Province of New York," CTP 8/19/5–5a; "Resolution against New York," CTP 8/46/2; Derek Watson, "The Rockingham Whigs and the Townshend Duties," *English Historical Review* 84 (1969): 561–65.

122. *PDBP* 2:473.

123. *PDBP* 2:467, 474.

124. *The Writings and Speeches of Edmund Burke,* ed. Paul Langford, 9 vols. (Oxford: Clarendon, 1981–2000), 2:59. See also Richard Bourke, *Empire and Revolution: The Political Life of Edmund Burke* (Princeton, N.J.: Princeton University Press, 2015), 305–7.

125. *SLGB* 7 Geo. III, c. *59; PDBP* 2:503, 512, 517; *PBF* 14:163–65; CGC 29:226–27; "London, May 14," *New-York Gazette or the Weekly Post-Boy,* July 30, 1767; Lee E. Olm, "The Mutiny Act for America: New York's Noncompliance," *New-York Historical Society Quarterly* 58 (1974): 210–11.

126. Gage to Carleton, April 19, 1767, TGP-AS 64; "Philadelphia, April 23," *New-York Mercury,* April 27, 1767; "Philadelphia, April 23," *Boston Evening Post,* May 4, 1767; "Boston, June 22," *Boston Evening Post,* June 22, 1767; "Captain Lynde Left London," *Boston News-Letter and New-England Chronicle,* July 2, 1767; "Extract of a Letter from New-Orleans," *New-York Mercury,* July 27, 1767; "New-York, August 24," *New York Gazette,* August 27, 1767; "New-York, September 3," *New-York Journal; or, the General Advertiser,* September 3, 1767; "New-York, October 15," *New-York Gazette or the Weekly Post-Boy,* October 15, 1767. See also Carol Lynn H. Knight, *The American Colonial Press and the Townshend Crisis, 1766–1770: A Study in Political Imagery* (Lewiston, N.Y.: Mellen, 1990).

127. "To the Publishers," *Boston Evening Post,* February 16, 1767. The same letter appeared in the *New Hampshire Gazette,* February 27, 1767; the *New-York Gazette,* March 5, 1767; and the *Providence Gazette,* March 6, 1767.

128. Gage to Bernard, December 15, 1766, TGP-AS 60.

129. *JHRMA* 43:229, 230, 243, 299. See also Shy, *Toward Lexington,* 254.

130. *JHRMA* 44:9, 56. See also *ARMA* 18:245.

131. Gage to Pitkin, January 8, 1767, TGP-AS 61.

132. *PRCT* 12: 541–43.

133. Pitkin to Gage, January 31, 1767, TGP-AS 61.

134. *PRCT* 12:544.

135. *Cantonment of the Forces in N. America 1766,* Shelburne Papers, 49:648, WLCL; "Plantations (1766)," WO 24/436; *CRGA* 17:312; Michael Craton, *A History of the Bahamas* (London: Collins, 1962), 151; René Chartrand, "Notes on Bermuda Military Forces, 1687–1815," *Bermuda Historical Quarterly* 28 (1971): 43.

136. Assembly Minutes, October 7, 1766, CO 40/12.

137. Bruere to Gage, March 23, 1767, TGP-AS 63. See also Assembly Minutes, October 11, 1766, March 21, 1767, CO 40/12.

138. Phillips to Gage, December 17, 1766, TGP-AS 60.

139. Phillips to Gage, March 24, 1767, TGP-AS 63; *JHCSC*-M 37.1:393. See also *JHCSC*-M 37.1:256, 373–76, 392, 453–54.

140. Wright to Gage, July 20, 1767, TGP-AS 67. See also *CRGA* 17:311–13.

141. Gage to Shirley, December 8, 1766, TGP-AS 60.

142. Gage to Shelburne, April 7, 1767, TGP-ES 9.

143. Gage to Wright, April 30, 1767, TGP-AS 64.

144. Gage to Bruere, May 31, 1767, TGP-AS 65.

145. *CRGA* 14:479–80, 483–85; 17:380, 382–83; "Savannah (Georgia) Nov. 4," *Virginia Gazette,* January 7, 1768.

146. Assembly Minutes, September 17, 1767, CO 40/12; Gage to Delacherois, October 14, 1767, TGP-AS 71.

147. Assembly Minutes, February 2, 1768, CO 40/12. See also Bruere to Gage, May 4, 1768, TGP-AS 76; Gage to Bruere, May 31, 1768, TGP-AS 77.

148. "Charlestown, April 29," *Georgia Gazette*, May 18, 1768.

149. Gage to Stapylton, January 8, 1767, TGP-AS 73.

150. Gage to Stapylton, June 11, 1768, TGP-AS 77.

151. *SLPA* 7:150–51.

152. "Tuesday Last the General Assembly," *New-York Gazette*, May 25–June 1, 1767.

153. *CLNY* 4:948. See also "To His Excellency Sir Henry Moore," *New-York Gazette*, June 1–6, 1767.

154. *VPNJ* (June 1767): 6.

155. *PBF* 14:234. See also *PSWJ* 5:704; *PBF* 14:175–79; Edgar Jacob Fisher, *New Jersey as a Royal Province, 1738 to 1776* (New York: Columbia University, 1911), 433–35; Larry R. Gerlach, "Soldiers and Citizens: The British Army in New Jersey on the Eve of the Revolution," *New Jersey History* 93 (1975): 5–36 21–22.

156. Gage to Barrington, October 8, 1767, TGP-ES 10.

157. *CLNY* 4:950.

158. *DCHNY* 7:994, 7:980, 8:63–64, 87–88; *PBF* 14:321; "Extract of a Letter from London, to a Gentleman in New-York," *New-York Gazette*, January 25, 1768; Olm, "Mutiny Act for America," 213–14; Varga, "New York Restraining Act," 251–55; Fisher, *New Jersey*, 434–35; *VPNJ* (April–May 1768): 5, 12, 27–29, 31–32.

159. *DCHNJ* 9:642–43, 10:12–13, 26–27, 41–48, 17:491–92.

160. *SLGB* 7 Geo. III, c. 41; 7 Geo. III, c. 46; 7 Geo. III, c. 56; Griffin, *Townshend Moment*, 126–32; Oliver M. Dickerson, *The Navigation Acts and the American Revolution* (Philadelphia: University of Pennsylvania Press, 1951), 195–202; Peter D. G. Thomas, *The Townshend Duties Crisis: The Second Phase of the American Revolution, 1767–1773* (Oxford: Clarendon, 1987).

161. "Letters from a Farmer in Pennsylvania, Letter XI," *Pennsylvania Gazette*, February 11, 1768. See also Griffin, *Townshend Moment*, 142–64; Milton Embick Flower, *John Dickinson, Conservative Revolutionary* (Charlottesville: University of Virginia Press, 1983); William Murchison, *The Cost of Liberty: The Life of John Dickinson* (Wilmington, Del.: ISI Books, 2013).

162. *PBF* 15:6–7.

4. Borderland

1. *DCB*, s.v., "Pontiac"; Gregory Evans Dowd, *War under Heaven: Pontiac, the Indian Nations, and the British Empire* (Baltimore: Johns Hopkins University Press, 2002), 5–11, 22–34, 41–53; Richard White, *The Middle Ground: Indians, Empire, and Republics in the Great Lakes Region, 1650–1815* (Cambridge: Cambridge University Press, 1991), 223–68; Michael A. McDonnell, *Masters of Empire: Great Lakes Indians and the Making of America* (New York: Hill & Wang, 2015), 207–38.

2. *JPC* 38, 194. See also Dowd, *War under Heaven*, 114–47; Timothy J. Todish, Brian Leigh Dunnigan, Robert Griffing, and Gary S. Zaboly, *A "Most Troublesome Situation": The British Military and the Pontiac Indian Uprising of 1763–64* (Fleischmanns, N.Y.: Purple Mountain, 2006); Richard Middleton, *Pontiac's War: Its Causes, Course, and Consequences* (New York: Routledge, 2007).

3. *JPC* 56, 120, 238. See also *JPC* 82, 156, 192–200; *CISHL* 1:171, 186, 246.

4. Evarts B. Greene and Virginia D. Harrington, *American Population before the Federal Census of 1790* (New York: Columbia University Press, 1932), 5.

5. Anthony F. C. Wallace, *The Death and Rebirth of the Seneca* (New York: Knopf, 1969); Daniel K. Richter, *The Ordeal of the Longhouse: The Peoples of the Iroquois League in the Era of European Colonization* (Chapel Hill: University of North Carolina Press, 1992); Daniel H. Usner Jr., *Indians, Settlers, and Slaves in a Frontier Exchange Economy: The Lower Mississippi Valley before 1783* (Chapel Hill: University of North Carolina Press, 1992); Andrew R. L. Cayton and Frederika J. Teute, eds., *Contact Points: American Frontiers from the Mohawk Valley to the Mississippi, 1750–1830* (Chapel Hill: University of North Carolina Press, 1998).

6. *PKT* 358.

7. Edward Kimber, *Itinerant Observations in America*, ed. Kevin J. Hayes (Newark: University of Delaware Press, 1998), 27–28. See also *PKT* 353–55, 368–69; Larry E. Ivers, *Colonial Forts of South Carolina, 1670–1775* (Columbia: University of South Carolina Press, 1970), 1–15, 43–44, 62–63, 70–72; William L. McDowell Jr., ed., *The Documents Relating to Indian Affairs, May 21, 1750–August 7, 1754* (Columbia: South Carolina Archives Department, 1958), 86–89; Wilber R. Jacobs, ed., *Appalachian Indian Frontier: The Edmond Atkin Report and Plan of 1755* (Lincoln: University of Nebraska Press, 1967), 12–19, 52; Paul M. Pressly, *On the Rim of the Caribbean: Colonial Georgia and the British Atlantic World* (Athens: University of Georgia Press, 2013), 12–17.

8. Matthew C. Ward, *Breaking the Backcountry: The Seven Years' War in Virginia and Pennsylvania, 1754–1765* (Pittsburgh: University of Pittsburgh Press, 2003), 71–72, 106–7, 195–99; James M. Johnson, *Militiamen, Rangers, and Redcoats: The Military in Georgia, 1754–1776* (Macon, Ga.: Mercer University Press, 1992), 25–44; J. E. Kaufmann and H. W. Kaufmann, *Fortress America: The Forts That Defended America, 1600 to the Present* (Cambridge, Mass.: Da Capo, 2004), 63–87; Stephen Brumwell, *White Devil: A True Story of War, Savagery, and Vengeance in Colonial America* (Cambridge, Mass.: Da Capo, 2004).

9. *TAC* 421. See also *TAC* 422, 444; Brady J. Crytzer, *Fort Pitt: A Frontier History* (Charleston, S.C.: History Press, 2012), 49; John Rocque, *A Set of Plans and Forts in America, Reduced from Actual Surveys* (London: Rocque, 1765), 23, 25, 28, 30; Lois M. Feister, "Building Materials Indicative of Status Differentiation at the Crown Point Barracks," *Historical Archaeology* 18 (1984): 103–7; Lawrence E. Babits and Stephanie Gandulla, eds., *The Archaeology of French and Indian War Frontier Forts* (Gainesville: University of Florida Press, 2014).

10. *CISHL* 1:337. See also Jacobs, *Appalachian Indian Frontier*, 41–43; *PSWJ* 4:240–46; Louis De Vorsey Jr., *The Indian Boundary in the Southern Colonies, 1763–1775* (Chapel Hill: University of North Carolina Press, 1961), 8–23; White, *Middle Ground*, 187–99; Alan Taylor, *American Revolutions: A Continental History, 1750–1804* (New York: Norton, 2016), 72–73.

11. *CISHL*, 1:3, 218, 281; 2:108–9, 125, 218, 444, 491–92; 469–70, 522; *TAC* 363, 473–76; Greene and Harrington, *American Population*, 187–91, 196–98, 205; Carl J. Ekberg, *French Roots in the Illinois Country: The Mississippi Frontier in Colonial Times* (Urbana: University of Illinois Press, 2000), 54–88; M. J. Morgan, *Land of Big Rivers: French and Indian Illinois, 1699–1778* (Carbondale: Southern Illinois University Press, 2010), 43–89; *Cantonment of His Majesty's Forces in North America, 11 Octr. 1765,*

MNA-LC; René Chartrand, *The Forts of Colonial North America: British, Dutch and Swedish Colonies* (Oxford: Osprey, 2010), 40, 43, 49–50; Paul W. Mapp, *The Elusive West and the Contest for Empire, 1713–1763* (Chapel Hill: University of North Carolina Press, 2011).

12. *CISHL* 1:43. See also *CISHL* 1:6–7; De Vorsey, *Indian Boundary*, 34–40; White, *Middle Ground*, 270–88; Patrick Griffin, *American Leviathan: Empire, Nation, and Revolutionary Frontier* (New York: Hill & Wang, 2007), 19–33; Eric Hinderaker and Peter C. Mancall, *At the Edge of Empire: The Backcountry in British North America* (Baltimore: Johns Hopkins University Press, 2003), 131–33; S. Max Edelson, *The New Map of Empire: How Britain Imagined America before Independence* (Cambridge, Mass.: Harvard University Press, 2017), 141–59.

13. *PA*, ser. 8, 6:5172.

14. Ivers, *Colonial Forts of South Carolina*, 70–72; Johnson, *Militiamen, Rangers, and Redcoats*, 42–43.

15. *MPCPA* 9:62.

16. Colden to Gage, November 28, 1763, TGP-AS 10; Franklin to Gage, November 30, 1763, TGP-AS 10; *DCHNY* 7:586–87; Penn to Gage, December 26, 1763, TGP-AS 11; Bouquet to Gage, May 27, 1764, TGP-AS 19; Gage to Murray, May 27, 1764, TGP-AS 19.

17. *MPCPA* 9:35. See also *MPCPA* 9:31–37; *SLPA* 6:293–301.

18. Gage to Bouquet, March 7, 1764, TGP-AS 16. See also *CLB* 1:250–51; Gage to Colden, December 4, 1763, TGP-AS 10.

19. Gage to Prevost, May 1, 1764, TGP-AS 18.

20. Cochrane to Gage, March 8, 1765, TGP-AS 31. See also Ivers, *Colonial Forts of South Carolina*, 42; Prevost to Gage, January 10, 1764, TGP-AS 12; Gage to Halifax, August 10, 1764, TGP-ES 2; *TBRSC* 30:146–47; *CRGA* 17:125–26.

21. Gage to Cochrane, April 1, 1765, TGP-AS 33.

22. James Thomas Flexner, *Mohawk Baronet: Sir William Johnson of New York* (New York: Harper, 1959); Fintan O'Toole, *White Savage: William Johnson and the Invention of America* (New York: Farrar Straus and Giroux, 2005).

23. *CISHL* 1:274, 278–79. See also *CISHL* 1:273–81, 327–42; *PSWJ* 5:442–45; De Vorsey, *Indian Boundary*, 40–43.

24. *Jonathan Carver's Travels through America, 1766–1768: An Explorer's Portrait of the American Wilderness*, ed. Norman Gelb (New York: Wiley & Sons, 1993), 74, 119.

25. *Lieut. Henry Timberlake's Memoirs, 1756–1763*, ed. Samuel Cole Williams (Johnson City, Tenn.: Watauga, 1927), 83–84.

26. James Adair, *The History of the American Indians*, ed. Kathryn E. Holland Braund (Tuscaloosa: University of Alabama Press, 2005), 407, 196.

27. Alexander Henry, *Travels and Adventures in Canada and the Indian Territories between the Years 1760 and 1776* (New York: Riley, 1809), 116–17. See also Charles E. Cleland, *Rites of Conquest: The History and Culture of Michigan's Native Americans* (Ann Arbor: University of Michigan Press, 1992), 47–48, 186–87; George E. Sioui, *Huron-Wendat: The Heritage of the Circle*, trans. Jane Brierley, rev. ed. (Vancouver: University of British Columbia Press, 1999), 94–95; Erik R. Seeman, *The Huron-Wendat Feast of the Dead: Indian-European Encounters in Early North America* (Baltimore: Johns Hopkins University Press, 2011).

28. *TAC* 472.

29. Henry, *Travels and Adventures*, 47.

30. *CISHL* 2:36. See also *JPC* 54; *CISHL* 2:176–77; Griffin, *American Leviathan*, 39–41.

31. *PSWJ* 5:512. See also Griffin, *American Leviathan*, 33–37.

32. *CISHL* 2:25.

33. *TAC* 517. See also *TAC* 530, 560.

34. *TAC* 387.

35. Bradstreet to Gage, May 23, 1764, TGP-AS 19; *JPC* 238; *TAC* 468; *CISHL* 1:441.

36. *CISHL* 2:353, 356, 168, 363. Walter S. Dunn Jr., *The New Imperial Economy: The British Army and the American Frontier, 1764–1768* (Westport, Conn.: Praeger, 2001).

37. *CISHL* 3:68, 2:483.

38. *CISHL* 1:201, 2:452, 488.

39. *PSWJ* 5:788.

40. *PSWJ* 5:234–35, 418–19, 480–1, 600–601, 659–60, 686; *CISHL* 3:76, 90; Johnson, *Militiamen, Rangers, and Redcoats*, 88–91; Griffin, *American Leviathan*, 50–54, 58–63, 78–79.

41. *PA*, ser. 1, 4:246. *MPCPA* 9:266–77; *CISHL* 1:523; Dowd, *War under Heaven*, 204–8; Griffin, *American Leviathan*, 74–78.

42. *CISHL* 1:515, 500. See also *CISHL* 1:508, 2:158; *PSWJ* 5:159, 224.

43. *PSWJ* 5:279. See also White, *Middle Ground*, 269–314; Dowd, *War under Heaven*, 213–25, 249–58; O'Toole, *White Savage*, 263–67; *DCB*, s.v., "Roberts, Benjamin."

44. *PSWJ* 5:333.

45. DCHNY 7:854, 858–59. See also *CISHL* 2:108, 489–91.

46. *CISHL* 1:396.

47. *CISHL* 2:199, 585; *DCB*, s.v. "Grant, Alexander"; Kaufmann and Kaufmann, *Fortress America*, 122.

48. "Estimate of the Charges of His Majesty's Forces in the Plantations and Africa, 1766–67," CTP 8/23/46; "Estimate of the Expenses of the Works at the Forts in the District of New York for 1766," CTP 8/28/18; *PSWJ* 5:368; "Estimate of the Expense for Providing the King's Barracks in North America, 1767," CTP 8/28/1; "Bills Drawn upon the Treasury and Warrants Drawn upon the Deputy Paymasters in America, 1765–66," CTP 8/2/3a; Dunn, *New Imperial Economy*, 155–74; Eric Hinderaker, *Boston's Massacre* (Cambridge, Mass.: Harvard University Press, 2017), 93–96.

49. "An Estimate of the Expense of Transporting Provisions for One Man for One Year from Albany," CTP 8/31/16.

50. *CISHL* 3:60, 2:374.

51. Pittman to Gage, February 24, 1766, TGP-AS 48.

52. Gage to Campbell, February 28, 1766, TGP-AS 48.

53. Campbell to Gage, May 31,1766, TGP-AS 52. See also *MJ* 286–91.

54. "Additions Proposed to Be Made to the Mutiny Act," enclosure in Gage to Ellis, January 22, 1765, TGP-ES 3.

55. *SLGB* 5 Geo. III, c. 33.

56. Gage to Barrington, October 10, 1765, TGP-ES 5.

57. *JCHSC*-M 37:188.

58. *JCHSC*-M 37:188–89, 203–5; Gage to Phillips, August 30, 1766, TGP-AS 56; Gage to Montagu, August 31, 1766, TGP-AS 56; John Shy, *Toward Lexington: The Role of the British Army in the Coming of the American Revolution* (Princeton, N.J.: Princeton University Press, 1965), 253.

59. *JCHSC*-M 37:256, 376.

60. Gage to Montagu, April 30, 1767, TGP-AS 64.

61. Gage to Phillips, December 14, 1766, TGP-AS 60; Füser to Gage, August 26, 1767, TGP-AS 69.

62. Wilkins to Penn, June 16, 1768, enclosure in Wilkins to Gage, June 16, 1768, TGP-AS 78.

63. *PA* 8th ser., 8:6772. See also *MPCPA* 9:684–85, 718, 10:17–20; *PA*, 1st ser., 4:395–98; Penn to Gage, October 16, 1770, TGP-AS 96; Gage to Wilkins, December 31, 1770, TGP-AS 99.

64. *PDBP* 2:51.

65. *SLGB* 5 Geo. III, c. 33.

66. Campbell to Gage, May 8, 1766, TGP-AS 51. See also Tiya Miles, *Dawn of Detroit: A Chronicle of Slavery and Freedom in the City of the Straits* (New York: New Press, 2017).

67. Gage to Campbell, June 15, 1766, TGP-AS 52.

68. Johnson to Gage, June 27, 1766, TGP-AS 53. See also *PSWJ* 5:573.

69. Gage to Hillsborough, August 12, 1769, TGP-ES 15.

70. Gage to Hillsborough, October 7, 1769, TGP-ES 16.

71. Gage to Cramahé, August 14, 1771, TGP-AS 105.

72. Gage to Cramahé, October 1, 1771, TGP-AS 107.

73. Gage to Hillsborough, July 1, 1772, TGP-ES 22.

74. Carl Van Doren, *Benjamin Franklin* (New York: Penguin, 1938), 356–60.

75. *CISHL* 1:261. See also Griffin, *American Leviathan*, 37–38.

76. Emphasis in original. *PBF* 12:398.

77. *CISHL* 2:203.

78. *PBF* 13:257; *CISHL* 1:375, 2:233, 318–20, 337–38, 364–68, 375–78, 400; *PSWJ* 5:196–98, 276–78; "Reasons for Establishing a British Colony at the Illinois," CO 5/67; James H. Merrell, *Into the American Woods: Negotiators on the Pennsylvania Frontier* (New York: Norton, 1999), 81–82, 100.

79. *CISHL* 2:248–50, 252, 257, 254.

80. *CISHL* 2:261, 270. See also Robin F. A. Fabel, "An Eighteenth Colony: Dreams for Mississippi on the Eve of the Revolution," *JSH* 59 (1993): 647–72; Griffin, *American Leviathan*, 54–58.

81. *PSWJ* 5:319.

82. *PBF* 13:424, 446–47. See also *CISHL* 2:375, 394–95.

83. *CISHL* 2:379. See also *CISHL* 3:3–6, 121–25; *PSWJ* 5:653–56, 6:185–86.

84. *PBF* 14:243.

85. *CISHL* 2:371, 375–76, 422–30, 454–59, 536–41, 3:12–21; Van Doren, *Benjamin Franklin*, 364–67; Jack M. Sosin, *Whitehall and the Wilderness: The Middle West in British Colonial Policy, 1760–1775* (Lincoln: University of Nebraska Press, 1961), 128–64; Patrick Griffin, *The Townshend Moment: The Making of Empire and Revolution in the Eighteenth Century* (New Haven, Conn.: Yale University Press, 2017), 139–42.

86. *CISHL* 3:17, 19. See also *CISHL* 3:77–81.

87. *CISHL* 3:13, 80.

88. *CISHL* 3:102.

89. *PBF* 14:325.

90. Shelburne to Gage, November 14, 1767, TGP-ES 10.

91. *PSWJ* 5:560.

92. *CISHL* 1:327–42, 2:152, 3:75–76, 89.

93. *CISHL* 3:43, 45.

94. *PSWJ* 5:449, 458–59, 646, 741, 744, 793; *CISHL* 2:450, 452; 3:75–76, 89–90, 156–58; De Vorsey, *Indian Boundary*, 36–47; Edelson, *New Map of Empire*, 159–73.

95. Barrington to Gage, October 10, 1765, TGP-ES 5.

96. *CKG* 1:438. See also Shy, *Toward Lexington*, 246–47.

97. *PSWJ* 5:188. See also John Richard Alden, *General Gage in America: Being Principally a History of His Role in the American Revolution* (Baton Rouge: Louisiana State University Press, 1948), 59–60, 68–72.

98. Gage to Shelburne, April 4, 1767, TGP-ES 9. See also *CISHL* 2:198, 318; Gage to Barrington, May 7, 1766, TGP-ES 6.

99. Whitehall Treasury Chambers, January 9, 1767, enclosure in Cooper to Gage, March 13, 1767, TGP-ES 9; "Mr. Knox Relative to American Affairs," DBP 296/5/3; "Proposals for Economy in N. America," CTP 8/31/26; Barrington to Gage, December 12, 1767, TGP-ES 10; *Autobiography and Political Correspondence of Augustus Henry, Third Duke of Grafton, K.G.*, ed. William R. Anson (London: Murray, 1898); *CISHL* 3:155; Flexner, *Mohawk Baronet*, 294–96; Margaret Marion Spector, *The American Department of the British Government, 1768–1782* (New York: Columbia University Press, 1940).

100. *PBF* 15:74. See also *PBF* 15:15–16; Franklin B. Wickwire, *British Subministers and Colonial America, 1763–1783* (Princeton, N.J.: Princeton University Press, 1966).

101. Barrington to Gage, January 8, 1768, TGP-ES 11.

102. *DCHNY* 8:7; *CISHL* 3:155; Hillsborough to Gage, March 12, 1768, TGP-ES 11; Shy, *Toward Lexington*, 291–94; Griffin, *American Leviathan*, 56–57.

103. *CISHL* 3:196, 198, 203. See also *CISHL* 3: 219–20, 245–47; Brian Leigh Dunnigan, *The Necessity of Regularity in Quartering Soldiers: The Organization, Material Culture and Quartering of the British Soldier at Michilimackinac* (Mackinac Island, Mich.: Mackinac State Historic Parks, 1999), 38–58.

104. Hillsborough to Gage, April 15, 1768, TGP-ES 11; TG-OB May 8–9, 1768; Gage to Montagu, June 24, 1768, TGP-AS 78; Gage to Wright, June 24, 1768, TGP-AS 78.

105. Gage to Wright, June 12, 1768, TGP-AS 77.

106. Gage to Shelburne, April 24, 1768, TGP-ES 12; Gage to Hillsborough, May 15, 1768, TGP-ES 12; *CISHL* 3:275–78.

107. *CISHL* 3:517. See also Hillsborough to Gage, April 15, 1768, TGP-ES 11; Gage to Hillsborough, August 17, 1768, TGP-ES 13; Gage to Hillsborough, November 8, 1768, TGP-ES 13.

108. *CISHL* 3:451.

109. *PSWJ* 6:404.

110. *DCHNY* 8:111–34; *PSWJ* 6:184–87, 411–13, 423–24, 436–37, 453–54, 464–65, 472–73, 480–81, 491–93; Griffin, *American Leviathan*, 83–86; Hinderaker and Mancall, *At the Edge of Empire*, 145–50; William J. Campbell, *Speculators in Empire: Iroquois and the 1768 Treaty of Fort Stanwix* (Norman: University of Oklahoma Press, 2012), 139–66; Flexner, *Mohawk Baronet*, 312–31; O'Toole, *White Savage*, 268–79; Ray A. Billington, "The Fort Stanwix Treaty of 1768," *New York History* 25 (1944): 182–94; Peter Marshall, "Sir William Johnson and the Treaty of Fort Stanwix, 1768," *Journal of American Studies* 10 (1967): 149–79.

111. De Vorsey, *Indian Boundary*, 60–74; Griffin, *American Leviathan*, 88; Woody Holton, *Forced Founders: Indians, Debtors, Slaves, and the Making of the American Revolution* (Chapel Hill: University of North Carolina Press, 1999), 3–28.

112. *PSWJ* 6:513.

113. *CISHL* 2:512–13; Barrington to Gage, April 4, 1768, TGP-ES 11; Gage to Campbell, June 24, 1768, TGP-AS 78; Gage to Browne, June 27, 1768, TGP-AS 78; Gage to Bruere, June 27, 1768, TGP-AS 78.

114. "The Humble Address of the Council & Assembly of the Province of West Florida" and Campbell to Hillsborough, October 25, 1768, enclosures in Hillsborough to Gage, December 10, 1768, TGP-ES 14.

115. Gage to Hillsborough, March 4, 1769, TGP-ES 14.

116. *TBRSC* 32:28.

117. *BMR* 22. See also *BMR* 5–6, 9, 29.

118. Gage to Dalrymple, June 24, 1768, TGP-AS 78.

119. Gage to Hillsborough, August 18, 1768, TGP-ES 13.

120. Tayler to Gage, January 20, 1766, TGP-AS 47.

121. Cheesolm to Gage, November 8, 1768, TGP-AS 82. See also Gage to Shelburne, April 24, 1768, TGP-ES 12.

122. Skynner to Gage, October 12, 1768, TGP-AS 81. See also James Moncrief, "Estimate for Repairing the Church of St. Francis, at St. Augustine, for Soldiers Barracks," CTP 8/28/6; "New-York, January 2," *Boston Chronicle*, January 2–9, 1769; Thomas Whitmore to Thomas Gage, August 22, 1768, TGP-AS 80; "From the Public Ledger, Aug. 25," *Boston Post-Boy*, December 25, 1769.

123. Ivers, *Colonial Forts of South Carolina*, 42, 70–72.

124. "The Memorial of the Merchants Trading to West Florida," Petitions (1768–71), CO 5/114. See also Neal Simmons, "The Divergent Colony: British West Florida," *Southeast Louisiana Review* 2 (2009): 5–34.

125. Durnford to Gage, March 6, 1770, TGP-AS 90.

126. "A General Abstract of the Expenses for the Several Proposed New Buildings and Repairs Now Carrying on for the Protection of the Town and Harbor of Pensacola, and Mobile in the Province of West Florida" (June 27, 1771), TGP-AS 104; David E. Narrett, *Adventurism and Empire: The Struggle for Mastery in the Louisiana-Florida Borderlands* (Chapel Hill: University of North Carolina Press, 2015).

127. Hillsborough to Gage, July 15, 1769, TGP-ES 15.

128. *CISHL* 3:409. See also *CISHL* 3:438, 449, 488, 491, 498, 509–11; Shy, *Toward Lexington*, 272–73, 328, 330–31.

129. *PSWJ* 6:430.

130. Gage to Hillsborough, October 9, 1768, TGP-ES 13.

131. *PSWJ* 6:433–34. See also *CISHL* 3:172, 527, 545, 564, 590–91, 596.

132. Gage to Hillsborough, March 5, 1769, TGP-ES 14.

133. *CISHL* 3:566. See also *CISHL* 3:548, 589–90.

134. *PSWJ* 7:76. See also Dowd, *War under Heaven*, 254–62; *PSWJ* 5:376, 643–44, 648, 673, 7:16, 98; *CISHL* 3:556, 561; Gage to Hillsborough, August 12, 1769, TGP-ES 15.

135. George Rogers Taylor, ed., *The Turner Thesis: Concerning the Role of the Frontier in American History*, 3rd. ed. (Lexington, Mass.: Heath, 1972); Herbert E. Bolton, *The Spanish Borderlands: A Chronicle of Old Florida and the Southwest* (New Haven, Conn.: Yale University Press, 1921); White, *Middle Ground*; Pekka Hämäläinen, *The*

Comanche Empire (New Haven, Conn.: Yale University Press, 2008); McDonnell, *Masters of Empire*; Kathleen DuVal, *The Native Ground: Indians and Colonists in the Heart of the Continent* (Philadelphia: University of Pennsylvania Press, 2006); Juliana Barr, *Peace Came in the Form of a Woman: Indians and Spaniards in the Texas Borderlands* (Chapel Hill: University of North Carolina Press, 2007); Karl Jacoby, *Shadows at Dawn: A Borderlands Massacre and the Violence of History* (New York: Penguin, 2008); Michael J. Witgen, *An Infinity of Nations: How the Native New World Shaped Early America* (Philadelphia: University of Pennsylvania Press, 2012).

5. Cities and Towns

1. Quoted in Anne H. Cresson, "Biographical Sketch of Joseph Fox, Esq., of Philadelphia," *PHMB* 32 (1908): 188. See also Charles E. Peterson, "Carpenters' Hall," *Transactions of the American Philosophical Society*, new ser., 43 (1953): 96–128.

2. *PA* 8th ser., 6:4825, 7:6047, 8:7099. See also *PA* 8th ser., 6:4858, 4879, 4884, 5062, 5154, 7:5658, 5662, 5788, 5916, 5921, 6068, 6288, 6421, 6450, 6557, 6586, 8:6704, 6709, 6722, 6726, 6876, 6894, 6899, 7003, 7014, 7022, 7027, 7128, 7133, 7145, 7151, 7283, 7290, 7299, 7304, 7385, 7568, 7587; Thomas Gage, "Rules and Directions, for the Good Government and Preservation of His Majesty's Barracks in North-America, and for Procuring and Issuing Fuel to the Troops Quartered Therein" (n.p., 1766?); John Russell Young, *Memorial History of the City of Philadelphia from Its First Settlement to the Year 1895*, 2 vols. (New York: New-York History Co., 1895–1898), 1:284–85; John F. Watson, *Annals of Philadelphia, in the Olden Time*, ed. Willis P. Hazard, 3 vols. (Philadelphia: Stuart, 1884), 2:168; John Shy, *Toward Lexington: The Role of the British Army in the Coming of the American Revolution* (Princeton, N.J.: Princeton University Press, 1965), 391.

3. Frank Allaben, *John Watts de Peyster*, 2 vols. (New York: Allaben, 1908), 1:13–28; *MCCNY* 6:117, 119–20, 128–29, 145, 153, 167, 205, 212, 219, 243–44, 256, 257, 282, 304, 328, 346, 352, 356, 7:35, 53, 59, 75; Valerie H. McKito, *From Loyalists to Loyal Citizens: The DePeyster Family of New York* (Albany: SUNY Press, 2015); John Braund, "Records Kept by Colonel Isaac Hayne," *South Carolina Historical and Genealogical Magazine* 10 (1909): 160; *SLSC* 4:251, 281.

4. Benjamin L. Carp, *Rebels Rising: Cities and the American Revolution* (New York: Oxford University Press, 2007), 225.

5. Carl Bridenbaugh, *Cities in Revolt: Urban Life in America, 1743–1776* (New York: Knopf, 1955); Gary B. Nash, *The Urban Crucible: Social Change, Political Consciousness, and the Origins of the American Revolution* (Cambridge, Mass.: Harvard University Press, 1979); Max Weber, *The City*, ed. Don Martindale, trans. Gertrud Neuwirth (New York: Free Press, 1958); Fernand Braudel, *Capitalism and Material Life, 1400–1800*, trans. Miriam Kochan (New York: Harper & Row, 1973); Stephen Graham, *Cities under Siege: The New Military Urbanism* (London: Verso, 2010).

6. Gage to Richmond, August 26, 1766, TGP-ES 7.

7. *MJ* 383, 385. See also "New-York, August 14," *Connecticut Courant*, August 18, 1766; *MJ* 368; TG-OB September 20, 1766, September 22, 1766; Joseph S. Tiedemann, *Reluctant Revolutionaries: New York City and the Road to Independence, 1763–1776* (Ithaca, N.Y.: Cornell University Press, 1997), 109–11; David Hackett Fischer, *Liberty and Freedom: A Visual History of America's Founding Ideas* (New York: Oxford University Press,

2005), 37–49; Paul A. Gilje, *The Road to Mobocracy: Popular Disorder in New York City, 1763–1834* (Chapel Hill: University of North Carolina Press, 1987), 52–58; Shy, *Toward Lexington*, 382–84; Joyce D. Goodfriend, *Who Should Rule at Home? Confronting the Elite in British New York City* (Ithaca, N.Y.: Cornell University Press, 2017).

8. *VPNJ* (April–May 1768): 22.

9. *JCHSC*-M 37, part 1: 426, 419. See also *SLSC* 4:205, 227, 253.

10. "Extracts from the Journal of Miss Sarah Eve," ed. Eva Eve Jones, *PHMB* 5 (1881): 34. See also *Travels in North America in the Years 1780, 1781 and 1782 by the Marquis de Chastellux*, trans. and ed. Howard C. Rice Jr., 2 vols. (Chapel Hill: University of North Carolina Press, 1963), 1:130.

11. "Philadelphia Society before the Revolution," *PHMB* 11 (1887): 279.

12. TG-OB January 24, 1767. See also TG-OB February 24, 1767, April 29, 1767, July 9, 1767, March 21, 1768, April 8, 1768.

13. TG-OB April 10, 1768. See also TG-OB March 6, 1767, April 29, 1767, July 7, 1767, November 10, 1767; "New-York, June 29," *New-York Journal; or, the General Advertiser*, June 29, 1769.

14. Clare A. Lyons, *Sex among the Rabble: An Intimate History of Gender and Power in the Age of Revolution, Philadelphia, 1730–1830* (Chapel Hill: University of North Carolina Press, 2006), 95, 110–12; Tiedemann, *Reluctant Revolutionaries*, 17; Carp, *Rebels Rising*, 67, 90–92; John Montresor, *A Plan of the City of New York* (1766), Maps 4-O-7, WLCL; TG-OB February 24, 1767.

15. "Philadelphia Society," 281.

16. "To the Printer," *New-York Journal*, August 31, 1769.

17. "Elizabeth-Town, New-Jersey, July 28, 1767," *New York Mercury*, August 3, 1767. See also Larry R. Gerlach, "Soldiers and Citizens: The British Army in New Jersey on the Eve of the Revolution," *New Jersey History* 93 (1975): 20–21; Shy, *Toward Lexington*, 382; Larry R. Gerlach, *Prologue to Independence: New Jersey in the Coming of the American Revolution* (New Brunswick, N.J.: Rutgers University Press, 1976), 68.

18. Roger Lane, *Policing the City: Boston, 1822–1885* (Cambridge, Mass.: Harvard University Press, 1967), 10–12; James F. Richardson, *New York Police: Colonial Times to 1901* (New York: Oxford University Press, 1970).

19. Hicks to Gage, March 24, 1767, TGP-AS 63. See also Tiedemann, *Reluctant Revolutionaries*, 109.

20. *MCCNY* 6:45.

21. *JCHSC*-M 37, part 2: 603.

22. Füser to Gage, May 31, 1767, TGP-AS 65. See also "Return of Small Beer (1767–68)," New York City Miscellaneous Manuscripts, NYHS; *PGW*, Colonial ser., 4:403–5; Füser to Gage, June 24, 1767, TGP-AS 66; TG-OB September 4, 1767.

23. TG-OB March 6, 1768.

24. Gage to Hicks, March 25, 1767, TGP-AS 63. See also Tiedemann, *Reluctant Revolutionaries*, 125–28.

25. *SLGB* 5 Geo. III, c. 33.

26. "Elizabeth-Town, New-Jersey, July 28, 1767," *New York Mercury*, August 3, 1767.

27. St. Clair to Gage, July 14, 1767, TGP-AS 67. See also Shy, *Toward Lexington*, 343–58.

28. Alexander Graydon, *Memoirs of His Own Time*, ed. John Stockton Littell (Philadelphia: Lindsay and Blakiston, 1846), 53.

29. Sterling to Gage, October 18, 1766, TGP-AS 58. See also *PA* 8th ser., 7:5944–45, 6034–35, 6085, 6141, 6421; *SLPA* 7:161–62; Scharf and Westcott, *History of Philadelphia*, 2:1011–12.

30. *MJ* 383. See also Franklin to St. Clair, July 13, 1767, enclosure in St. Clair to Gage, July 15, 1767, TGP-AS 67; Bridenbaugh, *Cities in Revolt*, 140, 243.

31. Gage to Barrington, September 13, 1766, TGP-ES 8. See also Shy, *Toward Lexington*, 172–76, 361–63.

32. Füser to Gage, July 4, 1768, TGP-AS 78.

33. Gage to Pitkin, May 14, 1767, TGP-AS 64.

34. "Extract of a Letter from Norfolk, in Virginia," *Boston Chronicle*, July 25–August 1, 1768.

35. *JCHSC*-M 37, part 2: 666. See also Perth Amboy to Gage, December 12, 1768, TGP-AS 83; *SLSC* 4:140, 201, 225, 251, 281.

36. Gage to Shelburne, January 23, 1768, TGP-ES 11.

37. "Last Sunday Evening the Royal Highland Regiment," *Pennsylvania Gazette*, July 30, 1767. See also Bull to Gage, August 23, 1768, TGP-AS 80.

38. Füser to Gage, February 20, 1767, TGP-AS 62.

39. "Id agere debemus," *New-York Mercury*, December 7, 1767.

40. TG-OB December 7, 1767. See also "City of New-York," *New York Chronicle*, October 26–November 2, 1769; "By Permission of His Excellency the Governor," *New-York Mercury*, December 7, 1767; *MJ* 364; Bridenbaugh, *Cities in Revolt*, 297–99; Gilje, *Road to Mobocracy*, 46, 247–53; William Dunlap, *History of the American Theatre* (New York: Harper, 1832), 30; Edwin G. Burrows and Mike Wallace, *Gotham: A History of New York City to 1898* (New York: Oxford University Press, 1999), 206, 218.

41. Emphasis in original. "New York, June 9," *New York Mercury*, June 9, 1766. See also "New-York, June 8," *New-York Mercury*, June 8, 1767; TG-OB June 2, 1767, June 4, 1767; "Philadelphia, June 12," *Pennsylvania Gazette*, June 12, 1766; "Charlestown, South-Carolina, June 1," *Postscript to the Boston Weekly News-Letter*, July 6, 1769; "Charlestown (South-Carolina) June 7," *New-York Gazette*, July 7, 1770.

42. *CISHL* 2:512–13; "Disposition and State of the Forces in North America," CTP 8/23/6; "Distribution of His Majesty's 26th Regt in the Province of New Jersey," enclosure in Thomas Gage to William Franklin, July 27, 1767, TGP-AS 68; Robert V. Wells, *The Population of the British Colonies in America before 1776* (Princeton, N.J.: Princeton University Press, 1975), 61–65, 133–43; Evarts B. Greene and Virginia D. Harrington, *American Population before the Federal Census of 1790* (New York: Columbia University Press, 1932), 101, 112.

43. Harry Piers, *The Evolution of the Halifax Fortress, 1749–1928*, ed. G. M. Self, Phyllis Blakeley, and D. C. Harvey (Halifax: Public Archives of Nova Scotia, 1947), 1–14; *TAC* 438; Serge Bernier et al., *Military History of Québec City, 1608–2008* (Montréal: Art Global, 2008), 199–200; André Charbonneau, Yvon Desloges, and Marc Lafrance, *Québec the Fortified City: From the 17th to the 19th Century* (Ottawa: Parks Canada, 1982), 384–88.

44. Gage to Shelburne, April 3, 1767, TGP-ES 9.

45. Gage to Carleton, March 28, 1767, TGP-AS 63.

46. James Robertson quoted in Daniel L. Schafer, ". . . Not So Gay a Town in America as This . . . , 1763–1784," in *The Oldest City: St. Augustine, Saga of Survival*, ed. Jean Parker Waterbury (St. Augustine, Fla.: St. Augustine Historical Society, 1983), 92.

47. Tayler to Gage, January 20, 1766, TGP-AS 47. See also J. Leitch Wright Jr., *British St. Augustine* (St. Augustine, Fla.: Historic St. Augustine Preservation Board, 1975), 6–7.

48. "Estimate of the Expense of Providing the King's Barracks in North America," CTP 8/28/1.

49. "List of Barrack Masters in America," enclosure in Gage to Barrington, March 11, 1768, TGP-ES 11.

50. "Estimate of the Expense of Providing the King's Barracks in North America," CTP 8/28/1; *The Twilight of British Rule in Revolutionary America: The New York Letter Book of General James Robertson, 1780–1783*, ed. Milton M. Klein and Ronald W. Howard (Cooperstown, N.Y.: New York State Historical Association, 1983); "Plantations (1767)," WO 24/441. Conversion of New York currency taken from "Estimate of the Expense Attending the Assistant Deputy Quarter Master Generals Department," CTP 8/28/10.

51. "Québec, February 9, 1767," *Pennsylvania Chronicle, and Universal Advertiser*, March 16, 1767. See also "Québec, June 11," *New-York Gazette, or the Weekly Post-Boy*, July 16, 1767; Bernier, *Military History of Québec*, 211, 214–19.

52. Tayler to Gage, January 10, 1768, TGP-AS 73; Tayler to Gage, February 14, 1768, TGP-AS 74.

53. "Québec, January 26," *New-York Mercury*, March 16, 1767.

54. Gage to Carleton, October 5, 1767, TGP-AS 70.

55. Quoted in Bernier et al., *Military History of Québec*, 211, 204.

56. "Québec, July 21," *Essex Gazette*, August 23, 1768. See also Carleton to Gage, April 27, 1768, TGP-AS 76; Bernier et al., *Military History of Québec*, 200, 210, 219; Thomas H. Raddall and Stephen Kimber, *Halifax: Warden of the North*, updated ed. (Halifax: Nimbus, 2010), 149–50; Wright, *British St. Augustine*, 12.

57. "Québec, February 9," *Pennsylvania Chronicle, and Universal Advertiser*, March 16, 1767.

58. Burns to Gage, February 8, 1768, TGP-AS 73. See also Bernier et al., *Military History of Québec*, 221–22; A. G. Doughty and N. E. Dionne, *Québec under Two Flags: A Brief History of the City from Its Foundation to the Present Time* (Québec: Québec New Company, 1903), 190.

59. *JHRMA* 44:246, 248, 238. See also *JHRMA* 44:229–31; Hiller B. Zobel, *The Boston Massacre* (New York: Norton, 1970), 68–69; *The History of the Colony and Province of Massachusetts-Bay, by Thomas Hutchinson*, ed. Lawrence Shaw Mayo, 3 vols. (Cambridge, Mass.: Harvard University Press, 1936), 3:122–30.

60. *PFB* 4:108.

61. Hillsborough to Gage, April 23, 1768, TGP-ES 11; CCL 5, 7–21; Massachusetts Papers, 1749–1777, MHS, vol. 1; *DCHNY* 8:58–59; Zobel, *Boston Massacre*, 65–70; Oliver M. Dickerson, *The Navigation Acts and the American Revolution* (1951; New York: Barnes, 1963), 198–200; Eric Hinderaker, *Boston's Massacre* (Cambridge, Mass.: Harvard University Press, 2017), 64–71.

62. Hillsborough to Gage, June 8, 1768, TGP-ES 12.

63. *PFB* 4:235, 258. See also Customs Commissioners to Gage, June 15, 1768, TGP-AS 78; CCL 2, 6, 22; Zobel, *Boston Massacre*, 70–85; Dirk Hoerder, *Crowd Action in Revolutionary Massachusetts, 1765–1780* (New York: Academic, 1977), 164–90.

64. *PFB* 4:253. See also Gage to Dalrymple, June 25, 1768, TGP-AS 78; *PFB* 4:219; Gage to Hillsborough, June 28, 1768, TGP-ES 12.

65. Barrington to Gage, August 1, 1768, TGP-ES 13.

66. Hillsborough to Gage, July 30, 1768, TGP-ES 13; Gage to Dalrymple, September 12, 1768, TGP-AS 80; *CKG* 2:35–36; *PBF* 15:127–28, 225–27; Bernard Bailyn, *The Ideological Origins of the American Revolution*, enlarged ed. (Cambridge, Mass.: Harvard University Press, 1992), 110–12, 131; Shy, *Toward Lexington*, 295–300; Zobel, *Boston Massacre*, 85–86; Hinderaker, *Boston's Massacre*, 71–75.

67. Hillsborough to Gage, June 8, 1768, TGP-ES 12.

68. *PFB* 4:304, 338. See also *LDJR* 174; *PFB* 4:291–92; Gage to Dalrymple, September 25, 1768, TGP-AS 81; "It Is Said G--r B--d," *Boston Gazette, and Country Journal*, September 26, 1768; Zobel, *Boston Massacre*, 89–95; John Philip Reid, *In Defiance of the Law: The Standing Army Controversy, the Two Constitutions, and the Coming of the American Revolution* (Chapel Hill: University of North Carolina Press, 1981), 14–15, 177–81; Nash, *Urban Crucible*, 116–19.

69. *RRCCB* 20:310.

70. CCL 45. See also *PFB* 4:338–39; *History of Massachusetts Bay*, 3:150–51.

71. Dalrymple to Gage, March 7, 1770, TGP-AS 90; *MJ* 407.

72. Dalrymple to Gage, October 2, 1768, TGP-AS 81.

73. BMR 2. See also *LDJR* 175; *PFB* 5:68–69; "Wednesday Morning Arrived Here from Halifax," *Boston Evening Post*, October 3, 1768; "Boston, October 3," *New-York Gazette; and the Weekly Mercury*, October 10, 1768; *History of Massachusetts Bay*, 3:146–62; Zobel, *Boston Massacre*, 96–101; Hinderaker, *Boston's Massacre*, 106–15; Shy, *Toward Lexington*, 303–6; Richard Archer, *As If an Enemy's Country: The British Occupation of Boston and the Origins of Revolution* (New York: Oxford University Press, 2010), 105–13.

74. *PFB* 5:72.

75. Gage to Dalrymple, October 2, 1768, TGP-AS 81. See also Shakespeare, *Macbeth*, 4.1.93.

76. BMR 3–4, 6–7, 21; Gage to Hillsborough, October 31, 1768, TGP-ES 13; CCL 52–54; *LDJR* 177.

77. BMR 9.

78. "Messieurs Edes & Gill," *Boston Gazette, and Country Journal*, October 31, 1768.

79. CCL 49–50.

80. Dalrymple to Gage, October 9, 1768, TGP-AS 81.

81. Gage to Hillsborough, October 31, 1768, TGP-ES 13. See also *WSA* 1:249–51; BMR 1–3, 5, 7, 11–12, 17–18.

82. BMR 11, 17–18, 20–21, 23, 26; *LDJR* 179–80; Zobel, *Boston Massacre*, 104, 107–12; Archer, *As If an Enemy's Country*, 124–27.

83. *CWS* 1:417. See also Bridenbaugh, *Cities in Revolt*, 115–17; Denver Brunsman, *The Evil Necessity: British Naval Impressment in the Eighteenth-Century Atlantic World* (Charlottesville: University of Virginia Press, 2013).

84. *WSA* 1:249. See also *WSA* 1:184–89; Mark Puls, *Samuel Adams: Father of the American Revolution* (New York: Palgrave Macmillan, 2006); Ira Stoll, *Samuel Adams: A Life* (New York: Free Press, 2008); John K. Alexander, *Samuel Adams: The Life of an American Revolutionary* (Lanham, Md.: Rowman & Littlefield, 2011); Zobel, *Boston Massacre*, 109–10; Hinderaker, *Boston's Massacre*, 115–26, 133–39.

85. BMR 38, 89, 39. See also BMR 15–17, 20–21, 35–37, 42, 47–48, 53–54, 57, 64, 71–72, 78–79, 84, 90–94, 106; Hoerder, *Crowd Action*, 190–203.

86. *BMR* 5, 125, 6. See also *BMR* 17, 51; Hinderaker, *Boston's Massacre*, 139–47.

87. *BMR* 19, 106. See also *BMR* 4, 11, 24–25, 31, 42–43, 51, 94, 110; "We Are Assured," *Boston Weekly News-Letter*, June 15, 1769; *LDJR* 182, 187.

88. *BMR* 97. See also Mackay to Gage, May 4, 1769, TGP-AS 85.

89. Gage to Mackay, May 15, 1769, TGP-AS 85.

90. *BMR* 109. See also *BMR* 103–4; *JHRMA* 45:117–18, 135–36, 138, 169–70; *WSA* 1:340–46.

91. *BMR* 15, 111, 94, 28, 75. See also *BMR* 7–8, 17–18, 20–21, 26–32, 34, 42–43, 47, 50, 53–54, 57–58, 61, 63, 71–72, 79, 84, 92, 96, 107–8, 117–119; Zobel, *Boston Massacre*, 132–51; Archer, *As If an Enemy's Country*, 129–37; Hoerder, *Crowd Action*, 204–15.

92. *BMR* 21, 79, 100, 114. See also *BMR* 34, 90, 93–94, 108, 118; "Boston, November 6," *Providence Gazette; and Country Journal*, November 4–11, 1769; Archer, *As If an Enemy's Country*, 131–32; Sharon Block, "Rape without Women: Print Culture and the Politicization of Rape, 1765–1815," *JAH* 89 (2002): 849–68; Thomas A. Foster, *Sex and the Eighteenth-Century Man: Massachusetts and the History of Sexuality in America* (Boston: Beacon, 2006), 63–64.

93. *BMR* 71, 114. See also *BMR* 21, 91, 108.

94. *BMR* 22, 5. See also *BMR* 9, 29.

95. Pomeroy to Gage, December 12, 1768, TGP-AS 83; Pomeroy to Gage, March 20, 1769, TGP-AS 84.

96. *BMR* 47, 123–27; Gage to Barrington, May 14, 1769, TGP-ES 15; Shy, *Toward Lexington*, 303–11; Zobel, *Boston Massacre*, 132–33.

97. *PBF* 16:192, 53, 17. See also *PBF* 15:191–93, 16:10–12, 33, 59, 237–38, 247–48; Carl Van Doren, *Benjamin Franklin* (New York: Penguin, 1938), 373–94.

98. "Roll 355 Lieut.-Gen. J. Robertson, North America (1 May 1765–30 June 1776)," AO 1/147/355; *BMR* 48; "Boston, December 5," *New-London Gazette*, December 9, 1768; Hinderaker, *Boston's Massacre*, 126–32.

99. Hillsborough to Gage, March 24, 1769, TGP-ES 14.

100. "Boston Intelligence," *Essex Gazette*, May 9–16, 1769.

101. *JHRMA* 45:180, 194. See also *JHRMA* 45:130–32, 168–72, 180, 192–94, 197–99; *WSA* 1:349–65; "American Grievances," *New-York Gazette or the Weekly Post-Boy*, August 14, 1769; Gage to Hillsborough, July 23, 1769, TGP-ES 15.

102. *PBF* 16:7. See also "Providence, October 8," *Connecticut Journal*, October 21, 1768, and *Pennsylvania Gazette*, October 2, 1768.

103. MacDonald to Gage, May 20, 1769, TGP-AS 85; Gage to Pomeroy, January 2, 1769, TGP-AS 83.

104. Mackay to Gage, June 19, 1769, TGP-AS 86.

105. "New York, December 22," *New-York Journal; or, the General Advertiser*, December 22, 1768.

106. "To the Printer," *New-York Journal; or, the General Advertiser*, March 16, 1769.

107. "New-York, December 29," *New-York Journal; or, the General Advertiser*, December 29, 1768. See also *CLNY* 4:1022–23, 1078; *HMWS* 1:62, 65–67; *DCHNY* 8:143–44, 157, 169–70; Tiedemann, *Reluctant Revolutionaries*, 128–31, 136–39; Leopold S. Launitz-Schürer Jr., *Loyal Whigs and Revolutionaries: The Making of the Revolution in New York, 1765–1776* (New York: NYU Press, 1980), 57–64.

108. Gage to Montagu, October 8, 1768, TGP-AS 81.

109. "Charlestown, December 27," *Georgia Gazette*, January 11, 1769.

110. Gage to Barrington, January 6, 1769, TGP-ES 14.

111. Gage to Haldimand, March 14, 1769, TGP-AS 84. See also *JCHSC*-M 37, part 2: 691; "Charlestown, South-Carolina, 10th July 1768," *Essex Gazette*, August 9–16, 1768; *TBRSC* 32:56–57; Jack P. Greene, *The Quest for Power: The Lower Houses of Assembly in the Southern Royal Colonies, 1689–1776* (New York: Norton, 1963), 389–90; Jonathan Mercantini, *Who Shall Rule at Home? The Evolution of South Carolina Political Culture, 1748–1776* (Columbia: University of South Carolina Press, 2007), 236–37; Robert M. Weir, *"A Most Important Epocha": The Coming of the Revolution in South Carolina* (Columbia: University of South Carolina Press, 1970), 32–38.

112. CGC 30:231.

113. *CKG* 2:84. See also *BMR* 26–27; "Charles-town, (S. Carolina,) Feb. 20," *New-York Journal; or, the General Advertiser*, March 30, 1769; Hillsborough to Gage, December 24, 1768, TGP-ES 14; Shy, *Toward Lexington*, 321; Peter D. G. Thomas, *The Townshend Duties Crisis: The Second Phase of the American Revolution, 1767–1773* (Oxford: Clarendon, 1987), 146–48.

114. *PDPB* 3:136.

115. Barrington to Gage, March 21, 1769, TGP-ES 14. See also Shy, *Toward Lexington*, 300–303; Andrew Jackson O'Shaughnessy, *The Men Who Lost America: British Leadership, the American Revolution, and the Fate of the Empire* (New Haven, Conn.: Yale University Press, 2013), 50.

116. "The Trumbull Papers," *Collections of the Massachusetts Historical Society*, 5th ser., 10 vols. (Boston: Massachusetts Historical Society, 1871–1888), 9:327.

117. SLGB 9 Geo. III, c. 18; *PDBP* 3:132, 134–40; CGC 31:46–62, 124–53; *CKG* 2:84; Thomas, *Townshend Duties Crisis*, 131–32; John A. Schutz, *Thomas Pownall, British Defender of American Liberties: A Study of Anglo-American Relations in the Eighteenth Century* (Glendale, Calif.: Clark, 1951), 218–21; Shy, *Toward Lexington*, 300–303.

118. *PBF* 16:80. See also *PBF* 16:69–70, 126–27.

119. Gage to Barrington, December 16, 1769, TGP-ES 16. See also *DCHNJ* 18:39, 101–3; *CRGA* 15:26–29; *VPNJ* (October–December 1769): 5, 61, 87, 90; Gerlach, "Soldiers and Citizens," 22–23; Edgar Jacob Fisher, *New Jersey as a Royal Province, 1738 to 1776* (New York: Columbia University, 1911), 435.

120. "Williamsburg, (in Virginia,) June 8," *New-York Gazette or the Weekly Post-Boy*, June 26, 1769. The same letter also appeared in *Boston Evening-Post*, July 3, 1769, and *Boston News-Letter*, July 6, 1769.

121. Gage to Barrington, June 10, 1769, TGP-ES 15.

122. *JCHSC*-M 38, part 1: 179, 25, 137. See also *JCHSC*-M 38, part 1: 19–20, 26–27, 84–85, 90–91, 136, 163–64, 178; Gamble to Gage, August 4, 1769, TGP-AS 87; Bull to Gage, August 19, 1769, TGP-AS 87; *TBRSC* 32:108–10; Mercantini, *Who Shall Rule*, 234–41; Weir, *Most Important Epocha*, 32–50; Greene, *Quest for Power*, 402–8.

123. "Mr. Holt," *New-York Journal; or, the General Advertiser*, November 16, 1769.

124. LBJW 309. See also *CLNY* 5:23–24; *CLB* 2:194–96; Tiedemann, *Reluctant Revolutionaries*, 139–45; Launitz-Schürer, *Loyal Whigs and Revolutionaries*, 72–82; Joseph Albert Ernst, *Money and Politics in America, 1755–1775: A Study in the Currency Act of 1764 and the Political Economy of Revolution* (Chapel Hill: University of North Carolina Press, 1973), 43–88, 251–74; Jeffrey Sklansky, *Sovereign of the Market: The Money Question in Early America* (Chicago: University of Chicago Press, 2017).

125. Gage to Barrington, January 6, 1770, TGP-ES 16.

126. Gage to Barrington, October 7, 1769, TGP-ES 16. See also "New York Resolve," January 15, 1770, TGP-AS 89; John Richard Alden, *General Gage in America: Being Principally a History of His Role in the American Revolution* (Baton Rouge: Louisiana State University Press, 1948), 65–69.

127. "To the Betrayed Inhabitants of the City and Colony of New-York," broadside, New York, 1769, NYHS. See also Patricia U. Bonomi, *A Factious People: Politics and Society in Colonial New York* (New York: Columbia University Press, 1971), 267–75.

128. "To the Public," broadside, New York, 1769, NYHS.

129. *CLB* 2:200.

130. Fischer, *Liberty and Freedom*, 44–45.

131. "To the Printer," *New-York Journal; or, the General Advertiser*, March 1, 1770. See also "New-York, Jan. 15," *Boston Evening-Post*, January 29, 1770; Lee R. Boyer, "Lobster Backs, Liberty Boys, and Laborers in the Streets: New York's Golden Hill and Nassau Street Riots," *New York Historical Society Quarterly* 57 (1973): 281–308.

132. "To the Printer," *New-York Journal; or, the General Advertiser*, March 1, 1770. See also "To the Public," *New-York Gazette or the Weekly Post-Boy*, February 5, 1770.

133. "Resolution, January 17, 1770," New York City Miscellaneous Manuscripts, NYHS. See also "To the Printer," *New-York Journal; or, the General Advertiser*, January 18, 1770; "New-York, January 25," *New-York Journal; or, the General Advertiser*, January 25, 1770; *MCCNY* 7:200–201.

134. Quoted in Boyer, "Lobster Backs," 296.

135. "New-York, January 15th, 1770," *New-York Gazette or the Weekly Post-Boy*, February 5, 1770. See also Albert Ulmann, "The Battle of Golden Hill," *New York Times*, September 17, 1898; Boyer, "Lobster Backs," 297–302; Tiedemann, *Reluctant Revolutionaries*, 147–49.

136. Whitehead Hicks, "To the Inhabitants of This City," broadside, New York, 1770, NYHS.

137. *HMWS* 1:73. See also "To the Freeholders, Freemen, and Inhabitants of the Colony of New-York; and to All the Friends of Liberty in North-America," *New-York Journal; or, the General Advertiser*, February 15, 1770; "To the Freeholders and Freemen and Inhabitants of the City and Province of New-York," *New-York Gazette or the Weekly Post-Boy*, February 26, 1770; "Mr. Printer," *New-York Gazette or the Weekly Post-Boy*, March 19, 1770; Launitz-Schürer, *Loyal Whigs and Revolutionaries*, 84–86.

138. *MCCNY* 7:204. See also Fischer, *Liberty and Freedom*, 46–47.

139. Gage to Hillsborough, February 21, 1770, TGP-ES 17.

140. Dalrymple to Gage, October 28, 1769, TGP-AS 88. See also Gage to Dalrymple, December 18, 1769, TGP-AS 88; Zobel, *Boston Massacre*, 164–79; Archer, *As If an Enemy's Country*, 164–81; Shy, *Toward Lexington*, 317.

141. *A Short Narrative of the Horrid Massacre in Boston* (New York: Doggett, 1849), 48. See also *LDJR* 197; Archer, *As If an Enemy's Country*, 182–85; Hoerder, *Crowd Action*, 216–34; Zobel, *Boston Massacre*, 182. On soldiers seeking civilian employment see Sylvia R. Frey, *The British Soldier in America: A Social History of Military Life in the Revolutionary Period* (Austin: University of Texas Press, 1981), 13–16; Shy, *Toward Lexington*, 37, 111; Sung Bok Kim, "A New Look at the Great Landlords of Eighteenth-Century New York," *WMQ* 27 (1970): 581–614.

142. Zobel, *Boston Massacre*, 184–200; Archer, *As If an Enemy's Country*, 186–202.

143. Murray to Smith, March 12, 1770, James Murray Robbins Papers, 1638–1899, box 6, folder 8, MHS.

144. *Short Narrative*, 33.

145. Hutchinson to Gage, March 6, 1770, TGP-AS 90.

146. Dalrymple to Gage, March 7, 1770, TGP-AS 90; *RRCCB* 23:57–58; Zobel, *Boston Massacre*, 200–209; Archer, *As If an Enemy's Country*, 202–6; Bernard Bailyn, *The Ordeal of Thomas Hutchinson* (Cambridge, Mass.: Harvard University Press, 1974), 156–64.

147. Gage to Dalrymple, March 12, 1770, TGP-AS 90.

148. Gage to Dalrymple, March 14, 1770, TGP-AS 90.

149. Dalrymple to Gage, March 27, 1770, TGP-AS 90.

150. Dalrymple to Gage, March 12, 1770, TGP-AS 90. See also "All the 29th Regiment and the Greatest Part of the 14th," *Boston News-Letter*, March 15, 1770.

151. Dalrymple to Gage, April 15, 1770, TGP-AS 91. See also Dalrymple to Gage, March 19, 1770, TGP-AS 90; Dalrymple to Gage, April 2, 1770, TGP-AS 91.

152. Gage to Barrington, September 8, 1770, TGP-ES 18.

153. Hutchinson to Gage, April 22, 1770, TGP-AS 91.

154. Gage to Dalrymple, April 9, 1770, TGP-AS 91. See also Gage to Hillsborough, April 10, 1770, TGP-ES 17; Gage to Barrington, April 24, 1770, TGP-ES 17.

155. "Oration by General Joseph Warren, 5 March 1770," John Collins Warren Papers, MHS.

6. Nation

1. *DNB*, s.v. "Long, Edward"; Andrew Jackson O'Shaughnessy, *An Empire Divided: The American Revolution and the British Caribbean* (Philadelphia: University of Pennsylvania Press, 2000), 4–6.

2. EL-*HJ* 2:310, 63, 204. See also EL-*HJ* 1:69, 155; 2:308–9; Robert V. Wells, *The Population of the British Colonies in America before 1776* (Princeton, N.J.: Princeton University Press, 1975),196; O'Shaughnessy, *Empire Divided*, 38; Trevor Burnard, *Mastery, Tyranny, and Desire: Thomas Thistlewood and His Slaves in the Anglo-Jamaican World* (Chapel Hill: University of North Carolina Press, 2004), 170–74; Alan Burns, *History of the British West Indies* (London: Allen & Unwin, 1954), 496; Suman Seth, "Materialism, Slavery, and the *History of Jamaica*," *ISIS* 105, no. 4 (2014).

3. EL-*HJ* 1:60, 69; Philip D. Morgan, *Slave Counterpoint: Black Culture in the Eighteenth-Century Chesapeake and Lowcountry* (Chapel Hill: University of North Carolina Press, 1998), 104–24; Dennis J. Pogue, "The Domestic Architecture of Slavery at George Washington's Mount Vernon," *Winterthur Portfolio* 37 (2002): 3–22.

4. Bruce D. Porter, *War and the Rise of the State: The Military Foundations of Modern Politics* (New York: Free Press, 1994), 105–7, 121–25; Charles Tilly, ed., *The Formation of National States in Western Europe* (Princeton, N.J.: Princeton University Press, 1975); Linda Colley, *Britons: Forging the Nation, 1707–1837* (New Haven, Conn.: Yale University Press, 1992); Lawrence Stone, ed., *An Imperial State at War: Britain from 1689 to 1815* (London: Routledge, 1994); Hagen Sculze, *States, Nations, and Nationalism: From the Middle Ages to the Present* (Oxford: Blackwell, 1996); Stephen Conway, *War, State, and Society in Mid-Eighteenth-Century Britain and Ireland* (Oxford: Oxford University Press, 2006), 193–226; Jeremy Adelman, "An Age of Imperial Revolutions,"

AHR 113 (2008): 319–40; Don Higginbotham, "War and State Formation in Revolutionary America," in *Empire and Nation: The American Revolution in the Atlantic World*, ed. Eliga H. Gould and Peter S. Onuf, 54–71 (Baltimore: Johns Hopkins University Press, 2005); Peter Thompson and Peter S. Onuf, *State and Citizen: British America and the Early United States* (Charlottesville: University of Virginia Press, 2013).

5. Alan Valentine, *Lord North*, 2 vols. (Norman: University of Oklahoma Press, 1967), 1:178–201; Peter Whiteley, *Lord North: The Prime Minister Who Lost America* (London: Hambledon, 1996), 77–95; Andrew Jackson O'Shaughnessy, *The Men Who Lost America: British Leadership, the American Revolution, and the Fate of the Empire* (New Haven, Conn.: Yale University Press, 2013), 47–54.

6. Barrington to Gage, July 1, 1770, TGP-ES 18. See also *PDBP* 2:243–45; *SLGB* 10 Geo. III, c. 15; Oliver M. Dickerson, *The Navigation Acts and the American Revolution* (Philadelphia: University of Pennsylvania Press, 1951), 195–202.

7. *PDBP* 3:273, 274, 276, 279. See also *PDBP* 3:270–96, 299–327; *CKG* 2:144–45; Barrington to Gage, April 2, 1770, TGP-ES 17; Valentine, *Lord North*, 1:204–5; John A. Schutz, *Thomas Pownall, British Defender of American Liberties: A Study of Anglo-American Relations in the Eighteenth Century* (Glendale, Calif.: Clark, 1951), 227–28.

8. Gage to Barrington, November 6, 1771, TGP-ES 21. See also CGC 33:125; *SLGB* 11 Geo. III, c. 11; 12 Geo. III, c. 12; 13 Geo. III, c. 24; *PDBP* 3:361, 364, 426, 475, 477; Gage to Barrington, May 12, 1770, TGP-ES 17.

9. Barrington to Gage, April 30, 1770, TGP-ES 17; John Richard Alden, *General Gage in America: Being Principally a History of His Role in the American Revolution* (Baton Rouge: Louisiana State University Press, 1948), 64.

10. Gage to Dalrymple, April 28, 1770, TGP-AS 91. See also Hiller B. Zobel, *The Boston Massacre* (New York: Norton, 1970), 204–5.

11. "At a Legal Town Meeting of the Freeholders and Other Inhabitants of the Town of Boxford, Legally Assembled on Thursday the 24th Day of May, A.D. 1770," *Boston Evening Post*, July 9, 1770.

12. *JHRMA* 47:70. See also Gage to Hillsborough, June 2, 1770, TGP-ES 17.

13. Dalrymple to Gage, September 24, 1770; TGP-AS 96.

14. Hillsborough to Gage, July 6, 1770, TGP-ES 18; Gage to Dalrymple, September 2, 1770, TGP-AS 95; Gage to Dalrymple, September 23, 1770, TGP-AS 96; *MJ* 399–410; *JHRMA* 47:94–95, 111, 149–50, 171–75; *PBF* 17:277–78, 286.

15. Zobel, *Boston Massacre*, 206–94; Richard Archer, *As If an Enemy's Country: The British Occupation of Boston and the Origins of Revolution* (New York: Oxford University Press, 2010), 207–25; *Legal Papers of John Adams*, ed. L. Kinvin Wroth and Hiller B. Zobel, vol. 3, cases 63 and 64 (Cambridge, Mass.: Harvard University Press, 1965).

16. *DCHNY* 8:246. See also *DCHNY* 8:260; Julius Goebel, *The Struggle for the Falkland Islands* (New Haven, Conn.: Yale University Press, 1927), 271–410.

17. Gage to Barrington, March 8, 1771, TGP-ES 19. See also Barrington to Gage, December 29, 1770, TGP-ES 19.

18. Hutchinson to Gage, May 13, 1771, TGP-AS 103. See also Wanton to Gage, May 14, 1771, TGP-AS 103; *PRCT* 13:422.

19. *JHRMA* 47:169, 175. See also *WSA* 2:61–62; *BMR* 61, 79; Saul Cornell, *A Well-Regulated Militia: The Founding Fathers and the Origins of Gun Control in America* (New York: Oxford University Press, 2006), 10.

20. *PBF* 18:125.

21. *JHRMA* 49:166; *DCHNY* 8:342.

22. *DCHNY* 8:259, 342; Jonathan Mercantini, *Who Shall Rule at Home? The Evolution of South Carolina Political Culture, 1748–1776* (Columbia: University of South Carolina Press, 2007), 211; James M. Johnson, *Militiamen, Rangers, and Redcoats: The Military in Georgia, 1754–1776* (Macon, Ga.: Mercer University Press, 1992), 68–74; Joseph Seymour, *The Pennsylvania Associators, 1747–1777* (Yardley, Pa.: Westholme, 2012), 118–23.

23. Valentine, *Lord North*, 1:208–12; Whiteley, *Lord North*, 95–100; Barrington to Gage, May 1, 1771, TGP-ES 20.

24. *CLB* 2:220.

25. *CLNY* 5:178. See also Gage to Barrington, July 6, 1770, TGP-ES 18; Gage to Hillsborough, July 7, 1770, TGP-ES 18; Hillsborough to Gage, September 28, 1770, TGP-ES 18; Gage to Hillsborough, December 7, 1770, TGP-ES 19; Gage to Hillsborough, January 16, 1771, TGP-ES 19; Gage to Dunmore, February 16, 1771, TGP-AS 100; "New-York, February 25," *Pennsylvania Chronicle*, February 25–March 4, 1771; *DCHNY* 8:202–3, 210–11; *HMWS* 1:80–81, 99–100; Joseph Albert Ernst, *Money and Politics in America, 1755–1775: A Study in the Currency Act of 1764 and the Political Economy of Revolution* (Chapel Hill: University of North Carolina Press, 1973), 277–80; Joseph S. Tiedemann, *Reluctant Revolutionaries: New York City and the Road to Independence, 1763–1776* (Ithaca, N.Y.: Cornell University Press, 1997), 154.

26. *DCHNJ* 10:272.

27. Gage to Hillsborough, February 5, 1772, TGP-ES 21. See also *DCHNJ* 10:201–3, 18:211, 213–15; *VPNJ* (September–October 1770), 39, 46–49; *VPNJ* (April–December 1771), 4–5, 7, 9–20, 26–33, 36–39, 57–58, 65–68, 71–73, 79; *VPNJ* (August–September 1772), 22, 24–25, 27, 38; Gage to Franklin, October 24, 1771, TGP-AS 107; Gage to Franklin, August 19, 1772, TGP-AS 113; Ernst, *Money and Politics*, 285–91; Larry R. Gerlach, "Soldiers and Citizens: The British Army in New Jersey on the Eve of the Revolution," *New Jersey History* 93 (1975): 24–32; Edgar Jacob Fisher, *New Jersey as a Royal Province, 1738 to 1776* (New York: Columbia University, 1911), 435–38; Larry R. Gerlach, *Prologue to Independence: New Jersey in the Coming of the American Revolution* (New Brunswick: Rutgers University Press, 1976), 72–79.

28. Barrington to Gage, March 4, 1772, TGP-ES 21. See also *SLPA* 8:241–42; *MPCPA* 9:684–85, 718, 10:16–20.

29. "New-York, August 20," *New-London Gazette*, August 20, 1770. See also Gage to Dunmore, April 14, 1771, TGP-AS 102; *CLB* 2:403.

30. "Extract of a Letter from Perth-Amboy, Dated Sept. 15," *Newport Mercury*, October 4, 1773. See also J. Thomas Scharf and Thomas Westcott, *History of Philadelphia, 1609–1884*, 3 vols. (Philadelphia: Everts, 1884), 2:966.

31. "Philadelphia, October 28," *Pennsylvania Packet; and the General Advertiser*, October 28, 1771; "Extract of a Letter from New-Jersey, Dated August 29," *New-York Gazette; or the Weekly Post-Boy*, September 10, 1770.

32. "New-York News Continued," *Supplement to Rivington's New-York Gazetteer*, June 10, 1773. See also "New-York, June 10," *Providence Gazette; and Country Journal*, June 15, 1771.

33. *LDJR* 98, 134, 246. See also *LDJR* 187, 204, 216, 229; "Friday Last Being the Anniversary," *Massachusetts Gazette; and the Boston Post-Boy and Advertiser*, May 31, 1773.

34. "Charles-town (South Carolina) June 7," *New-York Gazette; or, the Weekly Post-Boy*, July 9, 1770. See also D. E. Huger Smith, "Wilton's Statue of Pitt," *South Carolina Historical and Genealogical Magazine* 15 (1914): 18–38; "Charles-Town, (South Carolina)," *New York Journal, or the General Advertiser*, July 23, 1772.

35. *De Brahm's Report of the General Survey in the Southern District of North America*, ed. Louis De Vorsey Jr. (Columbia: University of South Carolina Press, 1971), 162. See also *CRGA* 15:394, 442, 542; Johnson, *Militiamen, Rangers, and Redcoats*, 79, 86–88, 92–96.

36. *TBRSC* 32:279, 281. See also *JCHSC-M* 38, part 2: 332–33, 340, 410–11; Larry E. Ivers, *Colonial Forts of South Carolina, 1670–1775* (Columbia: University of South Carolina Press, 1970), 42, 70–72; Hallowell to Maduit, December 5, 1773, Boylston Family Papers, 1688–1979, box 6, folder 11, MHS.

37. Penn to Gage, April 6, 1770, TGP-AS 91. See also *MPCPA* 9:583–89, 664–65, 679–80, 708–17, 746–59.

38. Gage to Penn, April 15, 1770, TGP-AS 91.

39. *DCHNY* 8:395. See also "New-York, May 6," *New-York Journal; or, the General Advertiser*, May 6, 1773; *DCHNY* 8:371, 393–94, 399, 451, 457.

40. *CRGA* 15:546; Johnson, *Militia, Rangers, and Redcoats*, 96–100.

41. Thomas Paine, *Common Sense*, ed. Isaac Kramnick (New York: Penguin, 1976), 107.

42. *DCHNY* 8:407; TG-OB January 1, 1774; Paul David Nelson, *William Tryon and the Course of Empire: A Life in British Imperial Service* (Chapel Hill: University of North Carolina Press, 1990), 120–21; "Governor Tryon's House in Fort George," ed. B. D. Bargar, *New York History* 35 (1954): 297–309.

43. Gage to Barrington, September 3, 1771, TGP-ES 21.

44. Marr to Gage, September 27, 1770, TGP-AS 96; John Marr, *A Plan of the Palace Barracks at Québec with the Environs, Relative to a Report of This Date, and an Estimate of the Expence of the Repairs Humbly Thought Necessary for the Year 1772* [1771], Maps 4-C-23, WLCL; Serge Bernier et al., *Military History of Québec City, 1608–2008* (Montréal: Art Global, 2008), 73; André Charbonneau, Yvon Desloges, and Marc Lafrance, *Québec the Fortified City: From the 17th to the 19th Century* (Ottawa: Parks Canada, 1982), 61–62.

45. Gage to Robinson, August 5, 1772, TGP-ES 22.

46. MacKenzie to Gage, July 1, 1771, TGP-AS 104.

47. "Charleston, November 22," *Massachusetts Spy*, January 14–17, 1771; James Moncrief, "Estimate for Repairing the Church of St. Francis, at St. Augustine, for Soldiers Barracks," CTP 8/28/6; James Moncrief, *Plan of the Soldiers Barracks at Present* [1767], Maps 6-K-11, WLCL; H. Burrard, *Sketch of St. Augustine and Its Environs* [1770], Maps 6-K-7, WLCL.

48. Patrick McRobert, *A Tour through Part of the North Provinces of America: Being, a Series of Letters Wrote on the Spot, in the Years 1774 and 1775* (Philadelphia: Historical Society of Pennsylvania, 1935), 17–18.

49. "Québec, July 1," *New-York Journal; or, the General Advertiser*, July 29, 1773.

50. "Halifax, October 16," *Boston News-Letter*, December 13, 1770.

51. Grant to Gage, February 18, 1771, TGP-AS 100. See also Murray to Murray, July 31, 1769, James M. Robbins Family Papers, 1638–1899, box 6, folder 7, MHS; *RPAC* 29a:21, 33–35; William Henry Atherton, *Montréal, 1535–1914*, 3 vols. (Montréal: Clarke,

1914), 2:15–16; Elizabeth Mancke, *The Fault Lines of Empire: Political Differentiation in Massachusetts and Nova Scotia, ca. 1760–1830* (New York: Routledge, 2005), 84–85.

52. Gorham to Gage, November 1, 1771, TGP-AS 107.

53. Hillsborough to Gage, April 18, 1772, TGP-ES 22. See also Gage to Marr, September 10, 1770, TGP-AS 95; Caldwell to Gage, August 7, 1774, TGP-AS 122; Corrance to Gage, August 17, 1770, TGP-AS 94; Gage to Bradshaw, August 5, 1771, TGP-ES 20; Gage to Prevost, August 20, 1771, TGP-AS 105.

54. DePeyster to Gage, May 5, 1775, TGP-AS 128. See also Gage to Bradshaw, August 5, 1771, TGP-ES 20; Caldwell to Gage, August 14, 1774, TGP-AS 122; Gage to Cramahé, March 24, 1773, TGP-AS 117; TG-OB May 26, 1773; Woody Holton, *Forced Founders: Indians, Debtors, Slaves, and the Making of the American Revolution* (Chapel Hill: University of North Carolina Press, 1999), 21–38.

55. Gage to Carden, September 9, 1772, TGP-AS 114. See also Gage to Bruce, April 1, 1771, TGP-AS 101.

56. Gage to Patterson, August 8, 1771, TGP-AS 105.

57. Gage to Dartmouth, December 2, 1772, TGP-ES 23. See also Williams to Gage, November 23, 1771, TGP-AS 107; Hillsborough to Gage, December 4, 1771, TGP-ES 21; Gage to Penn, November 2, 1772, TGP-AS 115; Gage to Edmonstone, December 17, 1772, TGP-AS 116; Gage to Haldimand, August 18, 1774, TGP-AS 122; John Shy, *Toward Lexington: The Role of the British Army in the Coming of the American Revolution* (Princeton, N.J.: Princeton University Press, 1965), 324–25, 403; W. M. Butler, "Historic Sites and Scenes in Randolph County, Illinois: Old Kaskaskia, the Drowned City; Fort Gage and the Traces of Old Fort Chartres, near Prairie Du Rocher," *Journal of the Illinois State Historical Society* 4 (1912): 459–68.

58. Sterling to Bassett, December 22, 1772, CO 5/154.

59. Barrington to Gage, September 2, 1772, TGP-ES 23.

60. Dartmouth to Gage, September 2, 1772, TGP-ES 23. See also Valentine, *Lord North*, 1:256–63; Robin F. A. Fabel, "An Eighteenth Colony: Dreams for Mississippi on the Eve of the Revolution," *JSH* 59 (1993): 658; Shy, *Toward Lexington*, 402–3.

61. Gage to Barrington, October 26, 1772, TGP-ES 23.

62. Philip Lawson, *The Imperial Challenge: Québec and Britain in the Age of the American Revolution* (Montréal: McGill-Queen's University Press, 1989), 108–45; Hilda Neatby, *The Québec Act: Protest and Policy* (Scarborough, Ont.: Prentice-Hall of Canada, 1972), 33–55; Victor Coffin, *The Province of Québec and the Early American Revolution: A Study in English-American Colonial History* (Madison: University of Wisconsin, 1896), 398–432.

63. Lawrence Henry Gipson, *The Great War for Empire*, 15 vols. (New York: Knopf, 1936–70), 9:232–76; Wells, *Population of the British Colonies*, 172–258; "General Estimate for Contingent Expences for the Islands of Grenada, the Grenadines, Dominica, St. Vincent and Tobago Which Probably May Be Incurred from Midsummer 1769 to Midsummer 1770," T 1/476/420; *TAC* 375–81; O'Shaughnessy, *Empire Divided*, 43–49; Cyril Hamshere, *The British in the Caribbean* (London: Weidenfeld & Nicolson, 1972), 186–201; Lennox Honychurch, *The Dominica Story: A History of the Island* (London: Macmillan Educational, 1995), 67–68, 70–71; Beverly A. Steele, *Grenada: A History of Its People* (Oxford: Macmillan Educational, 2003), 69–72; Gertrude Carmichael, *The History of the West Indian Islands of Trinidad and Tobago, 1498–1900* (London: Redman, 1961), 308–9.

64. An Act for Providing Oil and Candles for the Troops Doing Duty in His Majesty's Forts Nassau and Montague, and Establishing a Salary for the Storekeeper Thereof (1772), CO 25/4. For Bermuda see Assembly Minutes, February 15, 1769, CO 40/15; An Act for Renewing an Act Intituled An Act for Regulating the Militia of These His Majesty's Islands of Bermuda (1769), CO 39/9; Bruere to Gage, December 5, 1772, TGP-AS 115; René Chartrand, "Notes on Bermuda Military Forces, 1687–1815," *Bermuda Historical Quarterly* 28 (1971): 43–44. For the Bahamas see Assembly Minutes, November 11, 1768, December 22, 1768, January 18, 1769, September 5, 1770, November 19, 1770, November 30, 1770, February 5, 1771, February 12, 1772, April 9, 1772, April 14, 1772, CO 26/7; Gage to Hillsborough, December 16, 1769, TGP-ES 16; Gage to Shirley, August 30, 1770, TGP-AS 95; Hodgson to Gage, April 24, 1772, TGP-AS 110; Michael Craton, *A History of the Bahamas* (London: Collins, 1962), 140–41, 149–52; Michael Craton and Gail Saunders, *Islanders in the Stream: A History of the Bahamian People*, vol. 1 (Athens: University of Georgia Press, 1999), 139–44, 157–66.

65. Gage to Barrington, January 6, 1773, TGP-ES 23.

66. Gage to Barrington, April 13, 1772, TGP-ES 22. See also Gage to Barrington, May 4, 1772, TGP-ES 22; Gage to Barrington, July 1, 1772, TGP-ES 22; Gage to Barrington, September 2, 1772, TGP-ES 23; Gage to Hillsborough, October 6, 1772, TGP-ES 23; Dartmouth to Gage, December 9, 1772, TGP-ES 23; Alden, *General Gage in America*, 192–94.

67. Benjamin L. Carp, *Defiance of the Patriots: The Boston Tea Party and the Making of America* (New Haven, Conn.: Yale University Press, 2011), 7–22; Valentine, *Lord North*, 1:103–36; O'Shaughnessy, *Men Who Lost America*, 51–52.

68. "Messi'rs Fleets," *Boston Evening Post*, October 18, 1773.

69. TG-OB October 22, 1773.

70. "The Agents Since Find That the Tea Will Come," *Boston Post Boy*, December 6, 1773. See also "Extract of Another Letter from New York, December 1," *Pennsylvania Gazette*, April 20, 1774; DCHNY 8:407–8; Carp, *Defiance of the Patriots*, 65–69, 78–140; Alfred F. Young, *The Shoemaker and the Tea Party: Memory and the American Revolution* (Boston: Beacon, 1999); Nick Bunker, *An Empire on the Edge: How Britain Came to Fight America* (New York: Knopf, 2014).

71. Dartmouth to Gage, April 9, 1774, TGP-ES 24; Alden, *General Gage in America*, 194–204; Valentine, *Lord North*, 1:306–19; Whiteley, *Lord North*, 137–45; Shy, *Toward Lexington*, 406–10; Schutz, *Thomas Pownall*, 233–36.

72. *SLGB* 14 Geo. III, c. 19; 14 Geo. III, c. 39; 14 Geo. III, c. 45; Valentine, *Lord North*, 1:319–323; David Ammerman, *In the Common Cause: American Response to the Coercive Acts of 1774* (Charlottesville: University of Virginia Press, 1974), 1–10.

73. *SLGB* 14 Geo. III, c. 54. See also Barrington to Gage, May 4, 1774, TGP-ES 25; PDBP 4:318–19, 326–27, 405, 433, 438–41; "London, March 12," *Boston Post Boy*, May 2, 1774; PBF 20:228–29, 234n8, 547; Gipson, *Great War for Empire*, 12:131–32; Jack M. Sosin, "The Massachusetts Acts of 1774: Coercive or Preventive?," *Huntington Library Quarterly* 26 (1963): 235–52; Henry Longley York, *Henry Hulton and the American Revolution: An Outsider's Inside Look* (Boston: Colonial Society of Massachusetts, 2010), 307.

74. "London, June 18," *Virginia Gazette*, September 1, 1774.

75. JCC 1:71. See also "The Following Act for the Better Providing Suitable Quarters," *Boston Post Boy*, August 8, 1774; "Just Published and to Be Sold by Joseph

Crukshank," *Dunlap's Pennsylvania Packet or, the General Advertiser*, September 19, 1774; *JCC* 1:64, 69; Ammerman, *In the Common Cause*, 58, 66–68.

76. Don R. Gerlach, "A Note on the Quartering Act of 1774," *New England Quarterly* 38 (1966): 80–88.

77. *AFC* 1:88, 97. See also *AFC* 1:90; Woody Holton, *Abigail Adams* (New York: Free Press, 2009), 1–67; Diane Jacobs, *Dear Abigail: The Intimate Lives and Revolutionary Ideas of Abigail Adams and Her Two Remarkable Sisters* (New York: Ballantine Books, 2014), 3–57; Peter Orlando Hutchinson, *The Diary and Letters of His Excellency Thomas Hutchinson, Esq.*, 2 vols. (Boston: Houghton, Mifflin, 1884), 1:148–51.

78. *LDJR* 270. See also Gage to Haldimand, June 12, 1774, TGP-AS 120.

79. *LDJR* 273.

80. Gage to Maddison, June 12, 1774, TGP-AS 120. See also Gage to Dartmouth, May 19, 1774, TGP-ES 25; Gage to Barrington, June 26, 1774, TGP-ES 25; *JHRMA* 50:251–52, 261–91; *AFC* 1:108; *LDJR* 269–74; Gage to Lloyd, May 30, 1774, TGP-AS 119; Russell Bourne, *Cradle of Violence: How Boston's Waterfront Mobs Ignited the American Revolution* (Hoboken, N.J.: Wiley & Sons, 2006), 199–203; Dirk Hoerder, *Crowd Action in Revolutionary Massachusetts, 1765–1780* (New York: Academic, 1977), 276–93; Shy, *Toward Lexington*, 413n114. Numbers of troops based on returns from January 1, 1775, in David Hackett Fischer, *Paul Revere's Ride* (New York: Oxford University Press, 1994), 309.

81. TG-OB July 12, 1774, July 20, 1774.

82. *RRCCB* 23:223. See also *LDJR* 280.

83. "Extract of a Letter from a Gentleman at Windsor (Nova-Scotia)," *Boston Evening-Post*, September 12, 1774; *King v. Dyer*, July 5, 1774, TGP-AS 123. See also TG-OB August 2, 1774, August 12, 1774, September 26, 1774; "A Return of Men Deserted of the Royal Welch Fuziliers from 15th April 1773 to 28th June 1774," TGP-AS 120; Warrant, July 13, 1774, TGP-AS 121; "From the *Pennsylvania Journal*, August 17," *Essex Gazette*, August 30–September 6, 1774.

84. "Suffolk Resolves Portion," September 9, 1774, TGP-AS 123. See also Robertson to Gage, July 19, 1774, TGP-AS 121.

85. Gage to Barrington, August 27, 1774, TGP-ES 26.

86. Gage to Legge, July 13, 1774, TGP-AS 121; TG-OB July 11, 1774; Gage to Dartmouth, August 27, 1774, TGP-ES 26; *LDJR* 281; Fischer, *Paul Revere's Ride*, 309.

87. *Memorandums, for a Report* (n.p., 1774). See also TG-OB August 7, 1774, August 13, 1774.

88. "At a Meeting of the Selectmen and Committee of Correspondence, September 24, 1774," *Boston Post-Boy*, September 19, 1774; "Extract of a Letter from Québec, Dated September 18," *Rivington's New-York Gazetteer*, October 6, 1774. See also "Wednesday Night," *Boston Post-Boy*, September 12, 1774; *RRCCB* 23:229.

89. Lechmere to Lane, Son, and Frasier, September 28, 1774, Miscellaneous Bound Manuscripts, MHS. See also Gage to Randolph, October 20, 1774, TGP-AS 124; Hoerder, *Crowd Action*, 294–310.

90. Gage to Dartmouth, December 15, 1774, TGP-ES 27.

91. "Portsmouth, October 27, 1774," *New-Hampshire Gazette, and Historical Chronicle*, October 28, 1774; "Portsmouth, Nov. 11, 1774," *New-Hampshire Gazette, and Historical Chronicle*, November 11, 1774; "Boston, October 27," *Newport Mercury*, November 7, 1774; "Boston, November 24," *Boston Post Boy*, November 7, 1774;

"Boston, November 21," *Boston Post Boy*, November 14, 1774; David C. Hsiung, "Food, Fuel, and the New England Environment in the War for Independence, 1775–1776," *New England Quarterly* 80 (2007): 614–54.

92. *AFC* 1:151. See also *AFC* 147, 148n3, 149; Peter Charles Hoffer, *Prelude to Revolution: The Salem Gunpowder Raid of 1775* (Baltimore: Johns Hopkins University Press, 2013).

93. Gage to Barrington, September 25, 1774, TGP-ES 26.

94. Gage to Barrington, October 3, 1774, TGP-ES 26; Gage to Barrington, October 17, 1774, TGP-ES 26; *LDJR* 285–87; *JPCM* 41–48; Holton, *Abigail Adams*, 58, 68; Shy, *Toward Lexington*, 412–13; Fischer, *Paul Revere's Ride*, 309.

95. *RRCCB* 23:228.

96. *JPCM* 42–43. See also Bourne, *Cradle of Violence*, 203–10.

97. "To the Inhabitants of Connecticut," *New-London Gazette*, July 8, 1774.

98. "From the *Gentleman's Magazine* for November 1774," *Virginia Gazette*, February 16, 1775. See also "To the Author Who Stiles Himself an Englishman," *Virginia Gazette*, July 21, 1774.

99. Gage to Barrington, December 25, 1774, TGP-ES 27.

100. *CLNY* 5:493–94, 613; *DCHNY* 8:453–54; *VPNJ* (November 1773–March 1774), 192.

101. "The Committee Above Named Having Brought," *Dunlap's Pennsylvania Packet or, the General Advertiser*, July 25, 1774. See also Tiedemann, *Reluctant Revolutionaries*, 185–92; Leopold S. Launitz-Schürer Jr., *Loyal Whigs and Revolutionaries: The Making of the Revolution in New York, 1765–1776* (New York: NYU Press, 1980), 108–16; Fisher, *New Jersey*, 439–40; Gerlach, "Soldiers and Citizens," 34–35.

102. Hamilton to Moncrieff, July 11, 1774, enclosure in Haldimand to Gage, July 17, 1774, TGP-AS 121. See also Gage to Hamilton, July 23, 1774, TGP-AS 121.

103. *CLB* 2:370. See also Shy, *Toward Lexington*, 413; Tiedemann, *Reluctant Revolutionaries*, 193–204; Gerlach, "Soldiers and Citizens," 35; John Russell Young, *Memorial History of the City of Philadelphia from Its First Settlement to the Year 1895*, 2 vols. (New York: New-York History Co., 1895–1898), 1:341–42, 2:145.

104. *DCHNY* 8:544.

105. *VPNJ* (January–February 1775), 47.

106. *PA* 8th ser., 8:7177. See also *PA* 4th ser., 3:503.

107. "New-York, October 13," *New-York Journal; or, the General Advertiser*, October 13, 1774. See also Fischer, *New Jersey*, 440; Tiedemann, *Reluctant Revolutionaries*, 193–94; Edwin G. Burrows and Mike Wallace, *Gotham: A History of New York City to 1898* (New York: Oxford University Press, 1999), 213–14.

108. *PBF* 17:162, 18:28, 21:366–67. See also *PBF* 17:169–70, 277, 19:226; *JCC* 2:96–97, 111–23; Carl Van Doren, *Benjamin Franklin*, 520–32; Gordon S. Wood, *The Americanization of Benjamin Franklin* (New York: Penguin, 2004).

109. "Work Done by Captain Montresor in Boston, from December 1774 to March 1775," TGP-AS 127; Gage to Robinson, February 7, 1775, TGP-ES 27; Watts to Gage, February 20, 1775, TGP-AS 126; Fischer, *Paul Revere's Ride*, 309.

110. *JPCM* 87.

111. Cooper to Gage, March 30, 1775, TGP-ES 28.

112. *AFC* 1:182.

113. "Address of the Inhabitants of Marshfield to Governor Gage," February 20, 1775, TGP-AS 126.

114. *LDJR* 289; Middleborough, Plympton, and Halifax to Gage, March 10, 1775, TGP-AS 126; "Donations Received Since Our Last," *Boston Evening Post*, January 30, 1775; Marcia A. Thomas, *Memorials of Marshfield and Guide Book to Its Localities at Green Harbor* (Boston: Dutton and Wentworth, 1854), 56.

115. "Extract of a Letter from a Gentleman of Military Distinction in Connecticut Dated Jan. 24, 1775," *Boston Gazette, and Country Journal*, January 30, 1775.

116. Gage to Wentworth, February 6, 1775, TGP-AS 125. See also Wentworth to Gage, February 13, 1775, TGP-AS 126; Gage to Wentworth, February 23, 1775, TGP-AS 126; "Portsmouth," *New-Hampshire Gazette, and Historical Chronicle*, February 17, 1775; Fischer, *Paul Revere's Ride*, 52–57; Paul W. Wilderson, *Governor John Wentworth and the American Revolution: The English Connection* (Hanover, N.H.: University Press of New England, 1994), 245–53.

117. Gage to Terrey et al., March 31, 1775, TGP-AS 127.

118. Barrington to Gage, April 5, 1775, TGP-ES 28.

119. Graves to Gage, March 22, 1775, TGP-AS 127; *CRGA* 15:546–47, 17:773–74; Gage to Wright, April 16, 1775, TGP-AS 127; Colden to Gage, April 2, 1775, TGP-AS 127; Gage to Carleton, April 19, 1775, TGP-AS 127.

120. *JPCM* 121.

121. Dartmouth to Gage, January 27, 1775, TGP-ES 27. See also "Intelligence," March 3, 1775, TGP-AS 126.

122. Mark Puls, *Samuel Adams: Father of the American Revolution* (New York: Palgrave Macmillan, 2006), 165–71; Fischer, *Paul Revere's Ride*, 184–260, 313–15, 321–24; Robert A. Gross, *The Minutemen and Their World* (New York: Hill & Wang, 1976); Walter R. Borneman, *American Spring: Lexington, Concord, and the Road to Revolution* (New York: Little, Brown, & Co., 2014).

123. Gage to Carleton, April 21, 1775, TGP-AS 127.

124. Warren to Boston, April 22, 1775, TGP-AS 127. See also Gage to Graves, April 25, 1775, TGP-AS 128; Gage to Dartmouth, June 12, 1775, TGP-ES 29; Thomas Gage, "A Proclamation," June 12, 1775; Fischer, *Paul Revere's Ride*, 264–65.

125. *AFC* 1:200–201.

126. *LDJR* 295. See also "Extract of a Paragraph of a Letter from a Gentleman in London," *Essex Gazette*, October 25–November 1, 1774; Gage to Legge, April 23, 1775, TGP-AS 128; Gage to 22nd, 40th, 44th, and 45th Regiments, May 30, 1775, TGP-AS 129; Fischer, *Paul Revere's Ride*, 309.

127. Draft Letter from Eliot, May 31, 1775, Miscellaneous Bound Manuscripts, MHS.

128. *AFC* 1:204. See also *AFC* 1:204–6, 210–11, 217.

129. Legge to Gage, April 27, 1775, TGP-AS 128. See also Gage to Legge, April 24, 1775, TGP-AS 128; Gage to Carleton, April 27, 1775, TGP-AS 128; Legge to Gage, June 9, 1775, TGP-AS 129; Gage to Cooper, May 19, 1775, TGP-ES 29; Gage to Graves, June 15, 1775, TGP-AS 130; Ernest Clarke, *The Siege of Fort Cumberland, 1776: An Episode in the American Revolution* (Montréal: McGill-Queen's University Press, 1995), 5–6.

130. Gage to Dartmouth, April 22, 1775, TGP-ES 29.

131. *AFC* 1:202; Don Higginbotham, *The War of American Independence: Military Attitudes, Policies, and Practice, 1763–1789* (Bloomington: University of Indiana Press, 1971), 65.

132. "Intelligence," April 25, 1775, TGP-AS 128.

133. *AFC* 1:218, 205.

134. Inman to Inman, April 22, 1775, James M. Robbins Family Papers, 1638–1899, box 2, folder 29, MHS. Thanks to Kacy Tillman for this citation.

135. Colden to Gage, April 25, 1775, TGP-AS 128.

136. *JCC* 2:52.

137. Hamilton to Gage, May 25, 1775, TGP-AS 129.

138. Hamilton to Gage, June 8, 1776, TGP-AS 129.

139. Gage to Dartmouth, May 13, 1775, TGP-ES 29. See also Gage to Colden, May 23, 1775, TGP-AS 129; *CLB* 2:403, 416, 425; *HMWS* 1:222; *AFC* 1:189, 191; Tiedemann, *Reluctant Revolutionaries*, 220–34; Launitz-Schürer, *Loyal Whigs and Revolutionaries*, 155–63; Nelson, *William Tryon*, 128–35.

140. *AFC* 1:212. See also Steven Rosswurm, *Arms, Country, and Class: The Philadelphia Militia and "Lower Sort" during the American Revolution, 1775–83* (New Brunswick, N.J.: Rutgers University Press, 1987), 49–75; John Gilbert McCurdy, *Citizen Bachelors: Manhood and the Creation of the United States* (Ithaca, N.Y.: Cornell University Press, 2009), 172–73.

141. Martin to Gage, May 26, 1775, TGP-AS 129. See also Mercantini, *Who Shall Rule*, 239–44.

142. Gage to Dunmore, September 10, 1775, TGP-AS 135. See also Gage to Dartmouth, June 12, 1775, TGP-ES 29; Campbell to Gage, July 1, 1775, TGP-AS 131; Gage to Dartmouth, May 17, 1775, TGP-ES 29; Martin to Gage, July 6, 1775, TGP-AS 131; Gage to Tonyn, May 15, 1775, TGP-AS 129; Gage to Browne, May 15, 1775, TGP-AS 129; *PBF* 22:191–92, 551–53; Gerlach, *Prologue to Independence*, 255–72; Shelia Skemp, *William Franklin: Son of a Patriot, Servant of a King* (New York: Oxford University Press), 192–208; Gregory Evans Dowd, *Groundless: Rumors, Legends, and Hoaxes on the Early American Frontier* (Baltimore: Johns Hopkins University Press, 2015), 206–11.

143. DePeyster to Gage, June 16, 1775, TGP-AS 130. See also Shy, *Toward Lexington*, 419.

144. Marsh to Gage, June 20, 1775, TGP-AS 130. See also Carleton to Gage, June 28, 1775, TGP-AS 130; Clarke, *Siege of Fort Cumberland*, 6–11.

145. Bruere to Gage, September 28, 1775, TGP-AS 135.

146. Gage to Graves, September 8, 1775, TGP-AS 135.

147. Morden to Marsh, June 10, 1775, enclosure in Marsh to Gage, June 20, 1775, TGP-AS 130; Legge to Gage, July 28, 1775, TGP-AS 132.

148. Bruere to Gage, August 28, 1775, TGP-AS 134.

149. Gage to Legge, August 11, 1775, TGP-AS 133. See also Batt to Gage, June 30, 1775, TGP-AS 130; Francklin to Gage, August 18, 1775, TGP-AS 134.

150. Gage to Legge, June 7, 1775, TGP-AS 129. See also Gage to Legge, September 5, 1775, TGP-AS 135.

151. Carleton to Gage, July 27, 1775, TGP-AS 132.

152. Gage to Carleton, July 3, 1775, TGP-AS 131; *JCC* 2:109–10; Clarke, *Siege of Fort Cumberland*, 11–15; Harrison Bird, *Attack on Québec: The American Invasion of Canada, 1775* (New York: Oxford University Press, 1968); Robert McConnell Hatch,

Thrust for Canada: The American Attempt on Québec in 1775–1776 (Boston: Houghton Mifflin, 1979); Mark R. Anderson, *The Battle for the Fourteenth Colony: America's War of Liberation of Canada, 1774–1776* (Hanover, N.H.: University Press of New England, 2013).

153. *SLGB* 15 Geo. III, c. 15. See also *PDBP* 5:636, 651, 657; Pownall to Gage, April 15, 1775, TGP-ES 28; Valentine, *Lord North*, 1:355–61; *DNB*, s.v. "Percy, Hugh."

154. Gage to Barrington, June 12, 1775, TGP-ES 29.

155. Nathaniel Philbrick, *Bunker Hill: A City, a Siege, a Revolution* (London: Doubleday, 2013); Richard H. Brown and Paul E. Cohen, *Revolution: Mapping the Road to American Independence, 1755–1783* (New York: Norton, 2015).

156. JW-OB, July 7, 1775.

157. *AFC* 1:261. *AFC* 1:228, 232, 235–36, 239, 247–48, 369.

158. "Minutes of a Council Held at the General's," August 2, 1775, TGP-AS 133. See also JW-OB 10 August 1775, August 25, 1775, September 3, 1775; Selectmen of Boston to Pearson, August 4, 1775, TGP-AS 133; Dartmouth to Gage, August 2, 1775, TGP-ES 30.

159. *SLGB* 16 Geo. III, c. 11; *PDBP* 6:4, 391, 402, 453.

Epilogue

1. *The Diary of Elizabeth Drinker*, ed. Elaine Forman Crane et al., 3 vols. (Boston: Northeastern University Press, 1991), 1:218, 266, 267.

2. Patricia Cleary, *Elizabeth Murray: A Woman's Pursuit of Independence in Eighteenth-Century America* (Amherst: University of Massachusetts Press, 2000), 167–207; Mary Beth Norton, *Liberty's Daughters: The Revolutionary Experience of American Women, 1750–1800* (Boston: Little, Brown, 1980), 195–227.

3. *JCC* 16:298. See also *JCC* 3:288–89, 4:39.

4. *JHRMA* 52:118, 198, 277, 279, 53:43, 91.

5. *The Papers of Thomas Jefferson*, ed. Julian P. Boyd et al., 41 vols. (Princeton, N.J.: Princeton University Press, 1950–2014), 1:431. See also Pauline Maier, *American Scripture: Making the Declaration of Independence* (New York: Random House, 1997), 118.

6. Neil H. Cogan, ed., *The Complete Bill of Rights: The Drafts, Debates, Sources, and Origins* (New York: Oxford University Press, 1997), 216.

7. Marc W. Kruman, *Between Authority and Liberty: State Constitution Making in Revolutionary America* (Chapel Hill: University of North Carolina Press, 1997), 37–49; Gordon S. Wood, *The Creation of the American Republic, 1776–1789* (Chapel Hill: University of North Carolina Press, 1969), 271; Leonard W. Levy, *Origins of the Bill of Rights* (New Haven, Conn.: Yale University Press, 1999), 9–11.

8. Cogan, *Complete Bill of Rights*, 216–17.

9. Jonathan Elliot, ed., *The Debates in the Several State Conventions on the Adoption of the Federal Constitution* (Philadelphia: Lippincott, 1836), 3:410–11, 413.

10. Helen E. Veit, Kenneth R. Bowling, and Charlene Bangs Bickford, eds., *Creating the Bill of Rights: The Documentary Record from the First Federal Congress* (Baltimore: Johns Hopkins University Press, 1991), 12. See also Max Farrand, ed., *The Records of the Federal Convention of 1787*, 3 vols. (New Haven, Conn.: Yale University Press, 1911), 2:340n4, 341; Carol Berkin, *A Brilliant Solution: Inventing the American Constitution* (New York: Harcourt, 2002), 133–34; Levy, *Origins of the Bill*, 12–21, 29–43, 264.

11. Veit, Bowling, and Bickford, *Creating the Bill of Rights*, 185–86, also 39, 48, 179–80; Cogan, *Complete Bill of Rights*, 207–16.

12. Veit, Bowling, and Bickford, *Creating the Bill of Rights*, 4. See also Akhil Reed Amar, *The Bill of Rights* (New Haven, Conn.: Yale University Press, 1998), 59–63.

13. Engblom v. Carey, 677 F.2d 957 (2nd Cir. 1982), *on rem.* 572 F. Supp. 44 (S.D.N.Y. 1982), *aff'd. per curiam* 724 F.2d 28 (2d Cir. 1983). See also Amar, *Bill of Rights*, 220; William S. Fields and David T. Hardy, "The Third Amendment and the Issue of the Maintenance of Standing Armies: A Legal History," *American Journal of Legal History* 35 (1991): 393–431; Tom W. Bell, "The Third Amendment: Forgotten but Not Gone," *William and Mary Bill of Rights Journal* 2 (1993): 117–50; "Third Amendment Rights Group Celebrates Another Successful Year," *Onion*, October 5, 2007, www.theonion. com/third-amendment-rights-group-celebrates-another-success-1819569379 (accessed May 9, 2018).

14. Griswold v. Connecticut, 381 U.S. 479 (1965); Roe v. Wade, 410 U.S. 113 (1973); Lawrence v. Texas, 539 U.S. 558 (2003); Nancy Cott, *The Bonds of Womanhood: "Women's Sphere" in New England, 1780–1835* (New Haven, Conn.: Yale University Press, 1977).

15. Pub. L. 88–352, 78 Stat. 241.

16. Edwin F. Hatfield, *History of Elizabeth, New Jersey* (New York: Carlton and Lanahan, 1868), 392; William A. Whitehead, *Contributions to the Early History of Perth Amboy and the Adjoining Country* (New York: Appleton, 1856), 258.

17. John Russell Young, *Memorial History of the City of Philadelphia from Its First Settlement to the Year 1895*, 2 vols. (New York: New-York History Co., 1895–98), 2:153; J. Thomas Scharf and Thomas Westcott, *History of Philadelphia, 1609–1884*, 3 vols. (Philadelphia: Everts, 1884), 2:937; J. H. Easterby, *A History of the College of Charleston Founded 1770* (Charleston, S.C.: College of Charleston, 1935), 26–27.

18. *Minutes of the Common Council of the City of New York, 1784–1813*, 19 vols. (New York: City of New York, 1917), 1:278.

19. *The City of New Brunswick; Its History, Its Homes, and Its Industries* (New Brunswick, N.J.: New Brunswick Times, 1909), 38; Townsend Ward, "North Second Street and Its Associations," *Pennsylvania Magazine of History and Biography* 4 (1880): 178–79.

20. Harry Piers, *The Evolution of the Halifax Fortress, 1749–1928*, ed. G. M. Self (Halifax: Public Archives of Nova Scotia, 1947), 15–16; Brian Cuthbertson, *The Halifax Citadel: Portrait of a Military Fortress* (Halifax: Formac, 2001), 50–70; André Charbonneau, "Les Nouvelles Casernes: Haut lieu de l'histoire militaire à Québec," *Cap-aux-Diamants: La revue d'histoire du Québec* 58 (1999): 25–29; Merritt Roe Smith, *Harpers Ferry Armory and the New Technology* (Ithaca, N.Y.: Cornell University Press, 1980); United States Congress, House Committee on Military Affairs, "St. Francis Barracks" (Washington, D.C., 1922).

21. C. Edward Skeen, *Citizen Soldiers in the War of 1812* (Lexington: University of Kentucky Press, 1999); *SLGB* 31 Geo. III, c. 31; Desmond Morton, *A Military History of Canada* (Edmonton: Hurtig, 1985), 50.

22. Edward M. Coffman, *The Old Army: A Portrait of the American Army in Peacetime, 1784–1898* (New York: Oxford University Press, 1986); Colin G. Calloway, *The American Revolution in Indian Country: Crisis and Diversity in Native American Communities* (Cambridge: Cambridge University Press, 1995); James R. Jacobs, *The Beginning of the U.S. Army, 1783–1812* (Princeton, N.J.: Princeton University Press, 1947); Francis

Paul Prucha, *The Sword of the Republic: The United States Army of the Frontier, 1783–1846* (New York: Macmillan, 1969); Richard H. Kohn, *Eagle and Sword: The Beginnings of the Military Establishment in America* (New York: Free Press, 1975); Anthony P. Mora, *Border Dilemmas: Racial and National Uncertainties in New Mexico, 1848–1912* (Durham, N.C.: Duke University Press, 2011); Rachel St. John, *A Line in the Sand: A History of the Western U.S.-Mexico Border* (Princeton, N.J.: Princeton University Press, 2011).

23. Edward Rowe Snow, *The Islands of Boston Harbor: Their History and Romance, 1626–1935* (Andover, Mass.: Andover Press, 1935), 109–51; Stephen Jenkins, *The Greatest Street in the World: The Story of Broadway, Old and New, from the Bowling Green to Albany* (New York: Putnam's Sons, 1911), 118.

24. Roger Lane, *Policing the City: Boston, 1822–1885* (Cambridge, Mass.: Harvard University Press, 1967); Stephen Graham, *Cities under Siege: The New Military Urbanism* (London: Verso, 2010).

INDEX